The ROMANS

by
Dr. Robert Picirilli

Randall House Publications
114 Bush Road P.O. Box 17306
Nashville, Tennessee 37217

THE BOOK OF ROMANS

Preface

No generation of Biblical students has ever failed to appreciate Paul's epistle to the Romans as being the very finest presentation of Christian doctrine ever written. On the one hand, here is the Spirit's own inspired presentation of the need, provision, and meaning of redemption. On the other hand, here is the keen mind of Paul at his very best in arguing and expounding the very central truths of Christian teaching.

Would you understand man's sin? God's law? The Jews' history? Jesus' death? The sinners' salvation? The Christian's life? You must go to Romans if you would. No presentation of these, or many other Christian doctrines, will be complete unless the light of Romans shines brightly therein. One wonders what would be the power and integrity of Christianity without Romans.

Great minds have therefore always recognized the greatness of this book. Many have understood that their very systems of theology ought to be presented as commentaries on Romans, and so the publication of a commentary on Romans has more than once stirred the Christian realm with controversy. Sad to say, the commentaries have not always been as enlightening as the book itself. We will not ever fully plumb the depths of Romans; we recognize this even when we marvel at the marvelous clarity of the letter on the things we have to know.

Griffith-Thomas reports that Chrysostom had this epistle read to him once a week; that Luther called Romans "the chief book of the New Testament"; that Coleridge said it was "the profoundest book in existence"; that Melancthon painstakingly copied the letter twice by hand just to become more thoroughly familiar therewith. Romans is certainly worth becoming thoroughly familiar with. We offer these thirty-nine lessons to help you achieve that end.

About the Author

Robert Eugene Picirilli was born in North Carolina in 1932, to an Italian immigrant--nee Eugenio Picirilli--and his American wife--nee Lena Harrell. By reason of their separation, he was reared in rural South Carolina by an aunt and uncle, Alma ("Mom") and Oliver Weatherford.

Graduated from high school in 1949, he enrolled at age 16 at Free Will Baptist Bible College that fall, and received a B.A. degree in Bible there in 1953. His graduate studies were done at Bob Jones University, where he received the Master of Arts degree in theology in 1955 and the degree Doctor of Philosophy in New Testament text in 1963. Bob Jones University also awarded him an honorary Doctor of Divinity degree in 1967.

Mr. Picirilli's teaching career, except for one year as a graduate assistant at Bob Jones University, has been at Free Will Baptist Bible College, where he has taught New Testament Greek, Philosophy, and Biblical studies since 1955. He also served for a number of years, each, as Registrar and Academic Dean, retiring from administration in 1999 when he was named Professor Emeritus. He continues to teach part time. He was active in the Accrediting Association of Bible Colleges from 1958-1998, including service on various committees and stints as Vice President and President. He has taught in a number of situations abroad, most recently in the Chelyabinsk Affiliate of the Moscow Theological Institute in Siberia.

He insists that Biblical study is his primary interest and has written extensively in that field, both for his denomination and for others. He is active in the Evangelical Theological Society, especially in that society's southeastern section where he has often read papers and held its various offices. He has had articles published in a number of journals, including *The Evangelical Quarterly, Biblical Viewpoint, Journal for the Study of the New Testament*, and the *Journal of the Evangelical Theological Society*. In addition, he has been a regular columnist for *Contact* and has written many studies for the Free Will Baptist Sunday School curriculum. Books published include *Paul the Apostle* (Moody Press) and the commentaries on 1 and 2 Corinthians, Ephesians, Philippians, 1 and 2 Thessalonians, and 1 and 2 Peter in *The Randall House Bible Commentary* - a series of New Testament commentaries of which he is general editor. With four others he produced *The NKJV Greek English Interlinear New Testament* for Thomas Nelson.

Mr. Picirilli is also active as a preacher and in denominational affairs. He was ordained in 1953 and later served as interim pastor at Cofer's Chapel Free Will Baptist Church in Nashville, Tennessee, where he has been an active member since 1955. He served terms as assistant clerk, clerk, and moderator of the National Association of Free Will Baptists, where he has also filled a number of committee positions including, at present, a place on the Historical Commission. He has spoken at various denominational meetings (and to the National Association of Evangelicals) and preaches often in Bible conferences and local church settings.

Mr. Picirilli and his wife, Clara, live in Nashville, Tennessee, near Free Will Baptist Bible College. Five daughters graced the home and have presented them with nine grandchildren. Mr. Picirilli's hobbies include fishing, stamp collecting, and Free Will Baptist history. He is listed in several "personalities" publications, including *Who's Who in America*.

He characterizes himself as a "fundamentalist, without any particular modifiers." He believes that every word in the Bible was chosen by the human writers under the superintending and supernatural influence of the Holy Spirit, resulting in an inspired and inerrant Book. On this belief he bases his insistence that Biblical exegesis and exposition ought to have the place of absolute authority for both the theology and the life of the Church. That view of the Word of God is well demonstrated in these lessons on the book of Romans.

Contents

1 Paul Addresses the Romans

Study Text: Romans 1:1-7

Introduction
1. The Writer: a Carrier of the Gospel (Romans 1:1)
    a. His Consecration (verse 1a)
    b. His Commission (verse 1b)
    c. His Concentration (verse 1c)
2. The Writing: the Content of the Gospel (Romans 1:2-6)
    a. It Fulfils the Scriptures (verse 2)
    b. It Features the Savior (verses 3, 4)
    c. It Fosters Salvation (verses 5, 6)
3. The Written Ones: the Called in the Gospel (Romans 1:7)
    a. The Chosen Saints (verse 7a)
    b. The Cheerful Salutation (verse 7b)

INTRODUCTION

No doubt Romans is one of the most important of all the books of the Bible. W. H. Griffith Thomas reports that Chrysostom, one of the ancient church fathers, had Romans read to him once a week; that Luther, the great Reformer, called Romans "the chief book of the New Testament"; that Coleridge, a famous English poet, said Romans was "the profoundest book in existence"; that Melancthon copied Romans twice by hand just to get more thoroughly acquainted with it. Thomas himself says that Romans is concerned with "the deepest problems of Christian thought," "great theological principles," and "the prime secrets of the spiritual life." He adds: "A Christian life nourished on the Epistle to the Romans will never lack

1

the three great requisites of clear perception, strong conviction, and definite usefulness."

Hundreds of similar quotations could be found, agreeing on the special importance of Romans for Christian doctrine and Christian living. All this came about because Paul was writing to a church he had not yet visited. Nor had any other apostle. Therefore he felt the Roman believers needed thorough instruction in the basic matters of salvation and Christian experience. The Holy Spirit—as with all the Scriptures—directed Paul to give them, exactly and errorlessly, what they needed. We are humbly grateful that this was provided for us too.

The primary introductory facts about Romans will be dealt with in the Exposition that follows.

EXPOSITION

Your attention is called at the start to the general study-outline of Romans reproduced in the back of this book. Throughout this study, regular reference should be made to that outline. In particular you will be able to see how each section fits into the overall plan of the epistle. As you will see, for example, this portion is subsection A under the Introduction to the Epistle, and is entitled "Paul Addresses the Romans." These first seven verses of Romans in form match the standard letter-opening of Paul's day, in which the writer identifies himself and his readers and greets them with expressions about their well-being.

1. THE WRITER: A CARRIER OF THE GOSPEL (Romans 1:1)

Personal letters in the days of Paul always began with the name of the one writing. So do all of Paul's letters (unless he wrote Hebrews). By the way, the apostle probably had both names, Saul and Paul, from his birth, "Saul" being a Hebrew name and "Paul" a Greek one. Naturally the name Paul became the one most used of him since he specialized in missions to the Gentiles.

The writer of a letter often added identifying details about himself in the opening. Paul does this in verse 1 and mentions three specific things as follows.

His Consecration (verse 1a). Here Paul calls himself "a servant of Jesus Christ." The word translated "servant" means "bond-slave." This word represented a humble—and sometimes humiliating—position, but the early Christians deliberately and eagerly applied it to themselves. The word is the opposite of "free" (compare 1 Corinthians 7:21) and pictures the kind of slavery in which one is altogether under the control of some master.

2

In Barclay's commentary on *The Letters of James and Peter*, four things are listed as involved in the position of a Christian bond-slave: (1) inalienably possessed by God; (2) unqualifiedly at God's disposal; (3) unquestioningly obeys God; and (4) constantly in God's service.

Such observations do not mean that Paul and other Christians "serve" God against their own wills. You will remember that a slave happy in his master's service could voluntarily be bound to that master for life. The Christian has freely yielded himself to the possession and control of Jesus as his Savior and Master. And when Paul uses this word of himself, it does not set him apart from the rest of the believers, but identifies him as one of them. All believers have consecrated themselves to the service of Jesus Christ. Nor should it be assumed that all "slaves" were in a degraded position. Many were well regarded by their masters and given positions of responsibility and respect. It is, in fact, an honor to be in the service of Jesus Christ.

His Commission (verse 1b). The second thing Paul says of himself is that he is "called to be an apostle." Note that the words "to be" are in italics; the Greek literally says, "a called apostle." "Called" could be rendered "chosen": Jesus had selected or picked Paul to be an apostle. "Apostle" literally means one sent on a mission, an official representative. Paul was Christ's chosen emissary.

We can appreciate the conviction Paul had, that he was specially called by God. All men would be far happier had they such a sense of being divinely-chosen for their life-work. Every Christian ought to have such a consciousness.

If "servant" put Paul at one with his readers, "apostle" puts him in a place of official authority, and they must hear him. The usual opinion today is that the office of apostle passed away with the ones commissioned by Christ personally (cf. 1 Corinthians 9:1). By the way, Paul would probably not have been so willing to own himself a "slave" were Jesus not the Master, nor so bold to claim apostolic authority were Jesus not the Commissioner.

His Concentration (verse 1c). Third, Paul identifies himself as "separated unto the gospel of God." This phrase gives us Paul's own concept of the basic mission he had, the task to which he was completely devoted. "Separated" literally refers to the marking off of boundaries. Just as one might build a fence around his property and erect a sign declaring what or whose it is, so Paul regarded his life as wholly set apart for God's gospel. Anything else was "off limits," we might say.

It is never enough to be set apart *from* something; one must be set apart *to* something if there is to be a sense of meaning and purpose. Furthermore, all great men concentrate on *one* clear purpose. For Paul, the carrying of the gospel was the one thing for which he was called. "Gospel," by the way, means "good message,"

3

"good news." We will find that the content of the gospel is the very subject matter of this epistle. Some commentators use this phrase "the gospel of God" as a theme for the entire letter.

One further word before moving on: Paul was in Corinth when he wrote this letter. Compare Romans 16:23 with 1 Corinthians 1:14; Cenchrea (Romans 16:1) was a seaport suburb of Corinth. He was winding up his third missionary journey at the time, preparing to go to Jerusalem with a collection he had taken up in Macedonia and Achaia (Corinth was in Achaia) for the poor believers there. See Romans 16:25, 26. Thus the time was about A.D. 56. Paul had never been to Rome (Romans 1:13; 15:22), but hoped soon to be able to go both to Rome and Spain (Romans 15:24). Still, not knowing exactly when he might go, he writes so that they may be well instructed in spiritual things in the meantime. Such were the circumstances when Romans was written.

2. THE WRITING: THE CONTENT
OF THE GOSPEL (Romans 1:2-6)

These five verses are added to the usual Pauline letter-opening. Ordinarily Paul would go directly from verse 1 to the identification of those written, as in verse 7. You can see examples of this more usual way in 1 Thessalonians 1:1 or Colossians 1:1, 2.

Here in Romans, however, Paul delays the reference to his readers in order to give an introductory summary of the subject matter of the epistle. We get the feeling that he is so full of his subject he can hardly wait to get at it! And that subject is "the gospel of God." Paul will be writing about some good news from God. The reference to himself as "separated unto the gospel of God" is the thing that sets him off on the subject. You will notice that all of verses 2-6 is one lengthy sentence modifying "the gospel of God" in verse 1. We will subdivide this into three main things Paul observes about the gospel.

It Fulfils the Scriptures (verse 2). The first thing Paul reminds us of is that the gospel, this good news of God, is not altogether new. Indeed, the gospel was the subject of many promises delivered in Old Testament days by chosen prophets, and those prophetic promises are contained in the "holy scriptures." The entire New Testament makes a great deal over the fact that Jesus himself, and the salvation He brought, were but the fulfilment of what God often promised and the old saints longingly awaited. The Scriptures are "holy," by the way, because they are breathed from God (2 Timothy 3:15, 16).

It Features the Savior (verses 3, 4). The second thing Paul wants us to realize about the gospel is that it is about Jesus Christ. God's Son, the Savior, is the subject matter of the gospel. Gospel content is

4

the good news about Jesus Christ. These two verses, in fact, give us an excellent summary of the content of the gospel, emphasizing at least four facts.

(1) Jesus' identity as God's Son is indicated both in verse 3 and in verse 4.

(2) Jesus' identity as our Lord is referred to in verse 3.

(3) Jesus' incarnation is the main point of verse 3. "Incarnation" means, literally, "in flesh." The eternal second person of the Trinity ("the Word" in John 1:1) took on physical form (cf. Philippians 2:5-8). This incarnation means that the Divine One became human. Compare Isaiah 7:14 where "Immanuel" means "God with us."

Paul particularly connects the humanity of which Jesus partook with "the seed of David." This does more than give mere humanness to Jesus; it indicates that Jesus belonged to a specific tribe of humanity, a lineage that goes back to Israel's king. Jesus is heir to David's throne, the one in whom is perfectly and permanently fulfilled God's old promise to David that one of his descendants would never fail to sit on the throne.

The phrase "according to the flesh" has been subjected to varied interpretations. Probably it is not nearly so complicated as all that, and simply indicates the arena of activity in which the incarnation plays its important part. The physical world, the world of flesh and substance, is the realm in which the incarnation took place. Jesus Christ, God's Son, was a real, flesh-and-blood human being.

(4) Jesus' resurrection is the main point of verse 4. Paul sees this as the heart of the gospel (cf. Romans 10:9). Of course the doctrine of Christ's resurrection involves the doctrine of His death, and these two must be combined to understand the gospel. So the first thing clear about the resurrection here is that it is "the resurrection from the dead." As Paul puts it in 1 Corinthians 15:3, the gospel first says that "Christ died for our sins" and then that "he rose again the third day."

The second thing clear about the resurrection is that it served to underscore Jesus' identity as God's Son. The Greek word translated "declared" is a member of the same family of words as the "separated" in verse 1 (see above). Jesus was "marked" as God's Son by the resurrection. The phrase "with power" may equal an adverb "powerfully": Jesus was powerfully shown to be God's Son. The resurrection was a display of power, divine power, that answered all questions as to who Jesus was.

The third thing said here about the resurrection is that it was "according to the spirit of holiness." This phrase is parallel to "according to the flesh" above in verse 3, and has been subjected to just as many complicated interpretations. Again, the meaning is probably very simple: "the spirit of holiness" is "the Holy Spirit," and the whole phrase means that the resurrection took place in the arena where the Holy Spirit is operative. The important thing about the incarnation is that Jesus really became flesh; the important thing about the resurrection is that only the spiritual power of God's Holy Spirit could bring it to pass.

It Fosters Salvation (verses 5, 6). Now Paul moves to a third truth about the gospel, as to its purpose and the place of the minister of the gospel in helping achieve that purpose. Simply stated, the gospel is intended to bring men of all nations to obey the faith and be saved. In more detail, Paul speaks of how three different parties fit into this plan.

(1) *Jesus is the One who commissions the carriers of the gospel.* This fact is seen in the "by whom," which refers back to God's Son, Jesus Christ (verse 3). Paul intends for his readers to realize that the authority of the Lord Jesus lies behind his commission to preach and teach in the gospel; then they will take seriously this letter he is writing.

(2) *Paul, and other carriers of the gospel, receive their "office" from the Lord,* and thus their position and purpose are set for them by heavenly authority. The word "apostleship" means "the apostolic position." Notice that Paul links the word "grace" with this: his position of service as an emissary of Christ is a "grace," a position undeserved, but given him by God's sovereign favor. Paul frequently referred to his ministerial office as a "grace." Ephesians 3:7, 8 provides an excellent example and accurate explanation of what he means.

If the first part of verse 5 refers to the *position* Paul occupied, the last part summarizes the *purpose* of that place of service: to give faith a hearing among all nations, thus to give all men opportunity to hear about justification by faith and to hearken to what they hear. The word translated "obedience" literally means "to hear under," thus to submit to what is heard. "All nations" is significant: the gospel is for any man and Paul's office was unlimited by race or place. He was called to give faith a hearing everywhere and anywhere. So are we.

The phrase "for his name" literally means "in behalf of his name." This reminds us again that the gospel carrier is representing not himself but Jesus, the one who sends him forth.

(3) *The Romans are a part of the "all nations" to whom Paul was called to minister.* Verse 6 makes this point: the "whom" refers back to the "all nations" of verse 5. This statement accomplishes two things at the same time. First, it reminds the Romans of the thrilling salvation they have experienced as the "called" (chosen ones) of Jesus Christ, in spite of their Gentile background. More about this truth in the next verse. The "ye also" means "even ye," with a note of wonder at the inclusion of the Romans.

Second, it reminds the Romans they are among those to whom

6

Paul has been specially called to minister. Paul was a "chosen vessel . . . to bear my name before the Gentiles" (Acts 9:15). The Greek word "Gentiles" is, after all, the same as "nations." The believers in Rome are of those Gentile nations, and thus Paul is appropriately exercising his calling in writing them. It will be proper for them to receive his ministry as performed in this letter.

3. THE WRITTEN ONES: THE CALLED
IN THE GOSPEL (Romans 1:7)

As already mentioned, the standard letter form of Paul's time almost always called for three things in the opening. The first was the name of the writer, which Paul has given in verse 1. The second was the name of the one(s) written, and the third a wish for the well-being of the reader. Both these last two items are included in verse 7.

The Chosen Saints (verse 7a). Paul makes two interesting statements about the believers at Rome. First, he calls them "beloved of God." This means the same as if rendered "loved by God." They are to recognize themselves as objects of God's love. Only the Christian can truly accept this; all who truly accept this are thereby Christians. The phrase "dear children" in Ephesians 5:1 means the same thing: "beloved children"; so "walk in love" (Ephesians 5:2) means to live with the awareness we are objects of God's love. Anyone who has ever grasped the significance of Calvary cannot avoid this, for Calvary—more than anything else—convinces us of Heaven's love for us.

The second thing Paul says about the believers in Rome is that they are "called to be saints." Just as above in verse 1, the "to be" is italicized and thus not in the original Greek. This, then, means "called saints," "chosen saints." Just as Paul was called, selected to be an apostle (verse 1), so all who believe are called to sainthood.

You will find no limited sainthood here, such as that taught by the Roman church. All believers are "saints." "Saints" literally means "holy ones," "set apart ones." This refers not to believers as perfect or sinless, but as ones who are set apart for God, uniquely belonging to Him, possessed and indwelled by Him, and thus "holy" in its most usual scriptural sense (like the "holy mount" in 2 Peter 1:18, or the "holy ground" in Acts 7:33, or the "holy oil" in Numbers 35:25).

The Cheerful Salutation (verse 7b). In every one of Paul's letters (unless he wrote Hebrews), he greets his readers by wishing "grace and peace" to them (the Pastoral Epistles add "mercy" too). Compare First and Second Peter and Second John. We conclude that this was a standard Christian greeting in the early church. "Peace" was the usual Jewish greeting, and a word closely related to "grace" was a common Greek greeting. The Christians may have deliberately combined the two.

At any rate, only through Christ can real grace and peace be experienced. Grace is favor not deserved; all God does for man is by grace. Real peace comes only when there is "peace with God" (Romans 5:1). Grace and peace may come from God the Father, but only by the Son, our Lord Jesus Christ.

A few closing observations about the Roman believers. Some arguments have existed as to how there came to be a church in the Empire's capital. Paul had not been there. Nor had Peter, as some teach, else Paul would not have written them, building on another man's foundation (Romans 15:20). No doubt various ones went or returned to Rome after conversion elsewhere, perhaps some as soon as Pentecost (Acts 2:10). The clear truth is that most of them had been converted in other parts of the Empire under Paul's own ministry. The long list of names Paul greets in Romans 16 proves this, and the reference to Aquila and Priscilla (16:3) shows Paul had sent them to Rome as his own representatives in the ministry there. Paul definitely considered the Roman church as *his* church. And so, in hope of seeing them before long and yet not wanting to delay in teaching them, he wrote them this lengthy letter to build them up in their faith and in the understanding of basic gospel facts.

2 Paul's Ambitions for the Romans

Study Text: Romans 1:8-17

Introduction
1. His Sincere Interest (Romans 1:8-10)
   a. Praise for the Saints (verse 8)
   b. Prayers for the Saints (verses 9, 10)
2. His Spiritual Intentions (Romans 1:11-13)
   a. Establishment (verse 11)
   b. Encouragement (verse 12)
   c. Enlargement (verse 13)
3. His Salvation Incentive (Romans 1:14-17)
   a. A Compulsion (verse 14)
   b. A Commitment (verse 15)
   c. A Confidence (verses 16, 17)

INTRODUCTION

Let us review a bit. In the first section of study on this great epistle, we dealt with the part that is usually called the opening salutation, 1:1-7. There Paul identified himself, his gospel, and his readers. He is a chosen apostle; they are chosen saints. The connection between them lies in the fact that Jesus Christ has commissioned the apostle to minister in the gospel; and the Roman saints are proper objects of that ministry. Here lies the explanation why Paul is writing this letter. The Romans are expected to receive the letter in this light.

EXPOSITION

A reference to the outline of Romans in the back of this book will serve to help you see this part in its relationship to the entire study. We are still dealing with the Introduction to the Epistle; this part is subsection B, covering 1:8-17, and entitled: "Paul's Ambitions for the Romans."

1. HIS SINCERE INTEREST (Romans 1:8-10)

As seen in the previous section, Paul knew a great many of the Roman believers personally. Many of them had, no doubt, been converted under Paul's preaching in various places and had afterward moved to Rome. The lengthly list of names he calls in chapter 16 proves this. Paul therefore considered the church at Rome as one of his churches, even though he had not personally been there. The reference to Aquila and Priscilla in 16:3-5 most probably indicates that these co-workers of Paul had gone to Rome at his own urging to assist in getting the work established. Paul had used this couple in his ministry before, in a similar capacity at Ephesus, moving them there from Corinth (Acts 18:18, 19).

We are not surprised, then, that Paul had a special interest in the church at Rome, or that he kept himself informed of their situation. There would have been plenty of traveling back and forth from Rome into all parts of the Empire; no doubt Paul had contact with many who brought him word.

Praise for the Saints (verse 8). Most of Paul's letters begin with some words of thanksgiving. He never stopped showing gratitude for the grace of God and the people in whom that grace was displayed. We can learn a lesson from this trait. The particular thing he mentions for praise here is the Romans' testimony. Word of their faith had spread abroad.

Compare 1 Thessalonians 1:8, "in every place your faith to Godward is spread abroad." Paul appreciated it when the news of salvation was not kept quiet, but was joyfully told around. Both here in Romans and in 1 Thessalonians, Paul's statements should not be taken to the extreme. What he means most likely is that, everywhere there are believers, word had been gladly received about the number at Rome who had been converted. Again, such a statement offers no problems in view of the freedom of travel in the Roman Empire in Paul's day.

Prayers for the Saints (verses 9, 10). Paul's letters to his people are especially impressive in references to his prayer life. He tells every group he writes that he prays for them constantly, and we have no doubt this was so. Paul's intense concern for the spiritual welfare of his converts manifested itself in such praying; we ought to learn both these habits: the concern and the praying. We note several things in these two verses about Paul's prayers for the Romans.

(1) *The certainty* of his prayers is assured by an appeal to God as his witness (9a). This is an expression Paul used at times (cf. 9:1; 1 Thessalonians 2:10) when he wanted to make an especially convincing and serious claim about his own practice or motives. He had no fear of God's own investigation of his claim to regular prayers for the Romans.

Notice the parenthetic statement of 9a about God: He is the One Paul serves in the gospel. The word for "serve" here is not the usual one which means bond-service. This word means priestly service. And this is the reason for the phrase "with my spirit." Paul does not minister as did the Old Testament priests in physical ordinances and sacrifices of flesh. But he offers spiritual sacrifices; he performs a spiritual service in the realm of the gospel of Christ. The New Testament pictures all believers as priests and everything they do for God as spiritual sacrifices (see Philippians 4:18 and Hebrews 13:15, 16, for example).

(2) *The constancy* of his prayers is seen in the phrase "without ceasing" (9b). This adverb is used rarely in the New Testament, elsewhere only in Romans 9:2; 1 Thessalonians 1:3; 2:13; and 2 Timothy 1:3. It does not mean continuously, but regularly, consistently. Paul did not forget to pray for the Romans on a regular basis. The phrase "make mention of" means "remember." In addition to the "without ceasing," note the "always," thus doubly emphasizing Paul's faithfulness to remember the Romans in prayer.

(3) *The content* of Paul's prayer about Rome, in part, is made clear in verse 10. He had a passion to go to Rome personally, and he kept beseeching God to bring that to pass. The "now at length" points up the fact that Paul has long wanted to go. The "might" reflects a Greek word in the sentence that indicates uncertainty or indefiniteness. Paul still does not know when God might be pleased to send him to Rome. The "prosperous" journey probably means that Paul will feel himself "prospered" to be able to go; it will particularly please him.

We note, however, that Paul does not allow his eagerness for the journey to carry him away. The phrase "by the will of God" reminds us that Paul always submitted personal desires to God's will. He wants to make a visit to Rome, but only when and if God wills. We ought always to have such an attitude (cf. James 4:15). And, by the way, *any* trip "in the will of God" is a "prosperous" trip!

2. HIS SPIRITUAL INTENTIONS (Romans 1:11-13)

These verses begin by repeating the essence of verse 10, "I long to see you." They tell us exactly what Paul intended to do for the

Romans, why he wanted to visit them. And his aims are spiritual ones.

Establishment (verse 11). Paul's primary ambition for the Romans is their spiritual establishment. This word means "to make stable, strong," and it implies a degree of immaturity in the church. This immaturity would not be surprising. Most of the Roman believers were probably young Christians and so far no apostle had been there. We see in this desire Paul's concern that converts grow in the faith. He was never satisfied to win men and leave them. All his letters speak of his passion for spiritual strength, stability, and maturity.

Paul mentions a specific method he anticipates using to accomplish this end: "impart unto you some spiritual gift." This clause has been subjected to a variety of interpretations, depending on the exact meaning of "spiritual gift." We know that "the spiritual gifts" was a title often given to such technical functions as are listed in Romans 12:6-8; 1 Corinthians 12:28; Ephesians 4:11. Some interpreters think Paul means this here, and that he expects—by apostolic authority—to lay hands on some Roman believers to receive some of these gifts. On the other hand, "spiritual gift" is often used in a broader, less official sense to refer to any good thing God does for us, spiritually, by grace. So many interpreters take this to be the meaning here, understanding Paul to mean that he expects his ministry at Rome to bring spiritual blessings to the Romans.

Either way, Paul's main idea is quite clear. He knows that the establishment of the Roman believers cannot come except by God's gracious dealings with them. They need faith, knowledge, holiness, love—all the "fruits of the Spirit" (which are, in the broader sense, spiritual gifts). They may even need more official workers like Spirit-filled and Spirit-chosen preachers and teachers (which are spiritual gifts in the technical sense). Indeed, they probably need both and Paul expects that his ministry there could be used by God to help achieve these objectives and thus to help the Romans move on more steadily toward spiritual maturity.

Encouragement (verse 12). The word translated "comforted" has the idea of encouragement. There is a strong emphasis on reciprocal action in this verse. ("Reciprocal" means moving back and forth, sharing, exchanging; one returns to another what that one has given him.) To begin with, Paul refers to *"mutual* faith." He and the Romans share the same faith. Then he speaks of being comforted (encouraged) *together* by this mutual faith.

What he means is this: he will witness the Romans' faith and his heart will be encouraged; reciprocally, they will witness his faith and their hearts will be encouraged. A visit by him to them will produce such results: the faith of each will encourage the other. That is one of the things Christian fellowship does. Each of us can be an inspiration and help to the other and thus we mutually encourage each other in the faith.

Enlargement (verse 13). Another of Paul's intentions—if God permits him to visit Rome—is to fulfil a long-standing objective to reach out further in that direction with the gospel. Two factors are involved in this. First is the fact Paul has often made plans to go to Rome, and so a sense of personal accomplishment will result if his plans finally reach fruition. "Purposed" here means he actually made plans on several occasions. "Let" means hindered. So far he has been prevented from carrying out such plans. We are not told how he has been prevented, whether by Satan (as in 1 Thessalonians 2:18 in similar circumstances) or by the Lord's directions (as in Acts 16:6). Compare Romans 15:22, where Paul seems to indicate that the cause of Christ, his preaching at other places, was the hindrance.

The chief factor involved here is Paul's ambition for spiritual *fruit* at Rome. This "fruit" probably includes all the normal results of Paul's ministry, whether in the conversion of sinners or in the building up of believers in the faith. Both were important to Paul. Note, too, that Paul stresses the Gentile factor again (as in 1:5). His special calling was as a preacher for the Gentiles (Acts 9:15). The Roman capital was thus a proper city for Paul's ministry, being the heart of the Gentile world. Paul wanted to reach out yet farther with the gospel for the Gentiles, for this was his very commission (1:1). As indicated in 15:15-24, Paul felt he had now "fully preached" in the areas so far covered, and was ready to expand his field of endeavor to include Rome and Spain.

3. HIS SALVATION INCENTIVE (ROMANS 1:14-17)

Something propelled Paul, kept him going in his ministry. The reference in verse 13 to an enlarged ministry that will include Rome provides Paul an opportunity to share with his readers that incentive. In a nutshell, the gospel of Christ and Paul's relationship to it is the source of all his motivation including his desire to reach the Romans by visit or by letter.

A Compulsion (verse 14). The three "I ams" of Paul in these verses are quite famous. In the first of these, Paul acknowledges a debt, and by this he is compelled to preach the gospel anywhere and to anyone. A debtor is one who owes something: Paul is obligated to preach. Later in Romans he will instruct us to "Owe no man anything, but to love one another" (13:8). His own sense of obligation in the gospel does not contradict that admonition, for it is his love for men and concern for their salvation that provides the foundation on which this debt rests. Furthermore, his consciousness of Christ's love for all men makes him sensitive to his own obligation to carry the word of that love to them for whom Christ died (cf. 2 Corinthians 5:14, 15, 19).

The two pairs of words Paul chooses here make it plain he regarded his debt as to *all* men. "Greeks and Barbarians" include everybody. "Greeks" are those who speak the Greek language. "Barbarians" are those who do not. This word "Barbarian" was invented by the Greeks as a name for those who spoke no Greek, and whose languages were unintelligible to them, sounding like so much muttering ("bar, bar, bar"). The Greeks figured all "civilized" people spoke Greek, and so they used the word "Barbarian" with a hint of contempt and depreciation.

"Wise and unwise" (foolish) also includes everyone. The words probably carry the idea of knowledgeable versus ignorant. The Greeks considered themselves "wise," and others ignorant who were not instructed in their culture and philosophy. Likewise, the Jews considered themselves knowledgeable, and others foolish who were unlearned in the Mosaic system (cf. 2:17-20). Paul may well be thinking of both contrasts, or any others. Anyway, he is obligated to take the gospel to all, for neither the wise nor the foolish can be saved without it.

A Commitment (verse 15). The word translated "ready" does not deal with preparedness but with eagerness, willingness. This eagerness of Paul to preach the gospel at Rome can be explained on no basis other than his willing commitment of himself to the gospel ministry, a commitment from which he held nothing back. He was willing to go anyplace, anytime, to anyone.

And that included the Romans. Just as in 1:6, the "you also" may mean "even you," again hinting at the marvel that they are included among those who can be saved by the gospel. Indeed, any sinner can be amazed that he is included.

The phrase "as much as in me is" means "as far as my part is concerned." This indirectly refers back to Paul's qualification in verse 10, "by the will of God." In other words, Paul is willing and eager, but he will go to Rome only as God arranges it. His commitment to preach the gospel is not self-governing, but must itself be directed by the God whom Paul serves in the gospel (verse 9 above).

His Confidence (verses 16, 17). This third "I am" of Paul's brings us right to the heart of the lesson, and to the theme of Paul's entire Roman letter, for here he gives us a brief summary of the main truths about the gospel, truths he will expand in the letter.

(1) *Paul's enthusiasm* is clear in verse 16a. "Not ashamed" means "not made ashamed," "not put to shame." In other words, it means that the gospel never let Paul down. It never failed to work when properly applied. Paul was never disappointed by the gospel. And when one has such confidence in something, he can be enthusiastic and bold in presenting it. He does not need to be

ashamed of it when he has never been shamed by it. We can be sure that the gospel is such that we will never have to be ashamed of it. It never fails.

(2) *The gospel's effectiveness* is emphasized in verses 16b, 17. The word "power" is one that refers to ability. "Power of God unto salvation" means that the gospel says, "God can save." When Christ is preached, God can save.

Who then can He save? "Everyone that believeth." Two or three important things need to be noted about this. First, any person is a potential candidate for salvation. "Everyone" would be just as accurately translated "anyone." Second, faith (belief) is the one supreme condition man must meet. This is the only thing that makes the difference between those whom God saves and those whom He does not. Third, that faith is not one mere act of intellectual assent but a continuing and obedient trust in God through Christ. In Greek the word "believeth" is in the tense that involves continuing action. The basic meaning of "faith" is trust.

Paul reemphasizes the all-inclusiveness of his previous statement by adding "to the Jew first, and also to the Greek." In other words, nationality has nothing to do with it. Jew and Gentile alike are candidates for salvation by the gospel of Christ. Jew and Gentile alike can be saved by faith. There are not two plans or two peoples. Salvation by the gospel of Christ is for *anyone* who possesses faith in Christ.

You may delight in noting that this verse makes clear the gospel's supreme *person:* Christ; the gospel's sufficient *power:* to save; the gospel's simple *plan:* faith; and the gospel's selected *prospects:* any. This marvelous gospel salvation provided the incentive for Paul to preach. No wonder he was so bold and enthusiastic with the gospel! No wonder he wanted to enlarge his territory and include Rome too where yet others could experience salvation by his preaching!

Verse 17 states again the effectiveness of the gospel to save, but in different words that make the result more clear. "Therein" means "in the gospel." Something is "revealed" (unveiled) in the gospel: namely, "the righteousness of God." This phrase will become increasingly important in our study of Romans. For now, a brief definition must suffice. It means two things at once: how to get right *with* God, and that this righteousness is *from* God. In other words, God has provided righteousness for man, and by that provision man stands righteous before God.

This word "righteousness" is a judicial term; it means "to be found innocent by the judge." It is the same root word as "justification." The gospel reveals how man can stand innocent before God, how God has provided for man's justification.

Paul will tell us much more about this in the rest of the book. For now, he adds but one phrase as to the method which the gospel reveals by which man can be righteous with God: "from faith to faith." Interpreters argue over the exact significance of these words. "From faith" could mean that the "revelation" is seen by faith; and "to faith" could mean that it begets faith in the hearer. Leroy Forlines takes the meaning to be that "righteousness by faith is preached so as to beget faith." Either way, the main point is clear: faith is the method which the gospel reveals. Righteousness with God is based on faith.

Paul quotes Habakkuk 2:4 as further confirmation. That quotation means too that one only experiences justification by faith. To "live" in the sense meant here is to stand before God justified, spiritually alive. This Old Testament quotation makes it clear that faith has *always* been the method for justification, during the Mosaic age as well as now. Remember that Paul used this same quote in the same way in Galatians 3:11. Review the exposition on that verse if you have it.

3 The Heathen Need for Righteousness

Study Text: Romans 1:18-32

Introduction
1. An Ignorance Without Defense (Romans 1:18-20)
   a. A Universal Condemnation (verse 18a)
   b. An Unrighteous Concealment (verse 18b)
   c. An Understood Creation (verses 19, 20)
2. An Inexcusable, Wilful Departure (Romans 1:21-23)
   a. The Change (verses 21-23)
   b. The Causes (verses 21-23)
   c. The Consequences (verses 21-23)
3. An Inevitable World Degeneration (Romans 1:24-32)
   a. Unclean Activities (verses 24, 25)
   b. Unnatural Affections (verses 26, 27)
   c. Unacceptable Attitudes (verses 28-32)

INTRODUCTION

The first two sections have dealt with that part of Romans we call Introduction. Now we move into the body of the letter.

As suggested in the previous section, 1:16, 17 serve as excellent theme verses. Some like to say the theme is "the gospel of Christ" or simply "the gospel" (1:16). Others—this writer among them—prefer to use "the righteousness of God" (1:17) as the theme. The basic truth is still the same; you might even say that Romans tells us about "the good news of how to be right with God by faith in Christ."

At any rate, we will keep referring to "The Righteousness of God" as the theme of Romans. You will notice that our general

17

study-outline uses these words throughout.

Romans is most helpfully divided into five major sections (check the general study-outline). Five sections of study, beginning with this one, are devoted to Part 1 of Romans. In this first part Paul undertakes to show that all men, Gentile and Jew, are in desperate need for a God-provided righteousness. We have called Part 1 "The Righteousness of God: A Predicament for the Sinner" (1:18—3:20) Here Paul proves that all men are sinners, have failed to achieve righteousness, and stand before God guilty and condemned.

EXPOSITION

A quick reference to the general study-outline in the back of this book will show that this section covers subsection A under Part 1, entitled "The Heathen Need for Righteousness," covering the passage 1:18-32. As Paul sets out to show that the whole world stands quilty before God, he first deals with the world from a non-Jewish point of view: in other words, the Gentile or heathen world. And do not let the word "heathen" mislead you. Here it is being used of all mankind except the Jews, and that includes civilized and cultured men as well as backward, ignorant savages.

1. AN IGNORANCE WITHOUT DEFENSE (Romans 1:18-20)

Paul, in setting out to prove that the heathen world stands condemned before God, knows he will encounter an argument based on the ignorance of the heathen. He proceeds, therefore, to show that the world's ignorance of God is inexcusable.

A Universal Condemnation (verse 18a). Before giving us his reasons for declaring that men's ignorance of God is indefensible, Paul first makes a clear declaration that all men are under God's wrath. This is, after all, the fact he is going to prove, and this fact pointedly includes the heathen world.

1. *That God's wrath is revealed* is first made clear. We are not specifically told *how* "God's wrath from heaven" has been revealed, but the implication is that the fact is well-known and clear. In truth, the fact has been made known by more than one method. The Old Testament Scriptures have made it plain that God's wrath is presently upon all sinners, and that He will judge the sinful world (cf. Psalms 5:5, 9:17 for examples). The New Testament gospel also makes known the fact of God's unavoidable wrath for the unsaved. Perhaps this revelation in the gospel is particularly what Paul refers to here, thus tying in this verse with the previous one, and indicating that both the wrath and the righteousness of God are revealed in the gospel. Paul's "preaching" of the "gospel" generally included a

making aware of judgment: note Acts 17:22-31, for example, when in the sermon at Mars' Hill Paul says God "hath appointed a day in the which he will judge the world."

2. *That all sin is under God's wrath* is also made clear. The key word is "all" (which could just as easily be translated "every"). God's wrath is against every single manifestation of wrong in the universe, and it matters not whether those who practice that wrong are cultured or uncivilized, religious or pagan, Jewish or Gentile, well-taught or ignorant. "Ungodliness and unrighteousness" are probably intended to cover every sort of wrong, negative or positive, in attitude or practice. Ungodliness is impiety, a failure to be God-conscious; unrighteousness is wrongdoing.

An Unrighteous Concealment (verse 18b). This is Paul's first reason for his claim that the heathen are "without excuse" (verse 20): they "hold the truth in unrighteousness." "Hold" may mean *possess*, but more likely means *suppress* (hold down). Either way, the basic idea is the same: the fault for man's wickedness lies not so much in ignorance of the truth as in rejection of the truth. The truth is there, but has been held down, suppressed, set on, concealed, ignored, and rejected.

The phrase "in unrighteousness" is probably intended to show that man's love for wrongdoing is the cause for his suppression of the truth. He covers truth by the multiplicity of his unrighteous deeds. The picture is that of one who "keeps the lid on" something he would rather ignore, all the while busily involving himself in the wicked deeds that would be so unpleasantly exposed as evil if he would just let the truth out. Man does not want to let the truth out.

An Understood Creation (verses 19, 20). Paul now gives a second reason for saying the heathen world is "without excuse": God is well-revealed in nature. The creation of the world is adequate testimony to the existence and power of a divine Creator.

1. *The fact of this revelation* is indicated in verse 19, and is threefold. Fact one: some things about God can be "known" by revelation in nature. Fact two: man clearly possesses this revelation. Paul avows that this "is manifest in them." "Manifest" means open, plain, evident. Fact three: God deliberately and consciously revealed himself this way, as seen in the assertion "God hath shewed it unto them." "Shewed" is the same word as "manifest."

2. *The nature of this revelation* is seen in verse 10. Again, several items are indicated. Item one: the "creation" is the revealer. The phrase "from the creation" means both since and because of the creation of the natural world. The act of creation and the created world that exists from that act declare unmistakably that God exists.

Item two: this revelation makes "invisible" things clearly seen. God's "invisible things" refers to facts about God and His nature that are not themselves seeable with the physical eyes. But the created world gives such evidence that these facts are indisputably perceived.

Item three: this revelation actually produces understanding. That which is not visible to the physical eye is grasped by the mind. Paul is not saying that natural revelation *ought* to produce understanding, but that it *does*. "*By* things made" means "because of": because of God's handiwork, intelligent men perceive His existence.

Item four: the eternal power and Godhead (Deity) of the Creator are, in particular, the facts shown in natural revelation. In other words, creation clearly manifests the existence of an invisible God and His power to create the visible world. Further, the fact that He exists before the creation (His eternity) is also therefore clear.

Here are a few more words about the revelation of God contained in nature. The Bible regards such revelation as a fact. Psalm 19:1-3 is another excellent example. Paul used such an argument in his preaching to pagans (Acts 14:15-17; 17:22-31). The question often arises whether there is enough knowledge of God in natural revelation for men to be saved by. The answer is NO. But there is enough so that no man has any excuse for failing to seek sincerely the God of whom creation so eloquently speaks.

2. AN INEXCUSABLE AND WILFUL DEPARTURE (Romans 1:21-23)

In these verses Paul continues to show that any person who does not know God, even in heathen lands, is "without excuse." The "because" with which verse 21 begins connects with the last clause in verse 20. This is a third reason Paul has for his declaration of inexcusability: The world has wilfully departed from its original knowledge of God.

The Change (verses 21-23). Scofield calls this section the "seven stages" of Gentile world apostasy. The seven he means are (1) not glorifying God; (2) thanklessness; (3) vain imaginations; (4) darkened heart; (5) profession of wisdom; (6) becoming fools; and (7) changing "God" into images. Probably Paul did not intend so clear a marking between seven distinct stages. The main ideas involved are: a failure to glorify or be grateful to God when known (numbers one and two combined); a preference for "vain" (empty, worthless) imaginations rather than revealed truths, which resulted in spiritual darkness in their souls (numbers three and four combined); a preference for human wisdom over spiritually-discerned truth, resulting in foolishness and spiritual ignorance (numbers five and six combined); a perversion of the concept of God (number seven). In these factors are to be found both causes and consequences, as will be dealt with further below.

Let it be said that the "apostasy" referred to here is universal and that from two points of view. In the first place, this has

20

happened (past tense) in the history of the race in a sort of a once-for-all series of events. Beginning with the original knowledge possessed by Adam, even after the fall, the human race has departed from that knowledge so that many heathen are now in abject spiritual darkness.

But from another point of view, the "apostasy" Paul describes here continues to happen (present tense) in an ever-repeating cycle from place to place and time to time. Over and over again the process Paul outlines has repeated itself with individuals or communities or countries or nations. It has been often true that men have known God, but have wilfully departed from the knowledge and chosen perversion in preference.

The Causes (verse 21-23). Some of the factors outlined above are causes for human apostasy. Foremost among these is failure to glorify or be grateful to a God known. Let us all beware that such is the first step away from God.

Second is a preference for empty, human "imaginations" (reasonings) and natural wisdom over divinely-revealed and spiritually-discerned truth. Again, let us beware. The fact of moral depravity ought to convince us that we cannot substitute human reasoning for what God has said. That always leads to trouble.

The Consequences (verses 21-23). If some of the factors in these verses are causes of apostasy from God, others show the results. The "darkening" of the "foolish heart" and "becoming fools" both refer to the spiritual darkness and ignorance of men who have forsaken God and substituted empty, natural reasonings (cf. Ephesians 4:17-19).

Verse 23 in particular refers to the perverted concepts of God which result as seen in the worship of images. In a particularly pungent way, Paul shows how far-reaching this perversion reaches when idolatrous worship moves from images that are like men to images like birds, and then like four-footed animals, and finally even like reptiles!

By way of summary, we have seen three reasons for the assertion that all men, especially the heathen, are "without excuse": (1) wilful suppression of truth, verse 18; (2) wilful ignoring of creation's testimony, verses 19, 20; (3) wilful departure from knowledge of God, verses 21-23. Let this section forever silence those who raise doubts as to whether the "heathen" are lost. This passage—and the entire epistle—will be utterly meaningless if Paul does not mean that the unevangelized heathen are lost and in desperate need of the gospel. They are not lost as a special class; they are lost because all sinners are lost. The question "Are the heathen lost?" is the same as "Are men without Christ lost?" "The wrath of God is revealed from heaven against *all* ungodliness and unrighteousness of men . . . they are without excuse."

21

3. AN INEVITABLE WORLD DEGENERATION
(Romans 1:24-32)

Paul has affirmed both that God's wrath is upon all men and that men are without excuse in their condition, having wilfully forsaken God. Now he pursues this last theme at greater length, describing the degenerate and degraded condition toward which sinful man always inevitably moves once God has been left behind. Three times Paul says, "God gave them up (over) to . . . . " We will let these three serve as the basis for dividing the passage according to the three most prominent themes.

Unclean Activities (verses 24, 25). The phrase, "God gave them up" (all three times), does not mean God gave up on man, but that God allowed apostate mankind to be seized with various kinds of unrighteousness. From man's point of view, this is the inevitable consequence of wilful departure from the knowledge of God. From the divine standpoint, this is actually judgment on sinful men.

1. *The general nature of this uncleanness* is indicated in verse 24. Paul will be more specific below. For now, he is content to speak of the lusts from which the uncleanness derives and of the dishonoring of the body which results. "Lusts" are any strong passions, but especially those which stem from fleshly desires for self-indulgence. Sexual passions are not the only ones involved. The body is dishonored any time it is made the master instead of the soul and thus becomes the reason for various kinds of evil practices. Uncleanness is any kind of impurity, moral or religious. Paul is particularly condemning idolatrous worship.

2. *The cause for this uncleanness* is indicated in verse 25. In particular, a perverted concept of God is at the root. This is the same truth as has been indicated already in verses 21-23. "Changing the truth of God into a lie" means to exchange the true God for false idols. This in fact involves putting the creature in the place where only the Creator can rightly stand, as the objects of man's worship.

Such is the inevitable consequence when men depart from revealed truth. Their understanding of God will be distorted and perverted, and lies will replace the truth. Unclean activities, proceeding from unchecked fleshly lusts, will result.

Unnatural Affections (verses 26, 27). Paul now singles out one specific "uncleanness" for special mention: homosexuality. The Bible makes a point of condemning this sin as the ultimate sexual immorality. Our age is particularly in need of being reminded that homosexuality is gross perversion and wickedness. The farther men move from God, the more apt this sin is to be tolerated.

Female homosexuality is referred to in verse 16; male homosexuality in verse 27. Twice Paul stresses the word "natural," thus making the point that this sin is against nature. He also calls this "unseemly," which means "shameful" and "shameless" at the same time. In both verses the words translated "women" and "men" are not the usual ones, but the equivalent of our English "females" and "males."

Note in the last part of verse 17 that this is said to be a "meet recompense" of the error of men who departed from God. This fits in exactly with the explanation given above of "God gave them up": Man's seizure by such wickedness is part of God's judgment for forsaking Him.

Unacceptable Attitudes (verses 28-32). Here Paul speaks specifically about knowledge and the mind: man's way of thinking is thus the main theme. Man is wrong in his way of thinking about God and himself. Man's way of thinking is entirely unacceptable to God ("reprobate" means "rejected"). But God has given man over to this too.

1. *The cause for this judgment* is seen in verse 28. Just as already emphasized in verses 25 and 27b, man's rejection of God is the reason for God's abandonment of man to such perversion and evil as are indicated throughout this section. Verse 28a ("did not like to retain God in their knowledge") simply reinforces the idea already made plain, that mankind wilfully departs from the knowledge of God (verse 21), that mankind has wilfully ignored the testimony of creation (verses 19, 20), that mankind wilfully suppresses the truth (verse 18). Consequently God allows man to be possessed of a rejected way of thinking, a perverted attitude that produces all sorts of "inconvenient" (unbecoming, improper) practices (28b).

2. *The practices that result* are suggested in verses 29-31. Such lists are never intended to be complete, but to give examples. Nor are such lists usually in any certain order. Furthermore, such lists usually contain synonymous names for the same practice.

Twenty-three sins are included here. (1) Unrighteousness is the same as in verse 18, a general name for any wrong deed. (2) Fornication is any unlawful sexual relationship. (3) Wickedness is active working of evil, especially against others. (4) Covetousness is inordinate desire for what one does not have. (5) Maliciousness is absence of good, a bad disposition. (6) Envy is spiteful jealousy. (7) Murder is extreme hatred. (8) Debate, here, is strife. (9) Deceit is trickery aimed to hurt. (10) Malignity is the imputing of evil motives to others. (11) Whisperers are behind-the-back slanderers. (12) Backbiters are those who try to destroy others with their talk. (13) Haters of God probably means hateful to God, especially impious and wicked in the face of God. (14) Despiteful means insolent. (15) Proud means having an overblown opinion of oneself. (16) Boasters are the vainglorious. (17) Inventors of evil things are the contrivers or plotters of evil schemes. (18) Disobedient to parents is a violation of the fifth commandment. (19) Without understanding refers to the stupidity of the ungodly. (20) Covenant-breakers are those whose word is not good. (21) Without natural affection looks back to the homosexuality of verses 26, 27 and any other unnatural attachments and desires. (22) The implacable are those who will not commit themselves to others. (23) Unmerciful means hard-hearted, not moved with compassion on those in need.

W. H. Griffith Thomas adds this helpful observation: "It will be seen that the list refers to sins of inward disposition and outward act, to sins of thought, word, and deed, to wrong against self and against neighbor, as well as against God."

3. *The wilfulness of such practice* is indicated in verse 32. In particular, wicked men continue in such practices in flagrant disregard of the known fact that God will judge such deeds with death. This affirmation reflects both the clarity of revealed judgment as indicated above in verse 18 and the wilfulness of man's departure from God, as indicated especially in verses 18-23. In fact, Paul continues, not only do men continue to practice such deeds, but they take pleasure in others who join them in the practice. Throughout this section there has been an implied reference more than once to the fact that men's evils are worsened by their joint encouragement of one another in wrongdoing, and their joint participation in such evils (note verses 24, 27 in particular).

No doubt all that is said in 1:24-32 about the inevitable moral degeneration of the world is intended to describe the whole human race. Certainly not all men regress so far in wickedness as others; not even all the "heathen" (cf. 2:14, 15). But any person who rejects God is headed in the direction of the conditions here described. And pockets of humanity where such evil flourishes are but areas where the more definite rejection of truth has been manifested, and longer. These are but manifestations of the ultimate potential and destiny of all who do not know God. Wherever such evil has not been fully manifested, we can be sure, and grateful, that some of the knowledge of God has been better maintained.

In summary, you can easily see that 1:24-32 has as its theme the perversion that God has allowed to take over the world of fallen man. That perversion begins with wrong notions about God and then includes distorted ideas about man's own nature, leading to confusion and evil in worship and behavior.

4 God's Impartial Judgment

Study Text: Romans 2:1-16

Introduction
1. An Inescapable Judgment (Romans 2:1-5)
   a. An Inexcusable Hypocrisy (verses 1-3)
   b. An Impenitent Hardness (verses 4, 5)
2. An Individual Judgment (Romans 2:6-8)
   a. The Principle Indicated (verse 6)
   b. The Practice Illustrated (verses 7, 8)
3. An Impartial Judgment (Romans 2:9-11)
   a. The Practice Illustrated (verses 9, 10)
   b. The Principle Indicated (verse 11)
4. An Inevitable Judgment (Romans 2:12-16)
   a. Judgment for the Sinner (verse 12)
   b. Judgment by a Standard (verses 13-15)
   c. Judgment by the Savior (verse 16)

INTRODUCTION

We move now into the second chapter of this great epistle of Paul. We are still dealing, however, with the first major part of Romans (1:18—3:20) in which Paul's purpose is to show that all the world stands guilty and condemned before God and thus in desperate need for some way by which this guilt may be cancelled and the sinner justified.

In 1:18-32 Paul showed that this guilt and condemnation are

25

universal and include the heathen world in spite of its seeming ignorance of Biblical teaching. No doubt most of the believers in Rome were of Gentile, rather than Jewish, background; and Paul's words about heathen inexcusability were particularly appropriate to the culture whence they came.

But Paul was not content to show that the *heathen* needed a provision for salvation; the Jews too have as great a need. They are in the same human predicament as any others. Some of Paul's readers would certainly be Jewish; they must not feel that they are exceptions. They must understand their own guilt and condemnation and thus be convinced that they too can find salvation only by Jesus Christ.

Our study now moves us into the section in which Paul deals specifically with the Jewish need. This section covers 2:1—3:8, and we will devote three lessons to it.

EXPOSITION

A little time spent with the general study-outline in the back of the book will help you fit this particular section into the overall plan of Romans. Note that this is chapter 4, and comes under Part 1, subsection B: "The Hebrews' Need For Righteousness." This is the first of three sections under this heading, entitled "God's Impartial Judgment," dealing with 2:1-16.

1. AN INESCAPABLE JUDGMENT (Romans 2:1-5)

This section provides us with a good study of the principles of divine judgment, an important study for us whether or not we are interested in the question of Jewish guilt. The first of those principles, which Paul deals with in these verses, is that God's judgment is true and certain. No one, Jew included, is eliminated therefrom.

An Inexcusable Hypocrisy (verses 1-3). A careful reading of these three verses will show that there are three factors involved: (1) the Jews condemn the sinful practices of others; (2) but they, in fact, practice the same things; (3) consequently they stand, themselves, under God's certain condemnation. These points were particularly important for Jews in Paul's day, for the self-righteous Jews considered themselves "saved" by their meticulous observance of the Law. Paul knew that they too must be convinced of their need for the gospel. Just so in our time those who try to save themselves by their own moral efforts must be taught to recognize the sin they possess. Having enough knowledge of God's requirements to be able to "judge" others who sin does not excuse one from God's own judgment; such knowledge leads to hyprocrisy when one does not submit his own life to God.

In verse 1 the "thou" means the same thing as the "thou" in verse 17 and is thus particularly spoken to the Jew. Here the inexcusability of the Jew is seen on two counts. For one thing, he "does the same things," meaning he commits the same sins as his Gentile-heathen counterpart. Paul does not mean that the Jews go to the same excess of wickedness as the heathen, but we only need to recall Jesus' comparison of lust to adultery in order to remind ourselves that guilt is not dependent on eternal excess.

For another thing, the Jew "judges" ("condemns") the heathen for their wickedness. This ability to judge proves that the Jew *knows* God's law. Thus knowing, the Jew is doubly condemned, for he sins in the face of greater knowledge. The heathen know the eternal power and Godhead, seen in nature, and are condemned. How much more the Jews, who have sufficient knowledge of the Law to enable them to judge?

Verse 2 reiterates the fact that God's judgment is against men's wicked *deeds*, regardless whether they *know* His law. The key word here is "commit." When one does wrong, his enlightened judgment of others does not help him. That God's judgment is "according to truth" means just this: Judgment *will* come, and one's *true* situation will there be dealt with. Hypocritical pretense and judgmental condemnation of others will not fool God.

In verse 3 Paul exposes the foolishness of the notion that anyone guilty can escape the condemnation of God. Again he repeats the basic points already made: Those who have enlightenment about God's standards and are able to "judge" others who violate those standards, but themselves fail to measure up to the same standards, must expect the condemnation of God. There is neither excuse nor escape.

An Impenitent Hardness (verses 4, 5). In verse 4 Paul emphasizes the wickedness of impenitence in the face of God's goodness to the Jews. In verse 5 he explains the tragic "treasure" which the impenitent Jew is laying up for himself in consequence of his resistance.

In verse 4 "goodness" refers to all the good things God had done for the Jewish people, particularly the positive blessings bestowed on them. These include the revelations of himself given to them, the servants (like Moses and the prophets) who led them in the right, the choice of them as His people, the land given to them, the providential protection exercised so often on their behalf. "Forbearance" means "to hold off"; "long-suffering" means "to keep wrath far away." These words refer to all those times when God withheld from Israel the judgment and destruction she justly deserved. God's gracious dealings with men always include both these negative and positive elements. All these gracious dealings of God with the Jewish people should have led them to repentance; instead, they had resisted.

With verse 4 compare 2 Peter 3:9, where also God's long-suffering is seen as opportunity for repentance. God had been especially good to the Jews. Yet the Jews resisted His wooing, thus flaunting the very purpose of His blessings on them. Consequently, as in verse 5, the Jew's judgment is all the more inescapable and severe. Note the emphasis Paul puts on the word "wrath." The "day of wrath" is the day of judgment, the day when there will be "revelation of the righteous judgment of God." In that day God's judgment will be seen to be *right!* And the impenitent and hardened Jew can only look to that day as a "day of wrath" because that is what is in store for him then.

Notice the contrast between the "riches" of verse 4 and the "treasure" of verse 5. On the one hand, God's goodness, forbearance, and long-suffering; on the other, His wrath and just condemnation ("righteous judgment"). It ought not to be hard to choose between the two. In this light, how much worse the Jewish rejection of God! The Jew is quick to see and condemn the guilt of the heathen with their (obvious) practices but slow to see the same sinfulness at work within himself and manifested in his own (not-so-obvious) deeds. As the special object of God's "goodness," manifested in so many ways, he ought long ago to have repented. Instead he goes on with heart growing harder, condemning others, earning a store of divine wrath which is saved up for him against the judgment day. Impenitence in the face of God's goodness thus serves the double evil of hardening the heart and earning a more severe measure of God's wrath.

All that is said here in primary reference to the Jews can, without distortion, be applied to all men who possess a degree of spiritual knowledge not had in the heathen world—in other words, all who have had exposure to special revelation and so know more about divine laws and judgments. That very exposure is a token of God's goodness that would lead us to repentance. Continued resistance—especially when it includes self-righteous condemnation of others—earns us a "treasure" of divine indignation. We had best be careful how we count as trifles the rich mercies God has shown us!

2. AN INDIVIDUAL JUDGMENT (Romans 2:6-8)

The Principle Indicated (verse 6). The two key words in verse 6 are "each" ("every"), showing that justice will be individual, not national—as the Jew might think; and "deeds," which is in contrast with the Jew's confidence in *who* he is and the revealed *knowledge* he possesses. The principle then is two-fold. First, each person stands and answers for himself. It is not the *race* that is judged. Thus the

28

Jew gains neither advantage nor disadvantage. We might add, neither does the American citizen, the church member, or the one who is in a Christian family.

Second, the principle is that the individual's true self will be judged, as manifested in actual *deeds*. The Jews' expertise in knowing the Law will not help, nor will their religious identification or ritual observance. Profession is not important; practice is. Identification does not count; identity does. Knowing and saying and teaching and judging cannot substitute for being and doing.

The Practice Illustrated (verses 7, 8). Now Paul gives us two specific illustrations as to just how this principle of God's individual judgment will work in actual practice. There are, in fact, only two possibilities. There is no middle or neutral ground.

1. *Eternal life will be the reward of some*, as seen in verse 7. These are the ones who patiently wait for the reward that good work is promised and who seek for an incorruptible glory rather than an earthly one. Three things are clear about this group: (1) their manner of life: "patient continuance in well-doing"; (2) their objective: "glory and honour and immortality"; and (3) their reward: "eternal life." These are they who, when they stand before God in judgment, will be found to have practiced righteous deeds.

2. *Others will receive indignation and wrath*, as seen in verse 8. Here, in contrast to the previous group, only two factors are considered: (1) their manner of life, and (2) their reward. Obviously these do not have "glory and honour and immortality" as their objective. Three things are said about their manner of life: (1) they cause contention; (2) they do not obey the truth; but (3) they obey unrighteousness instead. The reference to "contention" is particularly related to the Jewish situation in Paul's day, but those who follow error always cause contention and division in opposing those who teach and follow the truths.

The reward of this group is "indignation" (fury) and "wrath": furious wrath. Note verse 5 again. The Jews are doubly condemned: by their deeds and by the light against which they have continued in these deeds. The same goes for all who sin against the light.

3. AN IMPARTIAL JUDGMENT (Romans 2:9-11)

In effect, these three verses repeat the previous three. Only now Paul restates himself in order to point up in a special way the fact that no one or no group will receive any special consideration at the judgment. In particular, the Jew will not. Jew and Gentile will face the judgment on the same basis.

The Practise Illustrated (verses 9, 10). In verses 6-8 Paul first stated the principle (6) and then illustrated how that principle would apply to two groups in practice (7, 8). Now, in restating this, he reverses the order, first repeating the two illustrations (9, 10) and then rephrasing the principle (11).

1. *Tribulation and anguish will be the reward of some*, according to verse 9. This is the same group as in verse 8 above. "Indignation and wrath" looked upon their reward from God's point of view. "Tribulation and anguish" sees it from the point of view of those judged. Tribulation is trouble; anguish is dire calamity. Their suffering is in view. In this verse their manner of life is more simply described than in verse 8; but "doing evil" means the same thing as "obeying unrighteousness instead of the truth."

2. *Others will receive glory and honour and peace* according to verse 10. This is the same group as in verse 7. Again, "eternal life" sees the reward from the viewpoint of the divine gift; "glory and honour and peace" look at the same reward from the viewpoint of the blessed person's happiness. Here "peace" is added to two words repeated from verse 7, and suggests permanence as well as tranquility. The description of the manner of life is almost the same as in verse 7.

The key phrase in both verses 9 and 10 is "to [of] the Jew first, and also to the Gentile." This addition provides the reason for repeating the illustrations so that special emphasis may be given the fact that race has nothing to do with the judgment. Jew and Gentile will stand on the same grounds.

The Principle Indicated (verse 11). In essence this restates the principle indicated in verse 6, but with a different phrasing and point of view. There the individuality is the point; here, the impartiality. That there is "no respect of persons" with God simply means that *who* a person is does not count. *What* he is is the only important thing. Distinctions of race—Jew versus Gentile—were particularly on Paul's mind when he gave us this principle. But the principle applies to all other identity distinctions equally as well: social, economic, national, or what have you. God treats all alike. All will be judged on the same basis.

4. AN INEVITABLE JUDGMENT (Romans 2:12-16)

These verses are similar to the first three verses of this chapter in that they insist on the certainty of judgment. The difference is that verses 1-3 spoke entirely of the Jews, while verses 12-16 stress the fact that judgment is an absolute certainty for all, Jew and Gentile alike.

Judgment for the Sinner (verse 12). This verse states the basic truth that will be expanded on in verses 13-15. That truth is this: All who sin will be condemned at the judgment, whoever they are, Jew or Gentile. Two groups are involved, then.

1. *Those who sin "without law"* will face this condemnation.

This group includes the Gentile and heathen world to whom the written law of God was not given. In Paul's day that involved practically all of the non-Jewish world. Today, since the Old Testament Scriptures have become part of the Bible of the Christian world, this group would involve the non-Jewish and non-Christian peoples as sinners "without law."

Paul's point is that these sinners, though not possessing the enlightenment of written law, will perish. This truth is based on the principle that actual guilt is the reason for condemnation, not anything else. Paul has already shown in chapter one that the heathen world is clearly guilty and responsible.

2. *Those who sin "in the law"* will likewise face the condemnation. This group in Paul's day was the Jewish people to whom the written law was given. The Jews possessed the revealed requirements of God, and yet they sinned, too (compare verse 1, again). By that law they will be judged and found guilty of sin.

Verse 12 makes it plain that the basis for condemnation at the judgment will be actual wrong-doing. Possessing or not possessing the written law will have nothing to do with it. Knowledge will not be the question; deeds will. All sinners—and surely Paul is implying that all have sinned—will be condemned.

Judgment by a Standard (verses 13-15). Now Paul makes it plain that both groups mentioned above will be judged by a clear standard.

1. *Jews will be judged by the written law,* and verse 13 tells us this. The phrase "hearers of the law" means the same as "in the law" in the previous verse: These are those to whom the written law has been given (Jews in Paul's frame of reference, but now including the "Christian" world). In calling this group "hearers," Paul subtly drives home the point that hearing is not enough; doing is required (cf. Matthew 6:24-27). only Jesus fulfilled the law

2. *Gentiles will be judged by the law of conscience*, a point made in verses 14, 15. (In our day, the Gentile Christian world would come under the first category rather than this one.) These "have not the law," meaning the written law of Moses. But Paul's teaching here is that even these possess *a* law, which we can call the law of conscience, and by which the Gentiles will be judged.

Paul cites three evidences that the Gentile, heathen world possesses such an unwritten law. (1) Their *deeds,* indicated in the clause "when the Gentiles *do* by nature the things contained in the law." Even the heathen, by their actions, show some consciousness of divine standards for human conduct. They show this both positively, in their own behavior; and negatively, in their efforts to atone for wrongdoing. (2) Their *conscience*, indicated in the clause "their conscience also bearing witness." This refers specifically to their sense of guilt (or lack of it) about their own deeds. (3) Their *judgments,* indicated in the clause "their thoughts the mean while

31

accusing or else excusing one another." This refers to their reckonings of guilt or innocence to others. Even the heathen judge each other. In all three of these then the heathen world manifests an inner law.

Do not be misled into thinking that Paul is teaching justification by works. First, he emphasizes deeds not because they are the basis of salvation but because they are the basis of judgment. Deeds stand in contrast to profession, race, knowledge, possession of the written law. Second, "justified" (13) refers not so much to actual salvation in this context as to the basis for judgment. Both Jew and Gentile possess "law." Both sin in spite of that knowledge. With both the *doing* will be the basis of their judgment, their trial at God's bar, not the *knowing*.

Third, Paul is implying one very important thing which lays a foundation for the remainder of the epistle. That is the fact that on the basis of deeds no one can be justified. The Jew has not kept the written law; the Gentile has not kept the law written in his heart. Who then can be saved? Paul will soon tell us of the righteousness God has provided in Christ, the one who kept fully both laws.

Judgment by the Savior (verse 16). Paul's concluding point is that the judgment day will feature Jesus Christ. All men, Jew and Gentile alike, will be brought face to face with Jesus Christ. The phrase "according to my gospel" simply means that Paul preaches this truth that all men will be judged by Jesus Christ.

That God will judge men in reference to Jesus Christ means two things. First, it means that Jesus will be the standard of judgment. We must remember that Jesus Christ in his earthly life was the perfect model of man as man ought to be. All our failures to measure up to the perfect humanity of Jesus Christ are but evidences of our sin. Second, this means that men will be judged in terms of their relationship to Jesus Christ. Compare John 16:8, 9.

We note in closing that all men will be judged in this same way, Jew and Gentile alike, and that all "secrets" will be made manifest then (1 Corinthians 4:5). The condition of one's *heart*, as shown by genuinely good *deeds*, is far more important than such external things as racial heritage or the possession of a written law. This principle has a double edge: It does not help the Gentile, who must face judgment by reason of natural revelation and conscience; the Jew has no advantage for he too will be "justified" by what is in his heart, not by what is on his Mosaic scroll.

5 The Guilt of Impenitent Jews

Study Text: Romans 2:17-29

Introduction
1. The Falseness of Jewish Confidence (Romans 2:17-20)
   a. Pride of Race (verse 17a)
   b. Pride of Revelation (verses 17b, 18)
   c. Pride of Responsibility (verses 19, 20)
2. The Fiction of Jewish Conduct (Romans 2:21-24)
   a. Their Reproachful Behavior (verses 21, 22)
   b. The Resultant Blasphemy (verses 23, 24)
3. The Failure of Jewish Circumcision (Romans 2:25-27)
   a. External Obedience Unsuccessful (verse 25)
   b. Equal Opportunity for the Uncircumcised (verses 26, 27)
4. The Facts about Jewish Character (Romans 2:28, 29)
   a. What Does Not Make a Jew (verse 28)
   b. What Does Make a Jew (verse 29)

INTRODUCTION

We are still studying that portion of Romans in which Paul proves that all the world stands guilty and condemned before God, and thus in desperate need of some provision for becoming right with God. In chapter one Paul showed that this applies to the Gentile, heathen world. In 2:1—3:8 he shows that the Jews are not exceptions, but share the same guilt and need. In the previous section (2:1-16), we saw that God's principles of judgment are such that Jew and Gentile alike stand under this condemnation. In this section

(2:17-29) we see that the actual situation with the Jews also makes it plain that they stand guilty and condemned.

We can imagine the anger of Jews who would read Paul's words in the passage covered in this study. They put such great confidence in their possession and knowledge of the Law, in their racial heritage, in their rigorous observance of Mosaic ritual, in their circumcision. Surely they were God's chosen, righteous! But Paul punctures their swollen pride and exposes the crumbling foundation of self-righteousness on which that confidence was built. The Jews too need the righteousness of God provided by Jesus Christ.

EXPOSITION

By noting the general study-outline in the back of this book, you will see that this is the second of three sections under the subsection, "The Hebrews' Need for Righteousness." This section dealing with 2:17-29 is entitled "The Guilt of Impenitent Jews" and has as its purpose to show that the actual situation of the Jews clearly shows their guilt before God.

1. THE FALSENESS OF JEWISH CONFIDENCE
(Romans 2:17-20)

As noted in the introduction, the Jews put great confidence in their own spiritual well-being, a confidence based on various things. Paul proceeds to show just how false and flimsy that confidence is.

Pride of Race (verse 17a). "Behold, thou art called a Jew," says Paul; and we can almost hear the indrawn breath of those whose chests swelled with pride in that name, "Jew." The word itself comes, of course, from the name of the tribe of Judah, the dominant tribe. It was applied, however, and with pride, to all Israelites.

"Abraham is our father," the Jews said with that same pride to Jesus (John 8:39). A few words later they showed they equated that with being children of God (John 8:41). After all, Abraham was the one God called to be father of a great nation, a nation to be known as God's chosen people (Genesis 17:7, 8; Exodus 19:3-6). The Jews understandably put great confidence in their racial heritage. Paul wants them to realize that to be "called a Jew," however, does not give one any special standing with God.

Pride of Revelation (verse 17b, 18). The second thing Paul mentions, in which the Jews put great confidence, is the Law. They had been given the Law as a special revelation from God through Moses. That fact added to their pride as a people specially chosen by God. Did that not make it evident they had special standing with God?

34

There are five clauses in this passage, all closely related and meaning about the same thing. (1) To "rest" in the Law (17b) means to bank on the Law as a source of confidence. Possession of the written law was the foundation of the Jew's sense of security.

(2) Possessing the Law, the Jews were consequently "instructed out of the law" (18b). The word translated "instructed" refers to a formal program of education. The Jews were especially careful to maintain a thorough system of education in the Law. The Rabbis taught that a father had three duties toward his son, and the first was to teach him the Law. The Jewish "public" educational system in Paul's day was built around the Law. All Jewish lads were well-instructed.

(3) In consequence of this thorough instruction, the Jews could rightly claim to "know God's will" (18). The Old Testament Scriptures made God's expectations of man quite clear. The Jews knew—if they did not correctly understand—God's standards and requirements.

(4) Further, this thorough instruction caused them to be able to "approve the things that are more excellent" (18). Literally, these words mean to "accurately test out the difference between good and evil." The Jews knew the Law and could put God's own standard of measurement by men's deeds.

(5) All this put together resulted in the Jews' "boast of God" (19). The word translated "boast" refers to a proud confidence. And all this rested on the privilege of possessing the Law. On this foundation the legalistic Jew could stand and confidently face God, little realizing (like that Pharisee of whom Jesus spoke in 18:9-14) how far from God he really was.

Pride of Responsibility (verses 19, 20). The Jews' pride in racial heritage and revealed law led to another source of confidence: a sense of responsibility to instruct others. When one has been given special revelation from God, it becomes his responsibility to teach others the content of that revelation, and to sit in judgment on others. So the Jews—partly correct—felt. Compare 2:1, 3.

1. *The nature of this responsibility*, as the Jews saw it, is indicated in 19, 20a. Four phrases are used, but all refer to the same sense of responsibility. "You see yourselves as guides for blind men," Paul says, "a light to those in darkness," "instructors of foolish (unknowing) ones," "teachers for babes." While it is true that the Jews entrusted with special revelation, should have instructed the rest of the world, Paul's phrases are carefully chosen to expose the wicked vanity and pride which the Jews had, creating a false confidence about their own situation and a boastful disdain of others. Thus, though Paul's descriptions of the Jews throughout the passage are all factually true, they are also ironic in revealing how the Jews wrongly felt.

2. *The basis for this responsibility*, as indicated in 20b, is the

Jews' possession ("hast") of the Law. This knowledge of truth from the revealed Law caused the Jews to recognize their responsibility to teach others. Again, that was a true recognition; but again Paul adds a touch of irony with his use of "form." The Jews had the form, the shape of knowledge and truth; but they missed its true spirit and essence.

So there is an element of truth in the way the Jews saw themselves. Indeed they did place their confidence in the Law. They *could* boast of their relationship to God and of His special blessings upon them. They *did* know His will. They *were* able to "accurately test out the difference between good and evil," and choose the good (verse 18). They certainly *were* instructed by the Law. They *did* have the capacity to guide the (spiritually) blind, to give light to those in (spiritual) darkness, to correct ("instruct") the foolish, to teach babes. They *were* possessors of the form of knowledge and truth contained in the Law.

But in all these marvelous possibilities the Jews had arrogantly and self-righteously twisted the truth they could have shared with the world. In teaching a kind of external salvation by law-keeping they had tragically missed the spirit and intent of the revelation with which God had blessed them. All their confidence, based on these things, was a false confidence.

2. THE FICTION OF JEWISH CONDUCT (Romans 2:21-24)

These verses stand in sharp contrast with verses 17-20. There Paul referred to all the glorious things which, if rightly followed, could have been such blessings to the Jews. Here he shows how far short the Jews have fallen in actual conduct. They who were so proud of legal righteousness are exposed as having only a fictional and hypocritical righteousness.

Their Reproachful Behavior (verses 21, 22). The Jews are hypocrites because they are guilty of violating their own teachings, the very standards of the Law they so proudly possessed. Paul makes this point by asking four pointed questions, and the implied answer for each one is "yes." By the way, several good commentators think these have been incorrectly translated as questions and should be simple statements of fact: "You teach others; you do not teach yourself!" etc. (The ancient Greek manuscripts do not have modern punctuation marks, so this is possible.) Either way, the point is the same.

There is strong contrast in verses 21, 22 between the Jews' *teaching* and their *deeds*. They teach ever so strongly against stealing, adultery, and idolatry, but they themselves are guilty of these very sins. Again, Paul's words are ironic: What excellent teachers the Jews are; a pity they have not taught themselves! Let us keep in mind that the Jews would not be as guilty as the heathen of open, excessive sins; but the motives and intents of their hearts brought them under equal condemnation (see Matthew 5:27, 28; 15:3-8; 23:25-28; etc.).

The Resultant Blasphemy (verses 23, 24). The tragedy of the Jews' hypocritical behavior is the reproach brought on the name of God. This is the point of verses 23, 24. By breaking the Law they proudly possess, they have given occasion for the Gentiles to speak evil about the God of the Jews. Verse 24 is a quotation from Isaiah 52:5, but it is an idea found often in the Old Testament. The misconduct of Israel was always viewed as an opportunity for Gentiles to mock their teachings and thus their God. And so with the Jews of Paul's day.

The idea also occurs in the New Testament in reference to Christians. Compare 2 Peter 2:2, where Peter indicates that "the way of truth shall be evil spoken of" (the same Greek word as in Romans) because of Christians who turn aside to follow false teachers. We must watch this principle in our lives as professing Christians. Whenever our lives do not match the teachings of Christ, His name suffers. The wicked take delight and comfort in our inconsistencies.

3. THE FAILURE OF JEWISH CIRCUMCISION (Romans 2:25-27)

The Jews not only placed a great deal of confidence in their possession of the law of Moses, they also took wrongful pride in the sign of circumcision passed down to them from Abraham. Paul turns now to that subject, in order to show that neither the Law nor circumcision exempts the Jew from condemnation. In no way is the Jew an exceptional case; he is as guilty before God and in need of righteousness as any other member of the human race.

External Obedience Unsuccessful (verse 25). The point here is that it is foolish for the Jews to put confidence in circumcision, because there is one very important condition for success they have failed to meet. The "if" in this verse introduces this essential ingredient. In other words, circumcision will be profitable to the person who succeeds in keeping the whole Law, and that includes a heartfelt, perfect obedience, not a mere external conformity.

In the clause "if thou keep the law," the Greek verb "keep" is one that means practice, observance. And it is in the tense that refers to continuing action. Regular, constant observance is in view. In the second "if" clause ("if thou be a breaker of the law"), the noun "breaker" (transgressor) is used, rather than the verb "break," referring to the name a person wears, the identity he bears, what he really is.

The point is clear, that *no* person, Jew included, has ever kept *all* the Law. As Paul says in Galatians 3:10, "As many as are of the works of the law are under the curse: for it is written, cursed is every one that continueth not in *all* things which are written in the book of the law." Compare James 2:10: "Whosoever shall keep the whole law, and yet offend in one point, he is guilty of all." The first "if" clause represents the situation as the Jews saw it on the surface. The second "if" clause represents the situation as it really was and is.

So Paul concludes that circumcision, to a breaker of the Law—and every Jew is one—is no better than uncircumcision. As people who have failed to observe the Law, the Jews have no basis for trusting in their circumcision to entitle them to special consideration from God.

Equal Opportunity for the Uncircumcised (verses 26, 27). What Paul teaches us in this passage is that an uncircumcised person (Gentile) has as much opportunity before God as the Jew. Because God is interested in *character*, not *ceremony*. Deeds and actions count, not names and knowledge and external rituals.

Paul says this is such a way as to give the logical "other side of the coin" to verse 25. If circumcision for a (Jewish) law-breaker is counted as uncircumcision, then uncircumcision for a (Gentile) law-keeper is counted as circumcision. The point is that circumcision does not help one be right with God, and so the Jewish confidence in that ceremony was misplaced. Circumcision failed to give them righteousness.

Again we must realize that the "ifs" in verses 26, 27 are as big as the first "if" in verse 25. The circumcised Jew cannot "keep the law" (25), nor can the uncircumcised Gentile "fulfil the law" (27). The condition is hypothetical as far as actual practice is concerned. The word "fulfil" in verse 27 means to carry out to completion. "Keep" in verse 26 means to guard. All these words involve the same basic concept of living up to the whole purpose and intent of the law, and neither Gentile nor Jew can do so. But if a Gentile ever did, he would, though uncircumcised, be far better off than the circumcised Jewish law-breaker. Neither circumcision nor racial ancestry matter with God. By the way, the phrase, "by the letter and circumcision," referring to Jewish transgression, probably means "in spite of keeping the letter of the Law and practicing circumcision," both of which can be mere external observance.

One further observation is that Paul may be hinting at truths he will make clearer later in the epistle. There is one method by which the "law's righteousness" *can* be fulfilled. This is only by Jesus Christ. Paul's implied point is that the uncircumcised Gentile can accept Christ as his righteousness and thus be in a position to judge the self-righteous Jew who in spite of "letter and circumcision" does transgress the Law.

4. THE FACTS ABOUT JEWISH CHARACTER (Romans 2:28, 29)

We could very well call these two verses "what makes one a real

Jew"—a Jew in fact, not in practice. Paul is going to show that spiritual character is what counts, not external ceremonies.

What Does Not Make a Jew (verse 28). This verse gives us the negative side. The key words are "outwardly" and "in the flesh" as contrasted with "inwardly" and "of the heart" in the next verse. This difference is applied to two areas of Jewish pride, both physical things.

First is racial ancestry. The Jews took great glory in their physical lineage. Being directly descended from Abraham, from Jacob (Israel), and from one or the other of Jacob's twelve sons was a source of confidence. They thought that this heritage entitled them to a special place with God. How startled they must be to hear Paul say that being a Jew is not a matter of physical (external) or fleshly lineage, but a matter of the spiritual condition of the heart!

Second is the sign of circumcision. The Jews likewise considered this a token of special favor from God. First given to Abraham (Genesis 17:9-14) circumcision had been commanded by God for every male Hebrew of every succeeding generation. The little surgical procedure had been carefully preserved by the Jews, and the circumcising of the eight-day-old boy was a reason for pride in every Jewish family. And now Paul makes the mysterious affirmation that being circumcised is also not a matter of a physical cutting away of the foreskin of the male, but a spiritual condition of the heart!

What Does Make a Jew (verse 29). Paul's statement must have seemed absolutely incredible to any Jew who read his letter. Why, being a Jew *is* being physically descended from Abraham! Being circumcised *is* a physical ritual! Or so they thought. But Paul—who had once thought the same way himself—now sees it differently. Being a "Jew" in the truest sense of the word and being "circumcised" in the best sense of the word are both matters of an inward spiritual condition.

It is not being a Jew outwardly that counts, then; it is being a Jew inwardly. This conclusion has tremendous importance and is rather like a two-edged sword. Negatively, it means that not all Jews, racially, are true Jews. In other words, not every Jew physically can lay claim to be spiritually what the name "Jew" was intended to imply. Positively it means that a Gentile physically *can* be a true "Jew." In other words, an uncircumcised non-Israelite can be spiritually what the name "Jew" was intended to imply.

The negative side of this truth was already implied in Old Testament times. Jeremiah, for example, spoke of the need for the Israelites to "take away the foreskins of your *heart*" (4:4), and he denounced Israel as "uncircumcised in the *heart*" (9:26). The positive side of this truth is evident in other New Testament passages. In Galatians 3:7, for example, Paul speaks of *all* who are "of faith," whether Jew or Gentile, as "Abraham's children."

In verse 29 "inwardly" means the same thing as "of the heart." Note the contrast between keeping the "spirit" of a regulation—its true intent and purpose, rather than the mere "letter"—that is, external observance without heartfelt conformity to God's deeper motivations. We must always be on guard about this principle in our obedience to the Lord. The reference to praise is intended to emphasize the fact that legalistic and external conformity bring human recognition, but not the praise of God, who sees the heart.

There is considerable disagreement among Bible interpreters whether all the promises to physical Israel have been yet fulfilled. Some, especially amillennialists, think that there will never again be a place of blessing for Israel as a nation, and that the "spiritual" Israel has completely and permanently displaced her as heirs of God's promises. Others, especially premillennialists, think that the future will again see physical Israel restored to a place of special service in God's hand, that a national remnant will occupy the original promised land and inherit the ancient promises.

Regardless which of these positions is correct, one thing is clear to this writer, at least. All saved people—Jew or Gentile—are Abraham's spiritual children, spiritually "Jews." Perhaps as some think, all God's promises to Israel are not being spiritually fulfilled within this "spiritual" Israel. Perhaps, as others insist, some of these promises will be fulfilled to a truly physical Israel in the future. Either way, whatever "Israel" inherits, *all* of the spiritual children of Abraham inherit, whether present or future.

In summarizing this section (2:17-29), we note that Paul has "knocked the props" out from under all the Jews' reasons for confidence. There are three of these in which they trusted: the *law* of Moses which had been so spectacularly given and almost lovingly preserved; *circumcision*, carefully observed from generation to generation since Abraham; and *physical lineage* as a Jew, with ancestry traced back to Israel himself, the one who wrestled with the Lord.

What Paul has said is that these do not count. The precious Law has been broken; fleshly circumcision and physical lineage are nothing more than profitless externals. What really counts is the true spiritual condition of the heart. And on this basis the self-righteous Jew stands as guilty and condemned as the Gentile-heathen.

6 God's Immutable Justice

Study Text: Romans 3:1-8

Introduction
1. A Question of Divine Favor (Romans 3:1, 2)
   a. The Question of Advantage Anticipated (verse 1)
   b. The Question of Advantage Answered (verse 2)
2. A Question of Divine Faithfulness (Romans 3:3, 4)
   a. The Question of Veracity Anticipated (verse 3)
   b. The Question of Veracity Answered (verse 4)
3. A Question of Divine Fairness (Romans 3:5-8)
   a. The Question of Justice Anticipated (verses 5, 7)
   b. The Question of Justice Answered (verses 6, 8)

INTRODUCTION

In the past three sections we have seen Paul's insistence that all the world stands in need of the salvation provided by Jesus Christ. In 1:18-32 Paul showed how the pagan world in particular is guilty and condemned before God. In chapter 2 Paul showed that the Jews are alike included in this universal condemnation. The principles of God's impartial judgment (2:1-16) and the actual condition of the Jews (2:17-29) both prove that the Jews are no exception.

Paul was well aware, however, that his Jewish readers would not take his accusations lying down. They would naturally be angered to hear him say that they were as guilty of sin as the heathen. They would be quick to offer arguments against his position.

Consequently, Paul devotes one more passage to the question of Jewish need. In this passage which we study in this lesson Paul anticipates the problems which the Jews will raise. He brings up the objections he knows they will offer and briefly answers each objection to his position. There are, in fact, three arguments with which Paul deals as will be seen in the study outline.

EXPOSITION

Before going into the details of the study, consult the general study-outline in the back of this book. There you will see that this study is the third and final one under the subheading, "The Hebrews' Need for Righteousness." This study, covering 3:1-8, is entitled "God's Immutable Justice." "Immutable" means unchangeable. The fact of Jewish guilt and the exclusive provision of righteousness in Christ do not change the immutable principles of God's righteous judgment.

1. A QUESTION OF DIVINE FAVOR (Romans 3:1, 2)

You will see that Paul's approach in this passage is to raise questions and then to provide answers. The questions he raises are those which he anticipates would be raised by Jews objecting to his position as stated in chapter two. The first question is that which is raised in verse 1.

The Question of Advantage Anticipated (verse 1). We can easily grasp the feeling behind this question. In chapter two Paul has indicated his position that the Jews are no better off, and are perhaps worse off, than the heathen Gentiles. Such a position will anger the Jews, and Paul knows it. They are going to be quick to object, to ask: "Paul, if it is true—as you say—that we Jews are as guilty as the heathen, then what good is it to be a Jew, anyway? If your position is correct, then there is no advantage in being a Jew after all!"

We might easily rephrase their question this way: "Did God bestow any special favor on the Jewish people?" The entire Old Testament would appear to indicate that He did. Certainly the Jews' feelings about themselves as God's chosen people were based on a consciousness of special divine favor. But Paul's view of Jewish unrighteousness and condemnation, as equivalent to or worse than heathen guilt, seems to contradict that view of the Jews as God's specially-blessed people. Is there a contradiction here? How is this to be explained?

The twofold question in verse 1 is all really this same question, phrased in two different ways. The first question uses the word "advantage," the second "profit": the two are synonyms. The "then" in the first question means "therefore" and looks back to the position stated in detail in chapter two. If that position is correct,

42

then was there any advantage to being a Jew? Or had the uncivilized black in Africa been as well off before God as the Israelite in Biblical times? This first phrasing of the question makes *race* the issue.

The second phrasing of the question makes *circumcision* the issue. Has there been any profit in circumcision? We can imagine the way the Jewish objectors would bristle with contempt for Paul as he raised this question. In particular, in 2:25-29 Paul had insisted that the circumcision of the flesh did not count with God, but the inward, spiritual "circumcision" of the heart. "Well then, Paul, if that is so, why were we ever circumcised? After all, Paul, *God* was the one who gave us circumcision! Surely there was some profit in it!"

The logic of these questions is obvious. Paul has insisted that physical descendancy from Abraham does not count with God, nor does physical circumcision. But it was God who chose Abraham's descendants, and God who commanded circumcision! What then?

The Question of Advantage Answered (verse 2). Paul does not attempt a thorough answer to the problem, but his brief reply touches on the chief ingredients of the solution.

2. *General advantage is admitted* by the words, "Much every way." These words simply declare that the Jews enjoyed great advantages in all sorts of ways. Paul does not, nor has ever intended to deny that. In other words, then, God *has* blessed Israel with special favor. The position of chapter two, that the Jews are guilty and condemned before God, does not contradict that.

Paul makes no effort to elaborate on all these advantages. Nor shall we. In a general way, however, we must make sure we understand the solution of the problem raised. On the one hand, for example, circumcision is an admittedly external act that engenders no favor from God, the position espoused in 2:25-29. On the other hand, God *did* command the practice and so there must certainly have been some value therein. The solution to that apparent conflict lies in the fact that circumcision had value only when properly understood and practiced as an outward sign of an inner, spiritual relationship with God. The Jews erred in placing value in the sign itself, just as they wrongly conceived the law to provide for salvation by rules-keeping.

God certainly did favor the Jews, and their racial heritage and circumcision were significant evidences of that favor, but the evidences were not to be confused with the favor itself or with the basis for the favor. Such is the point Paul wants clear. We, too, need to be constantly reminded of this truth lest we confuse divinely-given externals (like our ordinances, for example) with the inward spiritual experiences.

2. *A specific advantage is indicated:* "chiefly, because that unto them were committed the oracles of God." "Chiefly" means "foremost": This is the most important "advantage" Paul sees in the

special favor God bestowed on the Jewish nation. "Committed" means "entrusted." "Oracles" means "sayings."

The Jewish nation was entrusted with the written revelation of God. These "sayings" include, of course, all the messages ever brought by any prophet to whom God revealed his words for Israel. Most important among these, though, were those recorded, thus revealed and inspired. In particular, then, this "advantage" consists in the possession of the Old Testament Scriptures (though it would not require much stretching to include in these "sayings" the teachings of Jesus while on earth among the Jews).

Why was the possession of this revelation such an advantage? The answer is obvious: Because thereby the way to God was made plain. The Old Scriptures, even though not complete without the record of the Savior who was so clearly prefigured therein, made plain God's basic requirements of man and how man could please God by faith. The Jews alone possessed this record. Thus their opportunities for knowing and serving God acceptably—in comparison to the heathen world—were much enhanced. No doubt there was never a majority of the Jews really saved. Far too many of them wrongly understood the revelation. But there were many—hundreds of thousands, surely—who, even before Christ came, truly knew God and are in Heaven. There must have been precious few among the Gentiles. God certainly did favor the Jewish people.

2. A QUESTION OF DIVINE FAITHFULNESS (Romans 3:3, 4)

Again Paul uses the question and answer approach, the question being another he anticipates his Jewish opponents will ask. Verse 3 contains this second problem.

The Question of Veracity Anticipated (verse 3). The question raised here is one which logically follows the previous one. The first question looked at Paul's position from the standpoint of Jewish advantage; this one considers the implications from the standpoint of God's faithfulness to His promises.

The question asked in verse 3 will be clearer if the phrase, "the faith of God," is understood to mean "the faithfulness of God." (The Greek word used can mean "faith" or "faithfulness.") The point of the question is this: God had made, in his dealings with Israel, many wonderful promises to the Jews. But Paul has just taught, in chapter two, that the Jew stands guilty and condemned just like the heathen, headed for ruin and Hell, not for promised blessings. And Paul believes that Israel's unbelief is responsible for her lost condition. "Well, then," the Jewish objectors can ask, "Does Israel's unbelief—as you call it—void God's promises to Israel? Can God justly go back on His promises just because Israel has not had faith?"

44

You can see that this question involves God's immutability and veracity. We believe that God is immutable, that He changes not (Malachi 3:6). We believe in His veracity, that He always keeps his promises, that He is faithful to His Word (Isaiah 25:1). All through the Old Testament God had spoken of His special love for Israel, and always promised blessing to them. Yet Paul has now indicated, in chapter 2, that the Jews are as wicked as the heathen and headed for severe judgment. How can these two ideas be reconciled? Will God go back on His Word?

We should not overlook the fact that several words in verses 2, 3 are on the same root: "committed," "believe," "unbelief," and "faith." The Jews were *trusted* with the oracles of God (2). But they did not *trust* Him (3a). Will their lack of *trust* "nullify" ("make without effect") the *trustworthiness* of God (3b)?

The Question of Veracity Answered (verse 4). The answer Paul gives can be presented in the three following assertions, though all three mean basically the same thing.

1. *God is faithful,* regardless of the belief or unbelief of men. The exclamation "God forbid!" means that the answer to the question of verse 3 is an emphatic "No!" The faithfulness of God will never be nullified by anything men do. Any supposition that Israel's unbelief will cause God to go back on His promises to Israel is based on a misunderstanding. Paul never meant to imply any such thing.

2. *God is truthful,* regardless how much men lie. "Let God be true," Paul says, "even if every man must be found a liar." God always speaks the truth, and that includes His promises, even the old promises to Israel. Thus every promise can be counted on. Truthfulness is essential to faithfulness and vice-versa. For one to be truthful, he must be faithful to His pledged word; for one to be able to be faithful, he must speak the truth in the first place. God can be counted on both ways.

3. *God's pronouncements are right and just,* regardless of any accusations men might make against Him. Men may say God has not fulfilled His Word, but in every such instance they lie. God will always be "justified" in His sayings, which means He will always be "proved right." Paul represents this as though God himself had to stand before a judge to have His words tested; even so, God is "found innocent of wrong" (justified) in everything He has ever said. This is quoted from Psalm 51:4.

The problem, as we have seen it, lies in the fact that God had made great promises of blessing for Israel; yet Israel, because of unbelief, is under a curse. How are these reconciled? Two factors are involved. First, and most important, we have to understand that God's promises of blessing for men are always *conditional,* even though the condition may often be left implied rather than actually stated. Thus, when God promises blessing to Israel, we should realize that the fulfilment of that depends on whether Israel meets the condition man always must meet, faith. If Israel does not believe and is rejected and fails to receive the promised blessing, God's faithfulness cannot be questioned, for the conditional aspect was clear all the while.

Such is the case with many apparent scriptural difficulties. And we, like Israel, must remember that God's promised blessings to us are conditioned on our response in faith. Even the Christian cannot presume to hold God to promises of eternal salvation (as in John 10:28, for example) unless the required faith is maintained.

Second, we must also realize that Paul means that all God's promises to "Israel" *will* be fulfilled anyway. All interpreters agree that this is involved, though there are two different methods for arriving at this conclusion. Premillennialists believe the time is yet to come when a restored Israel will still inherit all the ancient promises as a nation. Amillennialists believe that the present church is a "spiritual" Israel that is now, in fact, inheriting these ancient promises so far as their spiritual content is concerned. Either way, God is not going back on His Word. Later in this epistle Paul will go into this in more detail (chapters 9-11).

3. A QUESTION OF DIVINE FAIRNESS (Romans 3:5-8)

Paul proceeds to the third objection he can imagine his Jewish readers will offer to his position, taught in chapter 2, that the Jews' need for salvation in Christ is as great as that of the heathen. Again, he approaches the matter in question and answer form.

The Question of Justice Anticipated (verses 5, 7). The two forms of this question in verses 5 and 7 are expressing the same objection, one Paul's Jewish readers will throw at him. He has just shown that the Jewish lack of faith in God will not set at nought the faithfulness of God. In men's lies the truthfulness of God becomes all the more evident. When men are wicked and sinful, the righteousness of God shines all the more brightly.

"Wait a minute!" some will say: "If our unbelief, our lies, our faithlessness, serve to commend God's righteousness, then is not our sin glorifying God? Is it not better that we sin? Why should God punish us for doing that which serves to magnify His goodness?"

This is a type of argument Paul evidently faced often in response to his preaching of the salvation of sinners by grace. As he puts it in Romans 5:20, "Where sin abounded, grace did much more abound." So some of his detractors, especially the self-righteous Jews, would reply: "Then it is better to be a sinner, than not—if what you preach is so!"

Jesus encountered this same attitude, you will recall. The Pharisees, in particular, frowned on His associations with "sinners."

He told them that He came to save "sinners," not those already righteous (Matthew 9:13). But, you see, if one carries that truth out to its logical conclusion, one might reason like this: Since only a "sinner" can be saved, and by that salvation the grace and righteousness of God are magnified, then it is *good* to be a sinner! How can God be fair and condemn sin, if sin commends His mercy? Logical or not, that is exactly the kind of argument Paul anticipates and deals with here.

The wording of this argument in verse 5 is this: "If our unrighteousness (wrongdoing) commends (establishes, evidences, holds together) the righteousness of God, then is it unrighteous (wrong) of God to take vengeance (literally, "bring wrath upon") upon us for our wrongdoing?" (The question is worded, in Greek, so as to expect a negative answer.) In verse 7 the wording is this: "If my lie (falsehood) caused the truth (veracity) of God to abound (flourish, excel, be pre-eminent), and thus glorifies God, then why am I to be judged (condemned) as a sinner?" Both wordings mean the same thing.

Before examining Paul's answer to this problem, we note two observations he makes about the argument.

1. *This is a natural man's argument.* The parenthetic "I speak as a man" in verse 5 means that the argument expressed in that verse is worded the way a man who does not understand spiritual things would word it. A spiritually-minded man would never dream of saying that God's salvation of sinners excuses those sinners for their unrighteousness.

2. *This is not what Paul taught.* The parenthetic insertion in verse 8 indicated that those who accused Paul of teaching "Let us do evil that good may come" were not reporting him correctly. Those who said Paul taught that were *slandering* (Greek: "blaspheming") him! The "we" means primarily Paul, but would include his co-workers.

The Question of Justice Answered (verses 6, 8). The answer, in summary, is that sin is never justified and God is always just. The argument of Paul's opponent will not hold water. We notice two closely related aspects of this truth.

1. *God is just in punishing sin.* Verse 6 particularly clarifies this. The exclamatory "God forbid" again shows that the question of verse 5 is an emphatic "No." God is not unrighteous in bringing wrath on sinners. God's justice is absolute and unchanging, and thus must never be questioned, even when we fail to understand. It *is* fair for God to condemn the sinner.

The rhetorical question in verse 6 is intended to reinforce this conclusion by showing how ridiculous would be the position implied in the question in verse 5. In other words, Paul answers his imaginary Jewish questioner with a question of his own: "If, as you imply, God is unrighteous to punish sin, how then shall God judge the world?"

In other words, if God cannot condemn the unrighteousness of the Jews, He cannot condemn the unrighteousness of anyone else! Remember the impartiality emphasized in 2:9-11.

2. *Man is never justified in sinning.* This is the directly-implied teaching of verses 7, 8. The way the question is worded in verse 7 implies that if the point of view of the Jewish argument *was* correct, then there would *not* be grounds to condemn him as a sinner. The foolishness of the conclusion shows the foolishness of the reasoning that would lead to such a conclusion.

That foolishness if further underlined in verse 8. Paul refers to the statement that some had slanderously attributed to him: "Let us do evil, that good may come." He had never taught such a blasphemous thing. But his point is this: If the reasoning of his imaginary Jewish opponent is correct, as stated in verse 7, that "my lie" has glorified God, then it *would* be true that we could say, "Let us do evil that good may come." Again, the foolishness of that conclusion proves the foolishness of the assumption. Any who slanderously say that Paul preaches such nonsense and any who would themselves offer such a wicked justification for their own sins will deserve the judgment they get (8b)!

Let us summarize Paul's answer to make sure the main truth is clear. The fact that God only saves sinners does not excuse sin. The fact that a sinner's salvation glorifies God will not exempt the unrepentant sinner from God's just condemnation. If there were some righteous and some wicked and God saved only the wicked, then one might accuse God of being unfair and conclude that sin is good. And Jesus' words in Matthew 9:13 might be harsh and unjust. But the fact is that all have sinned—Jew included—and God's offer of mercy does not in any way condone or excuse man's sin or relieve his guilt. God's justice in condemning the whole world stands immutable regardless of the Jews' advantages, or their failure to inherit the promises of God, or the glorification He receives in saving sinners.

48

7 Humanity's Need for Righteousness

Study Text: Romans 3:9-20

Introduction
1. A Universal Conclusion (Romans 3:9)
   a. Advantage Denied (verse 9a)
   b. Accusation Declared (verse 9b)
2. An Unrighteous Character (Romans 3:10-12)
   a. Failure in Righteousness (verse 10)
   b. Failure in Reasoning (verse 11a)
   c. Failure in Reverence (verse 11b)
   d. Failure in Rectitude (verse 12a)
   e. Failure in Respectability (verse 12b)
   f. Failure in Reformation (verse 12c)
3. An Unfearing Conduct (Romans 3:13-18)
   a. Deceit (verses 13, 14)
   b. Destruction (verses 15-17)
   c. Defiance (verse 18)
4. An Undeniable Condemnation (Romans 3:19, 20)
   a. What the Law Was Not For (verses 19a, 20a)
   b. What the Law Was For (verses 19b, 20b)

INTRODUCTION

This study brings us to a passage that is both the climax of and the conclusion to the first great part of Romans. As we have seen, the purpose of that first part (1:18—3:20) is to show a universal need for the righteousness of God as provided by faith in Jesus Christ.

If Paul was to persuade men of his gospel (that salvation could

49

be had by faith), he had first to convince men that they needed salvation. An ailing person will not seek treatment until first convinced of the illness. We must get people lost before we can get them saved. That is the reason Jesus said He came to save sinners, not the righteous.

And that is the reason Paul goes to such lengths in these first three chapters to prove that all the world stands guilty and condemned before God and thus in desperate need of some way to get right with God. In 1:18-32 he stressed the needs of mankind from the point of view of the pagan world; in 2:1—3:8 he dealt with the Jewish need, showing that they too are sinking into Hell. In the passage covered today Paul completes this section by summing all humanity—both the heathen and the Hebrews—into one whole and stating the inevitable and certain conclusion about humanity's need.

EXPOSITION

A brief glance at the general study-outline, in the back of this book, will show how this section fits into the overall scheme of Romans. As you can see there, this section covers the final subsection under Part 1 (3:9-20), and is entitled: "Humanity's Need for Righteousness." This passage is, in effect, a brief restatement of the main point Paul has been proving in Part 1.

1. A UNIVERSAL CONCLUSION (Romans 3:9)

This verse states the basic truth which is to be explained further in the remainder of the passage studied in this section. This is the conclusion toward which Paul has been pointing throughout the first portion of the epistle.

The "what then?" of this verse introduces this overall conclusion. The words mean, in effect: "What has all this proved?" What has the lengthy discussion from 1:18—3:8 proved? Paul moves from one point to another like a trained debater and with clear logic. Everything he has said prior to this verse leads to one clear and unmistakable conclusion, that all humanity stands justly condemned before God and in need of a righteousness it does not possess. Paul indicates his conclusion, answering that "what then?" in a twofold manner.

Advantage Denied (verse 9a). First Paul reemphasizes that his previous words have proved that the Jew has no advantage over the Gentile when it comes to standing before God. The "we" refers to the Jews and the "they" to the Gentiles. The Jews are no better off in this matter of guilt and innocence than the Gentiles. They cannot be treated as exceptions or exemptions. Whatever is to be said of one will also be true of the other. That is the point Paul has so carefully labored in 2:1—3:8 and which he restates now as his conclusion is expressed. The "No, in no wise" is an emphatic negative.

Accusation Declared (verse 9b). The essence of Paul's conclusion is this: *all* are "under sin." There are several factors about this worthy of note. First, the Greek word translated "proved" is a legal term that refers to the bringing of charges against someone. Paul is saying that his previous words (note the "before") have served to place this charge of universal guilt against men.

Second, the universality of the charge is seen in the words "both Jews and Gentiles." This serves to say again, as Paul has repeatedly hammered the truth home, that one is as guilty as the other. None are excepted, neither self-righteous moralists nor ignorant heathen.

Third, the phrase "under sin" is interesting. It means, in fact, two things: under the penalty of sin and under the power of sin. In other words, all men are sinners both as to their standing before God and as to their situation in life. All men stand under the judge's findings of guilt and the sentence He pronounces accordingly; and all men live in sin insofar as actual practice and experiences are concerned. Paul is lodging a charge against the entire human race: All wear the name "sinner"; all, alike, are guilty before God.

2. AN UNRIGHTEOUS CHARACTER (Romans 3:10-12)

Having stated his conclusion in verse 9, a conclusion toward which all his observations in 1:18—3:8 have been pointing, Paul now proceeds to cite final evidence of the charge he has lodged against humanity. The evidence given in 1:18—3:8 has been based mostly on the actual circumstances within the pagan and Jewish world. But now Paul turns to the infallible Scriptures to see what God himself has to say.

The words "As it is written" introduce these scriptural citations that confirm Paul's conclusion of universal sinfulness. Actually, these quotations continue throughout verses 10-18, and there are at least six Old Testament passages to which Paul refers. It would be easy to treat all of verses 10-18 under one heading, for they all prove the charge introduced in verse 9. But verses 10-12 prove the charge in a little different way from verses 13-18, and so we are dividing the passage into two sections.

More than one approach has been suggested for comparing verses 10-12 with verses 13-18. Some say that verses 10-12 deal with character in general, while verses 13-18 cover conduct in particular. There certainly seems to be an important element of truth in that distinction, and so we have tried to catch that truth in our outline.

Others have suggested that verses 10-12 state facts that are true of every individual in the whole human race, whereas verses 13-18 state conditions that are true of the human race in a general sense only, since not every human being is constantly "cursing" and "shedding blood" for example. There is certainly an element of truth in this observation, and we shall keep it in mind, even though that was probably not Paul's main thought.

Actually the comparison between verses 10-12 and 13-18 should emphasize the fact that verses 10-12 are mostly *negative*, while verses 13-18 are mostly *positive*. In other words, the first part shows what mankind has *not* done; the second part what he *has* done. On the one hand, he has *not* achieved righteousness, and so man in universal failure stands condemned of unrighteous character. On the other hand, he *has* practiced all sorts of sin, and so in universal wickedness stands condemned for unfearing (to use the words of verse 18) conduct. Both these truths should become clearer as we deal with the two sections individually.

Verses 10-12 show a universal failure. Man has—and certainly these observations are true of every single human being of all time (Jesus excepted)—absolutely failed to achieve a righteous character. There are at least six things Paul says man has failed to achieve, though each one does not present something entirely different from the others.

Failure in Righteousness (verse 10). Verses 10-12 are rather freely quoted from Psalm 14:1-3. Verse 10, therefore, does not specifically quote anything in the psalm, but is evidently stated by Paul as expressing the substance of the whole psalm. Therefore, we should take this first "failure" in the list as summing up all six. We remember that "righteousness" is a key word for the entire epistle, and Paul wants to make it very emphatic that man has unanimously failed to achieve righteousness.

The meaning of this could be stated in more than one way. Paul may be using the word in its judicial and legal sense: Thus man has failed to have right-standing before God, to be innocent or guiltless. Or Paul may be using the word in a more practical sense: Thus man has failed to practice what is right. Actually, both are true and neither can be separated from the other. The practical failure results in the judicial failure. This latter was probably uppermost in Paul's mind when he wrote the words.

Failure in Reasoning (verse 11a). The statement that "none understand" reflects the obvious intent of Psalm 14:2. This particular failure deals specifically with man's mental faculties, his rational powers. Man has not proved himself capable by natural and unaided reasoning to grasp truth about God, to attain trustworthy knowledge of God.

Failure in Reverence (verse 11b). The statement that "none seek God" likewise reflects the obvious intent of Psalm 14:2. If the

52

failure to *understand* speaks of man's mental faculties, the failure to seek God speaks of his spiritual faculties. Understanding God refers to awareness; seeking God refers to acknowledgment. That man does not seek God does not mean that men do not seek some god. Men are innately religious, but man's depravity has blinded him to the true God, and so his worship is misdirected. Man does not, therefore, seek, regard, respect, reverence, recognize the true God. The ancient question of Job (11:7), which would refer to all of verse 11, is still answered "No."

Failure in Rectitude (verse 12a). The words, "They are all gone out of the way," equal "They are all gone aside" in Psalm 14:3. "Rectitude" means straightness, uprightness. Man has failed to stay on the path ordered by God; he is not capable of walking right. All have turned aside, lost their way. Men's crooked ways and wicked deeds are ample evidence of this sad fact. After all, Psalm 58:3 applies to all mankind.

Failure in Respectability (verse 12b). Paul says, "They are together become unprofitable." This corresponds to Psalm 14:3: "They are all together become filthy." The Hebrew word translated "filthy" means "to be corrupt, to get spoiled." The Greek word translated "unprofitable" means "worthless, useless, good for nothing." These two involve the same basic idea. When something spoils, it has to be discarded as worthless.

Just so, man has failed to achieve the purpose and end for which the Creator made him. Sin has spoiled him, made him worthless and unprofitable. He has fallen from the respectable position he should have occupied to a rotten, worthless, rejected place.

Failure in Reformation (verse 12c). This last part of verse 12 exactly equals the last part of Psalm 14:3. It is an emphatic declaration that all men have failed to pull themselves out of the mire of sin and achieve true good. They have not been able to reform truly, and change their basically bad heart and character. Men always try to reform, and sometimes have external successes. But genuine reformation and the accomplishing of real good remains out of man's reach.

The word translated "good" is not the usual one. This one sees "good" or that which meets with God's favor, pleases God. Man is not naturally capable of pleasing God. "All our righteousnesses are as filthy rags" (Isaiah 64:6). Put this last failure with the first (verse 10), and we have both sides of the coin: Man achieves neither innocence before God nor positive good.

3. AN UNFEARING CONDUCT (Romans 3:13-18)

As already noted, if verses 10-12 are primarily negative and speak of universal failure, verses 13-18 are more positive and speak of what man *has* done. Thus Paul describes human conduct as wicked and not reflecting the fear of God (verse 18). It is true, of course, that not all men go so far into sin as others. In that sense, some of Paul's strong language here may not be altogether applicable to every single human being. But that point was probably not much in Paul's mind. What he *was* thinking was that humanity is universally and altogether wicked in its conduct and behavior. If all men have not yet gone to the same excess of sin, all men are headed there. At least relatively all men must be said to fit the description Paul gives here. And let us remember that Paul is still quoting Old Testament passages to confirm the conclusion drawn in verse 9.

Deceit (verses 13, 14). In these two verses Paul picks up truths from Psalms 5:9; 140:3; 10:7. All the quotations here involve the organs of speech: the throat, the tongue, the lips, the mouth. Paul probably selects these references because the poisonous deceit that issues from men's mouths is, after all, a reflection of *inner* wickedness, a deceitful heart.

Such was the case with Jesus' teachings, too. In Matthew 15:11 He startled his hearers by declaring that defilement results from what comes *out* of a man, not from what goes in! In Matthew 15:18 he explained this: "Those things which proceed out of the mouth come forth from the heart." As Jeremiah put it, "The heart is deceitful above all things, and desperately wicked" (17:9).

The "open sepulchre" is an opened grave. The nauseous corruption of such a place is easy to imagine. "Deceit" is trickery, guile. The "poison of asps" is the dreadful snakebite. "Cursing" is profanity. "Bitterness" is gall, jealous hatred. Taking it all together, Paul is saying that the heart of man is like an open grave, filled with the stench of pretense and hatred. And the spiteful speech of man often reveals this condition. But even when man glibly conceals the truth by controlling his tongue, the hateful heart is still there.

Destruction (verses 15-17). If the previous two verses emphasize *inner* wickedness, these three emphasize the *external*. If the mouth poetically represents the *heart* and its motives, now the feet (verse 15) and the "ways" (paths) of those feet represent *deeds* and the purposes behind them. These three verses are borrowed from Isaiah 59:7, 8.

The emphasis here is on man's hurtfulness to man, his warlike ways. The "swiftness to shed blood" referred to in verse 15 is willingness to murder and let us not forget that "whosoever hateth his brother is a murderer" (1 John 3:15). The sinner's feet (and *all* are sinners!) travel the path of killing (15) and destruction (16), causing misery (16) and war (17).

Defiance (verse 18). Here lies the explanation for man's wicked conduct: He does not fear God! Note too that the eyes are used poetically to represent this aspect of man's wickedness (from Psalm

36:1). Man looks toward Heaven with arrogance and defiance, assuming his independence and equality, instead of lowering his eyes in submission and acknowledgment.

The "fear of God" is used throughout the Bible to refer not to fright but respect for God. To fear God is to honor Him and His requirements, to stand in respect of judgment and retribution. The sinful race has lost that fear, and thus wicked behavior is unchecked.

With all these quotations in verses 10-18 Paul has clearly confirmed his conclusion that all men are sinners, guilty and condemned. The quotations chosen have shown convincingly not only that all men are sinners but also that men are altogether sinful. Corruption is universal in humanity. Paul could have added various other passages like Micah 7:2-4. Men are often prevented from reaching the extremes of sin of which they are capable either by conscience, or legislation, or fear. But the whole man is sick with sin, and all sorts of iniquity issue therefrom and testify to that sickness. We had better read these verses often, lest we forget who and what we really are.

4. AN UNDENIABLE CONDEMNATION (Romans 3:19, 20)

Paul has yet one clinching argument to use in establishing the truth of the conclusion reached in verse 9 that "all are under sin." That argument is the testimony of the law. These verses logically follow verses 10-18, because there Paul has been quoting from the Old Testament. Now he goes to the heart of the Old Scriptures, the Mosiac Law, and finds in that Law an irrefutable proof of his position. That proof is to be found in understanding the very purpose of the Law, a purpose which speaks clearly of man's sin.

These two verses are especially important because they tell us exactly why the Mosaic Law was given. Paul knew that many of his fellow-Jews tended to regard themselves as righteous because they "kept" the Law. Judaism was and still is a system of works-righteousness.

Those who read Paul's words about universal sinfulness might have replied in this way: "Sure, Paul, man is sinful and deserves condemnation. But God has given us the Law to correct our behavior and make us right!"

Then Paul could respond: "You are wrong. You cannot achieve righteousness by the Law, because you simply cannot succeed in keeping the Law (cf. Galatians 3:10)!"

And then the Jews might reply: "Well, Paul, even if we cannot keep it *perfectly*, surely God will be satisfied if we do our *best!* After all, He gave us the Law; He must have meant us to observe it! Surely that is the way to obtain right-standing with God!"

And that is exactly where Paul would make his point: "You are wrong because you have misunderstood *why* God gave the Law. It was *not* given for salvation!" We might add that there have been many who have not understood just why the Law was given. Paul answers that question in these two verses.

What the Law Was Not For (verses 19a, 20a). There are four main affirmations in these two verses: Two of them (the first part of each verse) have negative implications: the other two (the last part of each verse) have positive implications. We consider the negative first, and there are two.

1. *The Law was not for all.* Verse 19a makes this clear in saying that the Law spoke only to those under the Law. Moses' Law was never intended to be part of a universal plan for achieving righteousness. Whatever its purpose, it served a limited people for a limited period.

2. *The Law was not for justification.* Verse 20a makes this absolutely plain: "By the deeds of the law there shall no flesh be justified in his sight." "Justify" is built on the same root in Greek as righteousness; it means to acquit, find innocent, declare righteous. Paul is affirming a rule that stands for all times, Old or New Testament: God did *not* give the Law to serve as a means of achieving right-standing with Him.

Sometimes you hear it said, "Now that Jesus has come we are no longer saved by the law." But we never were! Paul touches on this same truth in Galatians 3:11 and 3:21. You may want to review the treatment of those verses in the study on Galatians.

What the Law Was For (verses 19b, 20b). The two positive clauses give us the same basic truth, only with a slightly differing emphasis.

1. *The Law was to convince of guilt.* Verse 19b makes this clear. Man has an innate tendency to claim innocence and defend his goodness. The Law closes such mouths. To man's every protestation of innocence, the Law replies, "Guilty!" The written Law does not *cause* guilt, of course; it causes *realization* of guilt.

2. *The Law was to bring knowledge of sin.* Verse 20b gives us, in the best possible words, the Bible's teaching on the true purpose of the Law (cf. Galatians 3:19, 22, and the study on the passage). Without the written Law, man would have a vague sense of sin, but the Law makes man's knowledge of sin specific, and shows him how exceedingly sinful he is. Compare Romans 7:7: "I had not known sin, but by the law."

So the Law was never intended to save. Unrighteous man cannot be made righteous by law-observance. This is the heart of 3:9-20. Man is wicked and out of contact with God. No one has achieved righteousness, either Jew or Gentile. The Law has only served its true purpose of revealing in detail the nature and extent of man's sin. Man stands condemned thereby, and cannot deny that condemnation. He must turn elsewhere for deliverance; he must seek yet another means of achieving righteousness before God.

8 Justification Is by Faith

Study Text: Romans 3:21-31

Introduction
1. Justification by Faith: The Concept (Romans 3:21-25a)
   a. Abandonment (verse 12)
   b. Acceptance (verse 22a)
   c. Access (verses 22b, 23)
   d. Atonement (verses 24, 25a)
2. Justification by Faith: The Consequences (Romans 3:25b-27)
   a. Establishing Heaven's Holiness (verses 25b, 26)
   b. Excluding Human Honor (verse 27)
3. Justification by Faith: Conclusions (Romans 3:28-31)
   a. A Conclusion about the Plan (verse 28)
   b. A Conclusion about People (verses 29, 30)
   c. A Conclusion about Purpose (verse 31)

INTRODUCTION

We have completed the first great part of Romans (1:18—3:20), in which Paul very carefully proves that all humanity—Jew and Gentile—stands guilty and condemned before God. Our previous study concluded with the observation that man must seek some means of achieving righteousness before God. That is the theme to which Paul turns now, starting at 3:21. He shows us exactly how God has provided for man to get right with Him.

If the first part of Romans showed the *need* for salvation, this second part (3:21—4:25) shows the *way*. Believe it or not, God has provided a method by which the guilty, condemned sinner can stand before Him innocent and free of any penalty! It is Paul's joy to relate that wonderful method in this section, and ours to study it.

EXPOSITION

The general study-outline in the back of this book will show just how we are going to deal with Part 2 of Romans and how this particular lesson fits into the pattern. Part 2 shows how God has provided righteousness through the Savior, Jesus Christ. This study is subsection A under that part and presents the plain and positive facts about that provision. It covers 3:21-31 and is entitled "Justification Is By Faith."

1. JUSTIFICATION BY FAITH: THE CONCEPT
(Romans 3:21-25a)

This particular passage ought to be regarded as one of the climactic portions of the whole Bible. The *method* of our justification is herein made plain. We are told exactly how a guilty sinner can stand righteous before God. Every believer ought to master well the four basic truths given below; these are the facts absolutely essential to the concept of justification by faith.

Before examining these facts individually, let us make sure one thing previously mentioned briefly is very plain. The Greek word translated "justify" and the Greek word translated "righteous[ness]" are really the same basic word. "Justify" actually means "to declare righteous." Thus, whenever we speak of justification by faith, this is the same as saying "righteous standing by faith." And do not forget that this means to stand before God innocent of wrongdoing, to be found by the divine Judge "not guilty."

Abandonment (verse 12). The first point Paul makes in defining the method of justification is a negative one; the remaining three will be positive. This negative point is that *justification is not by the law.* The phrase, "without the law," means "apart from the law." Webster defines "abandon" as "to give up with the intent of never again claiming one's rights or interests in." That is exactly what we must do in reference to the Mosaic Law. We must abandon all hope of ever saving ourselves by legal observances.

1. *The fact* itself is stated here in 21a: The righteousness God has provided is apart from the Law. That fact comes logically at the beginning of this discussion on the method of justification for two reasons. First, Paul has just been commenting on the true purpose of the Law, and his observations on that subject (verses 19, 20) make it appropriate to begin by saying that righteousness is not by the Law. Righteousness could not come by the Law: Such was not the Law's

58

purpose, and no one has kept it anyway.

Second, this fact comes appropriately at the start of this discussion because it is plain that one must abandon all false hopes for salvation before he will ever grasp the true way. The common hope of man is to save himself by his own efforts, and this hope led so easily to a distorted understanding of the Law's purpose. But all such hopes must be abandoned. Sinners cannot save themselves.

2. *The plainness of this fact* is seen in the words "is manifested," and this must be connected with the "now." Paul means that now it has been made plain that justification is apart from the Law. Now this truth must not confuse us: Paul is not saying that *now* we are justified apart from the Law. Justification has *always* been apart from the Law. Getting right with God has never been by any means other than faith, nor by any merit except that of Christ's atonement. But this fact is now, on this side of the cross, far more plain than it had ever been before. In former days the truth was contained in figures and types and shadows; now we possess the reality, the substance of the truth so plainly indicated at Calvary.

3. *The Old Testament testimony to this fact* is also indicated in this verse: "being witnessed by the law and the prophets." The fact of justification apart from the Law may not have been so plain then as now, but Paul wants us to know that this truth was taught in the Old Testament. The Old Testament was often wrongly understood by the Jews; but rightly understood it too gave witness to the gospel way of getting right with God.

Acceptance (verse 22a). The second great truth which Paul states, defining the method of justification, is this: *Justification is by faith in Jesus Christ.* Verse 22a, freely translated, reads: "The righteousness which God has provided comes by faith in Jesus Christ." This is the good news (gospel) of how to get right with God: Put faith in Jesus!

1. *The nature of faith* must be understood. Faith is never a mere intellectual assent to facts. Those who say one can have "faith" in Christ without showing any effects in his life are distorting the Biblical teaching. Faith means trust, reliance, confidence; and always involves a personal commitment to that in which one believes. Faith in Jesus is faith in a person, not a mere fact; and so saving faith is a personal commitment of oneself to Christ, based on confidence in Him and His work, which is in turn based on a conviction about the facts of who He is and what He has done. Genuine faith always involves these three elements: conviction, confidence, commitment. This is what it means to "receive Him" (John 1:12), or to accept Him.

2. *The object of this faith* is made plain: Jesus Christ. You need to realize that the phrase "faith of Jesus Christ" really means—both in the Greek and in the English construction—"Faith *in* Jesus Christ." This acceptance of Jesus Christ as one's salvation goes hand

in hand with the abandonment discussed above. One abandons all hope in self-efforts and casts all hope on Jesus.

Access (verses 22b, 23). The third great truth which Paul teaches us about the method of justification is that *it is freely and equally available to all.* All and any who believe have access into this graciously-provided "righteousness of God."

1. *The point of this equality* is especially clear in 22b: "unto all and upon all them that believe." Notice the repetition for emphasis. Though Paul does not come right out and say so, his point is that Jew and Gentile alike have access to the righteousness of God on the same basis.

2. *The reason for this equality* is likewise clear in 22b and 23: "There is no difference, for all have sinned." The obviousness of this conclusion has been attested so well in Part 1 of Romans. There Paul proved plainly that all are sinners. If all are sinners, then all must attain righteousness by the same method, faith. A person who was not a sinner might be saved by his own works, but the very fact that one has sinned eliminates that possibility for him. A sinner's only hope is in something other than himself. Such a provision has been made by God through Jesus, and faith is the requirement for that provision to be applied. Thus any and all may come by faith to Jesus and receive righteousness as a gift.

The connection between verses 22 and 23 is very precise. There is no difference in *men* (all are guilty), so there is no difference in the *provision* (all are invited). This is an important confirmation of our doctrine of universal atonement. God's provision is as universal as man's sin!

Verse 23 is a well-known testimonial to the universality of sin. Its grammatical constructions are important. In Greek "all have sinned" is a timeless expression that encompasses the history of the whole human race in one broad sweep: "Every man sins"—this is the meaning. The second part, "come short of the glory of God," is a different tense, and means "keep coming up short." This expression pictures the frustrating failure that is repeated over and over by man as he vainly keeps trying to achieve righteousness by his own efforts. The first is more positive: Sin is a violation of God's standard. The second is more negative: All man's best efforts fail to measure up to what God requires.

Atonement (verses 24, 25a). Now Paul proceeds to give us the fourth and most important fact about the method by which justification is provided: *Justification is by the death of Christ.* Paul does not go into great detail here, but three important factors are suggested by his words.

1. *Christ's death is an act of grace.* The phrase "by his grace" in verse 24 shows this. Grace is undeserved favor. No sinner deserves any act of favor from God, but God graciously acts on man's behalf. This is the reason the word "freely" can be attached to "justified" in

this verse. Man must be justified freely, as far as his part is concerned, because he really has nothing to offer: "In my hand no price I bring." But it was not "free" from God's side, or Christ's: "Simply to thy cross I cling."

2. *Christ's death is redemption.* Redemption, used in verse 24, refers to the price paid to bring liberty to the slave. (The word "ransom," often used, means the same thing.) We were enslaved by sin and Satan and could not free ourselves. We owed a sin-debt to God we could not pay—"Jesus paid it all," and by that payment bought our release.

3. *Christ's death is propitiation.* Propitiation, used in verse 25a, means the appeasement of wrath. The truth involved is that God's wrath is justly against man's sins (Psalm 5:5; 7:11; John 3:36; etc.). But Jesus—as when He calmed the storm on Galilee—calmed, appeased, satisfied the wrath of God. He did this by taking that holy wrath upon himself, by substituting himself in the sinner's place (cf. Isaiah 53:4, 5, 10, 11).

Someone has said that justification is by the death of Christ, in so far as its basis is concerned; that justification is by the grace of God, in so far as its cause is concerned; and that justification is by man's faith, in so far as its application is concerned. That observation provides a pretty good summary of what we have seen about the method of justification.

2. JUSTIFICATION BY FAITH: THE CONSEQUENCES
(Romans 3:25b-27)

In particular, Paul points up two consequences or implications of the doctrine of justification by faith. One of these relates to God; the other to man.

Establishing Heaven's Holiness (verses 25b, 26). The righteousness which God provided man had to be done in such a way as to be appropriate with the very nature and character of God. Before God is anything else, He is holy (just, righteous). Thus the method of justification must be in accord with this attribute. Paul refers to two particular problems relating to the holiness of God and shows that justification by the merits of Christ's death solves both those problems and thus clearly vindicates the holiness of God.

1. *The problem of sin before the cross* is dealt with in 25b. This verse needs explanation, because it is often misunderstood. The key to it is the word translated "remission," which means "letting go." The point is this: Prior to the cross God appears in His forbearance to have let sin go by unpunished and unatoned and men might have accused Him of failing to live up to His own holy nature which demands the penalty of punishment for sin. But the death of Christ

answers that once for all and—because Jesus had to bear God's wrath and pay the whole penalty—God's righteousness has been shown (declared) vindicated.

2. *The problem of justifying a sinner* is dealt with in 26. Every child of God ought to master the truth contained in the expression, "that he might be just and the justifier of him which believeth in Jesus." The death of Christ made that possible.

The problem consists in the fact that God cannot allow sin to go unpunished; His own holiness had to be satisfied. On the one hand, God could be *just* without providing an atonement for sin. Only then the sinner himself would have to bear the punishment for sin and thus no one could ever be saved, justified. On the other hand, God could not simply say to a sinner, "I know you are a sinner, but I will forget it and pronounce you innocent (justified) anyway." His own just nature would prevent that.

How then could a truly guilty sinner be pardoned and found innocent and God's own justice (righteousness) protected? The death of Christ provided the answer. By substituting himself in our place, Christ bore God's infinite wrath in our place and thus fully satisfied the requirements of divine justice (holiness). At the same time, provision was then made for the sinner's justification. It could now be said that any who accepted Christ's sacrifice by faith had therefore fully paid the penalty for their sins and could now stand guiltless before God. Thus God is both *just* and *justifier.*

Excluding Human Honor (verse 27). The second consequence or implication of the doctrine of justification by faith through the merits of Christ's death is one that relates to man. Man can receive no credit or get no honor for his justification. To Jesus Christ must go all the glory. Man's boasting is therefore excluded.

1. *The fact is stated* in 27a. "Excluded" literally means "shut out." There is no room for any individual to take any honor to himself for his salvation. All the work was done by Christ.

2. *The reason is given* in 27b. "Law" has the idea of "principle" or "basis." On what basis is human boasting excluded? On the basis of works? No, because that is the very way by which man is *not* saved. Paul's implication is clear: If good works (like Jewish legal observance, for example) provide the principle by which salvation is awarded, then the human being *will* be able to boast, to claim honor for himself.

But that is not the principle; faith is. Salvation is awarded to believers, not to practicers of good works. Consequently, man can take no credit at all. Now this observation must not be misunderstood. Some might wrongly take this to mean that it makes no difference how one lives even after placing faith in Christ's cross. Paul himself was sometimes misunderstood in that very way (cf. Romans 3:8).

It does matter how a Christian lives; good works are important.

But such works never play any part as a basis by which one is awarded salvation. The fact that you presently enjoy a standing of guiltlessness before God is not the result of your works, but is yours because you have faith in Christ's cross as the sacrifice for your sins.

Where do good works fit in? How are they important? What difference does it make how one lives? Simply this: They are necessary *evidences* of regeneration. As Ephesians 2:10 puts it, we are created in Christ Jesus *unto* good works. Good works never provide a basis or reason or cause or condition by which one is justified. If they did, man could "boast." But good works are the clear result of salvation, and the one whose life is not changed from practicing sin to practicing righteousness has no grounds to claim he had been justified by works.

3. JUSTIFICATION BY FAITH: CONCLUSIONS
(Romans 3:28-31)

These verses begin with "we conclude." The passage is, therefore, a summary restatement of the basic truths already covered in verses 21-27. There are three basic conclusions which Paul draws here.

A Conclusion about the Plan (verse 28). This verse in essence restates the truths first stated in verses 21, 22 about the plan of salvation, the method of justification. All that Paul has previously stated allows him now to state categorically how justification is awarded to any individual.

1. *The positive side* is expressed first. Justification is by faith. The results of Christ's work are applied to every person who puts faith in Christ. We should observe in passing that Christ died for all, but that the benefits of that death are applied only to so many as believe. Faith itself, however, is not a "work" in any sense and thus has no merit of its own. It is the condition though that men must meet.

2. *The negative side* is also restated (from verse 21). Justification is not by "the deeds of the law." One cannot earn salvation by keeping the Law of God, or by any other "works" for that matter.

This twofold summary of the plan of salvation is brief, but apt. This verse ought to be burned into the memory of every Christian. The truth indicated is exactly in accord with other New Testament teaching on the subject, as in Ephesians 2:8, 9 for example.

A Conclusion about People (verses 29, 30). Back in verse 22 Paul specifically emphasized that "all" receive justification (the righteousness of God) on the same basis, faith. He did not there single out Jews and Gentiles for special mention, though that was the point. Now he makes sure the point will be clear. The method of justification is the same for all, both for Jew and for Gentile. This conclusion logically follows his teaching on the basic concepts of justification as seen above and the insistence of the first two chapters that both Jew and Gentile are alike guilty and condemned. This conclusion about the people who must be justified by faith in Christ is indicated here in a twofold manner.

1. *Racial differences do not matter,* as seen in verse 29. The particular use of "Jew" and "Gentile" plays up this racial question. The word "Jew" was used with pride by those who could trace their ancestry back to one of the twelve tribes of Israel. "Gentile" was used by those same Jews to speak contemptuously of all who did not share their precious racial heritage. Paul's insistence that God is God of both makes it plain that both must approach Him on the same basis.

2. *Religious differences* do not matter, at least when those religious practices are external rituals. Paul makes this clear in verse 30 by singling out circumcision as the prime example. The Jews put great stock in their circumcision as a seal given them by God. Compare the earlier discussion on 2:25-29. Paul avows that both the circumcised Jew and the uncircumcised Gentile must be saved by faith.

A Conclusion about Purpose (verse 31). Paul's final conclusion relates to the consistency of his doctrine of justification by faith with the purpose of the Mosaic Law. This matter has already been discussed in detail in reference to 3:19, 20. Review that discussion.

Paul's point is simply this: Justification by faith does not contradict the Law, because the Law was never intended to serve as a means of justification. Many Jews wrongly understood that they would be saved by observing the Law as best they could; if that were true, then the Pauline gospel of justification by faith *would* contradict that purpose and thus "make void" (invalidate, set aside) the Law.

The truth, however, is that preaching justification by faith "establishes" the Law, fulfils the very purpose for which the Law was really given. The Law was given to make sin known (cf. 3:20) so that the sinner would recognize his guilt and flee to the Savior for forgiveness. Thus, when men are brought to Christ for justification by faith, the very purpose of the Law is being fulfilled.

9 The Failure of Efforts at Righteousness

Study Text: Romans 4:1-8

Introduction
1. An Illustrated Practice (Romans 4:1-3)
   a. How Abraham Was Not Justified (verses 1, 2)
   b. How Abraham Was Justified (verse 3)
2. An Indisputable Principle (Romans 4:4, 5)
   a. The Principle of Grace (verse 4)
   b. The Principle of Guilt (verse 5)
3. An Inspired Proclamation (Romans 4:6-8)
   a. The Principle in Question (verse 6)
   b. The Psalm Quoted (verses 7, 8)

INTRODUCTION

Our study of Part 2 of Romans continues. In this section Paul teaches us exactly how God has provided for man to be righteous. Throughout this study, keep in mind that the phrase "the righteousness of God" has a dual meaning. It means being right with God, righteous standing before God; and it means that God has provided this righteousness.

In 3:21-31 studied in the previous section, Paul presented the *positive* side of his instruction on how to have the righteousness of God. As we saw there, the answer is *faith*. Justification is by faith, at least as far as man's side is concerned.

This lesson brings us to the *negative* side of Paul's teaching about justification. Paul knew we would understand and appreciate the doctrine of justification by faith if we also are convinced that justification is *not* by any of man's own fleshly efforts. Both this and the next study, covering the greater part of chapter four, will come

65

from this negative section. In essence, Paul is going to show that justification does not come to a person by either of *three* things: (1) works in general; (2) circumcision; and (3) law-keeping in particular. This study deals with the first of these.

EXPOSITION

In order that the discussion above may be more clearly pictured, consult the general study-outline in the back of this book. There you will see that this study (no. 9) is the first of two under subsection B (Part 2). This lesson is entitled "The Failure of Efforts at Righteousness" and covers 4:1-8.

1. AN ILLUSTRATED PRACTICE (Romans 4:1-3)

A quick reading of 4:1-8 will show that Paul deals with works by using Abraham's experience as an illustration (1-3), by stating the principle he is proving (4, 5), and by citing David's testimony as confirmation (6-8). We should not miss the significance of Paul's choice of Abraham and David to back up his teaching. Abraham was, after all, the most revered Hebrew patriarch, the father of the Hebrew race. David was one of Israel's most famous heroes, the father of Hebrew royalty.

How Abraham Was Not Justified (verses 1, 2). Paul's use of Abraham, the original Hebrew, is particularly significant, not only for the Jews, but for all Bible-followers. From the Jewish point of view, Abraham's significance is obvious: He was the one called by God from Ur to break with his kindred and become father of a new people, a chosen people of God. This idea is probably the primary thing behind the fact that Paul here speaks of Abraham as "our father." Compare the typical Jewish attitude seen in John 8:39.

But Abraham's experience is significant for Gentiles who follow God, as well as for the Jewish nation. After all, it is the Abrahamic covenant which is regarded in the Bible as the basic covenant on which salvation is founded. This is the reason Paul in Galatians 3:6-9 makes such a point of the fact that *all* who are "of faith" are "the children of Abraham." Thus even saved Gentiles participate in the promises given to Abraham in the original "covenant" (compact, agreement, contract) of Genesis 12:1-3—at least in the spiritual aspects of those promises. For saved Gentiles too then, Abraham is "our father."

Therefore Paul will really have proved something if he can prove that Abraham was justified by faith and not by works. The arguments of all Jews will be silenced, as will the hope of any to earn righteousness before God by human efforts.

66

1. *Not by the flesh*. This is the point of verse 1, and is the basic truth involved in the entire lesson. Paul puts this in question form, and the answer he means for us to understand is "Nothing." What did Abraham accomplish by fleshly effort? Nothing. What righteousness was awarded him in consequence of fleshly deeds? None. Abraham achieved nothing, earned no standing with God by anything done in the flesh. We must face the truth that no one ever has or ever will.

The phrase "as pertaining to the flesh" means "according to the flesh" or "based on flesh." This refers to anything Abraham did that issued from fleshly motives or was performed by fleshly methods or resulted in fleshly accomplishments. The flesh is broader than the mere *physical* body. It encompasses anything natural as contrasted to the spiritual, anything done by ordinary human impulses as contrasted to that which is motivated directly by divine influence. Moule, in the *Cambridge Bible*, defines the "flesh" as "human nature in the fall as unrenewed and unassisted by divine special grace."

Paul could have referred to several specific matters in the life of Abraham as illustrations of fleshly effort. He might have mentioned circumcision, for example (and will do so a little later in the chapter). Circumcision is literally an action performed on the physical flesh. Circumcision does not purchase right-standing with God. Paul might have mentioned the decision Abraham made to produce a son by Hagar, hoping thereby to assist God in His promise of a seed. That decision was "according to the flesh"; not because it was lust for Hagar that motivated Abraham, but because Abraham's thinking represented natural human methods. That fleshly effort, that human energy bought Abraham nothing in God's eyes.

2. *Not by works*. This truth indicated in verse 2 is really another way of saying the same thing as that of verse 1. The "works" referred to here are any "deeds" performed by human effort, this meaning the same thing as the efforts of "flesh."

Verse 2 is in effect an argument to substantiate the point made in verse 1 that Abraham obtained no righteousness by deeds performed on a fleshly basis. Paul is saying, "Let us assume, now, that Abraham *was* justified by his own works, contrary to the position I have just stated. If that is the case, then Abraham *did* have grounds for boasting, contrary to what I have just taught (3:27). The only trouble with that assumption is that it does not match what *God* has said!"

So, for a moment, Paul assumes a position contrary to his own in order to argue against it. The position assumed leads to a conclusion that simply cannot be supported by the facts. Thus the position must not be correct at all: Abraham was *not* justified by works. The phrase "but not before God" means "but not according to God" and refers to the fact that God's own statements about Abraham's justification (which Paul is about to cite) do not match the assumption that Abraham was justified by works and thus has something to boast about.

Keep in mind that the verb "glory" here means the same thing as the "boasting" in 3:27. There Paul had asserted that justification by faith and through the atonement leaves man without any grounds for boasting. Here he says that if Abraham *was* justified by works, he *could* boast—and the assertion of 3:27 would be wrong. But God's words on the matter do not substantiate the assumption that Abraham was justified by works. Abraham had absolutely no grounds or basis for taking any credit or honor (glory, boasting) for his justification. He was not justified by his own "doings" (works).

In summary of verses 1, 2 let us not forget that "all *our* righteousness are as filthy rags" in God's sight (Isaiah 64:6). We can *do* nothing, so far as all natural human works and efforts are concerned, that even pleases God, much less that purchases innocence. The key words in Ephesians 2:8 are "not of yourselves," and these are followed in 2:9 by "not of works, lest any man should boast." We can take absolutely *no* credit for our salvation; we have done *nothing* to earn, deserve or merit justification. All of the natural, human, fleshly efforts of men to achieve righteousness only result in self-righteousness. Indeed, or shocking as it seems, all such efforts must be abandoned before God will award righteousness. Only when a person despairs of becoming righteous by his own works, and renounces all such efforts, and casts himself wholly and helplessly on the mercy of God by faith in Jesus Christ can he obtain righteous-standing before God! If that doctrine seems too strong for you, remember it is the inspired doctrine of Paul, and we should stand for it without apology.

How Abraham Was Justified (verse 3). At the end of verse 2 Paul's "but not before God!" was an assertion that the assumed "if" in verse 2 will not harmonize with what God himself says. So now in verse 3 Paul reminds us of exactly what God said about His justification of Abraham. The Scripture quoted here is Genesis 15:6 and shows clearly that God justified Abraham by *faith*, not by works.

You should recall that Paul used exactly this same quotation in Galatians 3:6 to make exactly this same point. (A review of the comments on that passage in Galatians would be helpful.) The words of Genesis 15:6 used in these two places are sometimes misunderstood. The "it" is just a carrier word and does not appear in the Hebrew or Greek original. "It" does not mean "faith." Faith is not counted as a substitute for righteousness. In fact, the word "for" is a carrier word too. All the verse means is this: Abraham believed (put faith) in God, and righteousness was reckoned his.

Faith is not righteousness nor a substitute therefor. Faith is not a "work" and has no merit. Faith is believing, accepting, trusting God. But faith is *man's* activity (not God's) and faith is the condition required if one is to be counted righteous before God. "Counted" means reckoned, regarded, imputed, put on one's account. Righteousness, you recall, means right-standing with God, guiltlessness before the divine bar of justice. When Abraham put his faith in God, this entry was placed on Abraham's record in Heaven: "innocent." And so it is with every person who puts faith in God.

2. AN INDISPUTABLE PRINCIPLE (Romans 4:4, 5)

These two verses state, as a matter of principle, the truth that Paul is discussing throughout this section. That truth has just been illustrated in actual practice by Abraham's experience (verses 1-3). Shortly this truth will be confirmed by a quotation from inspired Scripture (verses 6-8). Here, between those two citations, the logic of the principle itself is argued. This truth is, simply stated, the fact that justification is not by works but by faith.

The Principle of Grace (verse 4). Summed up, this verse simply declares that any idea of works-justification would involve God in a *debt* to man, instead of grace. And this is so obviously illogical that the idea itself must be discarded.

"To him that worketh" means anyone who works for what he can earn. "The reward" in Greek is a word that can refer to any sort of wages or earnings. What is actually stated in verse 4, therefore, is a universal principle that can apply in any situation, economic or spiritual: When anyone works for something and earns it by his labor, then the person who pays him does so not out of some gracious motive, but because he owes it to him. When your boss pays you what you have rightfully earned, he is not being gracious at all!

"Grace," you know, is *undeserved* favor, something good or kind done when that favor was not earned. So when one works for wages and gets paid, the payment is a matter of "debt" (obligation), not of grace. This universal principle Paul applies to our spiritual situation and to the justification of a sinner. The application is obvious and clear: If one earns justification by his deeds, this justification is not of God's grace, but God owes it in response to man's works to pay him with justification. That conclusion is preposterous!

Paul is quite right. God never bestows any favor on man in response to man's merit for man has no merit with God. Man is too much a sinner to deserve any kindness from Heaven. All the good things God does for men, salvation most of all, are absolutely and entirely gracious. Man's feeble efforts at self-righteousness never put any strings of obligation on God! We may earn wages in serving sin, and the wages of sin is death. But eternal life comes from God as a free gift! (Romans 6:23)

The Principle of Guilt (verse 5). If the manifest grace of God is one reason justification is not of works, another reason is to be seen in the obvious guilt of the sinner. Verse 5 particularly speaks of the fact that God justifies the ungodly (person: the word is singular). These words are quite pointed. You see, if justification came by *works*, then that is exactly the way it would come, and only those whose deeds were absolutely and perfectly guiltless could be counted so before God. Well, the point is that no one can claim that all his works have been truly innocent of all wrong. All are guilty, in fact, of gross sin. Then if justification were by actual deeds, none could ever be justified, save Jesus Christ himself. Thus justification by faith is proved correct because it is the only method that will work for ungodly sinners.

"To him that worketh not" provides the opposite of "to him that worketh" in the previous verse. It does not suggest that people ought to deliberately avoid doing good in order to be candidates for God's grace; indeed man is evil enough at his best. It does mean that man must renounce any efforts to earn God's goodness by his works. The one who clings to a hope that he can in some way merit justification will never cast himself wholly on Christ. So long as Naaman, for example, had clung to any hope that he could buy a cure elsewhere, he would never have dipped in Jordan, casting himself helplessly on the God of Elisha. The sinner must say, "In my hand no price I bring."

Faith is the condition for the sinner's justification. Paul indicates this twice in verse 5, using both the verbal form "believeth" and the noun "faith" (which are on the same Greek root). Verse 5 is simply affirming that the experience illustrated with Abraham in verse 3 is that which every sinner may have if he will, like Abraham, put faith in God by Jesus Christ. Again and again in human history that marvelous situation can occur when God "justifies the ungodly." Denny, in *Expositor's Greek Testament*, puts this well: "It is sometimes argued that God can only pronounce just, or treat as just, those who actually are just; but if this were so, what Gospel would there be for sinful men? . . . The paradoxical phrase, Him that justifieth the ungodly, does not suggest that justification is a fiction . . . but that it is a miracle."

Just as in verse 3, the latter part of verse 5 does not mean that faith itself is some meritorious work regarded by God as a substitute for righteousness. The expression is probably an abbreviated one, consciously borrowing the words of Genesis 15:6, quoted in verse 3, and means that the one who believes is counted righteous before God. Faith again is the condition any person must meet if the gracious declaration of God is to be applied to him individually. The situation of a believer is regarded by God as the situation of one righteous before Him. And as seen in the previous lesson, this is made possible because Christ put himself in the sinner's place and paid in full the penalty of all men's sins. A declaration of the believing

70

sinner's "innocence" is not a "fiction" indeed, but is made a true fact by the identification of the sinner with Christ.

3. AN INSPIRED PROCLAMATION (Romans 4:6-8)

Paul turns back to his Old Testament to confirm the truth he is teaching; this time to David, father of the Jews' royal family, rather than to Abraham, father of the Jews' race. What better evidence could one offer to any Jewish readers who disagreed with Paul? Or to us, for that matter, seeing we understand that what David wrote he wrote under the very guidance of God's Holy Spirit.

The Principle in Question (verse 6). This verse tells us exactly what point Paul expects the quotation from David to confirm. That point is "the blessedness of the man unto whom God imputeth righteousness without works."

"Blessedness" means "the blessed [happy] condition." "Imputeth" is the same word in Greek as "counted" in verses 3 and 5. "Righteousness" as always refers to the state of innocence, guiltlessness, right-standing with God. "Without works" means "apart from" works (compare "without—apart from—the law" in 3:21). Paul is simply saying that David himself (Greek: "even David") speaks of the blessed condition of the man who stands innocent before God totally apart from the actual works (deeds) of that man. That David speaks of this proves (1) that such a righteous standing is possible, (2) that it is awarded apart from works, and (3) that the man who experiences such is indeed blessed.

"Without [apart from] works" here definitely means that works is not the basis for the declaration of righteousness. The phrase in context probably even implies "in contrast to his actual deeds." One really guilty is indeed blessed who is given innocence.

The Psalm Quoted (verses 7, 8). Paul quotes Psalm 32:1, 2 in which the divinely-inspired David used three statements to describe the state of justification.

1. *Iniquities forgiven* (7a). "Iniquities" literally means "lawlessness." "Forgiveness" means "letting go," "sending away," "not regarding." Do not forget that God could not simply overlook sin. Our "forgiveness" is based on Christ's actual suffering of the punishment for our sins as our substitute.

2. *Sins covered* (7b). "Sins" in Greek are "missing of the mark." "Covered" is "covered up." What an interesting contrast this provides to Proverbs 28:13: "He that covereth his sins shall not prosper" (Achan, for example). But blessed—prosperous indeed—is the man whose sins *God* has covered with Christ's blood!

3. *Sin not imputed by the Lord* (8). Again, "impute" is the same as in verse 6 and as "counted" in verses 3, 5. To "impute" means to count, consider, reckon, regard. David is saying that there

are some whose sins the Lord does not count against them. Guilt for sin is not held on their accounts. David is implying, of course, that these actually sinned. How then came they to such a favored state wherein their sins are no longer counted against them? We know the answer: by the grace of God, manifested in the sacrifice of His Son, the merits of which are awarded to all who put faith in God.

Paul used these quotes from David because David made it so plain that he was speaking of the salvation of people who really were sinners. All three phrases make this clear. If these were sinners, they certainly were not justified by their works. Faith was the only avenue open to them.

A word, in closing, about "imputed righteousness." Some have argued—as implied in one discussion above—that, when God declares a real sinner "justified," this is only a "legal" declaration that contradicts the true facts of the case, that God finds the sinner innocent when he is really guilty. But such logical arguments are out of place, and miss the point. The fact is that Christ became the sinner's substitute and fully paid the penalty for the sinner's guilt so that the record really is cleared.

This truth is clarified wonderfully in 2 Corinthians 5:21, where we have a picture of what the theologians like to call "double imputation." There you will see how substitution and indentification with Christ are involved in justification. The sins of the sinner were "imputed" to (put on the account of) the Savior who had no sin of His own. And his righteousness, his right-standing with God, is "imputed" to (put on the account of) the sinner who had no righteousness of his own. *In Christ* the believing sinner really is righteous. And this is the grounds for God's justification of that sinner.

10 The Failure of External Religion

Study Text: Romans 4:9-15

Introduction
1. Justification Is Not by the Seal of Righteousness (Romans 4:9-12)
   a. Circumcision and Abraham's Salvation (verses 9, 10)
   b. Circumcision as Abraham's Seal (verses 11, 12)
2. Justification Is Not by a System of Ritual (Romans 4:13-15)
   a. An Affirmation (verse 13)
   b. An Argument (verses 14, 15)

INTRODUCTION

In Part 2 of Romans (3:21—4:25) Paul shows us just how God has provided for a sinner to obtain righteousness. He does so positively and negatively. In study 8 dealing with 3:21-31 we saw the positive side. Man can obtain righteous-standing with God by faith in the Savior.

In chapter 4, verses 1-15, Paul approaches this doctrine from the negative side, showing that justification is not by man's own fleshly deeds. Three things in particular Paul deals with: works, circumcision, and the Law. Justification is not by either of these, as important as each may be. In the previous study (4:1-8) we covered the first of these three; this study is concerned with the other two.

EXPOSITION

Paul's treatment of "works" in 4:1-8 is aimed at man's own

73

efforts at self-righteousness, whatever kind they may be. The treatment of circumcision and law-observance is more specific and is aimed at all external religion. As you can see in the general study-outline this study is entitled "The Failure of External Religion." This is the second of two studies under subsection B (Part 2), both of which teach that justification is not by the flesh. This lesson covers 4:9-15.

1. JUSTIFICATION IS NOT BY THE SEAL OF RIGHTEOUSNESS
(Romans 4:9-12)

The purpose of this section is to show that circumcision does not bring righteousness. The Jews placed great stock in this external sign. After all, God gave it to them as a token of His unique relationship to them. But many took the token as a method of pleasing God and that it was never intended to be.

Circumcision and Abraham's Salvation (verses 9, 10). Paul returns now to his use of Abraham, who is the basic illustration of all of chapter 4. No doubt Paul, who has referred both to Abraham and to David to confirm his doctrine of justification by faith, anticipates that some of his readers—especially Jewish ones—will point back to circumcision and Mosaic ritual as arguments against his position. "See," they will say, "Abraham had to do more than exercise faith!" So Paul must explain just why circumcision and legal ritual were given, and prove that those external religious practices were *not* the *means* of justification. Abraham is the logical example to deal with, since Abraham was the one to whom circumcision was first given.

1. *The question to be considered* is introduced in verse 9a, and it faces head-on the matter of circumcision. The "blessedness" Paul refers to is that of which he has just spoken in verses 6-8 (see the previous lesson). This is the "blessedness" of the justified state. So, Paul asks, can this blessed condition be experienced only by those who are circumcised? Or can this blessed, justified state be experienced by those who are uncircumcised also?

The Jews, who were so proud of their circumcision, were sure they knew the answer to such a question as this. Of course, circumcision was necessary to salvation! Of course, an uncircumcised Gentile was not saved! We can readily understand, though we do not agree with, their insistence if we just review the original provision for circumcision.

In the first part of Genesis 17, when Abraham was ninety-nine, the Lord restated the terms of His covenant with Abraham. Then, beginning with verse 11, the Lord directed Abraham for the very first time to establish the practice called circumcision, the cutting away of the "foreskin" of *every* Hebrew male-child at the age of eight days. "It shall be a token of the covenant betwixt me and you" said the

74

Lord (Genesis 17:11). "Every man child in your generations . . . *must* needs be circumcised," said the Lord (Genesis 17:12, 13). "And the uncircumcised man child . . . shall be cut off from his people; he hath broken my covenant" (Genesis 17:14).

We can almost hear Paul's Jewish antagonists reciting these famous words to Paul and ridiculing his position. "There," they would say, "can you not see it? It is as plain as the nose on your face! You simply cannot be saved apart from circumcision. Would you have us give up this precious practice that God ordained and that we have so faithfully kept all these generations since our blessed forefather Abraham?"

And we can almost hear Paul replying: "No, wait! I do not want you to give it up—at least not you Jews. God did command it for His chosen people in the flesh. But I want you to understand that you have wrongly interpreted the part circumcision played. You have taken God's 'token' and made it a means. And that is why we have to discuss the question whether the blessed, justified state can come only upon one circumcised."

2. *The time of Abraham's circumcision in relation to his justification* is considered in verses 9b and 10a. Verse 9b restates the fact that Abraham was reckoned righteous (justified) by God when he put his faith in God. This fact is repeated from verse 3; review the explanation of that verse in the previous study. It is a fact that believing Abraham was justified.

Now, Paul says, let us consider *when* he was declared righteous, in reference to the circumcision God commanded him to practice. Was Abraham reckoned righteous before or after he was circumcised? We can see Paul's sharp, logical mind at work; and, of course, he is led of the inspiring Spirit of God. The direction he takes is obvious. If Abraham was justified while he was yet uncircumcised, then that will prove that an uncircumcised person can experience the blessed state of righteous-standing before God. If, on the other hand, Abraham was not declared to be in right-standing with God (justified) until he was circumcised, the original question will have to be answered differently. The time element becomes the factor on which the answer will hinge.

3. *The answer*, both to Abraham's situation and to the original question of verse 9a, is given in 10b. The facts are quite clear: Abraham's justification came long *before* his circumcision. These facts, which Paul rightly assumes his Jewish readers will recognize, are easily proved. As we noted above, Abraham's *circumcision* came at the age of 99, recorded in Genesis 17. His *justification* in response to his faith, was clearly declared in Genesis 15:6, at least fourteen years earlier!

Two facts are clear by this answer. First, an uncircumcised person can experience the blessedness of justification. Abraham himself, the father of circumcision, is a prime example! Second, circumcision is therefore obviously not the *means* of justification, else Abraham could not have been declared righteous until he was circumcised. And Paul means for us to understand that what was true of Abraham is true for anyone else. Circumcision did not make a man right with God. An uncircumcised person—yes, a Gentile—can experience justification too.

Circumcision as Abraham's Seal (verses 11, 12). We can sense the quick indignation of Paul's Jewish opponents who would read the words of verse 10. "Hold on, Paul. If the uncircumcised can experience right-standing with God, then why be circumcised? Why did God give it in the first place?" Paul must answer this question. It is not enough for him to affirm that circumcision did not justify Abraham, he must explain what circumcision *did* do.

1. *Circumcision was a "seal" of Abraham's justification*, says Paul in verse 11a. Indeed, Paul uses two words here, "sign" and "seal." We might freely render Paul's words thus, to make the meaning clearer: "And he received circumcision as a sign, a seal of the righteousness which he already possessed, by faith, in his uncircumcised state."

The word "sign" refers to anything in general that signifies or indicates something. When Paul uses this word, he is actually quoting from Genesis 17:11: "It shall be a *token* of the covenant betwixt me and you." "Seal" means an image impressed on something for official identification, and Paul uses this word to explain more technically the word "sign" (token). The two words mean the same thing.

Paul's point is clear and important. Abraham was already righteous (justified) by faith when he was circumcised. Circumcision was, therefore, not the *means* of his justification, but a sign, a token, a seal thereof. As Griffith Thomas puts it: "It (circumcision) did not *confer*, but *confirmed* the righteousness .... It did not 'convey,' but 'attest.' It bore witness to an already existing righteousness." Circumcision was an identifying mark in the Jewish men's flesh that signified their covenant relationship with the Lord, and thus their right-standing with Him *if* they were true believers like Abraham. The faith put them there (and kept them there!); the circumcision was a testimony that they were there.

Perhaps this is a good place to discuss Christian baptism which is often compared to circumcision. In some ways the two are alike, though in other ways they differ. But as external religious ordinances they are similar. Baptism like circumcision is a token, a sign, a seal of a righteousness possessed by faith. The ordinance itself does not bring justification; and so, in that sense, it is not "essential" to salvation. It is not a *means* of justification. But again like circumcision it is an external action applied to the flesh that is intended in New Testament times to be a necessary testimony to the inner righteousness already obtained.

76

Stifler expresses this truth thus: "In no dispensation do rites bestow anything; they are the shadow, not the substance; they are a seal. But the seal is worthless apart from the matter or the document that it attests. The Jew had torn off the seal from the covenant, and then vainly boasted of this meaningless imprint."

Griffith Thomas adds: "This is not to set aside or even to derogate from the importance of divine ordinances. They are seals of promises to be embraced by faith. . . .Faith lays hold of the promise, and then the ordinance is the seal and assurance of its fulfillment, so that in their place and for their purpose, divine ordinances like circumcision (or baptism) are full of meaning, power, and blessing."

Need it be added that there were many Jews circumcised and many church members baptized who never put faith in God and were never cleansed from sin spiritually? This shows further that the ordinance is never the *means* of salvation and only has its real meaning when the individual has been justified by faith. And this is so for the Old Testament saints as surely as for New Testament saints.

2. *Abraham was "father" of all who believe, circumcised or not.* This truth is given emphasis by Paul in verses 11b, 12. This is the same truth Paul emphasized in Galatians 3:7 (you may want to review the comments on that passage). Here Paul specifically discusses Abraham's spiritual lineage in two groups.

First (11b), he asserts that Abraham, justified by faith and chosen by God to be the father of a spiritual covenant people and given circumcision as a seal thereof, became "father" of uncircumcised (Gentile) believers. Thus Paul makes it clear again that the blessedness of justification can be experienced by believers apart from circumcision. Indeed, an uncircumcised Gentile believer is an heir of the Abrahamic covenant! Paul is actually saying in the last clause of verse 11 that, if this were not so, then only the circumcised could have righteousness imputed to them. (Review the comments on "imputed" righteousness in the previous study.)

Second (12), Paul asserts that Abraham is spiritually the father of believing Jews too. Note that while Abraham is *physically* the father of *all* Jews; *only* those who put *faith* in God can rightly be said to be of his *spiritual* lineage.

In verse 11b Abraham is "father" of uncircumcised believers. In verse 12 he is "father" of some who are circumcised (Jews) too, but only if it can be said of them that they are not only circumcised but also exercised the same faith Abraham exercised even before he was circumcised. To "walk in the steps of that faith" of Abraham means to follow his example in faith, to put faith in God as he did. Thus, if a Jew is to claim Abraham as his father in the *truest* sense, he must have the saving faith that his circumcision is but a "token" of. In every way Paul has destroyed the claim of those who based their right-standing with God on their circumcision. Justification is not by circumcision.

2. JUSTIFICATION IS NOT BY A SYSTEM OF RITUAL
(Romans 4:13-15)

Justification is not by the observance of any other of the Mosaic rituals required by the law. Circumcision was but one of the external religious rituals practiced in Old Testament times. Moses' Law provided for hundreds of rules—moral, religious, civil—that were imposed on the Jews. Paul wants us to understand that justification cannot come by the observance of any part—or the whole—of the Law any more than it can come by circumcision.

An Affirmation (verse 13). In this verse Paul continues using Abraham as his illustration and plainly states the fact he wishes to prove that justification does not come by law-keeping. Several important factors must be noted in this verse.

1. *The promise to Abraham* is summed up by Paul as a promise "that he should be the heir of the world." The various commentators have differing opinions as to the precise meaning of this phrase. Some think it refers to the physical "earth" (compare Matthew 5:5), but the word here is the *cosmos* (perhaps the same "world" as in Romans 1:20). Probably the best understanding of this promise that Abraham would be "heir of the world" is that it refers to the universal, worldwide spiritual race of people who would be his "seed."

In Genesis 12:3 one of the promises of the original covenant with Abraham is: "In thee shall all the families of the earth be blessed." In Genesis 17:4 the promise is: "Thou shalt be a father of many nations." The point behind all this is that Abraham was promised a great spiritual lineage from all nations of the earth, a universal people (Jew and Gentile, as we have seen) who would be the very family of God. Ultimately, of course, that family will inherit and inhabit the *cosmos*, the universe—even if it will finally be a new Heaven and a new earth as described in Revelation. Thus, though an element of *place* is involved, Abraham's promise refers primarily to the worldwide *people* of whom he would be spiritually the father.

2. *The seed of Abraham will inherit this promise with him.* Paul does not pursue identification of this "seed" here, but in Galatians 3, especially verses 16, 29, he carefully identifies in a similar context this "seed" as first Christ himself and then all who are (Jew or Gentile) Christ's. Thus the seed of Abraham is the whole family of God. They "inherit" the promise given to Abraham in one sense when they are brought into that family by faith and in another sense when they with all the rest of that family come into the possession of the universe promised them.

3. *The promise was not possessed by the Law.* In the Greek order, the very first words of verse 13 are: "For not by the law." This is the point Paul is emphasizing. He does not explain himself, but the truth is obvious: Abraham was given this promise long before the Mosaic Law was given. His justification came before circumcision (verse 10), proving that circumcision was not the means of justification. So also the promise of a spiritual lineage was his before the Law, proving that the law was not the means whereby he would have a spiritual lineage. (Compare Galatians 3:16, 17 and the comments thereon in the study on Galatians.)

4. *The promise was possessed by "the righteousness of faith."* This phrase is a sort of abbreviated way of saying "the right standing before God that Abraham possessed by faith." Paul has proved, above, that Abraham was justified by faith (4:3). It was on this basis that the promise was given him. This means both that Abraham himself was given the promise by faith and that others come to be part of his lineage and heirs of the same promise as a result of their own righteousness (right-standing, justification) by faith. Faith, again, is the method for justification and inheriting all God's good promises to His people, not law-keeping.

An Argument (verses 14, 15). Paul now proceeds to give three logical arguments to back up the affirmation made in verse 13.

1. *Inheritance by law would void faith.* Paul's point is that we must adopt either faith or law-keeping as the means of justification and thus of inheriting with Abraham's spiritual lineage, the family of God. Faith and law-keeping exclude one another as *methods* of justification. True, a believer may try to observe the Law. Jewish believers in Mosaic times were expected to. Even now believers should observe the *moral* laws of God (though not the Mosaic rituals). But though a believer observes the Law, still one who would be saved by faith cannot at the same time try to be saved by his keeping of the Law (which explains the powerful words of Galatians 5:2-4).

2. *Inheritance by law would contradict promise.* The word "made void" applied to faith means "make empty," "render ineffectual." The word "made of none effect" applied to the promise means "to render idle," "annul." Thus both mean about the same thing, and the two expressions have the same point. Earning standing with God by law-keeping is the opposite of being awarded that standing by God's gracious promise.

Again, we cannot have both; one excludes the other. If justification were by law, if inheriting God's promises to Abraham's "seed" were by law, then faith and promise would be contradicted.

3. *Inheritance by law would violate the law's purpose.* This is the point of verse 15, and our understanding of this verse will be much helped by reviewing Romans 3:19, 20 and the comments on those verses. As Paul put it there, "By the law is the knowledge of

sin." In other words, the purpose of the Law is to bring *awareness* of sin, not *deliverance* from sin.

The same truth is taught in Romans 7:7: "I had not known sin, but by the law." Note also 7:13: "that sin by the commandment might become exceeding sinful." Without written law, there would still be guilt of sin, because there is at least the inner law of conscience (Romans 2:14, 15). But the written law was given so that man might have a very clear understanding of the exceeding sinfulness of man. As Paul puts it in 3:19, the Law was given that "all the world may become guilty before God."

The truth is this. The Law was to condemn, not to justify. Any doctrine of justification by law-keeping would serve to contradict this purpose and also would consequently dull man's understanding of his sinfulness by misleading him into thinking he can keep the Law well enough to be justified thereby.

This is what Paul means when he says, "The law worketh wrath." The Law reveals to man his own sinfulness and thus makes man aware he is rightfully condemned, under the wrath of God. Compare Romans 7:9: "When the commandment came . . . I died." The Law produces consciousness of sin, guilt, wrath, and death. That is its purpose. It cannot also serve as the means for deliverance from these.

The last part of verse 15 gives the same truth in other words. "Where no law is, there is no transgression" reminds us that it is the Law that serves to bring awareness of transgression and condemnation. Further, transgression is always measured against God's law, either the written or inner law. His law provides the standard by which all men's deeds are judged, and sin reckoned. That law, therefore, can never be the means of man's justification, since it reveals to all men that they have sinned. Justification is by no effort of man at self-righteousness, nor by any external religious or legal observances. Justification is by faith.

11 Justification by Divine Favor

Study Text: Romans 4:16-25

INTRODUCTION

In Part 1 of Romans Paul showed us the stark fact that all the world is lost. In Part 2, with which we are still concerned in this lesson, Paul shows just how God has provided for the sinner to be saved. The guilty sinner can stand before God guiltless; he can be awarded the righteousness of God!

In explaining this miracle of grace, Paul is both positive, telling us how man *can* get right with God; and negative, telling us how man *cannot* get right with God. The negative side helps us understand the positive better.

In 3:21-31 Paul began with a positive explanation of just how God has provided for man to be righteous before God. From man's

81

side, the method is *faith*. Then in 4:1-15 Paul turned to the negative showing that justification is not by works of self-righteousness (4:1-8); nor by circumcision or law-keeping (4:9-15). Man cannot save himself.

Now, in concluding this part of Romans, Paul returns to the positive, showing us once again the important principles in the method by which God has provided for man to get right with Him.

EXPOSITION

This study is subsection C, the last subsection under Part 2. (Check the general study-outline in the back of this book.) It covers 4:16-25 and is entitled: "Justification by Divine Favor." Paul's emphasis is on God's grace, a favor undeserved by man.

1. AFFIRMATION OF THE PURPOSES OF GRACE
(Romans 4:16, 17)

You will recall that Paul has used Abraham as his basic example of justification by faith and not by works throughout this chapter. That is still true in most of the passage we cover in this lesson.

Grace and the Promise (verse 16a). Some of the little logical progressions of verses 16, 17 are difficult to follow. Perhaps it is not necessary for us to be able to explain the exact connection between each phrase. The basic ideas are reasonably clear.

1. *The harmony of grace and faith* is first made plain here. The "it" refers back to "the promise" mentioned in verse 13. (You may want to review the comments on verses 13-15.) In verses 13-15 Paul spoke of a promise given to Abraham that provided for him to be father of a worldwide "seed" and that he and all his spiritual lineage would some day inherit the universe as the very family of God. Paul also made sure we understood that getting in on this spiritual lineage is not by the Law, for if inheritance were by the Law, then both "faith" and "promise" would be worthless notions.

Thus in 16a Paul begins the logical reaffirmation of his principles to which the negatives of verses 14, 15 have led. The "therefore" means based on the things just said. We might rephrase the words of 16a in this way: "What I have said proves that *inheriting* the promise God gave Abraham is by *faith*, in order that this might all be accomplished by God's *grace*." The entire statement looks back to things previously stated in the chapter.

The "it" means that Abraham received the original promise by faith, and that all who come to be part of the "seed" promised him do so by faith, and that he and they together will "inherit" by faith. Thus *faith* is the principle connected with the promise given to

Abraham in the covenant.

And, says Paul, the reason *faith* is the method on man's part (not law-keeping, or circumcision, or works, as earlier in the chapter) is so that *grace* may be the basis on God's part (not debt or obligation, as seen in verse 4). Paul's point is that faith and grace go together in harmony. Justification by works or circumcision or law-keeping on man's part would fit with salvation as a wage owed to man by God. Justification by faith, however, fits with salvation as a work of divine grace (favor undeserved by man).

2. *The harmony of grace and promise* is next made clear. Paul wants us to see that these three words go together appropriately: faith, grace, promise. They are all in accord; one calls for the other. Compare Galatians 3:18: "If the inheritance be of the law, it is no more of promise"; and Galatians 4:23: "He who was of the bondwoman was born after the flesh; but he of the freewoman was by promise." Paul means that the very idea of God's doing something for man by *promise* will of necessity mean that the promise is by *grace* (not obligation) and thus an object of *faith* (not works). (Compare also verse 14 above.)

3. *The certainty of the promise* results from the fact that it is by faith and grace. "To the end" means "with this objective (result) in view." God wanted the promise to be *sure, certain,* and *firm,* to the whole seed. Remember the "promise" referred to here is the one God gave to Abraham that he would have a worldwide (Jew and Gentile) seed in all nations and that he and his spiritual seed would inherit the world.

Paul is saying that this promise would fail to be certain if it were to be partaken of on the basis of works and law-keeping. If that were the basis, there would be no guarantee of success, simply because the Law is so difficult—indeed, impossible!—to keep. But since grace is the grounds on God's side and faith the condition on man's side, then the promise rests on a secure foundation. We can be sure of its fulfilment for all the intended seed.

Grace and the Provision (verses 16b, 17a). Paul has just said that grace makes the promise sure to *all* the seed, and the word "all" has two important points to it.

1. *The existence of the "seed,"* at all, is guaranteed by grace. The point here is that God's gracious provision is the basis for any and all to be included in the seed. God's grace makes the promise sure for the *whole* seed. In other words, had the provision of a seed for Abraham depended on law-keeping by those who aspired to "inherit" with Abraham, there would have been no "seed" at all.

This point has been made plain already by Paul's insistence that justification is *not* by the Law (3:20; cf. Galatians 3:11). No man can keep the Law, and so God's promise to make Abraham father of a great spiritual people from all nations would be absolutely empty if men were to participate in that promised seed by works. This point is made here again by Paul's reference to "not to that only which is of the law." This phrase refers to the Jews, who possessed the written, Mosaic Law. Even they, Paul is saying, have to be included in the Abrahamic promise by grace and faith. Only so is the promise sure of any content at all.

2. *The inclusiveness of the seed* is also guaranteed by grace. Thus by "all" Paul means both Jew and Gentile. The Jew, as just seen, is "that which is of the law." The Gentile is "that which is of the faith of Abraham": namely, they who are kin to Abraham only by faith and have no racial or legal standing to offer God. But both they—the Gentiles—and those who think their possession of the Law counts—the Jews—are included in Abraham's spiritual seed by faith and grace and promise.

This inclusiveness is triply emphasized in 16b, 17a: first, in the phrase, "to *all* the seed"; then in the clause "who is the father of us *all*"; and then in the parenthetic addition, "a father of *many* nations." All three of these stress the equal participation of both Jews and Gentiles in Abraham's spiritual seed by faith and the fact that only by this faith-grace method could such a promise be fulfilled. Abraham was promised an innumerable spiritual seed from all nations; all who are part thereof, who "inherit" with Abraham, are there by faith and in consequence of God's undeserved favor exercised in man's behalf.

Grace and the Power (verse 17b). The foundation for the grace of God (and the promise and faith that go with it) rests on the great power of God. The last part of verse 17 stresses this by pointing out the kind of God in whom Abraham put his faith.

The exact connection of "before him" (the "him" is God) is debatable, but probably reaches back to the idea of certainty in the previous verse: in other words, "that the promise might be sure . . . before Him in whom Abraham believed." The certainty of the promise has been established, certified in the very presence of God himself, the God in whom Abraham placed his faith.

Anyway, the character and power of God are the things emphasized here. Abraham did not put faith in a dead and powerless God, but in a God who has the power to back up any gracious promise He might be pleased to make. If salvation were accomplished by man's works, the power and ability of God would have nothing to do with it; but if by grace, then God is the doer, and He must be able to bring to pass what He has promised. Paul notes two things about the ability of the God in whom Abraham believed.

1. *The Raiser of the dead.* Interpreters argue over the meaning of this. Some think the point is that Abraham believed God would restore Isaac (cf. Hebrews 11:19), but that idea does not fit this context too well. More likely, Abraham's faith that God could give him a physical seed though he had passed the age of childbearing is involved (cf. verse 19, below). Abraham put faith in God's promise

of grace, because he knew God could "make alive the dead."

2. *The One who makes the future a fact.* The clause, "who calleth those things which be not as though they were," means that God sees the future which does not even exist yet and makes fact out of it. He makes the existent out of the nonexistent, the actual from the potential, the possible from the impossible.

The use of the word "calleth" emphasizes that God does this by His *Word.* God calls into existence things that do not exist. He speaks about things that are not yet and they come to be. This aspect of God's omnipotence (all-power) reminds us that the very existence of the future depends on God. His promises about the future are absolutely dependable!

In particular, as applied to Abraham, the promise of the seed is involved. God spoke of Abraham's "seed" when Abraham had no child at all. But that future reality was already fact with God, and its actual realization lay in God's hand. His word made it a certainty. This is the kind of God who stands behind all the gracious promises He makes to man, including especially the gospel-promises about our salvation and justification. Justification rests on God's grace; and God's grace rests on His unlimited ability to make reality of every promise. When man responds to such gracious promises by faith, the purposes of grace are accomplished.

2. ABRAHAM AND THE PROMISE OF GRACE
(Romans 4:18-22)

If verse 17 called to our attention the kind of God in whom Abraham believed, verses 18-22 direct our attention to the kind of faith Abraham had and to the gracious promise of God on which Abraham's faith rested.

The Contradictions of Abraham's Faith (verses 18, 19). Faith always has its testing, its obstacles to overcome. Abraham was no exception. God promised to give him a "seed" and for the immediate future that promise included a physical lineage. And Abraham, as we know the familiar story, had no children.

This obstacle, ordinarily no great hurdle, was a serious one in Abraham's case. Both he and Sarah his wife were beyond the age of normal childbearing. This is the matter which served to contradict the promise given by God, and in the face of that contradiction Abraham had to have faith. Paul feels that Abraham's faith was heroic and exemplary in this regard, and he reveals this by the various observations he makes.

1. *"Against hope."* This first part of verse 18 ascribes "hope" to Abraham, all the while saying it was "against hope." If that sounds paradoxical, it was intended to. The hope against which Abraham believed was *natural* hope. There could be no hope, no expectation

of childbearing according to any natural, human, fleshly consideration. The hope in which Abraham believed was *supernatural* hope, hope based on faith, hope based on confidence begotten by God's Word.

Hebrews 11:1 and Romans 8:24, 25 fit in well here. Hope and faith are inseparably tied. Each provides foundation for the other. Both relate to convictions for which other kinds, natural kinds, of evidence are inadequate. Both result from confidence in the God who makes future fact.

2. *"He considered not."* Verse 19 gives us two particular circumstances in Abraham's situation that ruled out natural hope: (1) the "deadness" of his own body; (2) the "deadness" of Sarah's womb. The first resulted from the fact that Abraham was nearly a hundred. Though men are generally able to father children at ages older than women's childbearing possibilities, still Abraham was now beyond that point. The second circumstance was even more serious and settled: Sarah was physically beyond childbearing capacity. Abraham "considered not" these objections. This does not mean he was unaware of them; he did not let them rob him of faith in God's promise.

The Confidence of Abraham's Faith (verses 20, 21). These verses present a picture of genuine faith, involving as it does not a mere intellectual affirmation but a heartfelt confidence in God. Three phrases emphasize this.

1. *"He staggered not."* This word "staggered" is the same as "wavering" in James 1:6 (which see). It refers to the doubts and conflicts of a person who cannot decide between two opinions, in this case whether to believer God or not. Unbelief is the father of such doubts. Genuine faith in God begets a settled confidence in His Word. Abraham was not tossed about in uncertainty whether God could make good on His promise.

2. He was *"strong in faith."* This is the opposite of the phrase in verse 19, "weak in faith." Abraham did not have a weak, infirm faith, but a strong, able, powerful faith. The next phrase gives the reason: "giving glory to God." The strength of one's faith is determined by the majesty and power of his God. Abraham held God in high esteem and a strong faith was the natural consequence.

3. He was *"fully persuaded."* The Greek word used here means full assurance, convincement, and certain confidence. We cannot fail to notice the conviction on which this solid persuasion stood so firmly, that "God is able to perform what He has promised." That conviction is like a spiritual rock of Gibraltar as a foundation for faith.

The Content of Abraham's Faith (verses 18, 21). These factors have already been noted, but are listed here for special mention.

1. *God's ability.* As just noted, verse 21b gives us one thing Abraham fully believed: that God is able to do what He promises.

Abraham was confident that God could give to him and Sarah a child, even though that might involve making the "dead" alive (verses 17, 19).

2. *Promised certainty.* Abraham not only believed God *could* do, he believed he *would* become father of many nations because God promised him such a seed (verse 18b). With Abraham, when God says something is so, it is as good as so!

The direct implication of all the Biblical passages on the subject is that God deliberately waited until Abraham and Sarah were past the age of childbearing so that the birth of Isaac would be *clearly* recognized as *His* work and not man's. This is exactly what Paul means in Galatians 4:23, for example, when he contrasts Isaac's birth "by promise" with Ishmael's "by flesh." Had Isaac been born to Abraham and Sarah under altogether natural and normal circumstances, who would have given *God* the credit? Here again is the idea that God's *promise* and God's *grace* are inseparably linked together and serve as objects for man's *faith*, producing in him the kind of *hope* Abraham had.

The Consequences of Abraham's Faith (verse 22). This verse repeats verse 3, which we have already studied and will not need to explain in detail again. In consequence of Abraham's faith, which is the condition man must meet, God declared him guiltless, righteous; God justified him. "Imputed" is the same as "counted." See the discussion on verse 3.

3. APPLICATION OF THE PRINCIPLES OF GRACE
(Romans 4:23-25)

Paul closes this discussion of Abraham's faith in God's gracious promise by applying the principles involved to our own situations.

The People to Whom Righteousness Is Available (verses 23, 24). Paul makes his point by being first negative and then positive.

1. *Negative: not for Abraham only.* This is the side presented in verse 23. What Paul says is that Genesis 15:6 (quoted in the previous verse and in verse 3) was not written for Abraham's sake alone. What he means by this is that Abraham was not the only one to whom the principle of justification by faith can be applied.

2. *Positive: for all who put faith in God.* This side of the truth is indicated in verse 24. If what happened to Abraham is available to others, Paul wants us to know it is available to all or any who will exercise faith in God.

The facts are these: Righteousness was put on Abraham's account when he believed in God. He did not earn or deserve this declaration of innocence but received it by God's undeserved favor, the gracious gift of God. That same method of achieving right-standing before God is available to all. Righteousness will be put on our accounts, too, if we but believe in God.

We note that Paul "defines" God a little more specifically as "him that raised up Jesus our Lord from the dead." Our faith in God has an even clearer object than did Abraham's, for we see Him as revealed in His Son Jesus and as powerfully demonstrated in the resurrection of Christ. Abraham understood, somehow, that God was a "Raiser of the dead"; we have seen that fact undeniably demonstrated in Jesus. Our faith rests on a firm foundation.

The Person by Whom Righteousness Is Available (verse 25). The last part of verse 24 leads naturally to this summary of the gospel fact about Jesus Christ on which righteousness by faith is based.

1. *Jesus' death* is fact number one. "Delivered" for our offences refers to this. This means He was "found guilty" of our transgressions and thus judged, in death, as our substitute (cf. 2 Corinthians 5:21). In some way of God's beyond our comprehension our sins were put on Him and He bore the righteous wrath of God in our place.

2. *Jesus' resurrection* is fact number two and these two facts stand together as the "heart" of the gospel (cf. 1 Corinthians 15:3, 4). That the Resurrection was "for" our justification means that it was required if there were to be any justification. The Resurrection was God's declaration that the sacrifice of the cross was sufficient and that it was accepted. The Resurrection is the divine declaration that a believing sinner is justified.

The entire lesson has shown us the way a gracious God acts. By His own favor, undeserved by man, He deigns to bless man. Abraham has provided an excellent example of the response of faith that is required to God's offer of favor. He believed the impossible because the gracious and able God said so. And so God made the impossible true, not only by giving a son to a couple too old to bear children (the promise) but also by declaring innocent a guilty sinner (justification/righteousness). Just so, we must believe the unbelievable, that we who are sinners are made righteous by His undeserved favor. Only we have a distinct advantage over Abraham: on this side of the cross we have a clearer understanding just how this impossible thing has come to be.

12 The Righteousness of God: A Possession of the Saved

Study Text: Romans 5:1-11

Introduction
1. Peace with God (Romans 5:1, 2a)
   a. The Meaning (verse 1a)
   b. The Method (verses 1b, 2a)
2. Perfection of Gladness (Romans 5:2b-8)
   a. Joy and Aspiration (verse 2b)
   b. Joy and Affliction (verses 3, 4)
   c. Joy and Assurance (verses 5-8)
3. Prospect of Glory (Romans 5:9-11)
   a. The Promised Rescue (verses 9, 10)
   b. The Present Rejoicing (verse 11)

INTRODUCTION

This section moves us into Part 3 of Romans. Perhaps a brief review of the first two parts will help prepare the way for the study. You are well familiar by now with the general theme of Romans, the righteousness of God. In Part 1 (1:18—3:20) Paul explained to us the sinner's predicament: All men—Jew and Gentile alike—stand guilty of sin and condemned before God.

In Part 2 (3:21—4:25) Paul explained just how a guilty sinner could stand guiltless (righteous) before God. That provision came by the work of the Savior, and man can be awarded that right-standing only by faith in God through Jesus Christ. This is Paul's doctrine of justification by faith.

Now Paul considers "justification by faith" as proved, and he can move on to explain the implications of that doctrine for the believer's experience. This he does in Part 3, which covers four

89

chapters, 5-8. We call this part "The Righteousness of God: A Possession of the Saved." Throughout these chapters Paul tells us what it *means* that we are justified by faith, just as in Part 2 he told us of the *method* of justification.

EXPOSITION

As this new part of the letter to the Romans is begun, a little time spent with the general study-outline should prove helpful (see the back of this book). You need to keep aware how each section fits into the overall pattern of the epistle. You will see that Part 3 of Romans has many subdivisions. Subsection A, which deals with chapter five, explains the results of justification. This lesson is the first of two under this heading and covers 5:1-11. It is entitled "The Believer's Possessions: Contents."

Almost everyone agrees that Romans 5:1-11 gives us a list of the results of justification. Verse 1 begins: "Therefore being justified by faith we *have*." These verses tell us what we possess, as believers and as "justified" by that faith. Thus Romans 5:1-11 is one of the most glorious of Scriptures. Justification involves far more than merely being declared innocent of wrongdoing by God, as wonderful and incredible as that is! Justification ushers man into a new relationship with God. Justification is the root and trunk of a tree that, once planted, bears all sorts of delightful fruits.

But though all agree that this passage gives a list of these possessions of the believer, not all agree as to the exact contents of that list. What words shall we select from 5:1-11 as the basic results of justification and around which we can organize our treatment of the chapter? Some interpreters (as in the Scofield Bible) see *seven* (or more) results, and include in the list: (1) peace, (2) access, (3) hope, (4) the love of God, (5) the Holy Spirit, (6) salvation from wrath, and (7) joy.

There is no doubt that all seven of these are wonderful items and are all part and parcel of what the Christian possesses in the Lord. The only problem with the list is that it fails to see the proper relationships between these words. Some of them, like "access," are looking back to the justification-event itself rather than pointing to a fruit of justification. Some of them are bases for others, rather than being equal results.

The more this writer has studied the passage, the more convinced he has become that there are *three* of these that are *most* prominent in the passage in catching the main emphases of Paul. These are peace, joy, and hope (cf. Romans 15:13). Nor can we say that they are treated in separate sets of verses. The coverage of the three is interwoven. "Peace with God" is mentioned in verse 1, but is also involved in verse 10. The word for "joy" in verse 11 is the same as "rejoice" and "glory" in verses 2, 3. The word "hope" appears in verses 2, 4, and 5; and the content of that hope is accurately expressed in verses 9-11.

These three will be used as a basis for the threefold division of this lesson. Though all three are intertwined, each has a section in which it receives the most emphasis; and that is the way in which we shall approach the subject.

1. PEACE WITH GOD (Romans 5:1, 2a)

Though the various interpreters disagree as to exactly how many "results" of justification to list from 5:1-11, they all agree about the first item on the list: "peace with God." There is no doubt about this, because "peace" is the noun object of the verb "we have."

The Meaning (verse 1a). Paul begins the verse by saying: "Therefore being justified by faith, we have." He assumes his doctrine of justification by faith has been proved in the previous part of his letter; the "therefore" looks back to that proof. Now he turns to the blessings believers possess as a result: "have" means "possess."

We possess peace with God, which is an obvious fruit of being found innocent by and before God (justification). This "peace with God" has a two-fold involvement. First, we are *at peace with God* and this is based on the truth that we were, before justification, at war with God. This truth, you will note, is clarified down in verse 10, which we ought to deal with now. There you see that we were *enemies* of God before we were saved. This idea, though unpleasant, is factual: God and man were enemies. Man, beginning with Adam, had planted his feet in a path of deliberate self-will and rebellion; and God's wrath was upon man for his sins. But the death of God's Son accomplished "reconciliation," a word that refers to the settlement of differences. Verse 11 uses the English word "atonement" (the same word, in Greek, as "reconciliation"). This word expresses the idea well: at-one-ment. Christ's death was the signing of a peace treaty between God and man, if you will. Compare Ephesians 2:14-17, which provides excellent commentary on this very subject.

Also involved in this "peace with God" is what is sometimes called *the peace of God.* The idea here is that we possess peace in our hearts in direct consequence of having settled things with God. Our relationship to God was one of enmity, and "there is no peace, saith my God, to the wicked," for "the wicked are like the troubled sea, when it cannot rest" (Isaiah 57:20, 21). But now having been declared guiltless and standing right with God (justification), we accept our innocence before Him, and our hearts are at last at peace.

The Method (verses 1b, 2a). Paul uses two phrases to define how we have come to possess this "peace with God."

1. *Through our Lord Jesus Christ* (1b). This brief phrase sums up all that Christ has done to make peace with God available to man. As just noted, verses 10, 11 are more specific about this, referring to Christ's death as reconciliation (atonement) between God and man. Ephesians 2:14 says: "He is our peace." Furthermore, His is the righteousness imputed to us when we believe (Philippians 3:9). He took our place, was identified as guilty of our sins and punished therefor (2 Corinthians 5:21). His death made peace.

2. *By "access" into God's grace* (2a). As pointed out earlier in the lesson, some interpreters take "access" as the *second* result of justification to be included in the list. They see the words "we have peace" (verse 1) and "we have access" (verse 2) as equal clauses, both stating what we possess as a fruit of justification by faith.

But this writer understands the order of the clauses differently, taking the first part of verse 2 as being parallel to "through our Lord Jesus Christ" (1b), and as added to show just how we have come to have peace. In other words, this "access" by Christ is the basis or reason for our peace.

The key to this is in understanding just what "access" Paul means here. The word "access" means being brought into or introduced to something. In Greek, the verb "have" is *perfect* tense, not present: "we have come to possess." *What* is it we have been brought into? The answer is "this grace wherein we stand." By "this grace" Paul means the state of justification-innocence which is ours by God's grace. "We stand" means literally "we have come to stand." Note *how* we have come to this: "by faith."

Paul is not speaking of an additional result of justification here (though, no doubt, free access to God is a result of justification, as in Hebrews 10:19). But he is pointing back to that justification-event itself as the basis of our peace. He is explaining what he meant when he said in verse 1 that "we have peace with God *through our Lord Jesus Christ*": because through Him we obtained access into this justified state in which we came to stand by God's grace and by our faith. By this we came to experience peace with God.

2. PERFECTION OF GLADNESS
(Romans 5:2b-8)

If "peace with God" is the first fruit of justification by faith, *joy* is the second. In this writer's judgment the verb "we rejoice" in verse 2b is parallel to the "we have peace" in verse 1; and thus this is the second basic result of "being justified by faith."

Joy and Aspiration (verse 2b). The clause "we rejoice in hope of the glory of God" means that hope is the foundation of our joy. Joy rests on hope. We will note (as has already been indicated earlier in the lesson) that hope and joy are interwoven from here on throughout the rest of these eleven verses. (It seems accurate, however, to emphasize the joy in verses 2b-8 and the hope in verses 9-11 as we are doing.)

What does "hope of the glory of God" mean? Probably this: "The hope [expectation, aspiration] we have that we will participate in the glory of God." Back in 3:23 Paul said that "We keep coming up short of the glory of God." That is a picture of the sinner's repeated and frustrating failure to measure up to the fulness of the image of God for which man was originally intended. But now Paul says we expect to reach that goal to which all men aspire: "When he shall appear, we shall be like him" (1 John 3:2; cf. Romans 8:18-25, where again "glory" and "hope" are related in the same way as here). And this confident aspiration, this hope, makes us glad.

Joy and Affliction (verses 3, 4). "And not only so" means that our rejoicing is not merely a momentary passion that is with us when we have our clearest picture of the glory of God of which we shall one day partake. There is more to it than that. Indeed, we rejoice in times of affliction.

The Greek word "we glory" (3) is the same as "we rejoice" (2). That "we rejoice in tribulations [afflictions]" means both that we are able to be glad even in spite of such circumstances and that we are glad *because* of such circumstances. The latter explains the first, and is true because afflictions are regarded as actually perfecting or intensifying or maturing our hope and thus our joy.

1. *Tribulation worketh patience.* The Greek word for "tribulation" originally meant *pressure*. Oppression, trouble, distress are indicated by the word. The same word is translated "affliction" in 2 Corinthians 4:17, which compares remarkably with the passage here. "Worketh" means an effect is produced. "Patience" is perseverance, bearing up under any sort of trying circumstances. The pressure-experience of trouble and affliction helps produce in a Christian the quality of perseverance, patience.

2. *Patience works experience.* Supply the same verb in both this clause and the next. "Experience" is a vague word. The Greek word refers to the results of a testing when the product has been tested out satisfactorily. Here, of course, the believer's character is in view. Griffith Thomas suggests we use "approvedness of experience." When something has been tested and has passed the test, confidence is the result. What Paul means is that perseverance through afflictions gives us confidence that we really are sons of God. We have, to use Thayer's words, "tried character."

3. *Experience produces hope.* And if persevering through afflictions works to produce within us a confidence confirmed by testing, then our hope of the glory of God is reaffirmed and strengthened. Then so will our rejoicing be intensified and perfected.

Joy and Assurance (verses 5-8). "Hope," "confidence," "assurance"—these words are closely related. We have just spoken of the first two and now we speak of the third.

1. *The reality of assurance* is seen in the first clause of verse 5: "hope maketh not ashamed." This simply means that our hope (our expectation, our aspiration to partake of the glory of God) *is not going to be disappointed*. We are assured that our hope is sound.

2. *The reason for assurance* is seen in the rest of this passage, 5b-8, all introduced by the word "because." And that reason can be summed up in these words: "the love of God." Paul takes time to discuss God's love at length, for in that love is the basis for our assurance that our hope will not be disappointed.

First, note this: "the love of God" means God's love for us.

Second, note that this love of God for us "is shed abroad" (Greek: has been poured out) in our hearts by the Holy Spirit who was given to us when we were saved. This probably means that the Spirit of God, when He convicted us, convinced us of God's love for us; and that, when He came to dwell within us at conversion, flooded our hearts with the assurance and experience of that great love.

Third, note that this love of God on our behalf was most convincingly demonstrated when Christ died for us. Verses 6-8 develop this truth. Compare 2 Corinthians 5:14.

In verse 6 "without strength" refers to the sinner's spiritual infirmity, his utter inability to do anything to deliver himself from the guilt and condemnation so thoroughly explained in Part 1 of Romans. "In due time" means the time ordained by God (cf. Galatians 4:4). The "ungodly" are the impious, those who do not reverence God.

In verse 7 Paul speaks of what is generally true of human circumstances. Both clauses express the same general idea. Men do not usually die for each other willingly, though on occasions one might be bold enough to risk his life and even die in behalf of one righteous or good. Even that, as plausible as it is, is rare enough to be the *exception* and thus cause for surprise. How much more amazing is it that Christ died for sinners!

In verse 8 Paul states this very surprising fact. The word "commend" means "introduce to" or "exhibit" or "show." The fact that Christ died in our behalf, even while we were sinners, displays the love of God for us. We note Paul's emphasis on the wonder of God's love for us when we see his threefold reminder that he loved us in spite of our weakness (6), in spite of our ungodliness (6), and in spite of the fact we were sinners (8). Had God loved man the way He made him, it would have been wonderful enough. But God loved man the way he became—sinful and rebellious. That is wonder beyond human comprehension. No wonder we have assurance that our hope will not make us ashamed, will not be disappointed; and no wonder we have joy as a fruit of justification!

94

3. PROSPECT OF GLORY
(Romans 5:9-11)

We come now to the third of the major results of justification to be gleaned from this passage, hope. In reality, "hope" has been mentioned three times already: as the basis for our joy (verse 2), as the product of afflictions and perseverance and tested character (verse 4), and as assured of not being disappointed by the demonstrated love of God (verse 5). But the actual *content* of that hope has been mostly left for now. This is the point of these final verses and they give us more detail about the original phrase used in verse 2. We have a hope, a prospect, of the glory of God.

The Promised Rescue (verses 9, 10). Back in verses 1, 2 the words "being justified" were followed by two present results: (1) "we have peace with God" and (2) "we rejoice." Now those very same words "being justified" are followed by a third result; only this is a promise about the future: "we shall be saved from wrath." This is the content of our hope and Paul wants us to be positively assured of this promise.

1. *The basis for our assurance* is the death of Christ. In effect, Paul states this twice in these verses. In verse 9 note that the promise is assured because we were "justified by his blood." The "blood," of course, means the shedding of Christ's blood in sacrificial death. Compare "justified by his blood" (9) with "justified by faith" (1). The one refers to the work which made justification possible; the other, to the condition man must meet for it to be applied. Compare also "faith in his blood" in 3:25 and see the comments on 3:24, 25 for an explanation how the death of Christ accomplished justification.

In verse 10 note that the promise of final salvation is assured because we were "reconciled to God by the death of his Son." This actually restates the same truth as above, though "reconciliation" is used instead of "justification." We have already taken note of this verse in our discussion on peace with God. Jesus' death accomplished reconciliation, thus solving the problem of enmity between God and man.

Note especially that the words "much more" are used with both statements. The point of these is that the promised salvation is actually *easier* for God to give us than the justification and the reconciliation already accomplished. If these *hard* things were done, how much more can we expect the prospective deliverance to be carried out!

2. *The nature of this assurance* is also twice stated. In verse 9 the words are "we shall be saved [delivered, rescued] from wrath"; in verse 10, "we shall be saved." Both refer to the same thing. The wrath referred to is that which will come in the day of the Lord on

those who are guilty before God. In Romans 1:18—3:20 Paul has shown that *all* the world stands guilty and condemned, expecting this wrath. But the accomplishment of justification-innocence by Jesus' death and by faith guarantees that we shall stand guiltless before Him in that day. And so we have no fear of the wrath of God, but expect the glory of God (verse 2). The wrath we deserved has been poured out on His Son as our substitute and so God's wrath is "propitiated" (3:25). We will be rescued from the great outpouring of His wrath that will come in the day of judgment (cf. 1 Thessalonians 1:10). That is *final* salvation and that is our assured and confident hope.

3. *The method of our deliverance* is likewise twice stated: "through him" (9) and "by his life" (10). Both refer to Christ's work, and the references include His death and resurrection (cf. 4:25). By the sacrificial atonement of His death and the confirmed power of His resurrection life we are assured of our hope for the glory of God and deliverance from the wrath to come.

The Present Rejoicing (verse 11). The words "we joy" are the same in Greek as "we rejoice" (verse 2) and "we glory" (verse 3). It is fitting that Paul close this section on the results of justification by returning once more to the joy we have in Christ based on our confident hope for final salvation. And once again Paul reemphasizes that the "atonement" (reconciliation) worked by Christ's death and resurrection is the basis for this joy.

Some interpreters like to point up the past, present, and future tenses involved in 5:1-11. *Past:* We have been justified by Christ's death and resurrection and by our faith. *Present:* Two results of justification that dominate our present experience are *peace* with God and *rejoicing. Future:* The third result of justification, the content of our *hope*, is deliverance from the wrath to come in final salvation. The tree that grows from the roots of justification bears wonderful fruits, indeed!

13 The Believer's Possessions: Comparison

Study Text: Romans 5:12-21

Introduction
1. The Universal Heritage of Death (Romans 5:12-14)
   a. The Inclusive Legacy: A Fact (verse 12)
   b. The Ineffective Law: A Failure (verses 13, 14)
2. The Unequal Heritages Distinguished (Romans 5:15-19)
   a. The Legacy of the Offense (verses 15-19)
   b. The Legacy of the Obedience (verses 15-19)
3. The Undeserved Heritage of Deliverance (Romans 5:20, 21)
   a. The Reign of Grace (verses 20, 21a)
   b. The Results of Grace (verse 21b)

INTRODUCTION

We have already seen that the fifth chapter of Romans presents to us the results of justification. From the first eleven verses of the chapter, we have taken note of the positive results listed by Paul as being the direct fruit of justification.

The last half of chapter five continues discussing the results of justification. The purpose of verses 12-21, however, is not to continue adding other results to the list but to help us appreciate the results already suggested. This Paul sets out to do by *comparing* these wonderful things we received from Christ in justification with the things we had first received from Adam as members of the human race.

Throughout this section Adam and Christ are regarded as heads of two races: Adam of the natural and Christ of the spiritual. From each there is a heritage passed on to his lineage. As head of the natural race, Adam's heritage is for *all mankind*. Christ's heritage is only for all the members of the spiritual family He has fostered. We will not find it too difficult to choose the more attractive of the two heritages.

EXPOSITION

A glance at the general study-outline in the back of this book will confirm that this study is the second on chapter five, which explains the results of justification. The first study dealt with the *contents* of the justified believer's possessions. This one is entitled "The Believer's Possessions: Comparison" and covers 5:12-21.

1. THE UNIVERSAL HERITAGE OF DEATH
(Romans 5:12-14)

The pattern of 5:12-21 is this: First Paul stresses the sin and death passed on to all Adam's posterity, then he compares the two heritages with each other piece by piece, then he concludes by stressing the grace and life passed on to all Christ's posterity. We will deal with these in this order, and verses 12-14 give us the first emphasis.

The Inclusive Legacy: A Fact (verse 12). Romans 5:12 should be committed to memory by every Christian because it is so important in whetting the keen edge of our appreciation of the situation from which Jesus has saved us. Here is stated in clear terms the fact of universal sin and death.

1. *"Original sin"* is first referred to by Paul with these words: "By one man sin entered into the world." The "one man," of course, is Adam, and the sin referred to is his original disobedience in eating of the forbidden fruit as described in Genesis 3. This was the first sin of any man and so by it sin "entered" the world.

2. *The original sentence* is next referred to in these words: "and death by sin." This harks back again to the original warning to Adam: "In the day that thou eatest thereof thou shalt surely die" (Genesis 2:17). And die Adam did in two senses: (1) physically the process of death began, though its result was slow rather than immediate; (2) spiritually death came then and there. The latter is more serious than the first and was so dramatically displayed when Adam ran in fear at the sound of God's voice, whereas previously he would have run forward with joy. He did not "know" God any longer as friend and as in fellowship (such a relationship to God *is* life!); he only knew dread and fear. He had died.

3. *Humanity's participation in the sin* is referred to with these

98

words: "for that all have sinned." The significance of these words is debated, and either of two interpretations may be adopted. Some see here a mere repetition of Romans 3:23 and thus a reference to each person's actual sin when he is alive. If this is correct, Paul means that each individual shows his identification with Adam's sin by his own sinful deeds.

More likely, however, is the view that Paul means we all sinned when Adam sinned. In Greek the verb is a simple past tense. If Paul is, as many feel, still looking back to the "original" sin, he is saying that all really participated in that sin with Adam. This is what the theologians mean when they affirm that all men are guilty of "original sin."

The theologians have different ways of explaining just how we all participated in Adam's sin. Two things are quite clear. First, in a physical sense we were all "in Adam" as far as the actual "seed" from which the whole race has sprung. (This seems to be what the writer of Hebrews means when he credits Levi with having paid tithes to Melchisedec while still "in the loins of" Abraham his physical ancestor. See Hebrews 7:9, 10.) This would not make us personally and consciously active "in Adam."

Second, it is also clear that Paul means we sinned when Adam sinned in the same sense as in saying we died when Christ died (cf. Romans 6:6, 8, for example). We bear an identification with Adam's deeds as head of the natural race just as we bear an identification with Christ's deeds as head of the spiritual race.

There may be even more to it than this. We shall leave the more complicated aspects of the discussion to the theologians. But two conclusions are simple and clear enough for us and seem well justified. First, at least in some sense we *sinned* in Adam and are regarded as equally guilty of his sin. We need a sense of guilt about this "mystical" reality. Second, we all *demonstrate* our participation in the sin of the race when we in our own consciously responsible lifetimes sin.

4. *Humanity's participation in the sentence* is affirmed in these words: "So death passed upon all men." And the truth of this confirms the truth of the previous point. Adam sinned and died. All sinned in Adam and all die. All men are subject to its twofold ravages: spiritual and physical death. That the sentence is universal proves that the guilt is equally universal. Such is the fact about the all-inclusive legacy we have received from Adam.

The Ineffective Law: A Failure (verses 13, 14). The point of these two verses, though they are a little difficult to follow, is that the Law itself had no effect on the universal sin and death just described. The Law (the Mosaic Law) did not *cause* sin and death, and the Law did not *cure* sin and death. The basic fact was not in any way changed by the giving of the Law. Perhaps we ought not to call this a "failure," since God never intended the Law as such a cure. But if men had any hope that "keeping the law" would deliver them from death, the Law failed. Paul proves that the Law did not change things by showing that the two basic facts are the same before as after the Law.

1. *Sin was present before*, as after. Verse 13 makes this point, specifically affirmed in the first clause: "Until the law, sin was in the world." We recall that Paul has proved earlier that the Law brought an intense knowledge and guilt of sin (3:19, 20). So all would agree that sin existed and was counted *after* the Mosaic Law was given.

But what Paul insists on here is that sin was also counted *before* the Law was given: "Sin was in the world." The last part of verse 13 can easily be misinterpreted. You might take it to mean that though sin existed before the Law, it was not counted. But that is not what Paul means. The last part of verse 13 is a general principle that sin is always a transgression of law (cf. 1 John 3:4). If there were no law at all, there would be no reckoning (imputing) of sin because there would be no sin!

So Paul's point is that men *were* guilty of sin before *the* Mosaic Law was given, thus proving that there was at least *some* law for man to transgress even before the Mosaic Law. (There is no "the" with "law" in the last part of the verse, as there is in the first part.) Paul is referring to that "law written in their hearts" already described in Romans 2:15. Thus sin was as factual and real before the Mosaic Law as afterward, even though the Mosaic Law most certainly clarified and intensified man's *knowledge* of his sin (Romans 3:20; 7:7).

2. *Death was present before*, as after. Verse 14 makes this point. The giving of the Mosaic Law did not change this part of the universal experience of sin and death either. That "death reigned" from Adam to Moses means that they who lived before Moses' Law died just as we who live after.

The clause "even over them that had not sinned after the similitude of Adam's transgression" refers to *all* who lived and sinned between Adam and Moses, as well as to all since Moses. The point is that there was something unique about Adam's "original" sin, and no subsequent sin is quite like it in that respect. That difference lay in the fact that Adam was the only one faced with the choice between life possessed and death, as an issue of a specific sin. To him, and him alone, was it said, "In the day thou eatest thereof thou shalt surely die." All others who have sinned have done so already dead! And that is exactly Paul's point: All men, even though not having been given the same choice Adam had, still died, thus proving that death had already been passed universally on a race universally guilty. The Mosaic Law neither caused nor cured this universal sin-death heritage gained from the first Adam.

2. THE UNEQUAL HERITAGES DISTINGUISHED
(Romans 5:15-19)

Verse 14, just studied, closed with a reference to the fact that Adam was a "type" of "the coming one." Paul sees certain similar principles in the fact that Adam and Jesus were "heads" of two different races, and in these similarities Adam serves as a type of Christ. With the last part of verse 14 serving as an introduction, Paul begins to draw the comparative picture in detail. As we shall see, the *principles* of comparison are quite similar, but the *results* stand in sharp contrast. Each passed on to his heritage a legacy, but what Adam passed on is quite different from what Christ passed on. Compare 1 Corinthians 15:45-49 in which the "first" Adam is compared to Jesus "the last Adam."

The Legacy of the Offense (verses 15-19). These verses need to be approached in a manner different from our usual procedure if their full effect is to be seen. Instead of subdividing them into two (or more) parts, we need to go through the whole passage twice, charting the key words on both sides of the contrast. Since Paul mentions first "the offense" of Adam, then we will look at Adam's heritage first. The picture is not an attractive one.

1. *Offense.* This word occurs six times in the passage in verses 15 (twice), 16, 17, 18, 20. The Greek word so translated carries a twofold idea involving a fall and a contradiction of the right. Trench suggests it carries the idea of falling back from goodness already experienced. That was certainly true of Adam, and his original sin is first referred to in verses 15, 17, 18. Humanity, likewise, has committed an abundance of trespasses against the revealed standard of God as seen in verses 16, 20.

2. *Death.* These verses emphasize again (cf. verses 12-14, above) that death is the consequence of sin for all, just as it was for Adam. Note verses 15, 17, and 21 where the point is thrice made.

3. *Sin.* The noun "sin" occurs twice (verses 20, 21), the verb "sin" once (verse 16), and the noun "sinner" once (verse 19). This Greek word refers to the missing of a mark, a good description of man's negative and positive failure to meet the requirements of God.

4. *Judgment.* This word occurs once, in verse 16, (supplied in

verse 18) and looks back to the reckoning Adam had with God as a consequence of sin. The *sentence* itself, which God pronounced, is the thing in view in the word.

5. *Condemnation.* This word is used twice (verses 16, 18). It is a compound in Greek built on the same root as "judgment." It affirms that the sentence was one of punishment, based on guilt. Adam's (16) and ours (18) are both referred to.

6. *Disobedience.* This word is used once, in verse 19, and again in reference to Adam's "original" sin. The Greek word means to go contrary to what one has heard, thus to substitute one's own way for God's direction.

We note that three of these words refer to Adam's (and our) sin: offence, sin, disobedience; three to Adam's (and our) penalty: judgment (sentence), condemnation, death. Such is the legacy passed on to all the human race from Adam and by reason of his sin.

The Legacy of the Obedience (verses 15-19). Again we look through the same verses, this time selecting the words that describe the heritage of the second Adam, Jesus Christ.

1. *Free gift.* The word so translated is used twice in verses 15, 16 (and supplied in verse 18). The Greek word is built on the same root as "grace," and refers to any *act of grace*, any specific favor (undeserved, of course) rendered to man by God.

2. *Grace.* This word, which refers to the general quality of undeserved favor from God to man, occurs five times in this section, in verses 15 (twice), 17, 20, 21. What we got from Adam we deserved; what we get from Christ is by God's grace.

3. *Gift.* This word appears three times, in verses 15, 16, 17, and sees a gift as an act of generosity, freely given, without price or return favor expected. (Technically, two Greek words are used in these three places, but they are both on the same root and involve the same idea.)

4. *Justification-righteousness.* We have already learned that these two are the same at heart. In verses 16, 18 we have (in English) "justification"; in verses 17, 18, "righteousness"; and in verse 19 "righteous." All these involve the same basic Greek root, though different forms of the word. They refer to innocence, guiltlessness, standing righteous before God.

5. *Life.* This occurs in verses 17, 18, 21. It looks back to Christ's resurrection, then on to our own spiritual regeneration, and finally to our eternal life.

6. *Obedience.* This word occurs once, in verse 19. In contrast to "disobedience" (above), it pictures submission to what one has heard, following the directions of God. In particular Paul is looking

back to the submission of Christ (Matthew 26:42; cf. Philippians 2:8).

Such is the gracious legacy of Christ that is passed on to all who become spiritual members of the race of which He was head. You will not have missed the fact that many of the words on either side of the contrast stand in direct opposition to words on the other side. Thus death—life; disobedience—obedience; and condemnation—justification.

You will also note a certain similarity in all the words on each side of the contrast. The truth is that all five verses are repeating the same basic truth. Thus each verse makes one statement about the effect of Adam's sin on the whole race: (15) "through the offence of one many be dead"; (16) "the judgment was by one to condemnation"; (17) "by one man's offence death reigned"; (18) "by the offence of one judgment came upon all men to condemnation"; (19) "by one man's disobedience many were made sinners."

Likewise each verse presents the contrast by making another affirmation about the effect of Christ's work for the whole spiritual race made up of those who believe in Him: (15) "the grace of God. . .by one man, Jesus Christ, hath abounded unto many"; (16) "the free gift is of many offences [all laid on Christ] unto justification"; (17) "they which receive abundance of grace and of the gift of righteousness shall reign in life by one"; (18) "by the righteousness of one the free gift came upon all men unto justification of life"; (19) "by the obedience of one shall many be made righteous." The same truth runs through all five repetitions.

3. THE UNDESERVED HERITAGE OF DELIVERANCE
(Romans 5:20, 21)

As already noted, the pattern of the passage is to close with a positive emphasis on the legacy of Christ. The key words are *grace* and *eternal life* in opposition to the key words *sin* and *death* in verses 12-14.

The Reign of Grace (verses 20, 21a). Back in verses 12-14 Paul spoke of the reign of sin and death as sin's consequence. Now he wants us to realize that grace has triumphed over sin and death.

1. *Grace has abounded.* Verse 20 presents an interesting picture of the triumph of grace over sin. First (20a) Paul tells us that "the law entered that the offence might abound." Do not hastily misunderstand this statement. It does *not* mean that there was more sin after the Mosaic Law was given than before. It *does* mean that the

knowledge and awareness of sin was increased by the giving of the Law. This statement is in accord with what Paul says about the purpose of the Law in various other places: Romans 3:19, 20; 7:7-13; Galatians 3:19. In particular Romans 7:13 has an expression that fits in well here: "that sin by the commandment might become exceeding sinful."

Without a detailed, written law sin exists and is judged (compare the discussion above on verse 13). But man's knowledge of sin would be vague and general. The Mosaic Law exposed man to specific knowledge about the multitude of his sins. Thus sin "abounded" as a result of the giving of the Law.

But, says Paul, "Where sin abounded, grace did much more abound." The Greek construction here is very emphatic: Where sin abounded, grace superabounded! If sin flowed free, grace overflowed. Grace flooded out sin. Grace outabounded sin. Sin in all its abundance is no match for the grace of God.

2. *Grace has reigned.* Verse 21a uses this word to describe the triumph of grace over sin. Sin abounded and grace superabounded (20). Sin reigned, but grace took over the throne and reigned instead (21a).

The clause "as sin hath reigned unto death" looks back to verse 12 where death is regarded as the universal consequence of sin. Verse 14 said that "death reigned." In other words universal subjection to death proves that sin has reigned universally. Death is unavoidable; it rules the race and mankind is not able to avoid its clutches or the sin that keeps it in dominion.

But grace, through the death and resurrection of Christ for sin, has supplanted sin and death on the throne. Those who put their faith in Him find themselves delivered from the dominion of sin and under the control of God's gracious dealings. Paul will say more about this in the next chapter.

The Results of Grace (verse 21b). Now that grace has triumphed over sin, two results are evident. Just as death demonstrates the dominion of sin, these two demonstrate the dominion of grace in the hearts of those who follow Christ.

1. *Righteousness.* This is the opposite of sin and guilt for sin. Men are delivered from the dominion and rule of sin when they are found righteous (innocent, justified) in Christ. By His work, sin's penalty has been paid, and sin's power broken. And men therefore stand righteous before God by faith in Jesus Christ and His atonement. Thus grace reigns instead of sin.

2. *Eternal life.* This is the opposite of death, the universal and inevitable consequence of sin. But they who put faith in Christ find

that the dominion of death has been broken with the dominion of sin, its cause. Not that men escape physical death; that much of sin's consequence must still be paid. But *spiritual* death is reversed by justification, and the justified one is *regenerated* spiritually (cf. Ephesians 2:5). Furthermore, the sting of physical death is removed by the knowledge of the resurrection (cf. 1 Corinthians 15:54-57). Most of all, the assurance of eternal life, as opposed to eternal death, is clear evidence that grace has reigned. The results of justification by faith in Christ's blood are indeed superior to the results of Adam's sin and humanity's participation in that sin and its consequences.

14 Our Baptism and Death to Sin: The Principle

Study Text: Romans 6:1-11

Introduction
1. Dead to Sin: the Issue (Romans 6:1, 2)
   a. A Question about Sin Anticipated (verse 1)
   b. A Question about Sin Answered (verse 2)
2. Dead to Sin: an Illustration (Romans 6:3-5)
   a. Affirmation (verse 3)
   b. Application (verses 4, 5)
3. Dead to Sin: the Implications (Romans 6:6-10)
   a. A Past Death (verses 6, 7)
   b. A Present Deliverance (verses 8-10)
4. Dead to Sin: an Invitation (Romans 6:11)

INTRODUCTION

As we begin chapter six of Romans, we "change gears" again. We are still in part 3 of the epistle which covers chapters five through eight. Chapter five, as studied in the previous two lessons, dealt with the immediate results of justification, listing and comparing them to the situation of the natural man.

Chapters six through eight continue to explain the effects of justification, but in a different way. Specifically, these chapters are concerned with the believer's new life as a justified person. In that new life the believer finds that he stands in an entirely new relationship to sin (chapter 6), to the mosaic system (chapter 7), and to the Spirit of God (chapter 8).

These are a marvelous three chapters, and they show us just what it means for the reality of justification by faith to be experienced in our daily lives. There is a firm foundation here for confident, victorious Christian living.

In other words, Paul's doctrine of justification by faith is no dead, lifeless doctrine. Nor is faith some cold, intellectual assent to mere historical facts. Possessing "the righteousness of God" effects a drastic change in the individual's life: "All things are become new" (2 Corinthians 5:17).

EXPOSITION

The general study-outline in the back of this book will be especially helpful in keeping you aware just how each of the eight lessons on chapters 6-8 fit together. As you will see there, all eight of these lessons (14-21) come under part 3, subsection B. The believer's new relationship to sin and life is dealt with in chapter six, and there are two lessons from this chapter. This lesson is entitled "Our Baptism and Death to Sin: the Principle" and is based on 6:1-11.

1. DEAD TO SIN: THE ISSUE (Romans 6:1, 2)

An earlier lesson, dealing with Romans 3:8 (lesson 6), pointed out that Paul often encountered opponents who insisted that his doctrine of justification by faith left one free to sin. Paul was always quick to deny such accusations. In 3:8 he called it a "slanderous report" to say he encouraged sinful living. Now he returns to that same subject to deal more thoroughly with the issue of sin in a believer's life.

A Question about Sin Anticipated (verse 1). We have seen before that Paul has a way of anticipating the questions his detractors will raise. That is what he does in these two verses. Notice the "them" which ties the upcoming discussion to what has just been said in the last part of chapter five. In 5:20, 21 Paul gladly exclaimed that though sin abounded, grace did superabound.

Having said this, Paul realizes that the old question is going to come up again: If the grace of God saves in spite of sin, then there is no need to discourage sin! Just let the grace of God take care of it. Paul never taught any such thing, but he was accused of it. And we can understand how the question arose.

The Jews of Paul's day taught that one should try to achieve righteousness by law-observance and good works. Paul said it could not be done, that the law was not given as a means of salvation, that no one ever kept the law, that only sinners could be saved, that self-righteous persons would not be saved. The Jews, horrified by such ideas, said: If that is right, then to sin is better than to try to do right! They were wrong, of course, but we can catch their logic.

107

Furthermore, both Jews and others might carry this logic over into a discussion of how the one justified by faith lives after his salvation. Paul taught that a man's sins were not imputed to him when he put faith in Christ (Romans 4:8), that justification was entirely based on saving *faith*, not on "works" at all (Romans 3:27, 28), that the grace of God was triumphant over all of a man's sins (Romans 5:20, 21). Some responded by saying: If that is so, then the one with faith can go on and live like the devil! If you do not have to obey God's commandments to be saved, then after you are saved you can still disobey. If the grace of God covers all sins, why worry about whether the believer lives in sin?

We can understand the logic in this, even though we know it is wrong. Many still say this, by the way. Some say it to "justify" sin in their lives, though they profess to be saved by faith alone, insisting that obedience and works make up part of the basis of salvation. Either of these is a misunderstanding and distortion of the truth.

This is the question that Paul anticipates in 6:1. "What shall we say then?" simply means: What are the implications of the truth just stated (in 5:20, 21)? The issue itself, the anticipated question is: "Shall we continue in sin, that grace may abound?" If grace out-abounds sin (as in 5:20), then should we go on living in sin, depending on the grace of God to triumph? Would that magnify God's grace and glorify Him?

A Question about Sin Answered (verse 2). Paul's answer to such a question is definite. "God forbid" means "absolutely not!" As might be said in our time, "no way!" Paul wants it firmly fixed that his doctrine of justification by faith does not condone sin. His teaching that grace out-abounds sin gives no excuse for continuing in sin. His strong insistence on faith as the sole basis for standing righteous before God does not leave one free to live in sin after obtaining that verdict of righteousness.

The basis for this definite negative is shown in the question Paul asks: "How shall we that are dead to sin, live any longer therein?" This question includes, in essence, two points, one a truth assumed and the other an implication of that truth. The truth assumed is that "we are dead to sin." The implication argued therefrom is that to live any longer in sin would contradict that truth. A life of sin is incompatible with death to sin. "Life" and "death" are opposites. One cannot *live* in sin and be *dead* to sin at the same time, just as one cannot sensibly speak of "square circles." The two terms are mutually exclusive.

This is the issue, then: Are we dead to sin, as believers, or alive to sin? And if we are dead to sin, how can we live any longer in sin? The answer, clearly implied, is that we cannot. But Paul is in no hurry to affirm this and go on to something else. He wants to deal with this closely. Proving and explaining the answer implied in verse 2 will be the purpose of the verses that follow. In particular, Paul is going to explain at length his assumption that we are "dead to sin."

2. DEAD TO SIN: AN ILLUSTRATION
(Romans 6:3-5)

In the previous verse Paul affirmed, by assuming it in his question, that believers are "dead to sin." This is a new concept, not yet discussed in the epistle. Paul proceeds to explain it now, and he first does so by the illustration of Christian baptism.

Affirmation (verse 3). The fact affirmed here is that we believers who "were baptized into Jesus Christ were baptized into his death." This affirmation has two parts: the fact itself, that we were baptized into Jesus Christ; and the implication of that fact, that we were thereby baptized into His death.

The question is often raised whether there is any reference here to the ordinance of baptism, or if Paul speaks only about the spiritual "baptism" of the believer into the body of Christ. We know that both are called baptism. The spiritual is referred to in passages like 1 Corinthians 12:13: "By one spirit are we all baptized into one body." Some interpreters prefer to avoid any discussion of water baptism here in Romans 6, perhaps because they fear any implication that water baptism is as significant as the baptism spoken of here.

You may want to side with them, and see only the *spiritual* baptism in these verses. But as far as this writer is concerned, Paul is referring to the *ordinance* of baptism both in verse 3 and in verse 4. Still, the outward ordinance is not of any saving merit. It is but an object-lesson, a symbol of the real thing. So if Paul is referring to water baptism, he is using the ordinance as a figurative representation of the truth baptism testifies to. (This is exactly the same way "baptism" is referred to in 1 Peter 3:21 where the word "figure" is very important.)

So when Paul mentions the fact that we were "baptized into Jesus Christ," he does not mean the ordinance itself placed us in union with Christ. He does mean that ordinance was a public profession and representation of the union with Christ we experienced by faith. In that sense we were baptized into Christ. And when we were, Paul wants us to understand Christ's *death* was the prominent thing. Our union with and identification with Christ, which was visibly portrayed in our baptism, was especially a union and identification with His death.

The emphasis Paul places on Christ's death is called for for more than one reason. First, the death of Christ was the basic "work" He performed for our redemption, as already emphasized in 3:24, 25. Thus this was the effective part of Christ's work which must be put on our accounts, so to speak, and by which justification is applied to us. Second, the dramatic thing about baptism is immersion, burial;

and thus the main point of the portrayal is identification with Christ's death and burial. This will be stated again in the next verse. Third, it is the believer's *death* to sin that Paul is explaining, and that "death" is part and parcel of our identification with Christ's. This too will be more thoroughly explained in the rest of the lesson.

Application (verses 4, 5). The principle affirmed in verse three is now given a two-fold, specific application.

1. The believer died with Christ, as is indicated in verse 4a. The "therefore" means that this statement (and the next) is based on the truth affirmed in verse three. The believer was baptized into Christ, and thereby baptized into His death (3); therefore this baptism was a burial of one dead.

The verb "we are buried" in Greek is simple past tense: We *were* buried with Christ by means of our baptism (again, baptism stands figuratively for the spiritual truth it vividly portrays in external form). This looks back to two historical incidents: to Christ's own death and burial, and to the believer's baptism when he was, in figure, identified and in union with Christ's death and burial.

Paul's point is right plain: Living men are not buried. When the believer submitted to that burial of immersion under water he was declaring himself a dead man, one dead and buried with Christ. The implication for his argument is clear: If the sinner died, does he yet live? Can the one baptized into Christ (assuming his water baptism *is* a true profession) live as a sinner?

One point should not be overlooked. There is a close parallel between Paul's meaning here and the idea in 5:12 (see the previous lesson). There Paul indicated we somehow participated in the sin of Adam, the head of the physical race. We were guilty of that sin and participated fully in its effects. Well, just as "we sinned in Adam" so we died when Christ did, and all the meritorious effects of His death are ours too.

2. The believer rose with Christ, as is indicated in verses 4b, 5. For the first time Paul is positive and refers to our new life as believers. Christ's death was not the end of His work. The resurrection was just as essential to the whole. Just so, we did not merely die when Christ died; we arose when He arose. Indeed, this latter is the *purpose* of the whole salvation experience, as indicated by the "that."

So we are not only identified with Christ in His death and burial, we are also identified with His resurrection. The believer testifies by his baptism that this is so, that a dead man was buried (the sinner) and a new man was raised to life. Note in verse four that the verb "we also should walk" is expressed (in Greek) in the tense that refers to decisive, crisis action. The time when the believer committed himself to that new walk is referred to. And this verb "walk" is the one that goes with the "that." This could be rendered as follows: "(in order) that . . . we might set ourselves to walk in newness of life." Again Paul is looking back to the time the believer took his stand for Christ.

Verse 5 basically repeats verse 4. The word "for" suggests a reaffirmation. Only the figure is different, using the idea of a planted thing. A seed put in the ground dies, and from it springs forth a new plant (cf., 1 Corinthians 15:36). Our "planting" together with Him then is the same as the "burial" of verse 4; our being in the likeness of His resurrection is the same as the newness of life of verse 4. The "shall be" does not look so much to the distant future or the bodily resurrection of that day, but to the present new spiritual life. We shall be, as Christians in the here and now, new persons, thus manifesting our identification with His resurrection. Some interpreters disagree with this and see a reference to the future bodily resurrection here. If so, Paul still means that our present life should be a *new* life, appropriate for people who expect this resurrection of the body.

If all this seems a bit complicated, look at it this way. The believer by his baptism declares that he buried, as dead, the person he used to be. He declares that he arose a new person with an entirely new and different life. And he declares that all this was effected by virtue of the death, burial, and resurrection of Christ. That declaration is totally out of keeping with the idea of continuing in sin, the basic issue under discussion.

Before leaving these verses, let us at least note that they provide the best single argument that immersion is the proper mode of baptism. Only by immersion is death, burial, and resurrection visibly portrayed. Only thus does the ordinance have its true significance.

3. DEAD TO SIN: THE IMPLICATIONS
(Romans 6:6-10)

Having explained "dead to sin" by the illustration, Paul now turns to the principles involved for more detailed discussion. The points being made are basically the same, only the implications of the basic truth are made plainer.

A Past Death (verses 6, 7). These two verses give us the essence of what was involved in our identification with Christ's death, already affirmed above in verses 3, 4a, 5a. Four statements are made, though these are not four distinct truths but different viewpoints of the same truth.

1. The "old man" was crucified with Christ. The verb "is crucified" (6a) is simple past time in Greek. And do not misunderstand "old man." The phrase simply means the sinner, the person he used to be before conversion, the way he lived formerly. (The term has exactly the same meaning in its two only other occurrences in Ephesians 4:22 and Colossians 3:9.) That person, that sinful way of life, died when Christ died.

2. *The sinful body was dethroned.* The phrase "body of sin" (6b) means "sinful body." The Greek word translated "destroyed" means to render powerless, ineffective, to sever relations with, break the hold of. Paul evidently uses "the sinful body" in much the same way he often uses "the flesh," seeing the fleshly body as the seat of depraved desires that pull the individual toward sin (cf., Galatians 5:17). This sinful body he regards as having been the master of the old man. But that hold was broken at conversion; the sinful body was removed from the throne. (Which does not mean the pull of the flesh is no longer felt; only that this force no longer is in control.)

3. *Bondage to sin was broken.* The word "service" refers to bondslavery. The idea here is quite similar to that of the previous clause: Sin was a slave master that held the old man in a helpless bondage. That bond of servitude was broken. By the way, the words "that we should" sound uncertain; the Greek says: "so as for us no longer to be serving sin."

4. *The penalty of sin was paid.* Verse 7 may not be clear to you without some helpful explanation. "He that is dead" means "the one who died": that is, the person who died with Christ. "Is freed" means "has been freed"; and the Greek word for freedom here is one that refers to *judicial* freedom, *legal* freedom, freedom from the penalty and guilt of a crime with which charged. It is, in fact, the same word as is usually translated "justified" in Romans. The one who died with Christ stands justified, having been found guiltless, innocent, free of the penalty of sin. After all, a man executed for his crime has made full payment. We were "executed" for our sins with Christ.

A Present Deliverance (verses 8-10). The previous two verses dealt with negative implications of the truth that we are "dead to sin." The penalty and dominion of sin have been broken. Now Paul turns to positive implications. If the negative ones stemmed from our *death* with Christ, the positive ones stem from our *resurrection* with Him.

1. *We live with Him.* Verse 8 makes this point. Again, "be dead" is simple past in Greek, "died." If it is true, as it is, that we died with Christ, then we believe (are confident) that we will live with Him too. Just as in verse 5, the remote future is probably not the time Paul is referring to: We shall, in our present Christian lives, "live" with Christ; we shall *not* continue in sin (cf., verse 1).

To "live" with Christ means to experience the effects of His resurrection-power, thus to be new persons, to "walk in newness of life" (verse 4). The resurrection of Christ testifies that He can give us new lives. We have declared, in identifying ourselves with Him by faith, that we are participating in that resurrection power.

2. *We have freedom from death.* Verses 9 and 10a make this clear. Christ himself is being spoken of exclusively in these two

112

verses, but Paul's implication is that this is true of us too by our union and identification with Him. The whole point of these verses is that once He died, death had no more claim on Him. This is seen by a threefold repetition: "dieth no more" (9); "death hath no more dominion" (9); and "he died once" (Greek: once-for-all; 10a).

Paul is probably viewing "death" in its punitive sense: death as penalty for crime, as execution. Once executed, Christ has permanent freedom from that penalty; He will never have to die again. The believer, identified with Christ, has all this on his account too. His subjection to death as a fair penalty for his sins is broken forever.

3. We live unto God. This truth in verse 10b is still being stated of Christ but applies to us as identified with Him. To be "alive unto God" is an interesting expression with depth of meaning. It involves at least two closely related truths. First it means justification, standing right and righteous before God. One "lives" only by right relationship with God. (Compare the explanation of Galatians 3:11 in the quarterly on that book if you have it.)

Second, to be "alive unto God" means not only *legal* "life," but also *practical* life. It means to be under His dominion instead of the old dominion of sin, to be conscious of His control in our day-to-day living. This is the outworking, in practice, of the righteous standing we possess before Him.

4. DEAD TO SIN: AN INVITATION
(Romans 6:11)

If verses 9, 10 referred specifically to Christ's experience, then verse 11 applies that experience to us. The verse is in effect an invitation of Paul's to his Christian readers. The invitation actually summarizes the whole truth covered in the first ten verses. Paul has been telling them what is true of a Christian. The believer *did* die with Christ and *is* alive with Him. The assumption of verse 2, that "we are dead to sin," is a fact. Consequently, Paul says, count on this as truth every day and live that way.

The verb "reckon" means consider, regard. In Greek the verb is in the tense that refers to continuing, habitual action. "Keep on regarding yourselves as *dead* men, in so far as sin is concerned, but as *living* men in so far as God is concerned. Because this is true *in Christ!*"

Now let us summarize the lesson. The question at issue is whether one justified by faith (as Paul preaches) can go on living in sin. No, says Paul. Because the believer has identified himself with Christ's death and resurrection. He has come to be in union with Christ in those redemptive acts. By virtue of Christ's death, the believer died. The sinful person he used to be died and was buried. The hold of sin was broken. The penalty of sin was paid. By virtue of

Christ's resurrection, the believer arose. A new person lived, freed from the old mastery and alive unto God, walking in newness of life. "That is a fact," says Paul: "Count on it! And in so doing you will see that you cannot continue in sin."

15 The Broken Dominion of Sin: Our Practice

Study Text: Romans 6:12-23

Introduction
1. The New Sovereign Who Reigns (Romans 6:12-14)
   a. The Possibilities (verses 12, 13)
   b. The Principle (verse 14)
2. The New Servitude We Render (Romans 6:15-18)
   a. Appeal (verse 15)
   b. Alternatives (verse 16)
   c. Appreciation (verses 17, 18)
3. The New Spirituality Which Results (Romans 6:19-23)
   a. A Forceful Injunction (verses 19, 20)
   b. The Fruit Inspected (verses 21, 22)
   c. The Final Issue (verse 23)

INTRODUCTION

The previous lesson got us started with chapter six; this lesson covers the rest of the chapter. Chapter six explains the justified believer's new relationship to sin. As we saw in the previous lesson, the believer has absolutely no justification for continuing in sin. The doctrine of salvation by grace does not excuse sin.

The principle involved is that the believer is a new person. The sinful person he used to be was crucified with Christ and a new person rose with Christ. To this truth the believer's baptism testified dramatically. Thus dead to sin, the believer cannot excuse living therein any longer.

If the first eleven verses of the chapter explained that important principle, the rest of the chapter applies the principle to our day-by-day practice. The wonder of our release from the bondage of sin is not merely a fact for intellectual admiration only. That wonder is intended for actual experience in our living. We can have victory over sin every day.

EXPOSITION

As you will see by reviewing the general study-outline, this lesson is entitled "The Broken Dominion of Sin: Our Practice." It covers 6:12-23, the second lesson on chapter six, which deals with the believer's new relationship to sin and life. All the lessons on chapter six through eight are emphasizing the *reality* of justification in our experience.

1. THE NEW SOVEREIGN WHO REIGNS (Romans 6:12-14)

If verse 2 was the main point of the first half of chapter six, as we saw in the previous lesson, then verse 14a is the key to the last half of the chapter: "Sin shall not have dominion over you." The entire lesson is an explanation of this truth.

As we have already seen in our study of Romans, Paul did not try to be as brief as possible in this letter. He took his time with each idea, presenting it carefully. Thus, much of 6:12-23 is repetitious with the basic ideas being stated over and over in slightly different ways. The emphasis varies, however, and this writer has attempted to catch that shifting emphasis in the outline. Thus, in verses 12-14 the emphasis is on the *servitude* we render to that sovereign. Again, in verses 19-23 the truths are the same while the emphasis shifts to the *fruits* of that servitude, the spirituality which results therefrom.

Someone has observed that the three key words in the whole sixth chapter of Romans are know, reckon, and yield. The first two of these we covered in the previous lesson. We *know* that our old sinful way of life was nailed to Christ's cross, thus depriving it of its power over us (verse 6). We also *know* that He rose from death and that we rose with Him as new creatures (verse 9). Consequently, we *reckon* ourselves dead to sin and alive to God (verse 11). We count on this as a fact that is true, both as we look back to Christ and our identification with Him and as we look to our present, everyday experience.

This lesson then is about the verb *yield*. In principle we know and reckon (count on) the facts of which we are assured. In practice then we simply have to choose what we will now yield ourselves to, what we will submit to, what we will obey. You will notice how often the verb "yield" occurs in 6:12-23: twice in verse 12, once in

16, twice in 19. "Obey" (or "obedience") occurs once in verse 12, twice in 16, once in 17. The Christian finds himself with an altogether new and different set of principles to guide him in choosing that to which he will yield himself. This lesson is about those new principles, and the first one is that the Christian has a new Master, a new Lord, a new Sovereign who reigns.

The Possibilities (verses 12, 13). There are but two possibilities faced by any human being for sovereignty over his life. One or the other of these two will reign as lord over every man.

1. Sin is the unsaved man's master. This is one possibility as presented in verses 12, 13a. Actually Paul uses two words for this master, "sin" (12) and "unrighteousness" (13a), but they mean the same thing. Likewise, the injunction, "let not sin reign," means the same thing as "yield not your members to unrighteousness." And the warning against "obeying" sin (12b) means still the same thing.

What Paul is saying then is simply this: The Christian must not allow sin to rule him. In the believer's choice as to the Sovereign power that will reign on the throne of his heart, he must not let sin be that choice. Sin is the power that rules the *sinner's* life, not the *Christian's.*

Lest this be misunderstood we must recognize that Paul is speaking to believers when he says, "Let not sin reign." The point is this: Even though a believer really has a new master and sin is no longer his master, he must be warned against listening to the sin that used to be his master. He must not obey sin as though sin were still his master for sin's rule has been broken.

To illustrate: A person who is a subject of the Queen of England might let another country's sovereign tell him what to do, but he should not. That other ruler has no right to exercise dominion over a subject of England. Just so, the dominion of sin in a believer's life has been broken. We are no longer sin's subjects. Sin has no right to rule. We should not listen to its suggestions.

The tense-action of the verbs in verse 12 is continuing action: "Do not let sin *go on reigning* in your mortal body, that ye should *keep on hearkening* to its lusts." We refuse to continue to hearken to the body's passions, and in so doing we assert that sin is no longer the sovereign to whom we yield the control of our lives.

This encouragement looks back to and is based on the fact asserted in verse 6 that when we died with Christ the sinful body was "destroyed" (dethroned). You see, before we were saved, sin had the upper hand. We were under its dominion, helpless to escape. But now that dominion has been broken; we no longer have to obey. Sure, the voice of sinful flesh still calls loudly, pretending to possess the lordship once clearly had. But we can and must ignore that call. We do not have to listen any longer. Compare Galatians 5:17.

Note that verse 12 mentions the "mortal body" and verse 13 our "members." Usually "mortal body" would mean that the body is subject to death. Perhaps here, as a result of verse 6, it means that the body is dead. At any rate, Paul views the body and its members (parts) as providing an arena in which sin can operate. We should make sure this does not happen. In verse 6 "it" refers to the body, and "thereof" to bodily (fleshly) passions. "Instruments" (verse 13) means "tools." If we let sin rule, if we let sin operate in our bodily parts, those parts become tools by which sin and unrighteousness carry out their work.

2. *God is the Christian's master.* This is the other possibility, the Christian's only acceptable choice, as seen in verse 13b. Again, Paul uses two words to name this sovereign power which reigns in the believer's life, God and righteousness. The results are the same. Again, the tense-action of the verbs is interesting. The first "yield" in verse 13 is continuing action: "neither go on yielding your members as tools of unrighteousness for [by] sin." The second "yield" is crisis action: "but enter a settled submission of yourselves to God." This is the clean break with the past that is descriptive of a genuine Christian; he has exchanged the old master, sin, for a new one, God. If before his members were tools for sin to produce unrighteousness, now those same members are tools for God to produce righteousness. And it all depends on what master we choose to yield to, to submit to, and to obey.

Note too that if the negative side (of verse 12, 13a) can be experienced as a result of having died with Christ (back to verse 6, again), the positive side can be experienced as a result of having risen with Him. This is clear in verse 13b when Paul adds: "as those that are alive from the dead." This looks back to verses 4 and 8.

The Principle (verse 14). The principle on which is based Paul's injunction to yield ourselves to the new Master, God, involves two things. First is a prohibition: "Sin shall not have dominion over you." This is probably an imperative: Sin *must* not have dominion over you. We must not allow sin to exercise lordship over us. We do not have to, because sin's power has been broken (back to verse 6).

Second is an assurance: We are not under law, but grace. This assurance is presented as both a reason we must not allow sin to exercise dominion and as a source of confidence that we do not have to be overcome by sin. If we were still under law, sin would continue to rule us, and that for two reasons: (1) "Law" does not deliver, but makes sin known (Romans 3:20) and thus makes sin "exceeding sinful" (Romans 7:13); (2) "Law" demands the penalty, and if we were still living there we would still be condemned to pay the penalty demanded thus still "ruled over" by sin.

But we are under grace, not law. Our "freedom from sin" includes deliverance both from its power and from its penalty. This deliverance, however, has not come from our own merit or efforts, but by God's undeserved favor. That same "grace" will continually provide victory so long as we yield ourselves as *His* servants, not *sin's*.

2. THE NEW SERVITUDE WE RENDER (Romans 6:15-18)

Verses 12-14 looked on our servitude from the Master's point of view. These verses look at the same subject from the servant's point of view. We have changed sovereigns; consequently, we have a new servitude.

Appeal (verse 15). This verse asks in different words the same question as was originally asked in verse 1 of the chapter. That question is, in fact, the subject under discussion in this entire chapter: Does the doctrine of salvation by grace give us excuse to continue in sin? As we have already seen, Paul's answer is an emphatic "no."

There is a difference, however, in Paul's tone here in verse 15 and that of verse 1. There he asked it as a question to be answered and answer it he has. Here he asks it again more as an appeal: "Shall we sin because we are under grace rather than law?" The answer, "God forbid," has this effect: "We must not!" The next verses will present Paul's reasons for this appeal not to use "grace" as an excuse for sin.

Alternatives (verse 16). Just as above in verses 12 and 13 Paul presents two possibilities in servitude, though again he is not neutral as to which he advises.

1. The principle of servitude is first indicated in 16a. That principle is this: "To whom(ever) ye yield yourselves servants to obey, his servants ye are." This is a general principle that applies in life universally: Whatever a person submits to, he is that person's (or thing's) servant. (This same principle is referred to in 2 Peter 2:19b.)

2. The possibilities in servitude are then named in 16b. There are only two: service to sin or service to righteousness. We may think there are more masters to choose from; there are not. We are either in service to one or the other. The word "God" does not occur here in 16b (as back in verse 13). One servitude is to "sin"; the other, technically, to "obedience." But this latter means "the obedience of God." Still, "righteousness" is the word Paul plays up.

The word for "servants" is *bond-slaves*. We saw the meaning of this word in 1:1 when Paul called himself a bond-slave of Christ. The bond-slave is obligated to give absolute obedience to his sovereign. That master rules him. In this life we can choose one of two such masters, sin or righteousness. Paul also hints here at the results: Sin's service brings death; God's service brings righteousness. But these ideas will be returned to for more emphasis.

Appreciation (verses 17, 18). Now Paul turns specifically to the experience of his Christian readers at home. He is grateful for their conversion, for their conversion means they have done the very thing he has been speaking of. They have exchanged one servitude for another.

1. Their former servitude is referred to in 17a: They were servants (bond-slaves) of sin. Paul is not glad of this, of course, but glad that they have been converted in spite of this.

2. Their change of servitude is referred to in 17b and 18. That change involves three things. The first is the method, the last two are the results. The method is in 17b: "Ye obeyed from the heart the form of doctrine (teaching) delivered to you." Paul is referring to his own preaching, no doubt, though any gospel preaching would qualify. The true Christians at Rome were those who "obeyed" (Greek: hearkened) from the heart the call of God in the gospel proclamation.

The results are in 18. One is negative; the other, positive. On the negative side, the believers were "set free" from servitude to sin. On the positive side, they were put in the service of righteousness.

We pause here long enough to observe that one does *not* have the privilege, in life, to choose to have *no* master! He may think he does but will be inevitably deceived. Indeed, when one believes *himself* to be his own master, he is really the bond-slave of sin.

This is as good a place as any to comment about one popular misunderstanding of the sixth chapter of Romans. The true interpretation of the chapter must take into consideration two points of view. On one side, Paul affirms here in verses 17 and 18 that his readers have swapped masters. Sin *was* on the throne; now righteousness *is*. Verses 3-8 also referred to that clear fact which *is* true of *all* Christians: They died with Christ and rose with Him. The sinful body was dethroned; Christians are no longer servants of sin (verse 6).

On the other side, Paul *exhorts* his readers not to do service to sin but to yield themselves servants to God and righteousness (verses 12-15 above; also verse 19 below). Some interpreters just do not seem to know how to balance out these two points of view. The truth is that every Christian *has* the new master and has broken with the old one. But it is *also* every Christian's daily duty to serve that new master and refuse the old one. The fact that he *can* do so is clearly proved in this chapter: The sinful body *has* been "destroyed" (verse 6). The truth is, that a Christian *does* obey his new master in so far as the general habit and practice of his life are concerned (verse 18). But even the best of Christians is often tempted to hearken again to his old master and needs regular encouragement that he does not have to and must not. This is what Paul is doing in this chapter, giving us both the assurance that the power of that old master *is* broken and the encouragement to refuse to hearken to him whenever he speaks. We are subjects now of a new Sovereign; we have a new servitude. Sin is never justified.

3. THE NEW SPIRITUALITY WHICH RESULTS (Romans 6:19-23)

In the two previous parts of the lesson Paul has stressed the new sovereign power in control of our lives and the new servitude we experience under that Sovereign. Now Paul turns to the results, the spiritual fruit that is produced in our lives in this servitude to God and righteousness.

A Forceful Injunction (verses 19, 20). Once more Paul urges his readers to yield themselves in full servitude to God. Only now, as throughout these last five verses, the results are especially in focus. First, however, Paul more or less "apologizes" for the manner in which he is presenting this truth (19a). He means that his use of a slave-master relationship is really an illustration borrowed from the human arena of action so that his readers can understand the truth he is teaching. Were they more spiritually mature, he could have put the truth to them in purer form without the illustration.

1. Their past servitude to sin produced the fruit of iniquity. This Paul reminds them of in 19b. This brief statement incorporates all the elements of the picture: their master, their bond-service to that master, and the fruit produced.

2. Their present servitude ought to be to righteousness and will produce holiness. And this is what Paul enjoins them to do. We must remember again the balance discussed earlier in this lesson: It is true both that Paul's converted readers *have* adopted this new master and that they *need* to yield in each practical moment—to this new master. As they do, they will find holy fruit produced instead of iniquity. In the past, as Paul reminds us in verse 20, their servitude to sin kept them free of righteousness; that is, no real righteousness was produced in their lives.

The Fruit Inspected (verses 21, 22). These two verses contrast the fruits produced under the old service and the new service.

1. The old servitude produced a shameful guilt, as seen in verse 21. Paul's question invites his readers to recall those fruits, knowing the memory will produce a sense of embarrassment. Indeed, the believer is ashamed of the things his old master, sin, produced in his life. His "members" were indeed yielded to that master as tools by which all sorts of iniquity were produced.

2. The new servitude produces a holy fruit, as seen in verse 22. In this servitude to God and righteousness, the believer's members become tools by which things holy are produced. These "holy" fruits are the good qualities that are spiritually-produced, "the fruits of the Spirit" (as Paul calls them in Galatians 5:22, 23). They are holy because they are produced by God for God's own glory and pleasure.

Paul also mentions the "end" of both these ways of servitude in verses 21 and 22, but we will save discussion on these for the next verse in which those "ends" are specially contrasted.

The Final Issue (verse 23). As just noted, Paul refers to the final outcome of the two servitudes in verses 21 and 22. Now he returns for particular emphasis to these facts.

1. *The end of the servitude of sin is death.* And this is more than physical death. Spiritual death is even more prominent here and certainly more significant. Serving sin, the way of life of the sinner, ends in eternal, spiritual death, the permanent separation of the soul from God.

2. *The end of the servitude to God is eternal life.* Again, the spiritual life is even more significant than the physical, though both are involved. This life is, of course, a permanent fellowship with God, for one "lives" by such a relationship to God.

We note the intentional contrast between "wages" and "gift." In the one case we receive what we have rightfully *earned.* In the other, what we have not deserved at all, a gift of God's grace. Still that gift had to be purchased by *some* merit, and so Paul adds that it was "through Jesus Christ our Lord."

16 Dead to the Law: Appreciating Conviction

Study Text: Romans 7:1-13

Introduction
1. The Present: a Broken Dominion (Romans 7:1-6)
   a. Introduction: the Problem of Dominion (verse 1)
   b. Illustration: the Partner's Death (verses 2, 3)
   c. Implications: a Permanent Deliverance (verses 4-6)
2. The Past: a Blessed Discovery (Romans 7:7-14)
   a. The Law and Conscience (verses 7, 8)
   b. The Law's Consequence (verses 9-11)
   c. The Law: Conclusion (verses 12, 13)

INTRODUCTION

As has been said earlier, chapters 6-8 are marvelous chapters describing the believer's experience of the reality of justification in his life. Such a justified believer finds himself in a whole new set of relationships. In chapter six (see the two previous lessons) Paul described our new relationship to sin: Our Christian baptism was itself a picture of this new relationship. The old man—the sinner—died and was buried with Christ. A new person arose with Him. Paul also presented this same basic truth under the analogy of a slave-master. We were in sin's bond-service, and thus our members were tools by which all sorts of shameful fruits were produced. But that dominion was broken by Christ, and we are freed to enter the service of a new master, God. In that servitude our members become tools for the production of a holy fruit. We do not now have to serve sin. We can have victory every day as we keep this knowledge in our consciousness, appropriate it, and yield ourselves to God.

Now in chapter seven Paul describes our new relationship to the Mosaic system, the law. Paul has already in this letter shown that the law was not the means of justification. But that truth by itself does not tell us enough. Just where do we stand, as ones justified by faith, in respect to the law? What is our attitude toward the law? Does the law perform any meaningful service now? Such questions as these are involved in chapter seven.

EXPOSITION

We will spend two lessons on this chapter. In the general study-outline, these are the two headings under subsection 2 of Part 3-B. This lesson, the first of the two, is entitled "Dead to the Law: Appreciating Conviction" and is concerned with 7:1-13.

1. THE PRESENT: A BROKEN DOMINION
(Romans 7:1-6)

The first thirteen verses of Romans 7 just naturally divide themselves into two sections. The point of the first six verses can be simply summarized by this: We are "dead to the law." The Mosaic system does not now have dominion over us. The significance of this truth will become clearer as we expound these six verses.

Introduction: the Problem of Dominion (verse 1). In the previous chapter (see the last two lessons) Paul has dealt with the question of *sin's* dominion. That dominion over the sinner was broken by Calvary and the believer's identification therewith (see 6:14a). Now Paul turns to the question of the law's dominion over a sinner. There is a close relationship between sin and law: 1 Corinthians 15:56 actually says "The strength of sin is the law." When sin has dominion, so does the law. If Paul has described the broken dominion of sin, he will now describe the broken dominion of the law.

Why do sin and the law go together so closely? Why does each support the other? One answer is that the law serves to make sin fully known: All the variety and excess of sin is fully exposed by the light of the law. And since the law cannot deliver from sin, then sin in effect thrives by the law. Another answer is that the law demands a penalty for sin. Consequently all who sin—and all have sinned—find themselves under the penalty. Thus the law is "reigning" over them, and that dominion finds its strength in the sin of which the transgressor is guilty. Thus sin and the law join hands in dominion over the unsaved man. And so Paul, having described the Christian as dead to sin and thus free from its dominion, now desires to turn attention to the Christian's new relationship to the law.

124

First, he wants us to understand the magnitude of the problem. This problem he introduces in the form of a rhetorical question in verse 1. The dominion of the law is an unpleasantly real problem for the sinner. Understanding this problem better will help us appreciate the deliverance from the law which the Christian has experienced.

1. The general principles by which any law operates are involved here. That Paul's readers will understand these principles is clear from two factors. First, the form of the question indicates that the principle he states are known to them. In Greek the question reads thus: "Or are ye ignoring, brethren, the fact that . . . ?" Second, Paul's parenthetic insertion affirms that his readers understand these principles. He is sure he is speaking to "ones who know law."

The word "law," in this parenthetic clause, has no "the" in Greek. Not just the Mosiac Law is involved, but any law. Those who understand how the law works will recognize the principles Paul is about to discuss.

2. The nature of the specific problem is that "the law has dominion over a man as long as he liveth." This statement must be examined closely in context to see what it does and does not mean. It does *not* apply to the Christian, as Paul will soon make clear. What Paul means is that the *unsaved* man is permanently under the law's dominion. This "dominion" remains in force so long as he lives. Man in sin cannot ever free himself from that dominion.

What is the "dominion" of the law over the sinner? That dominion consists of two things, at least: The law imposes on the sinner an obligation to keep its precepts, and thus to be something he is not capable of being; and the law sets and demands a penalty for its transgression. So long as the sinner lives he finds himself under the harsh mastery of these unreachable demands. Such is the magnitude of the problem faced by the unsaved man as he stands before the law of God, required to be something he cannot be, and sentenced thereby to death.

Illustration: the Partner's Death (verses 2, 3). The problem introduced in verse 1 was this: So long as the sinner lives, he is under the law's dominion. The obvious solution is that the sinner must die, and thus get free. That is the solution Paul is going to present. First, he prepares us for that solution with an illustration. The illustration concerns the bond created between man and woman at marriage. That bond can be broken by the death of one of the partners. Just so, the "bond" between the sinner and the law can be broken by the sinner's death. Such is the basic idea contained in the illustration of verses 2, 3.

1. The marriage bond is first described in verse 2a. Paul's point is simply this: A man and wife are permanently bound together, obligated to each other, by marriage.

Remember that this is but an illustration here, and thus not the best place to discuss whether anything but death can "break" the marriage bond that is certainly intended by God to be permanent. Jesus may have indicated that infidelity will also break the bond (Matthew 19:9). First Corinthians 7:15 may also indicate the bond can be broken, though the desertion there referred to most likely includes the infidelity spoken of by Jesus.

Regardless whether the marriage bond can be broken by such wrongdoing, that question is not involved in Paul's use of marriage here as an illustration. The point of the illustration is that the marriage bond is divinely ordained to be permanent, and the only circumstance that can break that bond without violation of God's ordained plan is death.

2. *That death breaks the marriage bond* is clear in verse 2b. "The law of her husband" means the obligation of the wife to give herself to her husband and to no other. The husband's death completely frees the wife of that bond.

3. *The implications of this* are clarified in verse 3, the point being this: The husband's death frees the wife to remarry. She may then give herself to another man without any guilt. In so doing she has not violated "the law of her (former) husband" because his death severed that bond. Had she married or otherwise given herself to another man while she was still obligated, bound, to a husband, then obviously she would be correctly reckoned guilty of adultery.

Verse 3 does not *necessarily* rule out remarriage in the case of those divorced on scriptural grounds. If Jesus' permission to divorce means that the bond is actually broken, then the man is no longer the woman's husband; and there can be no violation of that bond by remarriage. But many think that even the scripturally-permitted divorce does not actually break the "bond," and so remarriage can never freely take place. Such questions are still hotly debated, and it would be beyond the scope of this lesson and Paul's purpose for the illustration to argue these matters further.

Implications: a Permanent Deliverance (verses 4-6). Now Paul applies the illustration and makes the point he has been aiming for: The Christian has been fully set free from the "dominion" of the law. Just as the death of one marriage partner frees the other from the marriage bond, so the dominion of the law over the sinner has been broken by death. And, indeed, it is the sinner's death that has broken the bond between him and the law!

1. *The means of our deliverance* is indicated in verse 4. As already noted, death is that means. Verse 1 said that "the law has dominion over a man *as long as he lives*." But the sinner's death has freed him from that dominion!

And just how did the sinner "die"? "By the body of Christ"! The verb "ye are become dead" is simple past action in Greek: "ye died." The meaning is the same as it was in 4:4: We died with Christ. When His body was nailed to the cross, we died with Him there. We died to sin (chapter 6) and to the law (chapter 7).

We note that Paul pursues the analogy of the broken marriage bond one step further. The woman freed by her husband's death may marry another. We who died with Christ were freed from the law's dominion that we might be brought under the dominion of another, namely the risen Christ. The fruits of that new relationship are seen in holy lives; and these are indeed fruits "unto God," fruits that were never successfully produced by the law's dominion over us.

2. *Our former servitude* under the law is reviewed in verse 5. This reference to the past is suggested by the idea of the fruit produced from our new relationship to Christ. The contrast is clear: Under the law's dominion we were "in the flesh," and sin worked its operation in us and produced a "fruit" that was appropriate to death. The sinner's efforts to keep the law, whenever he makes such efforts, are of the flesh. And the flesh is corrupt and in servitude to sin. So sin operates freely in the unsaved man and produces an unholy fruit justly deserving of death.

And even in such a state, the sinner is "under the law." Indeed, this verse indicates that "the motions (passions, desires) of sin" were "by the law." This suggests that the law tends to create a climate in which sin operates freely. Indeed, it is not wrong to say that where the law is in force sin flourishes. If for no other reason, written law at least *exposes* a full variety of sins that would otherwise go unrecognized.

3. *Our present deliverance* is characterized in verse 6. That deliverance from the law's dominion came, as already made clear, by death. "That being dead" means that death (our death with Christ) broke the bond of obligation between us and law.

When that old dominion was broken, however, we were not set free to be neutral. We were brought into a new servitude, a servitude suggested already in verse 4, the servitude of Christ. The old servitude was a *legal* one ("the letter" means the written law). The new servitude is a *spiritual* one. This emphasis on "spirit" means several things: that the Holy Spirit lives in us and empowers this service, that the service involves spiritual things, that we serve and observe the very spirit and intent of God's abiding laws, and that even this keeping is from the spirit and heart instead of by legal obligation. Thus a holy fruit, a spiritual fruit, is produced in our lives by this new servitude to Christ.

The law with all its commands and ritual was never able to produce in men's lives such a genuine, spiritual fruit. Under the law, man continued to be overpowered by "the motions of sin." But the believer, justified by faith, finds himself in a new relationship to the law. He is dead to the law. The law's dominion is broken. He is in a new servitude to Christ that successfully produces in his life "fruit unto God."

2. THE PAST: A BLESSED DISCOVERY
(Romans 7:7-14)

All that Paul has said thus far might tend to make one think that the law only fostered sin and helped sin reign. If sin flourished when law was in force, then why was the law ever given? Would it not have been better to have no law at all? To such questions as these Paul now turns and takes a look at the past to see whether the law ever played *any* role helpful to man.

The Law and Conscience (verses 7, 8). Paul soon finds an answer for his search: The law has played a helpful role in man's history. As a sinner, man cannot appreciate or even understand that good thing. But Paul, as a justified believer looking back, can now grasp the significance of the law both for human history and for his own experience.

1. The question to be answered is suggested in verse 7a: "Is the law sin?" This question has been suggested by the previous discussion, which indicated that sin flourished under law and holy fruit was not produced in men's lives by the law. The question naturally arises then whether the very purpose of the law was one that really aided sin and hurt man. This is what Paul means.

2. The answer is given immediately after the question. "God forbid" is an emphatic "no." The law did not actually have a purpose on sin's side.

3. The explanation follows in verses 7b, 8. While the law was not for sin, the law did serve to make sin known, to provide occasion for sin, and to show that sin was alive. All three of these expressions mean, at root, the same thing; but we will do well to examine each individually.

First, the law made sin known. Verse 7b means this. Refer back to Romans 3:19, 20: "By the law is the knowledge of sin." This is the reason Paul says, "I had not known sin, but by the law." Sin exists without written law, but such law makes aware of sin, especially of its variety and extent. This is the Bible's most basic statement about the purpose of the law. In addition to Romans 3:19, 20 compare also Galatians 3:19, 22.

Paul gives the tenth commandment as a specific example. He could have used any other, but perhaps the tenth is most appropriate because it is the broadest in force. Covetousness—lust—is any inordinate desire. The commandment against that sin exposes much sin in us when properly understood.

Second, the law provided "occasion" for sin. Verse 8a indicates this. Probably "the commandment" referred to here is still the tenth one just mentioned. Once awareness of the meaning of "thou shalt not covet" was obtained, sin was provided a base from which it could work in every sort of situation. Not that sin actually began to exist only after law came but that the variety of possibilities for sin was only fully understood by the law. This is more a matter of awareness than existence of sin, even though we must admit that prohibitions tend to produce a desire for the forbidden in the minds of depraved men. "Concupiscence" means strong desire and is a synonym of covetousness or lust. Under the tenth commandment a man finds himself guilty of all manner of wrong desires.

Third, the law shows sin alive. The last part of verse 8 indicates this. Again, awareness is the main thing. Sin "lived" before the Mosaic system was given, but men were not so aware that sin lived. The effect of the law is to show that sin is very much alive and thriving. So in all three of these expressions we find that the law is an instructor of conscience. Man knows himself to be a sinner by the law.

The Law's Consequence (verses 9-11). If the law is an instrument, as just seen, of the knowledge of sin, then it logically follows that the law is an instrument of death. For the man who comes to see himself a sinner thereby comes to see himself dead.

Again, *awareness* is the emphasis. Man was both sinner and dead before Moses, but now he consciously experiences both as a consequence of the law's work.

1. Apparent innocence apart from the law is referred to in verse 9a. Every human being can, to one degree or another, look back to a time when—without the law's conviction of his conscience—he was "alive." That is, he *thought* himself alive.

2. The law as an instrument of death is seen in verse 9b. "When the commandment came" looks not so much to Sinai as to an individual's own experience of the conviction brought by the law to his conscience. In the face of law man finds himself a sinner and thus "dies." Dead already, but not aware of it, he now feels in his soul the doom and despair and the reality of his spiritual death.

3. That death is the consequence of law is the result of this discussion. This we see in verses 10, 11. Paul knows that the law was "ordained to life" and that its ultimate purpose is helpful toward God's purpose to give men life. But in his experience the law has only served to make death real, not life. He thought himself alive and enjoyed that "innocence" as mistaken as he was. The law spoke to his conscience, convinced him he was a sinner, and thus slew him.

The Law: Conclusion (verses 12, 13). Paul raised a question in verse 7, and gave it a quick, negative answer. He now states a conclusion in more detail.

1. The law is helpful. Verse 12 affirms this. Paul uses three words to emphasize the beneficial nature of the law: "holy, just, good." Let us not assume then that the law was bad, or its purposes in tune with sin, just because sin flourished under the law.

2. The reasons for this answer are given in verse 13. First, Paul uses the negative approach. The question and answer (13a) simply mean that the law ("that which is good") was not really the cause of death in itself. Then, in a positive approach, Paul gives us the solution. It was not the law which really effected the death, but the sin that the law exposed.

The law is helpful and good because it exposes sin. This is Paul's conclusion. "Sin, that it might *appear* sin" shows that the law brings *recognition* of sin for what it really is. "That sin . . . might become exceeding sinful" shows that the law brings awareness of the extent and variety and excess of sin, an awareness that sin is beyond measure, that sin pervades and spoils the whole of man's life, and that death has passed on all because all have sinned.

Thus the law is good in spite of the truth that sin flourished under the law. The law was never intended to solve the problem of sin, only to expose the problem for what it really is. The believer, and only the believer, justified by faith, can understand and appreciate this. In his old relationship to the law as a sinner, he was under its dominion (verse 1) and convicted and dead thereby (verse 9). Now, dead to the law and delivered therefrom, he can finally see that the law only helped him in that it made him aware of his sin so he could seek Christ and be saved.

The question is frequently raised whether verses 7-13 actually describe Paul's own individual experience or if he merely uses "I" to represent typical human experience. That question is probably fruitless, as interesting as it may be. True, Paul—as a Jew—was raised "in the law" and may never have known a time when he was "without the law" (verse 9). On the other hand, every human being—Jews included—shares to some extent the experience described here. Possessing the law "intellectually" does not guarantee that its convicting power will be manifested. For pious Pharisees like Paul, as well as for ignorant heathen, a time comes when a formerly-assumed innocence is smashed by the dreadful conviction, "I have sinned." And God's law serves as a powerful instrument in producing this knowledge of sin. This writer cannot help but feel that Paul is speaking out of a very real experience of his own in these verses, an experience that helped prepare for his own conversion and an experience that is typical of that of all men.

17 Delighting in the Law: Acknowledging Carnality

Study Text: Romans 7:14-25

INTRODUCTION

As we have seen in the previous lesson, the seventh chapter of Romans discusses the justified believer's relationship to the law. This, in turn, is just one of the believer's new relationships described in chapters 6-8. In chapter six we have already studied the believer's relationship to sin.

In 7:1-6 we saw that the believer is dead to the law. In 7:7-13 we saw the believer look back to the conviction which he experienced by the law. The law taught him about his sin and thus brought him an awareness of a need for the righteousness of Christ available by faith. The believer appreciates, therefore, the place of the law in the purpose of God. The law is good (7:12).

In this lesson we deal with 7:14-25, a passage about which there is considerable argument and difference of opinion. The problems involved in interpreting the passage will be discussed below in the exposition. This writer feels that the passage is still showing the justified believer's new relationship to the law. In a general way, the passage indicates that the law still plays a helpful role in keeping the believer conscious of the sinful inclination of his flesh.

EXPOSITION

A review of the study-outline should help keep the pattern of the lessons clear in mind. This lesson (17) is the second of two that explain the believer's new relationship to the system of law. The lesson covers 7:14-25 and is entitled "Delighting in the Law: Acknowledging Carnality."

1. A CONFESSION ACKNOWLEDGED (Romans 7:14-16)

The influence of the law is such that man is made aware of important things about himself and his nature. In these verses Paul brings out that awareness.

A Contrast (verse 14). In particular Paul sees a clear difference between himself and the law. That great difference brings home to him the truth about his human nature.

1. The law is spiritual. This truth carries over from the discussion in 7:7-13. There we saw that the law makes man conscious of his sins and so is an instrument that says to man he is dead. As unpleasant as such a ministry may be, it is beneficial to show a sick man he is sick and in need of medical attention. Consequently, Paul has said, the law is really good (7:12). In this sense the law is "spiritual" in that it conducts a spiritual ministry when it brings awareness of sin and spiritual death.

The law is "spiritual" in other ways too. Particularly, the law comes from God, who is Spirit; and the law is concerned with matters of the spirit. The law can only truly be kept within the heart and spirit of man and not by mere external observance. The law has spiritual intent and spiritual purposes. The nature of the law of God, when rightly understood, is a spiritual nature. This is the thing about the law that drives home to Paul a certain contrasting awareness about himself and about all men.

2. Paul is carnal. When Paul feels fully the spiritual nature, the

divine character and goodness of the law, then he feels most keenly his own human, fleshly, and sinful nature. This he now acknowledges.

We must stop here and examine the basic differences of opinion about this whole passage, 7:14-25. Obviously there is a sharp conflict being described herein, a conflict between good and bad. The question is, whose conflict is this? Is this the conflict which a *sinner* experiences, or is this a *Christian's* experience? And, if this is a Christian's conflict, is it the experience of a defeated, so-called "carnal" Christian? Or is this conflict experienced by a typical, normal Christian, like Paul himself?

Some believe this passage describes the conflict and defeat of a "carnal" Christian, one who "walks after the flesh" (as in Romans 8:1-5 or Galatians 5:16-21). They believe Paul is looking back, in these verses, to a time when he had been such a fleshly-minded Christian. This view has some glaring defects. The Bible knows nothing of the so-called "carnal Christian." True, Romans 8 and Galatians 5 speak of some who "walk after the flesh" and make a contrast between them and those who "walk after the Spirit." But that contrast is between sinners and saints, the lost and the saved, not between two types of Christians! Nothing further will be said in this lesson commentary about the view that Romans 7:14-25 describes the conflict of a defeated, carnal Christian, as opposed to a victorious, spiritually-minded Christian.

Others believe this passage describes the struggle experienced by an unsaved man. Many sound interpreters take this approach, including this writer's respected friend, Leroy Forlines. Those who approach the passage this way do not believe Paul is speaking personally of his own present situation at the time he wrote Romans. They believe that Paul used himself (the "I") only as a representative of the unsaved man, particularly the unsaved but sincere Jew who could see a great contrast between what the law demanded and what he could perform.

Admittedly, there are some aspects of these verses that would harmonize with the condition of the sinner. For one thing, the passage certainly reflects a sense of failure (verse 18b, for example) and "wretchedness' (24). Does a genuinely saved man have such feelings? For another thing, the very words of the verse before us (14b) are startling: Must a real Christian say "I am carnal, sold under sin"?

But the basic question is this one: Does a sinner really experience the kind of intense struggle described here? Sure, a sinner knows some battles between right and wrong. He has a conscience that smites him. He is subjected to moral teaching from various sources, including the laws of the land. But does a sinner *really* "delight in the law of God" inwardly (verse 22)? Does a sinner *really* want to do good only to find his sincere efforts at good frustrated by the evil within his flesh (verses 18-21)? Paul has already taught us that none seek God, that none do good (3:10-12). Forlines answers such objections by observing that Paul's words would really fit only the unsaved *Jew* who was "instructed out of the law" (Romans 2:18; note the same type of conflict in Isaiah 58:1, 2). According to Forlines, the sinner Paul represents is saying, "I am not my own master. My ideals, which I take from the law, are higher than my actions. I am in fact kicked around as a helpless victim of sin. By the law, I recognize my responsibility, but I am unable to perform it."

This writer, however, understands Romans 7:14-25 to describe the conflict experienced by the normal Christian. This is the view that will be presented primarily in the commentary on the passage though with frequent references to the other view just discussed above. If, in fact, the struggle described here is a typical Christian experience, then this is the same struggle as described in Galatians 5:17 (see the commentary on that verse).

There are several reasons for preferring this view. These reasons are only briefly summarized here and will be expanded on in the rest of the comments.

(1) Paul does use "I," most naturally interpreted to be himself.

(2) Paul uses present tense verbs throughout which stand in contrast to the past tense verbs in 7:7-13.

(3) Paul seems to "excuse" himself from the failures spoken of herein by blaming "the sin that dwells within" him instead of the real Paul (verses 17, 20). Can a sinner make such a distinction?

(4) Paul similarly distinguishes between the real self and his "flesh," a distinction that sounds exactly like Galatians 5:17.

(5) A sinner cannot truthfully speak the words of verse 22. Compare Psalm 1:1, 2.

(6) Even after Paul speaks of the secret of "victory" in verses 24, 25a, he still describes the same struggle in 25b.

If, however, the passage is going to be taken as descriptive of the typical experience of a Christian, Paul himself included, how can we explain satisfactorily the defeated-sounding words and the confessed carnality and sinfulness of verse 14? To that problem we now turn our attention.

What does Paul mean when he says, "I am carnal, sold under sin"? First, note the contrast between his own nature and the law's character. The law is a spiritual thing, manifesting divine character and goodness. "But I," Paul says, "am a fleshly creature, manifesting sinful human depravity in that flesh."

"Carnal" means, literally, "made of flesh." When a man—even a saint of God—beholds the very spiritual character of God manifested in the divine standards of the law, he can only confess he lives in a vessel of flesh and that this "flesh" is depraved and sinful, still unredeemed. And so he "groans" within himself, waiting (Romans 8:23). Paul's confession of "carnality," then, is not unchristian when that carnality is measured by the contrast with true spirituality and when that carnality is understood to be true of the depraved "flesh."

A Conflict (verse 15). Paul's acknowledgment of carnality takes on added dimension in terms of the conflict described in verse 15. Here is certainly expressed a sense of frustration that some find hard to reconcile with genuine Christianity. Paul will speak of this in more detail in verses 17-20.

For now, we note that the key to interpretation lies in understanding the way Paul uses "I." Sometimes, as clearly seen in verses 17, 18, he uses "I" but means his fleshly nature. That "flesh" is not the real Paul, though it is certainly part of him and his identity. Thus Paul experiences within himself a struggle, a warfare between his fleshly nature and his spiritual nature. I find, then, that there is an ever-present conflict: I want this, but do that; I want that, but do this. Understood in the light of Galatians 5:17, this kind of conflict is not at all unchristian. Indeed, the Christian is far more apt to experience this than a sinner who is spiritually dead!

We note that Paul does not say here in verse 15 which is the good and which is the bad (nor does he in Galatians 5:17). That is not the point; the point is that the conflict is very real and very frequent, between what the fleshly nature desires and the real Paul does, or (vice-versa) between what the real Paul desires and what the fleshly nature causes to happen. Please notice that Paul does not affirm himself guilty of any open sin or immorality as a result of this conflict. When the conflict involves good intentions, the struggle is mostly a matter of good intentions versus bad results. In all, the verb of "intention" occurs seven times (verses 15, 16, 18, 19, 19, 20, and 21), and always the intentions are good. The word for results (effects, accomplishments) occurs four times (verses 15, 17, 18, 20) and suggests not so much wilful wrongdoings as the failure of the results to match his good intentions.

A Consent (verse 16). The "if" clause in this verse simply restates the conflict already indicated in verse 15. If I have this conflict, Paul says, between good intentions and evil results, then I have to recognize (agree) that the law is good.

This is, after all, the purpose of this whole passage (7:14-25). The very nature of the struggle described testifies to the good character and purpose of the law. In other words, even for the Christian Paul, the law continues to set a spiritual standard which the fleshly nature of Paul resists and is, indeed, incapable of fulfilling. Thus the law serves a useful and beneficial function, even for the Christian, by keeping him constantly reminded of the sinfulness of his depraved, unredeemed flesh, and of the helplessness of fleshly, human effort to produce anything good. The law keeps the believer reminded of unredeemed flesh, and so reminded of his continuing need for God.

2. A CARNALITY ABHORRED (Romans 7:17-20)

Paul has acknowledged the sinfulness of his carnal (fleshly) nature, and the conflict caused thereby which in turn testifies to the goodness and spirituality of the law of God. Now he treats more closely that carnality, showing specifically the real root of the difficulty and the distinction between that "flesh" and the real self.

The Reason for the Difficulty (verses 17, 18a). Now Paul gets right down to the source of the conflict within a believer: unredeemed, unregenerate flesh is the culprit.

1. The true self's freedom from blame is indicated in verse 17a: "It is no more I that do it." Paul simply means that when evil results are accomplished against his good intentions, it becomes clear that the real Paul is not responsible.

2. The sinfulness that is responsible is then identified as "the sin that dwelleth in me." Then, to make sure this expression is clear, Paul explains that the "me" he refers to is, after all, his "flesh," not the real Paul. In that unredeemed, depraved fleshly nature is nothing good. This is the reason the flesh always "lusts against the Spirit" (Galatians 5:17).

The Reality of a Distinction (verses 18b-20). Paul proceeds to show now that there is a very real distinction to be made between the real Paul and his desires and intentions, and the fleshly nature that offers antagonism to those inner intentions (and indeed sometimes defeats them).

1. The difference in will and performance is seen in verse 18b. Paul's intentions for good are sometimes frustrated by failure to realize them.

2. The difference in intent and deed is about the same thing, and is indicated in verse 19. This basically repeats verse 15, already discussed. Again, what Paul wants and what is produced are often not the same.

3. The difference in the real self and the sinful flesh is again affirmed in verse 20, and again this is viewed as the source of the difficulty and struggle. This repeats verse 17. Thus Paul has said *twice* that the real Paul is not responsible, and *twice* that the sin that dwells in him (that is, in his flesh, verse 18) is responsible. This distinction Paul makes is one of the strongest reasons for taking this passage to describe a Christian's conflict. A sinner has no such excuse. But who of us has not experienced that helpless feeling that often results when we have seen our own good intentions frustrated by a failure and inability to produce the kind of results really desired. At such a time the believer's soul cries out: "That is not the real me!"

3. A CONFLICT ASSESSED (Romans 7:21-23)

The same conflict between the believer's spiritual "inner man" and his sinful, unredeemed flesh is still in view. Paul examines the principles involved in that conflict. He sees two "laws" at work, opposing each other.

The Law in the Mind (verses 21, 22). The expression "the law of my mind" in verse 23 refers to the law of God, acknowledged in the inner man as good and right.

1. The law is experienced in the conflict. Verse 21 is a bit difficult, but this is what it probably means. The English says "a law," but the Greek has "*the* law," and surely means the Mosiac Law, the law of God, as in the next verse. What verse 21 means then is this: Whenever I experience the conflict between good intention ("I would do good") and the evil that dwells in my flesh ("evil is present with me") I discover in that experience the law of God. The real me, and the sincere inner intention for good, testifies to the presence and goodness of the law of God. Again (compare verse 16, above), this shows me the good work of God's law in exposing the sinfulness and failure of flesh, even the believer's flesh.

2. The law is appreciated by the inner man. Verse 22 makes this point clear: The believer's "inner man" (the real self) takes pleasure in God's law. He finds that he wants what God wants. His fleshly nature may hinder him from measuring up fully to the stature set by divine standards, but this stature is what his heart wants anyway, and so again the goodness and spirituality of the law is confirmed.

The Law in the Members (verse 23). The "members" here mean the same thing as "flesh" (verse 18) or "dead body" (verse 24). Paul finds in these unredeemed bodily parts another law, "the law of sin." "Law" is used here in the sense of principle. Another principle, another powerful force is at work in Paul as in all believers. That principle is the flesh which unchangingly pulls the believer toward evil (Galatians 5:17 again). This conflict, between Paul's "mind" and his "members," is the same as that which has already been described above.

4. A CONCLUSION ACCEPTED (Romans 7:24, 25)

Paul is ready now to summarize the picture he has developed.

A Present Distress Endured (verse 24). The conflict is real and normal. It continues, unpleasant though it may be.

1. A cry of wretchedness is sounded in 24a. "Wretched" means, literally, "torn." This is a graphic picture of the conflict, the antagonistic warfare between flesh and spirit.

2. A cry for deliverance is sounded in 24b. The answer of the "who?" will be given in the next verse. Here the emphasis belongs on the phrase "the body of this death," which means "this dead body." Again, Paul has "the flesh" in view, the "members"—all these mean the same thing. And these cries are but the "groanings" of Romans 8:23: "We ourselves groan within ourselves, waiting for ... the redemption of our body."

A Promised Deliverance Expected (verse 25a). "Through Jesus Christ our Lord" answers the "who" of the previous verse. We will be delivered from these dead bodies when Jesus returns, but for now we are "waiting" (Romans 8:23). We shall not be rid of the conflict until the flesh too experiences the redemption.

A Present Distinction Explained (verse 25b). This final conclusion applies to the here and now of Christian experience while we await the promised deliverance. In essence, these words merely repeat what Paul has been saying throughout the passage: The conflict goes on.

The "I myself" is the *real* "I" of previous verses in contrast to the flesh. The spiritual, regenerate Paul will go on delighting in the law of God, his true intentions matching the divine standards represented therein. Paul's unredeemed flesh will go on in its sinful depravity, lusting against the Spirit, until the final redemption and resurrection of the body. Victory in such a conflict is not gained by denying the conflict nor by trying to escape the conflict now, but by acknowledging and understanding it and depending on God rather than on the flesh in which nothing good dwells.

Let us summarize the truths involved in this lesson thusly: (1) The Christian is still "in the flesh." This is what "I am carnal" means (verse 14).

(2) "The flesh" (also called "my members" and "this dead body" in verses 23, 24; cf., "the sinful body" in 6:6) is depraved and thus controlled by sinful inclination. This is what is meant by such expressions as "sold under sin" (14), "sin that dwelleth in me" (17, 20), and "captivity to the law of sin in my members" (23).

(3) A Christian therefore has conflict between his spiritual nature (also called "inner man" and "the mind" in verses 22, 23) and this unredeemed fleshly side.

(4) This conflict results at times in the frustrations of a Christian's inner desires.

(5) But the nature of the intention shows that the failure does not stem from the real self, but the sinful flesh.

(6) This very awareness of the presence of evil in the flesh, coexisting (not peacefully!) with good intentions in the heart confirms the goodness and spirituality of the law of God.

(7) Deliverance from the conflict will not come until the Lord returns and redeems the sinful body, thus the conflict is accepted as normal Christianity.

We can only add here that a true Christian is not defeated by that conflict. Nor does he accept living in sin because of it. The next chapter will proceed immediately to show that a genuine believer, though "in the flesh," does not "walk after the flesh."

18 The Presence of the Spirit in the Believer

Study Text: Romans 8:1-13

Introduction
1. Overcoming by the Spirit (Romans 8:1-4)
   a. Victory in Legal Standing (verse 1)
   b. Victory over the Law of Sin (verses 2, 3)
   c. Victory in a Life of Sanctification (verse 4)
2. Opposition to the Spirit (Romans 8:5-8)
   a. The Mind of the Sinner (verses 5-8)
   b. The Mind of the Saint (verses 5-8)
3. Occupancy by the Spirit (Romans 8:9-11)
   a. A Possession (verse 9)
   b. A Present (verse 10)
   c. A Promise (verse 11)
4. Obligation to the Spirit (Romans 8:12, 13)
   a. A Debt Cancelled (verse 12)
   b. A Destiny Considered (verse 13a)
   c. A Death Commanded (verse 13b)

INTRODUCTION

Chapters six through eight of Romans deal with the experience of justification in the life of the believer. Such a justified believer finds himself in a new world with new relationships. Chapter six explained the new relationship to sin. Chapter seven explained the believer's new relationship to the law.

In chapter eight these new relationships continue. And in this chapter we are shown our new relationship to the Spirit of God and to the providential love of God in our daily lives. Justification by faith is much more than a cold, legal transaction. When we put faith in Christ we are found innocent before God; and at the same time, God's Holy Spirit is put in our hearts. His presence there makes a tremendous difference in our practical lives.

You will remember that the previous lesson in covering 7:14-25 emphasized the struggle that a believer experiences. This struggle reflects a confict between his spiritual, regenerate nature and his unredeemed flesh. That lesson concluded with an affirmation that the believer is not defeated by this struggle. Nor must he allow the flesh to control him and cause him to live in sin. Chapter eight shows just how this victory is experienced even though the basic antagonism between flesh and spirit goes on.

EXPOSITION

We will have four lessons on chapter eight, all under the heading, "The Believer's New Relationship to the Spirit and Love." As you will see from the study-outline in the back of this book, this lesson is the first of those four, covering 8:1-13, and is entitled: "The Presence of the Spirit in the Believer."

1. OVERCOMING BY THE SPIRIT (Romans 8:1-4)

These verses indicate the basis for Christian victory: That basis, as the previous chapter has led us to expect, is not by the flesh, but in following the Spirit of God.

Victory in Legal Standing (verse 1). Paul first reminds us of the basic truth that has undergirded Romans all along: The believer is, after all, a *justified* person. He is not under divine condemnation. He has been found innocent before Heaven's bar of justice.

This assertion is particularly appropriate to link together the previous chapter with this one. There a distressing conflict was seen to be the experience of a believer, a conflict between the real self, the regenerate spirit, and unredeemed flesh. Verse 25b served as a summary statement of that situation, typical and normal of all Christians: I myself—the real me—serve the law of God. My flesh is still subject to the depraved desires of sin.

Now, says Paul, we must not let that fact discourage us. We are not condemned. The presence of sinful inclination in the flesh is not a basis for condemnation to those who are in Christ. Note that Paul uses "them which are in Christ Jesus" as his identification for Christians.

The clause "who walk not after the flesh, but after the Spirit" also identifies all Christians. This clause will be repeated at the end of verse 4, and we shall comment about its significance in more detail there. For now, suffice it to say that all true Christians "walk after the Spirit" (though some more consistently than others, of course), and this is the basis for practical, daily Christian victory too.

Victory over the Law of Sin (verses 2, 3). Paul now moves more into the matter of practical victory than legal, righteousness in life more than righteousness in standing. The Holy Spirit's presence in us makes this possible.

1. *Freedom from the law of sin and death,* as seen in verse 2, means at least two things: (1) deliverance from eternal death as the penalty of the broken law; and (2) deliverance from the power of sin and dominion of spiritual death over our lives.

"The law of sin and death" means, more or less, what Paul has already stated in Romans 6:23, "The wages of sin is death," or 5:12, "Sin entered the world, and death by sin." Also included is "the law of sin in my members" of 7:23. In other words, the law of sin and death is that all men—in their natural state—are ruled by sin and are spiritually dead because of it and destined for eternal death too. That universal "law" is unbreakable in so far as natural man is concerned.

But Paul avows that the believer has broken free from that universal law! How? By "the law of the Spirit of life in Christ Jesus." This also involves the same two aspects just mentioned, the legal and the practical. We are "freed" from the law of sin and death in that Jesus bore the penalty in our place. We are therefore no longer sentenced to die. More important here though is the practical side. The Holy Spirit has entered our hearts and restored us to life, raised us from spiritual death. By that Presence and Power, the chains of sin have been broken; we are not any longer enslaved by sin's power. In essence, this verse reviews the sixth chapter.

2. *Overturning the law's inability* is another aspect of our victory over sin. Verse 3 refers to this, even though the wording is somewhat abbreviated. Basically, the verse means this: What the law could *not* do, God *did* by the sending of His Son.

What was it the law could not accomplish? The production of real holiness in living. The law offered no assistance to men as to how the law could be kept. The law said, "Thou shalt not," but never helped man in his helplessness to obey. Paul says that this failure lay in the fact that "it [the law] was weak through the flesh." In other words, man's fleshly depravity rendered him incapable of keeping the law.

But we have been freed from this inability too! God has sent His own Son to rescue humanity from humanity's own failure. To accomplish this, Jesus had to become flesh, though He was not sinful. This is the reason Paul says Christ came in the *likeness* of "sinful" flesh. Christ's human nature was like that of Adam before the fall, but it was real human nature nonetheless. The words "for sin" probably mean what Scofield's marginal note suggests: "as an offering for sin." At any rate, Christ, by the sacrifice of His body for

141

sin judged sin. As Denney puts it: "In the death of His own Son, who had come in our nature to make atonement for sin, God had pronounced the doom of sin, and brought its claims and its authority over man to an end." We *can* now become, by this work of Christ applied to our hearts by the Spirit, what the law could never have made us.

Victory in a Life of Sanctification (verse 4). We recall that the previous chapter pictured a distressing antagonism between "the inner man" and "the flesh." The inner man delights in the law; the flesh is dominated by urgings toward sin. Can righteousness, holiness, be successfully manifested in real life then? Or does "the flesh" render this impossible?

Paul answers these questions in no uncertain terms: The righteousness of the law is fulfilled in us who walk after the Spirit rather than after the flesh! "The righteousness of the law" means the righteous standard set by and represented in the law of God. The law is, after all, truly spiritual (7:14) and good (7:12). The sinner, living in the flesh completely, cannot at all manifest such righteousness in his life. Furthermore, even the saint's fleshly nature will be antagonistic toward such a standard.

Still, Paul insists, the believer can experience victory. Practical righteousness can be fulfilled in his daily life. The answer lies in the fact that the believer walks after the Spirit, not after flesh. Thus the sinful inclination of flesh is no hindrance when one walks by the impulses of the Spirit.

This word again: The clause, "who walk not after the flesh, but after the Spirit," applies to *all* Christians. A few interpreters do not agree. They say that some Christians walk after flesh and some after the Spirit. But the following verses make it clear that Paul is contrasting sinners with saints, not one type of Christian with another. Sinners walk by flesh; saints walk by the Spirit. Neither does so with perfect consistency, of course, but the general habit of life is thus. Following the Spirit's impulses in our daily lives then will free us from sin's control. A sanctified, holy, righteous life will be the result.

2. OPPOSITION TO THE SPIRIT
(Romans 8:5-8)

Paul feels we will understand "walking after the Spirit" better if he clarifies the contrast between those who live thus and those who live by the flesh, in enmity toward God, opposed to spiritual things. This he does by comparing the two "minds."

The Mind of the Sinner (verses 5-8). Throughout these verses Paul makes several descriptive statements about "the carnal mind." *Mind* means attitude, way of thinking, outlook, philosophy of life.

Carnal, as we have seen, means fleshly. In 7:14 Paul spoke of himself as "carnal," meaning he still possessed, even as a Christian, a depraved fleshly side to his nature. But here "the carnal mind" refers to the sinner as will be obvious from the things said about "this carnal mind." In the seventh chapter that same Paul who was "carnal" did have a "mind" that delighted in God's law (7:22, 23, 25). But here "the carnal mind" refers to the one whose inner man is dominated by the impulses of the flesh, thus clearly the sinner. The expression "the carnal mind" refers to the same people as those who "walk after the flesh" (8:1, 4), who "are after the flesh" (8:5), who "are in the flesh" (8:8).

1. *He "minds" the things of the flesh* (verse 5). This means he is interested in and attached to fleshly things.

2. *He is dead* (verse 6). This probably refers both to present spiritual death and to the destined eternal death.

3. *He is an enemy of God* (verse 7). This shows that a sinner is meant. Compare 5:10.

4. *He is not subject to God's law* (verse 7). He does not submit to or observe that law, nor can be.

5. *He displeases God* (verse 8). Indeed, he cannot please God, considering his enslavement to flesh. Even his attempts at right doing are like filthy rags in God's eyes (Isaiah 64:6).

The Mind of the Saint (verses 5-8). Again, throughout these verses "the spiritual mind" is repeatedly set in contrast to "the carnal mind." This "spiritual mind" is that which is possessed by the Christian. This is "the inner man" of a regenerate person. This is the one who "(walks) after the Spirit" (8:4, 5), one who is "in the Spirit" (8:9).

1. *He "minds" the things of the Spirit* (verse 5). He is interested in and pursues spiritual things.

2. *He has life* (verse 6). He has been raised from spiritual death by the regeneration of the Spirit. He is spiritually alive and destined for eternal life.

3. *He has peace* (verse 6). This is in contrast to the "enmity" in the heart of the sinner. He is at peace with God (Romans 5:1) and thus has peace within.

4. *He is subject to God's law.* Paul does not state this, but the contrast in verse 7 implies it. Romans 7:22 actually stated it, as did 7:25.

5. *He pleases God.* Again, the contrast implies this (verse 8). When a desire for righteousness comes from the heart, God is pleased. Such desires, when genuine, are motivated by the Holy Spirit, not by self-centered (fleshly) impulses.

3. OCCUPANCY BY THE SPIRIT (Romans 8:9-11)

Paul turns now to another manner of describing our new

relationship with the Spirit, that relationship that enables us—though in the flesh—to "walk after the Spirit." The point here is the marvelous truth that *we are indwelled by the Holy Spirit.* Nothing short of that would make it possible for us to live by spiritual rather than fleshly impulses.

A Possession (verse 9). The indwelling of the Holy Spirit is, first of all, a token that one belongs to Christ. This verse clarifies two things. First, those "in the Spirit" are those who possess the Spirit, and they are in contrast to those "in the flesh" as described in verses 5-8. This makes clear again that the contrast throughout this entire passage is a contrast between sinners and saints.

Second, the verse makes it emphatically clear that all Christians possess the Holy Spirit (and, in turn, are Christ's possession). The Spirit of Christ is certainly the Holy Spirit.

A Present (verse 10). This verse speaks of our present experience of life because of the indwelling presence of the Holy Spirit. We note several aspects of this present situation.

1. The Spirit's indwelling makes Christ himself real in us. It is interesting to note that Paul moves so easily from the *Spirit* in us (verse 9) to *Christ* in us (verse 10). But this is the way it is. Christ dwells in us by the Spirit. The Spirit ministers the presence of Christ within us. Various Scriptures speak of the reality of Christ's presence in the Christian's heart. In Galatians 4:19 Paul speaks of his desire that "Christ be formed in" his readers. The Spirit of God does this work. Colossians 1:27 speaks of "Christ in you, the hope of glory." Indeed, Jesus promised that the Holy Spirit would "not speak of himself" but would "glorify me" (John 16:13, 14). That very verse indicated that the Spirit would make the things of *Christ* real to the believer. In John 15:16-18 Jesus certainly seems to say that His sending of the Spirit to his followers would be, in one sense, His own coming to them.

2. The Spirit's indwelling counteracts the deadness of the body. This first part of verse 10 should not be misunderstood. Paul does not mean that the presence of the Spirit *causes* the believer's body to be dead by reason of sin. Nor does he mean that the Spirit's presence *corrects* or *changes* this to make the believer's body alive. No, what he means is that the Spirit indwells the believer *in spite* of his dead body, and that spiritual life is imparted to the believer in opposition to that dead body.

In other words, read the verse this way: "If Christ is in you, then it is true that your body is dead, as we have seen; but in spite of this the Spirit gives you life in the inner man." That the believer's "body" is dead has already been made clear in 7:14-25, especially verse 24.

3. The Spirit's indwelling gives life. This is the counteraction of the dead body, and the last part of verse 10 indicates this. That "the Spirit is life" means he regenerates the inner man; He restores from spiritual death (Ephesians 2:5). The believer is alive and destined for eternal life. The phrase "because of righteousness" is parallel to and in contrast to "because of sin." Probably "because of" means "as an effect of" in both phrases; but no doubt the idea of intended results is also loosely interwoven. Sin produced the death of the body (the flesh), and thus sin is produced. Righteousness (especially the righteousness of Christ) produced life in us by the Spirit, and righteousness is produced as a result.

Verse 10 really harks back to chapter seven. "It may well be," says Paul, "that you live in a 'dead body,' a fleshly nature inclined to sin. But when the Spirit forms Christ in you, the inner man lives and rules the man, and genuine righteousness is produced in your life."

A Promise (verse 11). Not only is there *present* life in the inner man despite the deadness of the body, the presence of the Spirit indwelling us constitutes also a promise to redeem the body too! Even the dead body, the flesh, will experience the life now possessed only in the inner man. This is what verse 11 teaches us.

1. The Spirit raised up Jesus, as indicated in 11a. This reference to Christ's bodily resurrection serves as a basis on which to affirm the promise of our own bodily resurrection. It is quite interesting how the Scriptures unanimously tie these two togehter (cf., 1 Corinthians 15:20).

2. The Spirit will raise our bodies. Verse 11b anticipates verse 23 below. Together these verses continue the line of thought introduced in the previous chapter (7:24, 25). For now we live with a regenerate inner man and an unredeemed, dead body. Inevitable antagonism results (7:14-25). One day, though, the conflict will be finally resolved by the redemption of the body. Then even the body will share in the spiritual character now experienced only by the inner man.

The final solution then for the problem of chapter seven will be the redemption of the body. The present solution is to be found in walking after the Spirit who lives within us and enables us to overcome the fleshly nature we must continue to endure.

4. OBLIGATION TO THE SPIRIT (Romans 8:12, 13)

The conclusion to Paul's discussion is now at hand. The problem introduced in chapter seven lies in the fact that we are presently still bound to a body of unredeemed, depraved flesh. The solution is to be found in the presence of the Spirit of God in us, who fosters in us (in the inner man) a "spiritual mind," and who is responsible for righteous impulses that will lead us, when obeyed, to live righteously in spite of the fleshly nature that "lusts against the Spirit" (Galatians 5:17). These ideas Paul now states in summary form, introduced by the word "therefore."

A Debt Cancelled (verse 12). The first summary conclusion is this: We are no longer obligated to the flesh. We owe the flesh nothing. We do not have to live according to its impulses. The flesh is still "there" with its lusts (Galatians 5:17, again, as also Romans 7:14-25). But we do not have to obey it. Its hold is broken. Compare Romans 6:6: The sinful body has been dethroned.

A Destiny Considered (verse 13a). "If ye live after the flesh, ye shall die" is a general principle that warns all men where flesh will take them. It is an axiom much like Romans 6:23: "The wages of sin is death." In this sense, Paul's words do not apply, first force, to the *believers* Paul was addressing. As we have already seen, the believer does *not* "live after the flesh." The believer "walks after the Spirit" (verse 4). Therefore Paul's words apply first to any reader who *is* living according to the impulses of the flesh. Any such reader had better consider that eternal death is his certain destiny.

Still, in another sense, Paul's words do apply to all believers as a warning. True, the believer has been freed from the hold flesh had over him. The sinful body has been dethroned. Another master has taken control. He no longer *has* to heed the call of flesh and sin. But *can* he heed that call? Indeed—as we all know from tragic experience—he can. The believer too needs the warning then that to obey the flesh leads ultimately to death. If the believer allows flesh's impulses to get the upper hand, again he faces the awful prospect of apostasy and eternal death (cf., 2 Peter 2:19-22). The believer then must be on guard.

A Death Commanded (verse 13b). And here is the very method by which the believer can combat the tug of the flesh and keep the victory he has been granted by the Holy Spirit. He must "mortify" (put to death) the deeds of the body. So long as he continues thus, life, not death, is his destiny.

The sinful body has already been dethroned; its chains of mastery over us broken by the power of Christ and presence of the Spirit. Thus all the believer needs to do is "kill" each and every impulse that comes from the flesh as it arises. Were the believer still alone and dependent on his own energy, he could not do this. But "through the Spirit" who lives within him he can. Every time the flesh rears his ugly head, lop it off. Every time he calls out, silence him. Pay no heed to any suggestion he offers. He has no hold on you. You owe him nothing. A new master lives within. He is the divine Spirit. You owe Him complete obedience. He will aid you in resisting and in mortifying each impulse of the flesh. By that method you can have everyday victory and live for God, walking after the Spirit. The antagonism of sinful flesh need cause you no defeat.

19 The Position of Sonship for the Believer

Study Text: Romans 8:14-17

Introduction
1. Sonship: an Indication of Privilege (Romans 8:14)
   a. The Guidance of the Spirit (verse 14a)
   b. The Guarantee of Sonship (verse 14b)
2. Sonship: an Intimate Position (Romans 8:15)
   a. It Is not a Position of Servitude (verse 15a)
   b. It Is a Position of Son-Placing (verse 15b)
3. Sonship: an Inner Pledge (Romans 8:16)
   a. The Manner of This Witness (verse 16a)
   b. The Message in This Witness (verse 16b)
4. Sonship: the Inheritance Promised (Romans 8:17)
   a. The Fact of This Inheritance (verse 17a)
   b. The Features of This Inheritance (verse 17b)

INTRODUCTION

Chapter eight of Romans describes the justified believer's new relationship to the Holy Spirit. In the previous lesson we examined verses 1-13 and took note of some aspects of that new relationship. In particular, the believer is indwelled by the Holy Spirit, as was seen in verses 9-11. Therefore the believer comes to be spiritually-minded, as opposed to his former carnal-mindedness. The believer is thus interested in and concerned about spiritual things. Verses 5-8 made this clear.

Further, the former dominion of the sinful flesh is broken, and the believer finds himself free therefrom and alive by the Spirit (verses 2, 10). Consequently, he is no longer indebted to the flesh,

147

but owes allegiance and obedience to the Holy Spirit (verse 12). By the Spirit then he can put to death every day the deeds of the flesh, obeying instead the righteous impulses of God's Spirit within him (verse 13). This is what it means to "walk after the Spirit" (verses 1, 4).

Today's lesson continues with the subject, developing still more interesting aspects of the Holy Spirit's ministry in the life of the one justified by faith. In particular, the passage covered will emphasize the believer's place in the family of God. The Holy Spirit's ministry is especially important in testifying to that place.

EXPOSITION

A quick check of the general study-outline in the back of this book will show how this lesson fits into the pattern of Romans. Note that we are still concerned with part 3 of Romans (chapters 5-8) in which the meaning of justification, as possessed by the believer, is explained. Chapters 6-8 point up the reality of justification in the believer's experience, indicating that the believer finds himself in a whole new set of relationships: to sin, to the law, to the Spirit of God. This lesson is the second of four, from chapter eight, that describe our new relationship to God's Spirit and God's Love. This lesson covers 8:14-17 and is entitled "The Position of Sonship for the Believer."

1. SONSHIP: AN INDICATION
OF PRIVILEGE (Romans 8:14)

This verse introduces the subject of the believer's sonship in God's family and the matter of the Spirit's involvement in making this sonship a reality in the believer's experience.

The Guidance of the Spirit (verse 14a). This first part of verse 14 refers to *as many as are being led* (continuing action) *by God's Spirit.* First we note that this looks back to the first thirteen verses (see the previous lesson) and especially to the phrase used in verses 1 and 4: "walk after the Spirit." As we noted there, that phrase is a general description of all Christians; and this observation is further confirmed by the verse before us.

Verse 13 also spoke of *living* after the Spirit, which means basically the same thing as *walking* after the Spirit. The essence of verses 1-13 was to show that the believer has a new and powerful force operating within him, the Spirit of God. This force contradicts the flesh and impulses the believer toward righteousness instead of evil. The believer—though not always perfectly, of course—follows these impulses and thus walks, lives after the Spirit. This is at the heart of what Paul means here in verse 14 when he speaks of being led by the Holy Spirit.

Surely, though, this leadership has further ramifications. More is involved than overcoming the lusts of the flesh (verse 13). Perhaps then, *guidance* is the best word for it has much broader and more positive implications. It is not stretching the context to see in this clause the wonderful truth that Christians have, in the Spirit, a guide they can trust. This Guide gives perfect direction in all matters about which the Christian is concerned. Long ago Jeremiah called out to God, in despair of his own sufficiency: "It is not in man that walketh to direct his steps. O Lord, correct me" (Jeremiah 10:23, 24). The Spirit of God solves the problem of man's inability to guide himself aright.

How does this guidance come? Both by inner impulses and by the revealed, written Word of God. Jesus spoke of the Spirit who, when He is come, "will guide you into all truth" (John 16:13). The foundation for that ministry of the Spirit was fully laid when He infallibly guided the apostles in the recording of the New Testament revelation, just as He had earlier guided the prophets of the Old. In our time, with the revelation done, the Spirit generally works for our guidance through the Word. This does not discount the significance or wonder of those mystical, inner convictions by which the Spirit impresses us individually about the will of God. Such impulses, however, are not of the Holy Spirit if they contradict the spirit of the written Word. Nor can these individual promptings be raised to the level of general authority for the church, possessed by the written Word.

The Guarantee of Sonship (verse 14b). The leadership of the Spirit referred to in 14a is a guarantee, an evidence of sonship. The individual who finds himself led by the Spirit obtains from that very experience an assurance that he is a son of God.

This means, in essence, that the victory over sin referred to above is this evidence. As already observed, to be "led by the Spirit" is to be guided into righteousness as opposed to following the flesh's lusts. This is "walking after the Spirit" as described in verses 1-13. The believer finds this new force at work within him, leading him successfully in a direction quite the opposite of his former way of life. This victory is an indication of his position as a son of God. *No one has any basis for assurance he is God's son if his life has not taken on this new direction!*

As we have seen, this guidance includes more than the changed direction of one's life away from the flesh's lusts to the Spirit's inclinations. This leadership includes, for example, illumination about the truth (cf., John 16:13, above, with 1 Corinthians 2:14). Thus the believer experiences the "spiritual understanding"—particularly of the Word—that can only be the work of the Spirit.

And by that leadership into truth he gains assurance he is a son of God.

We also said above that this guidance includes mystical inner impulses for the individual about God's will. Such impressions too add to one's conviction that he is a son of God. Now this does not mean that one should doubt his Christianity if he is not always being mysteriously "impressed" to do all sorts of strange, odd things he would not otherwise do. We all know that some believers develop greater sensitivity to the inner impulses of the Spirit than others. And there are excesses. Some think every inner impression, every idea that occurs to them, is the voice of the Spirit. They get quite a thrill from doing even ridiculous things as a result of such impressions. Such inner feelings must be evaluated and disciplined against foolish excesses. Especially must "inner voices" be tested by the written Word. On the other hand, some of us—to avoid excess—ignore all inner voices and thereby never develop sensitivity to the mystic impressions that really originate with the Holy Spirit. Such insensitivity robs one of an important evidence of his sonship.

Paul's emphasis here is on the *privilege* of being a son in *God's* family. The very word used—*son*, as opposed to *child*—stresses this rank and privilege. More about this will be given below. For now, note that Paul's point is this: God would not put his blessed Spirit within to lead you were you not now His son.

2. SONSHIP: AN INTIMATE POSITION
(Romans 8:15)

The *fact* that we are sons of God has already been indicated in verse 14. That fact is evidenced by the presence and leading of the Spirit in our lives. Now Paul turns to the *nature* of our sonship. What kind of position do we occupy in God's family as His children?

It Is Not a Position of Servitude (verse 15a). You will note that this verse has two parts, one negative and one positive. Paul just tells us what our position is *not*. This contrast will help us understand and appreciate better what the position *is*. You will also notice that each half of the verse has two parts too: Paul first characterizes the position by a word naming its nature, and then he expresses the *result* of such a position.

1. We are not servants. The word "bondage" means bond-service, slavery, servitude. This is the nature, the character, of the position we did *not* receive when we were saved. The Holy Spirit is *not* a spirit of servitude. His presence in our hearts does *not* testify that we bear such a relationship to God as bond-slaves.

Of course we *are* in voluntary servitude to God, and the Bible often uses this word to name our relationship to God. But we are not *mere* bond-slaves. Nor is the Spirit given to us to witness to that side of our relationship. Thus that servitude is not the point here.

You will notice that Paul says we did not receive this position *again*. This word reminds us that the position of the believer under the law *was* one of servitude. But we have been delivered from that Mosaic system. Paul has made this clear in chapter seven. This fifteenth verse, in both halves, reflects concisely the very same truths as were outlined in detail in Galatians 3:24—4:7. Note Galatians 4:7, for example, where also the former servitude under the law is contrasted to present sonship. More about this will be said in a moment.

2. We are not afraid. The phrase "to fear" describes the result of a position of bond-service. This is true in a general sense: A slave obeys his master from fear, not from love. Such is not our relationship to God. This is also true specifically of the particular servitude referred to here, the servitude of the believer under the law. We can easily imagine the fear, the dread, the awe, with which the Old Testament believer offered his sacrifices and observed meticulously the required ritual. Such is not our relationship to God. Our relationship to God, made real in our hearts by the Spirit, does not beget fear.

It Is a Position of Son-Placing (verse 15b). The word translated "adoption" literally means *son-placing*. This is the same word that was used in Galatians 4:5, a passage in which the same truths are under discussion as here. Throughout the following discussion it would be helpful to compare and review the commentary on Galatians 3:24—4:7.

1. We are adult sons of God. The "son-placing" (adoption) was not performed on someone *not* born into one's family. It was done to one's natural child, especially in families of wealth and prestige. A small child, not old enough to be on his own, was generally put under the watchcare of a slave. But when that child became of age, he was placed in a new position in his own family. That occasion was often marked by a special ceremony and made an occasion for festivity. That occasion was called the son-placing (adoption). Afterward, the child was no longer a child, but a son, treated as an adult, a full-fledged member of the family, with all the equal rights and responsibilities of membership in the family.

You will remember that Paul in Galatians 3:24—4:7 uses that very circumstance as a parallel to the change from the Mosaic dispensation to the New Testament dispensation. The law was like that guardian assigned watchcare over the little child ("schoolmaster" in Galatians 3:24; cf., 4:2). Thus Old Testament believers lived under a system that was immature, a system comparable to that by which children are controlled. That system engenders servitude, and fear (Galatians 4:1, 3, 7). But when Jesus came, believers were delivered from that childhood and experienced the "adoption" (Galatians 4:4, 5). Believers are now dealt with as mature sons with all the rights and responsibilities that relate thereto. This is what Paul refers to here in Romans 8:15. The Spirit's presence in us is testimony to that adoption.

We are in God's family by virtue of regeneration. We enjoy the rank and privilege of responsible members of His family by virtue of adoption (son-placing). One word more: Denney indicates that this "son-placing" is a word that "serves to distinguish those who are made sons by an act of grace from the only-begotten Son of God." In other words, Jesus *is* God's Son by nature; we are not, but are *put* there, *placed* in God's family anyway. No doubt this observation is valid.

2. We call on God as Father. This result of the son-placing is in contrast with the fear that results from a position of servitude. A servile relationship begets fear. A relation of sonship begets the intimacy and confidence to call to one's father.

"Abba" is the Hebrew (Aramaic) word for Father. The repetition serves to translate this. Paul probably thought of "abba" (even though he was writing in Greek) because Hebrew was the language spoken in his own home, and by which he had first and habitually addressed his own father. (Hebrew may probably also have been the language he was most accustomed to use in personal prayer.) It is also possible that the Hebrew word had connotations of intimacy and confidence not possessed by the Greek word. Some take this even further, suggesting that "abba" was the word of a lisping baby, barely able to talk, like our "da-da." But the picture Paul is giving us here is not a helpless infant but of a confident son. No doubt, however, that the filial love is there, as opposed to fear.

Indeed, this writer believes that Paul is thinking primarily of a prayer relationship. In other words, the Spirit in us impresses us to call out to God, to call on God as our Father in prayer. The word "cry" means "call out." This prayer has then the element of intimacy, for it stems from that relationship of family love. It has also the element of confidence, in that one understands his right to ask of his Father.

Again borrowing a word from Denney, "We have not only the status, but the heart of sons." Something within impels us to call out to God as our Father. That is the work of the Holy Spirit.

3. SONSHIP: AN INNER PLEDGE
(Romans 8:16)

We have here the marvelous doctrine that the Spirit of God testifies in our hearts that we are children of God. This is not merely the *evidence* we get from the Spirit's presence and leadership and prompting to call on God in prayer as Father. Those things, already noted in verses 14, 15, are certainly included. But verse 16 goes beyond this evidence to an active *work* of the Spirit within, bearing witness that we are God's children.

The Manner of This Witness (verse 16a). Translated literally, this clause says: "The Spirit himself bears joint-witness with our spirit." This declaration involves two interrelated facts.

1. Our own spirits bear witness (testify) to our membership in God's family. There is no need here to enter an involved discussion about the technical distinctions between body, soul, and spirit. For practical purposes, man's "spirit" is that dimension of his nature, that part of him, that is related to God. This is the highest side of man.

Man without Christ is spiritually dead; he is not in a living relationship to God. At conversion, he is spiritually regenerated (born again), raised from spiritual death, made alive, restored to a living relationship to God. Compare Ephesians 2:1, 5. Thus the believer's spirit gives testimony that he is a child of God.

2. The Holy Spirit gives joint-witness. He gives testimony along with that borne by our own regenerated spirits. Those two witnesses coincide and strengthen each other. This is an active work of the Spirit of God, whispering mystically in our souls that we are God's children. This inner pledge swells within our souls by His promptings, yielding confident assurance of salvation. To quote Denney again: "Our own spirit tells us we are God's children, but the voice with which it speaks is, as we know, prompted and inspired by the Divine Spirit itself."

The Message in This Witness (verse 16b). This inner witness confirms, as we have seen, "that we are the children of God." We notice that the word here is "children," not "sons" (as above in verses 14, 15). In other words, the previous verses have dealt with the specific kind of position we occupy in the family; but this verse deals with the basic fact that we are members of God's family. We are God's children. (This is the word used in John 1:12.)

4. SONSHIP: THE INHERITANCE PROMISED
(Romans 8:17)

We have already noted comparisons between these verses and Galatians 4:1-7. Here, as there, Paul concludes his treatment of our sonship in God's family with a reference to the inheritance we are entitled to as a result of that sonship.

The Fact of This Inheritance (verse 17a). This fact is simply indicated: If (since) we are God's children, then we are heirs. Compare Galatians 4:7: "And if a son, then an heir of God."

Such heirship was more significant to those of Paul's day than to us. For us, inheritance is something that speaks entirely of the future. We wait until our parents' death to inherit. But in Paul's background the word had connotations of a present relationship as well as a future experience. In the system of "adoption" referred to above (the son-placing), the son was already regarded as being in some sense a co-owner of his father's possessions after the adoption. (Perhaps this is the very reason the prodigal son could say, "Give me the portion that belongs to me." Not that his father had to accede to the request, but there was a relationship that made the request significant.)

We *are* (not "shall be") God's heirs. This speaks then both of the future and the present. We have now the kind of standing in His family as heirs. That is present experience. And, though Paul does not take time to spell it out here, he is implying what he spells out in Ephesians 1:14, that the Spirit is an "earnest" of this inheritance. God has given His Spirit as His guarantee He will deliver on His promise. This fact heightens our appreciation of the present side of this truth.

The Features of This Inheritance (verse 17b). Paul gives two features:

1. We are heirs of God. This feature has already been emphasized. Here, then, emphasize the identity this gives us as heirs of *God.* How much more important this, than to be heirs in the wealthiest family on earth!

2. We are joint-heirs with Christ. We noted above, the distinction between Him as natural Son of God and ourselves as sons placed there by grace. Still, we inherit with Him!

Paul presents two ideas that stand together in this matter. First, he points out that we are presently suffering together with Christ. In one sense, this is part of the inheritance, but probably Paul sees this more as in contrast to the inheritance, as that which presently must be endured while we wait for the future inheritance.

Second, Paul observes that we will be glorified together with Christ. This is the essence of the inheritance for which we look. The Scriptures never tell us much about the "glory" we expect to receive. Passages like Revelation 21, 22, where the heavenly glory is described, in part, are certainly to be included in our thoughts about this glorification. But perhaps it is more important to stress that this inheritance is glorification *with Christ. He* will be glorified; we will participate in that glorification with him. Maybe 2 Thessalonians 1:10 puts it best: "He shall come to be glorified in his saints." At any rate, the Spirit's presence in our hearts serves as unshakeable confidence we are God's sons and heirs with His Son.

20 The Promised Salvation of the Believer

Study Text: Romans 8:18-27

Introduction
1. Hope: the Spirit and Our Inheritance (Romans 8:18-25)
   a. Theme: a Comparison in Glory (verse 18)
   b. Travail: the Creation's Groaning (verses 19-22)
   c. Triumph: the Christian's Glorification (verses 23-25)
2. Help: the Spirit as Our Intercessor (Romans 8:26, 27)
   a. The Saints' Ignorance (verse 26a)
   b. The Spirit's Intercession (verses 26b, 27)

INTRODUCTION

Chapter eight of Romans is a marvelous one indeed. Our approach to this chapter is following this theme: the justified believer's new relationship to the Holy Spirit and to the love of God.

Already we have examined many facets of this new relationship. The believer is indwelled by the Holy Spirit (verse 9). The believer is led by the Spirit (verse 14). The believer is given inward witness by the Spirit that he is a mature child of God, an heir with Jesus (verses 14-17). The believer is enabled by the Spirit to "put to death" the deeds of the flesh in his daily walk (verse 13). Consequently, the believer is one who lives and walks after the Spirit (verses 1, 2, 4, 10, 13).

The Christian life then is not merely an intellectual persuasion that one is reckoned justified by faith. The Christian life instead is a life controlled and empowered by the presence of God's Spirit in one's heart. That Presence is a dynamic force that produces in the believer's life a practical righteousness in spite of the fact that the

155

believer's fleshly nature is still unredeemed and lusts for sin (7:14-25).

We continue in this lesson to examine more facets of the believer's new relationship to God's Spirit.

EXPOSITION

Lest these several lessons on chapter eight get "lost in the shuffle," keep checking the general study-outline in the back of this book. There you will see that this is the third lesson on the chapter, covering verses 18-27, entitled "The Promised Salvation of the Believer."

1. HOPE: THE SPIRIT AND OUR INHERITANCE
(Romans 8:18-25)

The previous lesson covered verse 17. There the subject of our inheritance as mature sons of God was introduced. The Spirit's presence in our hearts bears witness to that sonship and thus to that inheritance. This is the theme Paul follows up in 8:18-25. The key word is "hope." Paul speaks of "the glory which shall be revealed in us," "the manifestation of the sons of God," "the glorious liberty of the children of God," "the redemption of our body"—these are the elements of that "hope." This is the inheritance we shall possess as full-fledged members of God's family. The Spirit of God is given us as an "earnest" of that inheritance (cf., Ephesians 1:14), as the "firstfruits" thereof (Romans 8:23).

Theme: a Comparison in Glory (verse 18). This verse states, in a nutshell, the general truth that will be expanded on in verses 19-25. The verse also connects up closely with verse 17 and serves to tie in this new theme with that of verses 14-17. Paul has just made the point that our ultimate joint inheritance with Christ must wait while we presently jointly suffer with Him. Now he is ready to speak at greater length about that expected glory, and he makes the transition to this theme by comparing the present suffering to that promised salvation. In essence, verse 18 accomplishes two things.

1. There is a promised glory. This is called "the glory which shall be revealed in us." This expression sums up the content of the promised inheritance of verse 17. It encompasses all that is awaiting us in final salvation, including the redemption of the body—as will be discussed below. This expression is our "hope."

This promised glory then is the time of our glorification. Second Thessalonians 1:10 speaks of this in these terms: "When he shall come to be glorified in his saints." Thus this full glorification of the believer awaits the second coming of Christ and will be accomplished by the transforming power of the glorification of Christ. Indeed, it is He who will be glorified, and our glory will be a participation in His. Perhaps the summary in 1 John 3:2 is as good an explanation as any: "When he shall appear, we shall be like him; for we shall see him as he is." That is the time when we shall be fully "conformed (in body and spirit) to the image of his Son" (Romans 8:29).

2. *Present sufferings are insignificant by comparison.* The value, significance, importance, and weight of present sufferings are as nothing when compared to the weight of the promised glory. So says Paul in 18a, and so he often said. Compare 2 Corinthians 4:17 where our present "affliction" is seen as "light" and "but for a moment," in contrast with the "glory" that is "weighty" and "eternal." These sufferings include all normal and natural afflictions as well as those imposed on us by persecution. None of them are important when compared to the eternal glory we expect.

Travail: the Creation's Groaning (verses 19-22). In these verses Paul presents his first proof that the promised glorification of the believer rests on solid ground. That proof consists in what Denney calls "the sighing of creation." The natural realm—all the created universe—experiences this painful sense of expectation for deliverance, thus confirming the truthfulness of the believer's future hope.

1. *What the creation awaits* is indicated in verse 19. First, let us note that the word "creature" does not refer to the individual created object but to the created universe as a whole: "creation," as we say. Creature (verses 19, 20, 21) is the same Greek word exactly as "creation" in verse 22 (compare Romans 1:20). This "creation" is the whole physical universe, including all things animate and inanimate except for the spiritual side of human nature. Paul poetically personifies this "creation" as though it consciously partook of man's hope. Of course creation is not conscious, but it will partake of the final glorification.

Two words are used to express the *nature* of this expectancy. One is "earnest expectation"; the other, "waiteth for." Both are rare and expressive words. The first is said to mean "to wait for in suspense"; the second, "to wait perseveringly." The picture is of intense expectancy, waiting with head and arms outstretched, almost imploringly. The universe is waiting for something.

The *content* of this expectancy is contained in these words: "the manifestation of the sons of God." These "sons of God" are us, the believers. The manifestation means the full revelation, the unveiling of the finished product. We are sons of God now, and our legal standing by "adoption" (see verse 15 in the previous lesson) is that of mature sons. But we are not yet, in fact and experience, fully conformed to the image of His Son, nor can that be complete until the body too experiences the redemption and is renewed in His likeness. Then we will be fully revealed as God's sons. Like a roomful of admirers awaiting the unveiling of the master's latest painting, the world stands with bated breath awaiting the uncovering of God's sons!

2. Creation's present subjection is indicated in verse 20. Paul looks back to a specific time when the creation was put in subjection to (subordinated under) "vanity." The time referred to is obviously the time when sin entered the world, the time of the fall of man as described in Genesis 3. There it is recorded that the ground was cursed as a result of Adam's sin (Genesis 3:17-19). No doubt the entire universe was affected in ways beyond our knowledge. We really have no way of knowing how extensively or severely the physical world was affected, but we know enough to be sure that things in general are far different from what they were in the innocence of Eden.

What does "made subject to vanity" mean? Well, "vanity" means emptiness, meaninglessness. Denney says, "The idea is that of looking for what one does not find—hence of futility, frustration, disappointment . . . . Sin brought this down on creation; it made a pessimistic view of the universe inevitable." This is exactly the truth expressed in Ecclesiastes: "Vanity of vanities; all is vanity" (Ecclesiastes 1:2). Solomon goes on in that ancient book to show that all of his life's natural pursuits are like blind alleys, leading nowhere.

The latter half of verse 20 shows why this subjection to vanity was made. The "him" referred to is God: He is the one who put the creation in subjection to vanity. The curse was delivered for His sake, because His righteous character must be upheld by the severe punishment of sin. The punishment fell on man, because man was guilty. But there were effects on the whole creation, originally intended for man's occupancy and dominion, even though that creation was not conscious and thus not wilfully participating in man's sin. The "in hope" makes it clear, however, that God's curse—both on man and creation—is not utterly hopeless. There is an expected glorification; and just as creation was affected by the curse so it will be affected by the glorification.

3. Creation's expected deliverance is indicated in verse 21. This hopeful outlook gives the content of the "hope" with which verse 20 ended. We note, first, that the creation is now in "the bondage of corruption." This phrase matches the "subject to vanity" of the previous verse. All that exists experiences corruption, deterioration, and decay. Death, as the curse of sin, passed on all things as on man. The world is passing away, says John (1 John 2:17). The physical universe is "enslaved" by this corruption, helpless to free itself, just as man the sinner is helpless to break the control of both moral and physical corruption. Sin has brought rottenness to all the world.

But the creation will be delivered (set free, set at liberty) from this slavery. The Second Coming will bring a "regeneration" of all physical things, just as of the human body (compare Matthew 19:28). Then there will be no more corruption, no decay, and no death.

We notice in 21b that the time of this "making new" (Revelation 21:5) coincides with "the glorious liberty of the children of God." In other words, then, it will only be when man experiences the full and perfect liberty of final glorification that the world too will have such liberty. Man cannot experience this, of course, until the redemption of the body. We note then that the world's destiny has always been linked with man's. The world is, after all, for man. When man fell, the world was cursed. When man is finally and fully restored, so will the world be. Denney says: "When man's redemption is complete, he will find himself in a new condition . . . : this is Paul's faith, and the sighing of creation attests it." Revelation 21, 22 describes this new earth in detail.

4. Creation's waiting pains are indicated in verse 22. Two verbs are used to describe the anguish of the personified creation as it waits for the final glorification to come. The first is "groaneth," a word that describes the kind of agony caused by pressure. The second is "travaileth in pain," which literally refers to the pains of childbirth, labor pains. This suggests "the travail out of which the new world is to be born" (Denney). The word "together" means that all the universe, in all its parts, unites in this distress awaiting the coming redemption. "Until now" suggests that this has been true always since the fall; there has been no relief. But relief will come.

Triumph: the Christian's Glorification (verses 23-25). Verses 19-22 have spoken about the "groaning" expectation of the creation for the promised final redemption. Now Paul moves to the similar "groaning" in the spirit of the Christian. This is Paul's second proof that the confident hope of the believer rests on solid grounds.

1. The believer's inner yearning is described in verse 23. There are several things about this yearning that are worthy of careful notice. First, there is a comparison made with the sighing of creation described above. The "not only they, but ourselves also" indicates this. The "they," by the way, has been supplied; it would have been better if the translators had supplied "the creation." At any rate, the Christian shares in his spirit ("within ourselves") the groaning of the whole creation.

Second, note that the Christian's yearning is especially related to his possession of the Spirit of God as "firstfruits." Thus the Christian's yearning is intensified, stronger than the sighing of the creation. Thus too the Christian can feel this yearning in a clearly defined way in his spirit ("within ourselves") and not merely feel the vague anticipation of the creation. That the Spirit is "firstfruits" means that His presence is something like a "foretaste of glory divine" (to borrow the words of Fannie Crosby). He is not subject to corruption. His nature is already like that for which the present, transient order sighs. Thus we have already experienced a little of the glory for which we are destined when all things are made new. In fact, the Spirit as "firstfruits" and the Spirit as "earnest" (Ephesians 1:14; 2 Corinthians 5:5) present basically the same truth: God has already given us part of the inheritance promised in final salvation, both as foretaste and as guarantee of His earnestness, His sincere intention to deliver on His promise. And this blessed Spirit whets the edge of our hope and desire to an ever-increasing sharpness.

Third, the specific thing we are yearning for is "the adoption, to wit, the redemption of our body." The *adoption* was dealt with in the previous lesson (verse 15). In one sense, we have already received the adoption. We have already been placed as mature sons in the family of God. But in another sense that adoption will not be perfectly experienced until the *whole* man—body as well as spirit—participates in the redemption. Denney compares the situation with Christ himself who, though He was certainly God's Son always, was "declared to be the Son of God with power . . . by the resurrection from the dead" (Romans 1:4). Just so, we will be fully and perfectly manifested as the sons of God (see verse 19, above) only when our bodies have been raised.

Redemption literally refers to a bought freedom. The body's redemption, effected by the work of Christ, will be actually experienced at His return. That redemption includes two things: restoration to life (resurrection) and renewal (regeneration). The new body will be unlike the present one, released from both physical and moral decay, no longer subject to death or sin's temptation. Second Corinthians 5:1 calls the new body "a building of God, an house not made with hands, eternal in the heavens." First Corinthians 15:42-53 makes an interesting comparison between the old and the new bodies. The new body will be "spiritual," and will possess incorruption, glory, power, and immortality. In short, as already noted, it will be "fashioned like unto his glorious body" (Philippians 3:21).

2. *The believer's hope* is discussed in verses 24, 25. Paul has just said that we are "waiting for" the redemption of our body. This "waiting" is the essence of our hope. Hope is not a mere desire, in this case, but a confident expectancy of our final glorification and inheritance as God's sons.

First, we note that this hope is closely related to our salvation. Many interpreters believe "we are saved *in* hope" would be a better translation than "we are saved *by* hope." Either way, the point is clear: The very nature of our salvation involves hope, because present salvation would be meaningless without the final salvation we await.

Second, the nature of hope is clarified in 24b. Hope is not sight. Hope relates to that which is yet unseen, an expectancy about the future. What a person already sees, already possesses, already experiences, he does not need hope for.

160

Third, Paul affirms that the Christian's hope is therefore one that engenders patient waiting. Patience here is perseverance under any sort of trying circumstances or opposition. This patience can only result from confidence. Our hope is a confident one. The Spirit of God makes this hope real within us. We will experience the final glorification, the inheritance of the sons of God.

2. HELP: THE SPIRIT AS OUR INTERCESSOR
(Romans 8:26, 27)

Some interpreters have suggested that these two verses present yet a third proof that our hope for final glorification rests on solid grounds: "The intercession of the Spirit which helps us in our prayers . . . lends words to our longing" (Denney). This view would make the prayers in which the spirit helps us a very specific sort of prayer, namely the prayer for final, perfected salvation. No doubt the Spirit can help us in such prayers as that too, but there seems no need to limit these verses to so narrow an interpretation. All our prayers are included here.

The Saints' Ignorance (verse 26a). The Spirit's intercession for us is first presented in the light of our own limitations. These limitations make His help all the more important and essential.

1. The Spirit's response to our infirmity is indicated first. The infirmity referred to here looks back to the previous verses in which our present situation is contrasted to our promised salvation. We await the redemption of our bodies, but while we wait we still have these "earthen vessels" (2 Corinthians 4:7). The present body is corrupt and weak (1 Corinthians 15:42, 43). Further, as we have seen so clearly indicated in 7:14-25, the present body is "carnal," subject to depraved, fleshly lusts. All this is part of our body's sickness, and all this makes the Spirit's help crucial.

The word "likewise" probably looks back to verse 23. On the one hand the Spirit's presence in our infirm bodies creates hope; likewise His presence within provides help in intercession.

The word "helpeth" is extremely interesting. Literally, the Greek word means "takes up together on the other end." The picture presented is that of one who has a load to carry. Our infirmities do so burden us. But the Holy Spirit picks up and helps us carry that burden. He helps by sharing the load.

2. Our ignorance in prayer is then indicated. Specifically, "we know not what we should pray for as we ought." This is part of our infirmity. Technically this does not mean that we have absolutely no knowledge, ever, as to the objects of our prayers. But we often do not know *how* to pray, in specific situations. We simply do not always know what is needed or how God's ultimate will is to be worked out step by step. Our human ignorance prevents such confident knowledge. Indeed, our own motives cannot always be discerned by us, or trusted. We are too much affected by sin.

The Spirit's Intercession (verses 26b, 27). At least three facts about the Spirit's helpful intercession are clear here.

1. *The character of His intercession* is seen in 26b: "with groanings that cannot be uttered." These groanings (same word as in verses 22, 23) are unspeakable in the sense that *we* cannot put them into words. As Dale puts it, "His intercession for us—so intimately does He share all the evils of our condition—is a kind of *agony.*"

2. *The understanding of the Father* is seen in 27a. Though *we* are not able to frame in words the Spirit's intercession, yet we are assured that God the Father understands. In other words, we do not have to be able to frame perfectly the prayers we know are needed, especially when our human ignorance prevents our understanding as to what is needed. But the Father, who searches our hearts, where the Spirit lives and from which place He intercedes, understands the mind of the Spirit. There is direct "mental telepathy," we might say, from the Spirit within us to the Father in Heaven, even when we are not enabled to put our prayers in words.

3. *The perfection of the Spirit's intercession* is indicated in 27b and is given as the reason for the successful presentation of this intercession to the Father: This intercession is in perfect harmony with God's will. This perfection is possible only because He *is* God and has perfect knowledge of God's will. Such prayer would never be possible from us, because we can never—in our presently limited conditions—have perfect knowledge of His will. And so James reminds us: "Ye ought to say, If the Lord will, we shall live, and do this, or that" (James 4:15). Even our Lord set such an example in prayer (Matthew 26:42). But though our prayers can never ask perfectly for God's will (except by an expression of surrender to His undiscerned will), we can be reassured by the knowledge that there comes from the Spirit who lives in our hearts such perfect prayers.

21 The Present Security of the Believer

Study Text: Romans 8:28-39

Introduction
1. God's Purpose for the Believer (Romans 8:28-30)
   a. A Present Good (verse 28)
   b. A Promised Goal (verses 29, 30)
2. God's Providence toward the Believer (Romans 8:31-34)
   a. The Believer's Safety (verse 31)
   b. The Believer's Supply (verse 32)
   c. The Believer's Standing (verses 33, 34)
3. God's Protection of the Believer (Romans 8:35-39)
   a. A Question Asked (verses 35, 36)
   b. A Question Answered (verses 35-39)

INTRODUCTION

The previous lesson closed with verse 27 where we were told that the Spirit's unspeakable intercession, which comes from our hearts, is in perfect accord with the will of God. Paul now moves logically to speak in greater detail about God's will for us and our relationship to that will.

Up to now chapter eight has spoken in detail of the believer's new relationship to the Spirit of God. The last part of the chapter, which we cover in this lesson, follows logically: our new relationship to the plan of God, the purpose of God, the will of God, and the providence of God—all these are ways of saying the same thing.

But there is still one more way of saying this, using the word Paul uses in verse 39: the *love* of God. God's providential purpose for our lives is always an expression of His love. His plan, His will, is formed by His love. The believer, justified by that faith, finds himself an object of that love. He finds that God has a purpose for him and that the providence of God is working things toward the accomplishment of that purpose. In such an understanding there is a sense of great safety and security: If God be for us, who can be against us?

163

EXPOSITION

As will be shown in the general study-outline, this is the final lesson (of four) on chapter eight. It is entitled "The Present Security of the Believer" and covers 8:28-39. As already noted, the emphasis in this lesson is on the believer's new relationship to the love of God as manifested in His purpose and providence toward us. Such love, such purpose, and such providence teach the believer that he is safe in that place. You are aware that some Christians teach a doctrine commonly called "the eternal security of the believer." That is not the Biblical teaching. The Bible teaches a *present* security of the believer, a safety he experiences now and so long as he continues to exercise saving faith. That "security" is not unconditionally guaranteed nor does it violate the individual's moral freedom—even after conversion—to serve or reject God. But the Christian finds great comfort in knowing that he is safe from the devil's clutches or power so long as he continues to want to serve God and manifests that desire in saving faith. Such truths as these ought to become clearer as the lesson develops.

1. GOD'S PURPOSE FOR THE BELIEVER
(Romans 8:28-30)

The key word in these verses is found in verse 28: "purpose." The love of God toward the believer is specifically expressed in a benevolent, gracious plan for the believer. The sinner could not say this; he could not be involved in the wonderful truths of these three verses. The child of God can. This is one of the new relationships of the person justified by faith.

A Present Good (verse 28). This is a famous and favorite verse, and rightly so. Its declarations are marvelous indeed. Here we are told that the purpose of God lies behind a present, practical, daily outworking of good in the lives and circumstances of believers. Three often-used questions can be used to help us plumb these inviting depths.

1. Who? Some people misunderstand this verse and mistakenly think that only some Christians are included in the facts stated here. Who is included? The verse says "them that love God." You must realize that this phrase is meant to include *all* believers. There is no such thing as a Christian who does not love God. The verse does not mean to limit the truths expressed here to some select group of Christians, special servants of God. No, "them that love God" is just another way of saying "Christians." (The same was true, you recall, of "them . . . who walk not after the flesh, but after the Spirit" in verse 1 of this same chapter. It would be interesting to make a collection of all the phrases used in the Bible to characterize Christians.)

2. *What?* The verse states a fact that is true about "them that love God." What is promised them? Here it is: "All things work together for good" to these believers. The verb "work together" will be more meaningful to you if you read it in continuing action, as it was no doubt intended: "All things are working together unto good." All the continuing, daily circumstances and events of a believer's life are involved here.

Some New Testament Greek manuscripts read these words this way: "God is working together all things for good." That reading was not original, but it certainly expresses the correct idea. All things do not work together for good according to some blind fate or accidental happenstance. The verse is simply telling us that God is in control of the circumstances of a believer's life, and that He guides all these circumstances so that they work in harmony toward the good God intends for us to experience. On the one hand, it may take a great deal of faith to rely on that truth, especially when a young Christian must experience difficult and trying circumstances beyond his understanding. The longer we serve Him and the more we see Him at work in such happenings, the easier it becomes for us to relax and trust His hand.

3. *Why?* The last part of verse 28 tells us the basis for this truth: God's *purpose* for us is, in fact, the "good" that He works all things toward. God's plan for us lies behind His providential control of the circumstances of our lives.

We need to link this first verse of this lesson with the previous lesson and with verse 27 which closed that lesson. You will remember that verses 26, 27 described the "unspeakable" intercession which is carried on for us and from our hearts by the Holy Spirit. At the very end of that Paul assured us that the Holy Spirit's intercession for us is "according to the will of God." This will is identical with the purpose here mentioned. Here is part of the explanation how God providentially controls all the circumstances of our lives toward the working out of His "good" purpose for us: From our hearts there always come the perfect prayers of the Spirit that are in perfect accord with that will and purpose. God hears Him pray and reckons that prayer ours that His plan will be perfectly worked out in us all the time.

Note too that the phrase "them who are called according to his purpose" is also a description of *all* Christians. The "call" referred to here (as will become clearer in verse 30) is not a call to special service, as to the ministry or mission field. This is the "call" to God's final purpose and goal for the believer. Every Christian has been called to that purpose, and God providentially directs the events of a believer's life toward the accomplishing of that purpose. This does not mean we should sit down and do nothing toward spiritual development, of course. It does mean that we can rest assured that the circumstances and events of our lives cannot stop us, if we do not wish it so, from achieving the spiritual goals God has for us. What security there is in such knowledge! What comfort and encouragement there is here, even when we are faced with "tragedy" and difficulty! Just remember that there are no real "accidents" in the believer's life!

A Promised Goal (verses 29, 30). These verses speak specifically of the good purpose God has for us, presenting that purpose as an ultimate goal toward which our spiritual development is headed. The nature of that goal is indicated, as are the basic steps involved in reaching toward that goal.

1. God's *ultimate goal* to be reached in the believer's life is emphasized in verse 29. Again, we can break this verse up into its essential parts by considering the who, the what, and the how.

The *who* is seen here: "[those] whom he did foreknow." As with the two phrases in verse 28, this includes all believers. In fact, that is exactly what the words mean: Those whom God foresaw would put faith in Christ and be saved. For these God set a purpose. To "foreknow" means to know in advance. God foreknows all things perfectly. But His advance knowledge of an event does not *cause* that event any more than our after knowledge causes the things we know. He knew from before the foundation of the earth who would put faith in Him, and He determined to do certain things for them.

The *what* is found in these words: "He also did predestinate [them] to be conformed to the image of his Son." This is the ultimate goal toward which the believer's spiritual development is headed: conformity to the image of Jesus himself. God's plan is that the believer develop finally into the likeness of Jesus Christ. This does not mean that we shall become gods as He is God. But we shall "be like him" when He returns (1 John 3:2) and thus "bear the image of the heavenly [one]" (1 Corinthians 15:49).

What exactly does Paul mean by these words? Is he speaking of spiritual or bodily conformity? Both! We will partake of His holy character and of the kind of glorified body He possesses. Both sides are essential to the full "manifestation of the sons of God" already spoken of in verse 19.

We need not be upset by the word "predestinated" here. This verse is not telling us that God predestinated some to believe and others to reject Christ. The Bible never speaks of man's faith or rejection of God in any terms except those that speak clearly of man's freedom to choose and responsibility for his choice. No, what we are told in verse 29 is that God has predestinated a certain goal, a certain ultimate glorification *for those who believe.* "Predestinated" is not all that special a word, anyway. All it means is foreordained, preplanned. The verse is telling us that God's plan for the believer is not a new thing or an accident. Before man was ever made God

166

foresaw that sin would come. He also foresaw that some would put their faith in Him for redemption from that sin. In eternity, He made His plan and settled His purpose for those who would believe. He determined even then to bring the believers to a final glorification in which they would be conformed to the image of His Son.

Thus man's freedom is quite real. He can get in on that plan or resist it. Indeed, even after conversion man still has such moral freedom. But those who persist in saving faith can rest assured that God has planned for them from all eternity to partake of this final glorification. Such is the foreordained destiny of the faithful.

The *why* of this pre-determined goal is also seen in this verse: "that he [Jesus] might be the first born among many brethren." In other words, God has planned to bring all true, persevering believers into conformity to the image of His one Son so that that Son would have many brethren to share with Him the position of perfect sonship to the Father. Compare again verse 17. Denney adds: "The idea of Christ's dignity as firstborn among many brethren who all owe their salvation to Him is sublimely interpreted in Hebrews 2:10-13."

2. *The chief steps of salvation* are listed in verse 30, as working together toward that final goal. Four stages are indicated here. First is the "predestination," looking back (as explained above) to God's plan made before the foundation of the world.

Second is the "call." Of course the gospel call goes out to all men. But Paul is thinking especially about the truly saved here. Only in the hearts of those who respond in faith is the gospel call truly effective. This call includes the preaching of the gospel, with its invitation to "whosoever will," and the convicting work of the Holy Spirit, the "drawing" Jesus spoke of in John 6:44. God must always take the initiative in man's salvation.

Third is justification. We have spoken of this gracious act of God much in our study of Romans. When the individual puts faith in Christ in response to the gospel call, then he is declared innocent before Heaven's bar of justice. He stands righteous before God, justified by faith.

Finally will come glorification. Paul is thinking of the future, final glorification that has been on his mind in the earlier parts of this chapter (verses 18-25, especially). But he speaks of this future glorification in past tense because he regards it as an already accomplished fact. When God says something will be so, it is as good as already so, and God's goal is to bring persevering believers into perfect conformity—body and spirit—to the image of His Son. Consider it done! The believer can rest in this secure confidence.

2. GOD'S PROVIDENCE TOWARD THE BELIEVER
(Romans 8:31-34)

Verse 28 has already indicated that God is working all things together for good to the believer. That truth involves the *providence* of God, a doctrine that simply means God is in control of affairs. Indeed, providence is "God, conceived of as guiding men through his prescience, loving care, or intervention" (Webster). Verses 31-34 bring us back to that doctrine to consider some of the comforting implications thereof. Keep in mind that God's providential control of the circumstances of a believer's life is primarily a manifestation of His love.

The Believer's Safety (verse 31). The providence of God assures the believer that he does not have anything to fear from men or circumstances antagonistic toward him.

1. A question is raised in 31a. "These things" look back to the facts indicated in verses 28-30, namely that God has an ultimate plan for the believer and controls the circumstances of his life toward that goal. The question asks what we shall say in reference to these truths. What are the implications of the doctrine of God's purpose and providence for the believer? These implications will be indicated in the following words.

2. The answer indicates the first implication: God is "for" us and therefore we have assurance of His providential love. We consequently have nothing to fear from any opposing circumstances or antagonists. The fact that God is for us means exactly what verse 28 has already affirmed. Well, then, since He has a plan and guides all things toward the accomplishing of that plan, we need not fear. We are safe from all opponents. God is all-powerful; no enemy of ours is, not even Satan himself. No force in the universe—including evil—can operate without God's permission. Even Satan is limited to acting as God wills to permit him. Thus God will permit no circumstances to occur in our lives except those that will work helpfully toward the accomplishment of the goal God has for us. Indeed who can be against us? No one!

The Believer's Supply (verse 32). Now we have another implication of the doctrine of providence: God will give us everything we need.

1. The basis and evidence of our confidence is indicated first: God has given His Son for us. The point of Paul is that this is the *supreme* gift of love. The greatest act of love ever conceived was done when God gave His Son to bear our sins and rescue us from Hell. That God "spared not" His Son means He withheld not even this unimaginable gift. That He "delivered him up" means He permitted Him to become the sin-bearer, to die for our sins.

2. The assurance gained from this act is then indicated: If God has given so great a gift for us, we need not doubt He will give everything else we need. Nothing else, in fact, will be so startling as the sacrifice of His Son. God will supply all we need for the fulfilment of the ultimate good goal He has for us. Should we fail to achieve that goal, it will be through no lack of divine provision for every need.

What does the "all things" include? Everything we need, whether material or spiritual. Philippians 4:19 may speak primarily of material needs. Second Peter 1:3 speaks primarily of spiritual provision: God has freely given everything needed to maintain spiritual life and godliness, to move in steady progress toward the perfection of spiritual maturity.

The Believer's Standing (verses 33, 34). Now a third implication of the doctrine of God's providential love for us is indicated. Not only will God—on our side—deliver us from all enemies, and not only will God give us everything we need, especially for spiritual development; but God will resist all efforts to bring us under condemnation, and thus rob us of the justified standing we have found by faith.

1. The declaration of God is behind our standing, as seen in verse 33. God is the one who has justified us. We have stood before the bar of Heaven and been declared innocent of guilt or wrong by the omnipotent Judge of the universe. That is the doctrine of justification that has been so clearly outlined in the earlier chapters of Romans.

We may be sure there are those who yet would like to reverse the verdict of God. Indeed, Satan himself is unanimously depicted in the Bible as the "accuser of our brethren" (Revelation 12:10). The Book of Job is an excellent illustration of Satan's efforts to overthrow the justification of men by Heaven. But we need have no fear that Satan or anyone else can lodge any charge against us that will hold up in court. God has already declared us innocent! The word "elect," by the way, emphasizes the gracious selection God has made. Salvation is not of ourselves, but by His choice. He has chosen all who put faith in Jesus.

2. The work of Christ is also behind our righteous standing with the Father. Note that three aspects of His work are mentioned: His death for our sins, His resurrection, and His exaltation to the right hand of God where He intercedes in our behalf. Compare Hebrews 7:25, where especially His intercession is seen as the guarantee of our salvation standing.

Consider then that all our antagonists have no chance of bringing us again into condemnation. Should Satan hurl any charge against us to God, the death, resurrection, and intercession of Christ himself will answer for us. He died to bear all our sins and pay the full penalty demanded because of our guilt. He rose to declare our justification. He represents us as our Advocate at the Father's hand. Can Satan prosecute us successfully when God's own Son directs the defense? Again we are given confidence about the secure standing we have in Christ with God so long as our present faith continues.

169

3. GOD'S PROTECTION OF THE BELIEVER
(Romans 8:35-39)

And now we come to the final verses of this chapter. They do not introduce new thoughts so much as restate the ones already presented in verses 28-34. That restatement expresses our confidence that God is our Protector, that believers are safe from all opposing forces in Him. That confidence is expressed poetically; the verses are much like a song.

A Question Asked (verses 35, 36). These two verses introduce a very real and important question. The previous verses have answered us that God is on our side, that God has justified us, that God has a glorious goal for us, that He controls the circumstances of our lives for that good goal. Well, then, so far so good; but Paul knows that adverse circumstances do come our way, that we do suffer. What about this?

1. *The form of the question* in 35a does not ask why or whether we must endure affliction, but whether such afflicters can succeed in coming between us and the loving protection of God. Can any of our antagonists—Satan included—take us from the effective working (verse 28) of that love?

2. *The types of affliction we may endure* are suggested by the partial list in 35b. Be assured this verse means we *are* subject to such. Paul himself had experienced all of them in abundance! (See 2 Corinthians 11:23-27, for example.) "Tribulation" is pressure, oppression, especially as imposed by opponents. "Distress" is, literally, to be without a place, or in a narrow place: not knowing where to turn, hindered, confined, and limited by opposition. "Persecution" is pursuit, relentless opposition. "Famine" and "nakedness" are being without proper food and clothing. "Peril" is danger, threatening men or circumstances. "Sword" is the threat of execution for the cause of Christ.

3. *A Scripture confirming the certainty of affliction* is cited in verse 36. The verse is Psalm 44:22. There the psalmist had wondered why God permits his faithful servants to undergo such difficulties. Paul knows we must, if we are in fact faithful to God ("for thy sake"). "We are killed all the day long" means the same thing as "I die daily" (1 Corinthians 15:31) and "in deaths oft" (2 Corinthians 11:23). It means that Paul—and others—are continuously in actual jeopardy of life for the cause of Christ, like sheep scheduled for the slaughter. Does such affliction mean that the servant of God has, in fact, been removed from the loving protection of God?

A Question Answered (verses 37-39). With ringing assurance Paul affirms that the answer is "No." No force outside the believer can threaten him, can remove him from the loving, providential protection of Christ and God.

1. *Assurance of victory* is expressed in verse 37. "All these

things" looks back to the various kinds of affliction listed in verse 35. In all such circumstances, the believer can be "more than conqueror." As Denney expresses the meaning of this, "These trials not only do not cut us off from Christ's love, they actually give us more intimate and thrilling experiences of it."

Note the method of this abundant victory: "through him that loved us." Specifically referred to is the love manifested in Christ's death. Our victory comes only as we allow His victory to become our experience. Compare Philippians 4:13.

2. Assurance of abiding in God's love is expressed in verses 38, 39. Paul's "persuasion" is confidence, assurance. The list of antagonists given here is intended to restate—though more completely—the list in verse 35. Not only will *those* affections not separate us from God's love, none will! Death may be the threat of death; life, the offer of life or "the pride of life" (1 John 2:16). Angels, principalities, and powers stand for the various orders and ranks of angelic beings, especially here the wicked ones who are our supernatural enemies (compare Ephesians 6:11, 12). Things present and things to come include any existing or potentially threatening circumstances. Height and depth look to anything that exists above or beneath us. "Any other creature" means exactly that: anything else; but this serves to remind us that all our enemies are, after all, creatures of God and subject to His control. All the more reason they must fail to come between us and the loving protection of God manifested in our behalf for Christ's sake and by reason of His redemptive work. From every point of view then the providential love of God reassures us of our safety as believers.

One final word. Those who teach the doctrine called "eternal security" (that believers can never fall away from grace) make use of this passage. They overlook the fact that Paul is referring to all the host of enemies arrayed against the believer's soul. None of those enemies can overthrow us. But our secure place in God's hand depends on the maintenance of saving faith. Our freedom is not taken away. Still, the verses speak volumes of comfort and confidence to us *as believers*, and based on these verses we can put away our fears. God's love is powerful and His providence in perfect control of all the circumstances of our lives. He will not permit the enemies of our soul to separate us from that love.

22 God Ignores Flesh

Study Text: Romans 9:1-13

Introduction
1. A Concern that Includes the Fleshly Israel (Romans 9:1-5)
   a. A Weighty Passion (verses 1-3)
   b. Wasted Privileges (verses 4, 5)
2. A Choice that Ignores the Fleshly Israel (Roman 9:6-13)
   a. The Rejection of the Physical (verses 6-8a)
   b. The Requirement of the Promise (verses 8b-13)

INTRODUCTION

We enter now the fourth great section of the Book of Romans. First we saw the universal *need* for righteousness (1:18—3:20). Second we saw the divine *provision* for righteousness: justification by faith (3:21—4:25). Third we saw the meaning of the experience of righteousness (5:1—8:39). Now Paul turns to an especially vexing subject, the *Jewish rejection* of the righteousness of God (chapters 9-11).

This particular subject comes up in a very natural way in Romans. The Jews had their own ideas how to be right with God. The observance of the Mosaic Law was the essence of their "method." But Paul, in order to prove his gospel teaching that righteousness is by faith, has had to show that the Jewish understanding was wrong. So, in earlier chapters, he has made clear that justification was never by law (3:20) and that Jews need salvation by faith in Christ as much so as Gentiles (3:9).

The only method, then, of being right with God for *anyone*— Jew or Gentile—is by faith in Jesus Christ. But the Jews, as a whole, have rejected Jesus Christ as Messiah, Savior, and Lord. What

172

happens then to Israel? What shall we say about all the promises God had made to the Jews? Such natural questions as these are behind these three chapters. In essence, Paul shows that the Jews have failed to achieve the righteousness of God because they have tried to substitute their own self-righteous works. This is the reason we have entitled Part 4: "The Righteousness of God: A Prohibition to the Self-Righteous."

EXPOSITION

A key verse of these entire three chapters (9-11) could well be 9:14: "Is there unrighteousness with God?" The basic purpose of these chapters seem to be to answer that question, to show that God is righteous (just) even in His relationship to the rejected Jews. These chapters defend God, as it were, in His actions toward Israel. Especially is this true of chapter nine. You will see, by checking the general study-outline in the back of this book, that we will have three lessons on chapter nine. The whole chapter is subsection A under Part 4, dealing with "Israel's Rejection and the Divine Propriety" (properness, rightness). This first lesson from chapter nine covers verses 1-13 and is entitled, "God Ignores Flesh."

1. A CONCERN THAT INCLUDES THE FLESHLY ISRAEL
(Romans 9:1-5)

Paul introduces this part of Romans with a personal reference. He has a burden for his "kinsmen according to the flesh" in spite of the fact that they have rejected God and He, them (the two sides of this cannot be separated). He would like to see them saved, and he wants that fact to be clearly understood even though he is going to have to say some frank things about Israel's unbelief and responsibility for her rejected place.

A Weighty Passion (verses 1-3). The Jews are Paul's own countrymen, his own people. The burden he feels over their rejection of Messiah and destiny is natural. The expression he gives to that burden here is a moving one and a challenge to us all about our lack of concern for the lost.

1. The truthfulness of his expression is affirmed in verse 1. Three times Paul says this for emphasis: (1) I say the truth, (2) I lie not, (3) my conscience bearing me witness. To the first of these he adds "in Christ," which "means that he speaks in fellowship with Christ, so that falsehood is impossible" (Denney). "My conscience bearing testimony with me in the Holy Spirit" (literal translation) means that Paul is sure the Holy Spirit has stirred his conscience to

recognize that what follows is indeed a truthful expression of his feelings.

2. The nature of his concern is clarified in verse 2. "Great heaviness" means great grief. "Continual sorrow" refers to uninterrupted pain. The pangs of grief Paul feels for Israel weigh heavily on him. He is never free from that burden. Weiss calls attention to the triple intensity indicated here: from "heaviness" to "sorrow," "from great" to "continual," from "I" to "my heart." We cannot miss the keenness thus shown.

3. The extent of his feeling is expressed in a startling way in verse 3. The expression does not quite mean "I *do* desire to be cursed from Christ for Israel's sake," else that could have been easily said. Paul means he could wish this curse on himself if it would be helpful and right to do so. But let us not soften the words too much. Paul's feelings are deep and self-sacrificing: He *could* go to Hell for his racial brethren were that possible!

Appropriate comparison has often been made with the emotionally-charged words of Moses: "If thou wilt forgive their sin—and if not, blot me, I pray thee, out of thy book" (Exodus 32:32). Some have said that it must be left to men of the stature of Moses and Paul to offer such "reckless" prayers. Perhaps. But all of us ought to be moved by such examples to a deeper commitment to the lost, to such sacrificing of selfish interests as *can* effectively be made for their rescue.

Wasted Privileges (verses 4, 5). Paul's feelings of compassion for the Jewish nation are heightened by his recall of their former prominence and blessings at the hand of God. Those who have stood so high in the service of God have now rejected God's Son and the righteousness offered by that Son. Thus the tragedy of their present lost condition is compounded by an awareness of their former privileges and standing as a nation. The several words and phrases in these two verses are but a list of various elements of Israel's former blessedness.

1. Israelites. The name recalls their descent from Jacob, specially renamed Israel, "prince with God" (Genesis 32:28). This name, then, speaks especially of their relationship to God, their spiritual prerogatives.

2. The adoption. "Pertaineth" (supplied) is not needed: "whose is the adoption" would be adequate. This refers to Israel's special, former position as God's "son" (Exodus 4:22). Remember that the Greek word for "adoption" literally means "son-placing" or position of sonship.

3. The glory. This probably looks back to the visible "glory" formerly displayed in the tabernacle-temple "holy of holies," the "Shekinah" glory (cf., Hebrews 9:5 and Exodus 40:34).

4. The covenants. These are the marvelous pacts and promises God made with the key figures in the Israelite heritage: men like

174

Abraham (Genesis 12:1-3), Jacob (Genesis 28:1-4), and David (2 Samuel 7:8-16).

5. *The giving of the law.* This was the greatest "covenant" of all, made with the whole nation, at Sinai. Note Exodus 19:3-8 in particular, words which immediately preceded the law itself in Exodus 20.

6. *The service.* This looks back to the priestly ministry and tabernacle-temple worship system, including all the rituals, ceremonies, and sacrifices involved.

7. *The promises.* The Old Testament was filled with promises to the chosen people, and each stage was the fulfilment of earlier promises. All are included here, like that which promised to make of Abraham's loins a great physical nation—a promise already fulfilled. Any yet unfulfilled are also included. But especially in Paul's mind here were, probably, the messianic promises.

8. *The father.* These are the hero-patriarchs, especially Abraham, Moses, and David. The Jews took pride in these "fathers" (note John 8:39), and indeed they were blessed to have the leadership of great men of God.

9. *The Christ. Christos* is merely the Greek translation of the Hebrew word that means "the anointed one," the *Messiah*. Messiah was scheduled to come, in the flesh, of Jewish descent. That was the greatest privilege of all, the supreme blessing accorded the nation of Israel. Note, by the way, that three things are said of Christ: He is (1) "over all," (2) "God," and (3) "blessed forever." These expressions testify to His deity, His lordship, and His right to eternal praise.

The recitation of these great blessings of the Jewish people causes one to ask, can such a blessed people now be rejected from divine favor? As incredible as that is, it is true. And Paul is going to explain exactly how such rejection accords with God's justice. That is what the rest of this lesson—and indeed all of chapters 9-11—is about.

2. A CHOICE THAT IGNORES THE FLESHLY ISRAEL
(Romans 9:6-13)

In these chapters Paul will present several factors that prove God is just in rejecting Israel. The verses before us now for study in the remainder of this lesson present *one* of those factors. In essence, Paul's point is this: God's choice of men to bear His name has never been and never will be based on considerations of a fleshly nature. That is an important principle. That principle only *seems* to have been violated by God's choice of the Jews by physical descent. In truth, as Paul is about to show, the principle was *not* violated. Physical descent was not the basis of this selection, even in Old Testament times.

The Rejection of the Physical (verses 6-8a). These verses tell us clearly that even the selection of Israel to God's favor was not based on fleshly, physical descent. Paul's proof of this point is quite interesting.

1. *God's word is effective apart from considerations of fleshly descent.* This is indicated in 6a. What Paul means probably is that his indications about Israel's "lostness" (verses 1-3) should not be taken to imply that *no* fleshly Israelites are saved. Indeed, some are, but not merely because they are Israelites according to the flesh.

2. *The true Israel is not fleshly Israel.* This is what 6b means. The first "Israel" uses the word in its truest sense, with all the scriptural implications proper to the people of God. The second "Israel" uses the word in its basic racial sense, physically descended from Jacob (Israel). In other words, not all those descended from the original Israel are truly Israelites in the fullest sense.

3. *Not all Abraham's descendants were chosen.* This point, made in verse 7, is a specific instance and illustration of the truth just stated in 6b. The point here is that Abraham had two sons, physical descendants, Ishmael and Isaac (and several others, as in Genesis 25:2). But not all Abraham's physical descendants were chosen, only Isaac. The quotation here is from Genesis 21:12.

The point is clear from the illustration. Another illustration will be given below (concerning Jacob and Esau). God's choice of people for His blessing and name is not based on fleshly descent.

4. *The children of God are not chosen by fleshly descent.* This summary of the truth is contained in verse 8a. Paul's wording of it is such as to show this is a universal, timeless principle. Never has it been so that God's children are chosen by physical relationships. Perhaps this is what John means in John 1:12, 13 when referring to the sons of God as those born "not of blood [lines]."

We must face up to the lesson taught here as we view the Old Testament situation. That persons were racially descended from Abraham or Isaac or Jacob did not entitle them to a place as children of God. Racially they (those from Jacob, at least) were of "the chosen people." But spiritually they were not necessarily of the ones chosen for the true family of God. Only those of national Israel who put saving faith in God were also of His spiritual family. We cannot do more than guess what percentage of physical Israel was also in the true, spiritual Israel. There is no reason to think they were in the majority!

Why has Paul told us this? To make it plain that God's present rejection of the Jews is neither surprising nor in violation of any of God's principles. God owes the fleshly Israel nothing on that basis. He has never dealt with men on that basis anyway.

The Requirement of the Promise (verses 8b-13). If God's selections are not based on physical considerations, then what *are* they based on? The answer is to be found in His gracious promise.

1. The principle of promise is stated in 8b as a direct opposite to the principle of physical descent. "Promise" here represents a gracious work of God, done for man not because man deserves or earns (or inherits physically) something from God, but because God has simply said (cf., "word" in verse 6) He would do it.

Remember that in 4:13-16 Paul has contrasted "promise" with works and law-keeping. What one gets by works is owed him (4:4). If one inherits by law-keeping, faith and promise have no place (4:14). But if God's blessings are of grace (undeserved and unearned favor), then the promise is the foundation of the blessings (4:16). Those same ideas are involved here. None become children of God by racial descent or by works. God's only children are those He graciously chooses in fulfilment of His gracious promises to call out a people for His name.

2. The illustration of promise by Isaac is recalled in verse 9. Paul has already dealt with this particular illustration in chapter four. He did so at length in Galatians 4:22-31, where also the concept of "promise" is prominent (Galatians 4:23, 28). The point is that God deliberately waited until after Abraham and Sarah were past the age of child bearing. Then He fulfilled His promise by miracle so that it would be clear *He* had worked, not they. Only so could it be clear that the work was done by God and by gracious promise. They did not deserve or earn the favor: God graciously kept His word and chose to give them a son of His own choice, other sons were to be rejected. Thus the physical, the fleshly, the human will had nothing to do with this gracious work of God.

3. The illustration of promise by Jacob is recalled in verses 10-13. "Not only this" means that here is a further clear illustration of the principle of promise as opposed to fleshly descent. In summary, here are the facts. When Rebecca had conceived by Isaac, twins were in her womb (verse 10). Before they were born (verse 11) God indicated His choice of Jacob over Esau (verses 12, 13). Thus again is made clear the fact that God deals not with men on the basis of fleshly descent, else both Jacob and Esau would have received equal blessings. But, in fact, another physical descendant (like Ishmael, verse 7) was rejected. Again, then, is reinforced the lesson of the whole passage, that fleshly descent places no special claims on God for His favor, not even where the Jews are concerned.

Some of the theological implications of verses 10-13 must be given closer attention. As already noted, the main lesson is clear: Only children of *promise* are chosen seed, not necessarily the fleshly descendants of Abraham. But the intricate details of the illustration are too interesting to overlook.

The point is that God did make a choice in the matter of the twins Jacob and Esau. Note the *time* of that choice: before they were even born (10, 11a). Note the *basis* of that choice: God's own purpose, not their deeds (11b). Note the *results* of that choice: The natural order was reversed and the younger (Jacob) was chosen over the elder (Esau). Two problems in particular arise from these basic facts, as follows.

First, there is the problem of the words "loved" and "hated." We would hear no objections to the first, but the second raises questions. Did God hate Esau? And hate him even before his birth? When Esau was an innocent fetus? The answer is yes, as the record specifically says in verse 13, quoting from Malachi 1:2, 3. The correct understanding of these words will help us: They mean, at heart, *choice* and *rejection*. The Greek words used here do not express emotion so much as action. We are not being told that God *felt* love and hate in the human sense so much as that He chose one and rejected the other. He committed himself to Jacob (love), and withheld that commitment from Esau (hate). We could probably get a more accurate picture of the verse by reading: "Jacob have I chosen, but Esau have I rejected." That is what is always involved when one chooses between two.

The second problem follows the first and is more important: It is the problem of predestination. Those who believe in God's unconditional, arbitary predestination of all things like to use these verses. Understandably so, since the verses seem to suggest at first glance that God's choice between Jacob and Esau was entirely arbitrary and capricious.

But let us not stop with that "first glance." A closer investigation will show that God's preselection of Jacob over Esau can *not* be used to substantiate Calvinistic doctrine about predestination of the individual to Heaven or Hell. In the first place, the selection of Jacob referred to here was not so much a selection to *personal salvation*. Rather, this was "national" election. Jacob was being chosen as the heir of Isaac (and Abraham) through whom the promised national line would be continued. Not Jacob's eternal but his earthly destiny was primarily involved. We must be cautious about extending the illustration of Jacob's selection as Isaac's heir so as to apply it to personal salvation. After all, what Paul is illustrating is that physical descent was not the basis of the choice, even for "the chosen people."

In the second place, we must consider that even these verses, as startling as they are, do not tell us there was *nothing* about Jacob and Esau that conditioned God's choice. Paul only affirms that God's choice was *not* based on their *works* (the verb "done" in verse 11). This writer happens to believe that God chose Jacob and rejected Esau, even before their births, because He foresaw the difference in their attitudes toward spiritual things—their *faith in God*, no less.

If we must speak of personal salvation, let us remember that the Bible's unanimous declaration is that salvation is not by works. But, following that, the Bible does *not* say that salvation is by *nothing!* What the Bible *does* say is that salvation is *by faith!* As we look back on the Genesis account we recall easily the interest of Jacob in the birthright and spiritual things, along with Esau's flippant disregard of such considerations. Was that difference a *result* of God's selection of Jacob (as some would say), or was it in fact a manifestation of faith of Jacob which was the *cause* of God's preselection of him. The latter alternative is more in keeping with the Biblical picture, and there is really nothing in these verses to contradict such a view. This approach respects both God's sovereign right to choose whom He wills and man's moral freedom to believe or reject God.

What we have in verses 10-13 is a clear picture of the principles Paul is emphasizing. One of Isaac's sons was rejected, the other chosen (just as with Isaac himself and his brother Ishmael). That decision was not based on physical descent or fleshly works. That choice was by the gracious promise and purpose of God. All God's selections of people for His blessings are so based. This does not eliminate the requirement of faith; that condition is in perfect accord with the principle of promise as seen in Romans 4:13-16. Faith is not a work of merit and does not constitute an obligation. Faith is man's acceptance of God's sovereign and free offer of favor. This is what verse 11 means when it refers to "the purpose of God according to election." Election is selection, choice. God's purpose is a free choice of men. The verse continues by saying that the outcome of this is that the one who calls (God) will consequently get the glory and credit, not the man who works (cf., 4:4 again).

And so Paul has effectively given us his first line of argument explaining and defending God for rejecting unbelieving Israel. God never intended to choose men for His favor by racial, physical, fleshly descent. He always chooses by gracious promise. Consequently, the present rejection of Israel violates no principle of God's dealings but follows the same pattern clearly established in the rejection of Ishmael and Esau.

23 God's Inherent Freedom

Study Text: Romans 9:14-24

Introduction
1. God's Sovereign Power: Affirmation (Romans 9:14-18)
   a. Introduction (verse 14)
   b. Illustrations (verse 15, 17)
   c. Implications (verse 18)
2. God's Sovereign Power: Application (Romans 9:19-24)
   a. An Inquiry (verses 19, 20)
   b. An Illustration (verse 21)

INTRODUCTION

With the previous lesson we began a new section of Romans, Part 4, in which Paul deals with particular questions related to the Jews' situation. All of the teaching in Romans has insisted strongly on the idea that justification—being right with God—is by faith in Christ's work rather than by man's work. Righteousness does not depend on the keeping of the law.

The question, then, is this: Where does this leave the Jews? What about God's "chosen people"? The second and third chapters of Romans especially have made it clear that they are lost like all the rest of the races. The favor they once knew is no longer theirs. In a manner of speaking, God has turned from them.

Such is the fact that Paul deals with in this part of Romans. His main purpose is to make clear that the Jews as a whole are rejected and to explain exactly why. We can almost imagine someone asking Paul, "Has God done right in rejecting Israel?" (Compare 9:14, the first verse of this lesson.)

180

In essence then this section defends God's justice, explaining why He has rejected Israel from favor and that He has acted right in doing so. In the previous lesson we saw one of Paul's arguments in defense of God: namely, that God never has dealt with men on the basis of racial descent anyway. In today's lesson we see the second argument of Paul, based on the doctrine of God's sovereignty.

EXPOSITION

Check the gereral study-outline in the back of this book to keep the pattern of these lessons clearly in mind. There are three lessons on chapter 9 of Romans, all defending God's propriety (proper behavior) in rejecting Israel. This is the second of the three lessons, entitled "God's Inherent Freedom," covering 9:14-24.

1. GOD'S SOVEREIGN POWER: AFFIRMATION
(Romans 9:14-18)

The purpose of these verses is to make crystal clear the fact that God is an absolute sovereign. This word *sovereign(ty)* will be used frequently in this lesson, so we had better define it now. That God is a Sovereign Being means He is absolutely *free* to do as He pleases. That freedom is *inherent* within His own character. ("Inherent" means inborn, a part of His very nature.) God's sovereignty involves the idea that His actions come wholly from His own pleasure. His decisions are made entirely on the basis of His own will. His freedom to act as He wills is not limited or conditioned by any considerations outside himself. He is not under obligation to anyone or any principle except for His own character. Included in this sovereignty is the truth that He is omnipotent, so He is not limited by considerations of power either. He can do anything He wills to do. No other being in the universe—not man or angel or devil—is truly sovereign. To be sovereign in this truest sense is to be God.

Introduction (verse 14). This veres introduces the section by raising the basic question that lies behind this whole part of Romans. Paul has anticipated that some might accuse God of dealing unfairly with men because national Israel has now been rejected from favor. Or they might think Him unjust in having chosen Jacob over Esau—the illustration in verses 10-13 with which the previous lesson concluded.

So *the question* is: "Is there unrighteousness with God?" The word "unrighteousness," as used here, means not acting right in His dealings with men. Has God acted unjustly, unfairly in making choices like those referred to in verses 6-13? Was He doing wrong when He chose Isaac and rejected Ishmael? Did He wrong Esau when he rejected him and selected Jacob instead? Has God acted unrighteously in turning aside from the "chosen nation," Israel?

The answer is quickly affirmed, even without waiting for further proof. "God forbid" is an emphatic negative, meaning something like our "absolutely not!" or (as the younger generation puts it) "No way!" The point is clear: We *know* God has not acted wrongly, even if we can not always understand why He acts in the way He decides. The discussion above about sovereignty said God is not obligated to anything except His own character. But He *is* obligated to His own character. And His very character is right-eousness. We know then even before we start that God has not acted unrighteously in anything He has ever done. So, whether we can figure out exactly why He chose Isaac over Ishmael and Jacob over Esau, we are already sure He acted right in doing so. We are already positive God has acted righteously and justly in rejecting Israel.

Before moving on, let us anticipate briefly what Paul is about to tell us. He is not ready yet to indicate the *reasons* God has acted in certain ways. No, but he is going to insist on God's *right* to act any way He chooses. That right is the sovereignty we have spoken of. We cannot always figure out God's reasons. Sometimes we can; sometimes we cannot. It does not matter; God has a right to act as He pleases. That sovereign right cannot be argued. But one thing has already been made clear here in verse 14: God only has a right to act right! As we begin to explore God's sovereign power, His inherent freedom to do as He wills, we will keep this qualification in mind. Only remember that even this qualification comes from within His own character, not from anyone or anything outside Him.

Illustrations (verse 15, 17). Paul is ready now to illustrate God's sovereign right to act as He wills. He uses two illustrations, both chosen from Old Testament circumstances during the life of Moses.

1. God's words to Moses given in verse 15 are quoted from Exodus 33:19. The circumstances were these: While Moses was on the mountain, Israel had sinned and judgment had fallen. Now Moses was imploring God to restore the people to His favor and go with them again toward the land of promise. Moses' prayer is recorded in Exodus 33:12-16. God speaks, answering, in verses 17-19. And it is in this answer that God affirms the principle of His sovereign right and power to act according to His own pleasure and will. No man has a right to impose on God for His mercy. God owes mercy to none. The entire section in Exodus is a clear statement of the fact that any mercy shown by God to man is *by grace*, undeserved favor (note Exodus 33:13, 16, 19 in particular).

These particular words to Moses are significant then for two reasons. First, they state clearly the principle: God acts as He wills, completely free. He shows mercy and compassion to whomever He chooses. His sovereign right to do this cannot be gainsaid. Second, these words are significant for Paul's context in Romans, dealing as he is with the matter of Israel's rejection, because even in the Exodus context the words made clear that God was not showing mercy to all the race of Israel. Even in the wilderness, when we might think all the nation was automatically entitled to His favor, He said: "I will shew mercy on whom I will shew mercy." In other words, He wanted it clearly established that neither Moses nor Israel had any special claims on Him that took away His sovereign right to act as He chose. Nor will He show mercy to all of them, just because they were Israelites in the flesh. That is never the basis of His dealing with men, as we saw clearly in the previous lesson.

2. *God's words to Pharaoh* given in verse 17 are quoted from Exodus 9:16. We remember those circumstances well: Pharaoh had resisted the efforts of Moses to get the Israelites released from Egypt. One plague followed another. With each, Pharaoh would appear to relent, but afterward he would harden his heart. The particular words quoted here from Exodus 9:16 came after the sixth plague, the boils.

What God said to Pharaoh, as recorded here in Romans 9:17, is quite strong, and we need not try to avoid the facts. Our understanding of these facts will increase as we go on farther, both in this lesson and the subsequent ones. For now, Paul wants to emphasize the fact that God acts according to His own will, with an inherent freedom that is not limited or conditioned by man's doings. So He boldly declares to Pharaoh: I raised you up for the very purpose that is being fulfilled in My dealings with you. My purpose was to display My power, in order that the fame of My name might be spread abroad.

God was as much as saying to Pharaoh: I am in control of these events. My purpose is being fulfilled. My sovereign power is behind all that is going on. Your stubborn resistance will not thwart My will. In fact, your resistance itself is in accord with My will, because this contest allows Me to give an even more impressive display of My power. God's sovereign control over earth's events was in no way threatened by Pharaoh's puny resistance. Indeed, God had an unquestioned right to bring Pharaoh to the throne at that particular time so that by his evil resistance God's power would be all the more clearly demonstrated and declared.

Implications (verses 16, 18). The implications of each illustration are briefly stated in verses 16 and 18, both of which say about the same thing. The implications are two, and these are closely related.

1. *God shows mercy to whom He pleases and hardens whom He pleases.* Verses 18 and 16b indicate this. More about this will be given in the following discussion, but for now we must not resist the basic principle so clearly stated. When God shows mercy to a particular person (like Moses and the Israelites He forgave in Exodus

33), He does so in keeping with His sovereign right to act as He wills. He is gracious, compassionate, and merciful toward whomever He wishes. Likewise, whenever He withholds His gracious influence from a man and thus hardens his heart (like Pharaoh), He does so in keeping with His sovereign right to act as He wills. He rejects from His favor whoever He wishes. His own free, good (and righteous) pleasure is the basis, within Him, for choosing to bless some and reject others.

2. *The mercy shown some is not by their own character.* Verse 16a indicates this. The "him" here is the one shown mercy. The word "willeth" refers to the man's resolve, his *disposition.* "Runneth" refers to the man's behavior, his *deeds,* his daily conduct in the course of life. Paul is quite clear: When God determines to show mercy to particular individuals, it is not because there was an inclination about them that was different from others. Nor was their behavior any more righteous than others. Conversely, those whom God rejects from favor are no worse in will or conduct than others!

These words may be difficult to accept, at first. But a deeper examination will help us. First, we must remember that this conclusion has already been established earlier in Romans by Paul's insistence, in 3:22, 23: "There is no difference, for all have sinned." In other words, the fact that some are saved—shown mercy—and other lost—hardened—cannot be based on a difference among men. All men are alike sinful in will and ways. Romans 3:9-20 made it plain that all are depraved and wicked, evilly inclined in their very natures. In essence, none are worse than others or better than others. That God has shown mercy to some and hardened some, therefore, cannot be based on supposed differences in the men's character. Consequently, the showing of mercy must be by God's sovereign right, by His will not man's will. You may object that there is surely a difference in the lives of sinners and Christians, of course. But that difference comes *after* they are saved, *after* God has "shown mercy," not before.

Second, remember that this is the very question that involved the Jews. They insisted they had a claim on God's favor because of their efforts at law-keeping. Paul has already proved this wrong (chapter 2). Thus the point Paul is making here in chapter 9 has particular significance in the discussion of the rejection of Israel, even if Israel claims to have earned His favor by keeping His law. No one ever earns God's favor. All are sinners. He owes mercy to none. Not even Israel has any claim on Him by conduct or character. God's mercy to men is not shown by reason of their character, for none have the kind of character that deserves mercy. (And if they did, it would not be mercy or grace, but debt! Do not forget Romans 4:4.)

True, the Calvinists use these verses to support a doctrine of absolute predestination. But, in truth, they are taking the verses too far. On the one hand, we are being told that God rules us in His

184

sovereign power as Creator and Lord of the universe as He pleases. He is merciful to whom He will and withholds mercy from whom He will. We, as His creatures, have no right nor power to question Him or resist His treatment of us.

But on the other hand, the verses do not go on and tell us *how* God pleases to deal with men. He has a right to choose whom He pleases and reject whom He pleases; that is so. He does not save some and reject others by any fleshly considerations or by their works; that is so. He saves whom He pleases and damns whom He pleases, and all alike are sinners. We *could* ask then this question: On whom *does* he please to show mercy? The answer would be, as we know it from elsewhere in the Scriptures and from earlier in this book: He pleases to deal with men on the basis of *faith*. He chooses freely and in sovereign power to save those who believe by Jesus Christ. But Paul is not ready for that point yet in the dimension here in chapter nine. He is first concerned to establish clearly that God is a Sovereign Being who inherently possesses the freedom to deal with men in anyway He pleases. We must first yield to that truth, and then we will not question His rejection of Israel even if we cannot figure out exactly why He did so.

2. GOD'S SOVEREIGN POWER: APPLICATION
(Romans 9:19-24)

The principles involved in God's sovereign right to deal with men as He pleases have been firmly laid down in the previous verses. Now we come to deal with the application of those principles in specific questions that men might raise. In particular, men might raise one very obvious question. They could read what Paul has just said about the sovereignty of God and react in a huff by asking: If it is all of God and He runs everything like He wants it, then whatever we do is His fault and He cannot complain, can He? Such a question attacks the justice of God, denies human responsibility, and puts the blame for sin on God. But still such questions are asked, and by them men often mean to ridicule the very doctrine of divine sovereignty.

An Inquiry (verses 19, 20). Actually the question is in verse 19 and an answer in verse 20. The question is (like many in Romans) an *anticipated* question, one Paul imagines some objector might ask. Indeed, it is a question that has been asked from time to time.

1. The question has two parts, as seen in verse 20. "Why doth he yet find fault?" The one who raises this question is simply implying that God has no basis or reason for blaming a man for anything he does if, as Paul has taught, everything is ordered by the will of God. If God has mercy on whom He will and hardens whom He will, then He cannot very well blame me, can he? That is what some would say, since Paul's teaching *appears* to remove human responsibility. (But—as we will see more clearly later—human responsibility is not really done away with by Paul's teaching.)

The other part of the question, "Who hath resisted His will," implies that God is responsible for everything we are and we could not be any different. That implication also is wrong and is based on a misunderstanding of the doctrine of sovereignty. But there have always been those who would like to use such a doctrine as an excuse to escape any personal responsibility or blame and blame God for everything.

2. *The answer* in verse 20 is not a direct one. It does not attempt to explain the reasons behind God's decisions. Indeed, the answer itself is in the form of two questions with obvious implications. "Who are thou that repliest against God?" means simply that no man has a right to talk back to God. "Shall the thing formed say to him that formed it, why hast thou made me thus?" The answer is "no": The creature has no right to question what the Creator does with him.

Note again that Paul is still not indicating where the true explanation of God's actions lies. He will do that later. For the time being, he wants us to realize that it really does not matter whether we can ever find such an explanation or not. God does not have to explain himself to us. The Sovereign Ruler owes nothing to His created subjects. What matters at this point in the discussion is that we must submit to His right to rule us according to His will.

An Illustration (verse 21). To strengthen his point, Paul uses the well-known illustration of the potter and clay. The lesson is quite obvious: A potter has a sovereign right over a piece of clay. He owes nothing to the clay. He can make it into any kind of vessel (container) he wishes.

A "vessel unto honour" is a container that will be used for something honorable, like a dish for eating or a pot for cooking or a vase for lovely flowers. A "vessel unto dishonour" is one that will be put to uses regarded as unattractive, like a garbage pail or trash can. (The same distinction applies in 2 Timothy 2:20, 21.) All Paul means is that a potter can make a lump of clay into a garbage pail or a cooking pot, as he suits his fancy. His right to do this as he chooses cannot be questioned.

The implications of this illustration, in so far as they relate to God's sovereignty over man, are obvious and will be clearly spelled out in the next three verses. Before passing on to those verses, though, let us remember that the illustration is especially appropriate for Paul's use in discussing the Jewish rejection. You will recall that Jeremiah used the potter in much the same way and particularly as an illustration of God's sovereign rule over Israel. See Jeremiah 18:1-6 and note particularly these words: "as seemed good to the potter." God has the right to make of us what seems good to Him.

The Implications (verses 22-24). The implied answers to the questions in verse 20 and the implications of the illustration of the potter (verse 21) are now clarified. There are two:

1. *The primary implication* indicated in verses 22, 23 is that God's sovereign power is rightfully displayed in both of the kinds of "vessels" He makes. Verse 22 deals with one kind of vessel, "vessels of wrath." These are the men for whom the wrath of God is their final destiny. Such men God endures in His long-suffering, but they are headed for Hell, "fitted for destruction." Verse 23 deals with the other kind of vessel, "vessels of mercy." These are the men on whom He has mercy. They are headed for Heaven, "prepared unto glory." In both groups, the sovereign power of God is displayed.

Once again, Paul does not say *how* some came to be chosen as one, and some the other, or even whether there was any reason. We know there *is* a how, a reason, a basis by which God decides for one against the other. But we know it from other Scriptures, not from here. What we have to know here is that God has a sovereign right to "make" both kinds of vessels "as He pleases." And what we have to know is that the purpose and power of God are manifested in *both* groups!

He does not desire for any to perish (2 Peter 3:9), but He wills to destroy some (as we know, those who reject Christ). And in such "vessels of wrath" His holy wrath against sin and awesome power are displayed—to His everlasting glory—when they go to Hell. Likewise He wills to save some (as we know, those who exercise saving faith). And His rich mercies are displayed—to His everlasting glory—when these go to Heaven. In this sense both groups display the sovereign will and glory of God. And neither group has any right to challenge the actions of the Sovereign who deals with men as He pleases.

2. *The secondary implication* is added on in verse 24. The point here is that the "vessels of mercy" will include both Jews and Gentiles, a point made frequently in Romans (as in 3:30, for example) and a point with special bearing on the context here in the ninth chapter. Remember that Paul is defending God's righteousness in rejecting national Israel from His favor. Well, his point here is that God's "calling," His selection of men as vessels of mercy, is not based on racial considerations.

In conclusion, let us make sure we understand what we have learned so far. We have learned that God deals with men *as He pleases*. His sovereignty assures Him the right to do so. But we have not learned *how* He "pleases" to deal with men. We have learned how He does *not* please to deal with men: not on a racial basis; not on a basis of man's goodness or wickedness (since all have sinned). We will learn soon that God is pleased to deal with men on the basis of man's faith or unbelief. That is also God's right, to name a condition and deal with men on that condition. His sovereignty is not at all impaired when He does so.

Keep in mind then that Romans 9:14-24 is only *part* of a complete picture. The picture will be filled in more completely in the following lessons. What Paul wanted us to be sure of here is that we cannot attack God for rejecting Israel since God is sovereign and does as He pleases. Even if we cannot find an explanation why God has rejected Israel (we *will* find one later), we still cannot "reply" against God. He is perfectly free, by nature, to deal with men as He pleases.

24 God Insists on Faith

Study Text: Romans 9:25-33

Introduction
1. Expectation: the Prophecies of Israel's Rejection (Romans 9:25-29)
   a. Quotations from Hosea (verses 25, 26)
   b. Quotations from Isaiah (verses 27-29)
2. Explanation: the Principle behind Israel's Rejection (Romans 9:30-33)
   a. Israel's Replacement in Favor (verses 30, 31)
   b. Israel's Rejection from Favor (verses 31, 33)

INTRODUCTION

Our study of chapter nine is completed in this lesson. You will recall that Paul is defending God's rightness in rejecting Israel. The question Paul is answering is, in fact, given in 9:14: "Is there unrighteousness with God? God forbid."

Two of Paul's arguments have been presented in the first twenty-four verses and dealt with in the two previous lessons. The first argument was this: God never has dealt with men—not even Israel—solely on the basis of physical race. As 9:8 puts it: "They which are the children of the flesh, these are not the children of God." God cannot be accused of dealing unjustly with the Jews then, for He never promised to save all Jews in the flesh.

Paul's second argument was this: God is a Sovereign and has the right to deal with men as He pleases, even with Israel. After all, as 9:18 puts it, "He hath mercy on whom he will have mercy." Again, He has not wronged Israel in this rejection, because He has no obligation to "Israel" anyway. His sovereign freedom gives Him the right to accept or reject Israel as He pleases.

The arguments continue in this present lesson. Indeed, two more arguments are presented by which any accusation that God has dealt unjustly with Israel can be proved wrong.

EXPOSITION

A brief glance at the general study-outline will serve to show how this lesson fits into the overall pattern. This is the third lesson on chapter nine, entitled "God Insists on Faith," covering 9:25-33. You will recall that the previous lesson emphasized the truth that God, as a Sovereign, has the independent right to act as He pleases, to deal with men on whatever basis He chooses, so long as that basis does not violate His own righteous character. We were told in 9:14-24 that God shows mercy to whomever He wishes. There is no denying that truth, but that truth is not complete until we are informed just whom He wishes to show mercy to. This lesson serves the purpose of answering that question. God wills to show mercy to men who put faith in Him. Thus His sovereign right to act as He pleases and man's responsibility to choose or reject God are both maintained.

1. EXPECTATION:
THE PROPHECIES OF ISRAEL'S REJECTION
(Romans 9:25-29)

As noted in the introduction above, Paul has already defended God's present rejection of Israel on two counts, His rejection of fleshly considerations and His sovereign right to favor whom He pleases. Now Paul turns to a third basis for defending God's rejection of the nation of Israel. That basis is a prophetic one. The point is simply this: God has predicted all along that the time was coming when He would turn aside from Israel. Consequently the present rejection of the Jews was to be expected. How can we impugn God for doing exactly what He has been telling us all along He would do.

Quotations from Hosea (verses 25, 26). In the main, verse 25 reflects Hosea 2:23, and verse 26 reflects Hosea 1:10. The situation and circumstances of Hosea's prophecy are quite interesting. He prophesied to Israel (the northern kingdom) and Judah (the southern kingdom) at about the time Israel was being overcome by the Assyrians and a similar judgment loomed on the horizon for Judah.

As you may recall, Hosea was instructed to marry Gomer, a wife who proved unfaithful, thus dramatically depicting the unfaithfulness of the chosen people, Jehovah's "wife." To Hosea and Gomer were born children that were given special names by God, names that testified to the things God promised to do for and against Israel and Judah.

Without getting too involved in Hosea's original prophecies, we need at least to examine their basic original intent. The two children born to Hosea and Gomer were Lo-ruhamah and Lo-ammi. The names meant "no mercy" and "not my people." The names testified to the judgment of Israel and Judah which was soon to come in the form of captivity by heathen nations. God would no longer extend mercy; He would not continue to own His people.

In 1:10 and 2:23, however (the passages quoted here in Romans), God promised that even though He was about to cast away His people in this threatening captivity, the time would later come when He would once again claim them as His people (1:9, 10a), yet later He would restore them as His sons (1:10b). Though He was about to take away mercy (1:6), yet later they would experience His mercy again (2:23). Thus the original words of Hosea indicated, first, that the impending captivity would end and that a restoration would come. We know that such a restoration came about 70 years after the captivity of Judah when once again the Jews returned home under the renewed mercies of God.

But though that was the original and primary intent of Hosea's words in 1:10 and 2:23, Paul sees in those words a deeper significance. This secondary implication is the one he is mostly concerned with in Romans. The original words of Hosea were: "I will call them my people, which were not my people" (Romans 9:25; Hosea 2:23), and "In the place where it was said unto them, ye are not my people; there shall they be called the children (sons) of the living God" (Romans 9:26; Hosea 1:10). To Paul this is a clear prophecy that the Gentiles, which were formerly not God's people, would come to replace, in God's favor, those who formerly were. That Paul interprets the words this way is clear from 9:24, which introduced this quotation, and from 9:30, which shows the Gentiles attaining to the righteousness Israel has failed to achieve.

It seems reasonable to conclude then that Hosea's original prophecy had a *dual* meaning. The near fulfilment lay in the restoring from captivity of the fallen Jews. The long-range fulfilment lay in the rejecting of national Israel from God's favor, and the replacement of them by Gentiles not previously known as His people.

Thus there are two reasons Paul uses these words from Hosea. One is to show that it is no surprise that God would reject the chosen race from His favor. Indeed, He had done so before, in Hosea's day. And that ancient captivity was but a forewarning that He would do so again, as has now come to pass. The second reason Paul uses these words is to show that Gentiles would replace Israel in favor. This too should not be surprising in the light of Hosea's prediction that those not called God's people would come to be called His people. And both these aspects show that God has never obliged himself to keep Israel in favor just because she is Israel. God's former actions and His prophetic utterances make this clear. He has plainly declared He would reject Israel. We should have expected it. As Denney expresses it: "The Jews cannot quarrel with the situation in which they find themselves when it answers so exactly to the Word of God."

Quotations from Isaiah (verses 27-29). Again there are two quotations given, this time from the prince of Israel's prophets. Verses 27, 28 give us Isaiah 10:22, 23; verse 29 is from Isaiah 1:9.

The time of Isaiah's ministry was roughly the same as Hosea's, though Isaiah prophesied entirely to Judah, the southern kingdom. Exactly the same four kings of Judah describe the period of Isaiah's ministry (in 1:1) as for Hosea (in 1:1). Isaiah, like Hosea, had to warn of the coming judgment of God's people. His prophecy, of course, is in much more detail than Hosea's. Both of them looked beyond the coming captivity too to the immediate restoration of the Jews and to long-range events. Isaiah was especially involved in messianic prophecy.

The two passages of Isaiah quoted here in Romans both speak, primarily, of a remnant. That is the reason Paul selects them. ("Seed" in Romans 9:29 is "remnant" in Isaiah 1:9.) In Isaiah 10:22, 23 (Romans 9:27, 28), we read that "A remnant of them shall return" ("be saved" in Romans). In Isaiah 1:9 we read that "Except the Lord of hosts had left unto us a very small remnant ("seed" in Romans), we should have been as Sodom, and we should have been like unto Gomorrah."

In the original prophecies these promises served two purposes. First, they indicated that destruction was coming, that the people of God were going to be judged and cast off, in spite of the Lord's former relationship to them. That casting off was the captivity to come. Second, the prophecies also served to give hope that not all the chosen people would be wiped out. A "remnant is like a small amount of cloth left over from the main bolt of goods. A "seed" (Romans 9:29) is a little saved by which the plant can be regrown. Thus God was promising, by Isaiah, that at least a small group would be saved to return to the land after the captivity from which a new generation could spring and on whom His mercies could again be poured.

But, you see (as with Hosea's prophecies), Paul is taking a much longer look. He sees a deeper and more far-reaching lesson in Isaiah's words. First, he detects a principle there, one by which God would deal with Israel not just once but often. What God did in the captivity, in casting off Israel and preserving a remnant, God would do again. And Paul understands that God has, in fact, done that again now that the Jews have rejected Messiah and are cast aside.

Second, Paul sees in the emphasis on the "remnant" that the

majority of the nation was to be cast aside. That is the basic reason he uses the prophecy here. Isaiah's words clearly showed that time(s) would come when God would cast aside all but a remnant of Israel.

Once again then there ought not to be cause for surprise or resistance that the Jews are now cast off from favor, as a national entity. God has done so often before, and all those times simply forewarned of this time. Only a remnant of the Jews can expect salvation, and there are those who receive Messiah by faith—as Paul will shortly make clear. All this substantiates, as did the quotations from Hosea, the main argument of the passage: God's rejection of Israel as a body is nothing new or surprising. He has done so before and prophesied of doing so in the present. He has never acknowledged any obligation to maintain all Israel in His favor just because they were of the race.

Verse 28, by the way, rephrases Isaiah 10:22b, 23. In neither place is the language very clear. Nor is this part essential to the main point Paul is making in Romans. Apparently Paul quotes it just to be complete in his quotation. Basically the words tell us that God's purposes are always fulfilled. He has started a work and will finish it. Even the judgment and casting off will not stop the fulfilment of His plan in righteousness, and the preservation of the remnant is a testimony to that.

2. EXPLANATION:
THE PRINCIPLE BEHIND ISRAEL'S REJECTION
(Romans 9:30-33)

Paul now moves to yet a *fourth* argument by which he defends the rightness, the propriety of God's actions in rejecting national Israel from His favor. That argument is this: God has rejected Israel, in principle, because of Israel's unbelief. Israel has attempted to please God by works rather than by faith. This is Israel's failure, and this is the real reason she has fallen from the favor of God. This is, in fact, the main argument of Paul, the one he has been heading for all along, and the one he will enlarge on at great length in the next chapter. Here he states the truth briefly.

Israel's Replacement in Favor (verses 30, 31). The truth here is two-fold.

1. The Gentiles have attained righteousness. Verse 30 makes this plain: Gentiles have replaced Jews in the favor of God. Three things are clear about this. First, the Gentiles' former situation: they "followed not after righteousness." This is in contrast to the Jews, who sought righteousness by law-keeping. The Gentiles did not, in their natural state, pursue getting right with God. Second, the Gentiles' new situation: They "have attained to righteousness." They enjoy right-standing before God. They have been declared innocent before Heaven's bar of justice. Third, the method of the Gentiles' success: "even the righteousness which is of faith." Here is the basic principle involved, as has been made so clear throughout Romans: faith. That is the method by which one can be right with God. The Gentiles, who had no method by which to pursue righteousness, have accepted, by faith, righteousness as a gift from God.

2. *The Jews have not attained righteousness.* Verse 31 makes this plain: The Jews have lost their place in God's favor to the Gentiles. Again, three things are clear. First, the Jews' former situation: They "followed after the law of righteousness." Unlike the Gentiles, they sought right-standing with God. They did so according to a specific system, the law. Only they failed to realize it was a system by which they could not succeed. Second, the Jews' present situation: Israel "hath not attained to the law of righteousness." Though they sought it diligently, they have not come to enjoy right-standing with God. Third (by implication), the reason for their failure: They used the wrong method, substituting law-keeping for faith. This reason Paul will give in detail in the next two verses. Before moving there, though, note that verse 30, in referring to the Gentiles, uses "righteousness" while verse 31, in referring to the Jews, uses "the law of righteousness." The reason for this is that the Jews sought the kind of righteousness presented in the law and failed even to attain that. They could not keep it after all.

Israel's Rejection from Favor (verse 32, 33). These two verses give us exactly the reason for Israel's rejection. The word "Wherefore" means this, and thus introduces the cause for the failure stated in the previous verse.

1. *The basic principle behind their rejection* is plainly indicated in verse 32a: They substituted law works for faith. In other words, they pursued righteousness, but by the wrong methods. They desired the favor of God, but figured to earn that favor by their own efforts at observing the Mosaic system. And there they failed, because one does not ever earn or deserve God's favor. He does not work that way. And even if He did, man cannot succeed in keeping the law anyway. Such a method then is doubly doomed to fail.

"They sought it not by faith"; there is the tragedy. Righteousness was so easily available to them had they—like Abraham (Romans 4:3)—put faith in God and depended on Him to save them. Faith pleases God. Works do not.

2. *The personal element in their rejection* is indicated in verses 32b, 33. In principle, they did not put faith in God. Their unbelief doomed them. But there is something more specific than this involved in Israel's unbelief. There was not just a general lack of faith in God that lay behind their failure to achieve righteousness. No, there was a specific and well-defined case of unbelief that accounted for their rejection from God's favor. That unbelief consisted in Israel's rejection of Jesus, their Messiah.

194

Jesus is the "stumblingstone" and "rock of offence" (the two expressions mean the same thing) referred to in 32b, 33. Paul gets these expressions from another prophetic utterance, this time associating together such declarations as are in Isaiah 8:14 and Isaiah 28:16. Compare also Psalm 118:22. The idea is clear: God would lay a stone of His choosing in Israel, a stone intended to be the chief cornerstone, the foundation of His building a people of righteousness. That "stone" was the promised Messiah, the one by whom real blessings and permanent righteousness would come.

And the method for experiencing Messiah's blessings was to be *faith:* "Whosoever *believeth* on him shall not be ashamed." ("Be ashamed" means "put to shame"; compare "make haste" in Isaiah 28:16, which means basically the same thing, "put to flight.") The one who puts faith in Messiah will not have to run from God in fear; he can stand confidently in God's presence, in the favor of God. That is true righteousness.

But the ancient prophecies had themselves warned that this stone would become a stone over which the Jews would stumble. ("Offense" means stumbling.) And, indeed, that is what has happened. The Jews have rejected the very one God had sent to provide them salvation, the "Messiah" (anointed one), Jesus. Consequently, God has rejected them from His favor, and a people (Gentiles) who would put faith in Christ have been received into favor in their place. Here lies the explanation of Israel's rejection.

In concluding our study of this lesson, we need to make sure two elements of its importance are clear. First we should review the pattern of the entire chapter nine and how this section (verses 30-33) fits into that pattern. Paul is defending the justice of God in rejecting Israel, and he has listed at least four primary arguments to support the divine propriety in this rejection. First, God does not deal with men by the fleshly race they represent (verses 6-13). Second, God is a sovereign who deals with men as He pleases (verses 14-24). Third, God has been telling, all along, that He could turn from the "chosen race" and bring Gentiles into His favor instead (verses 25-29). Finally God has rejected Israel because Israel has first rejected Him in her failure to put faith in God's Anointed Savior (verses 30-33). You see how each of these reasons supports the others and all work together logically to give a complete picture.

The other element of importance is this: The truth contained in the last reason (verses 30-33) is absolutely necessary to complete the picture of sovereignty presented in verses 14-24 above (see the previous lesson). Without verses 30-33 we might get a wrong notion from verses 14-24 (as, in fact, Calvinists are apt to do). There we were informed that God deals with men as He pleases. He is sovereign. He chooses some and rejects others as He wills. He has been pleased to reject Israel from favor. Israel has no right to "talk back" to God protesting this rejection. After all, He is Creator and she is creature. The potter can make of the clay what He wishes. He shows mercy to whomsoever He wills to show mercy.

That picture is absolutely accurate, but it is not complete. It does not tell the whole story. For, while it is clear that God deals with men as He pleases, that fact alone does not tell us how He pleases to deal with men. As sovereign, He exercises mercy when He wishes. So far, so good. But when and on whom does He will to show mercy? Well, He has willed *not* to show mercy to those who pursue righteousness by their own self-righteous works. That method would conflict with His sovereignty, for then man could earn His favor and He would be obligated to something other than His own character.

Again then when and on whom does He will to show mercy? The answer is, on those who will accept the righteousness He offers as a free gift by faith in Christ. Faith is the principle. He insists on faith. He wills to save those who put faith in Him. You see then that only when the picture is completed by *both* elements do we fully understand just why Israel has been rejected. *From the point of view of divine sovereignty* Israel's rejection requires no other explanation than that He chose to reject her. He has that right and if we could find no further explanation we would still have to be content with that. But we are now given a further explanation, one *from the point of view of human responsibility:* Israel has been rejected *because* she sought righteousness by works rather than faith. God's sovereignty establishes the *right;* but unbelief is the *reason.* Romans 11:20 confirms this beyond question.

25 Righteousness by Faith: God's Provision

Study Text: Romans 10:1-11

Introduction
1. Self-Righteousness: the Way of Failure (Romans 10:1-5)
   a. Importunity over the Jews (verse 1)
   b. Ignorance among the Jews (verses 2, 3a)
   c. Imitation by the Jews (verses 3b, 4)
   d. Indebtedness for the Jews (verse 5)
2. Salvation: the Way of Faith (Romans 10:6-11)
   a. An Observation about Achievement (verses 6, 7)
   b. An Observation about Availability (verse 8)
   c. An Observation about Application (verses 9, 10)
   d. An Observation about Access (verse 11)

INTRODUCTION

The three chapters of Romans 9-11 form a unit that deals with the matter of the Jews' rejection. Paul was especially conscious of the situation in Israel for he was a Jew. Furthermore, he constantly faced antagonism from the Jews everywhere he preached, and so his consciousness of the situation was kept alive throughout his ministry. He knew that many Jews read this very letter, and he wanted to be sure they would understand his position.

For such reasons he covers carefully the question whether God is righteous in rejecting Israel—the chosen people—from His favor (9:14). In chapter nine (the previous three lessons) Paul has outlined his basic arguments defending God's justice. He has argued that God never promised to favor men solely by fleshly descent, that God's sovereignty gives Him the right to act as He pleases, that God had clearly forewarned Israel about this rejection. Most important, Paul has argued (verses 30-33) that the basic cause of Israel's rejection lies in Israel's own error: She has sought righteousness by works—self-righteousness—rather than that which God has made available by faith.

Chapter ten, which we cover in this lesson and the next, undertakes to expand at length on this last argument. Israel's error is one of method: They have overlooked God's own provided method, righteousness by faith. They have substituted a method that does not work righteousness by works. This chapter is an especially thorough treatment of the method that succeeds and that has been rejected by Israel: righteousness by faith.

EXPOSITION

Pay attention to the general study-outline in the back of this volume. There you will note that chapter ten is subdivided into two lessons dealing with Israel's rejection of the divinely-provided method of righteousness. This first lesson covers verses 1-11 and is entitled "Righteousness by Faith: God's Provision."

1. SELF-RIGHTEOUSNESS: THE WAY OF FAILURE
(Romans 10:1-5)

Before emphasizing the positive side, the righteousness that is possible by faith, Paul indicates the negative. He reveals exactly why Israel has failed to achieve right-standing with God. In a nutshell, that reason is this: Israel has attempted to substitute her own self-righteous works in place of the faith which God has designated as the only condition for the gracious awarding of righteousness to men by Christ.

Importunity over the Jews (verse 1). Paul begins this description of Jewish failure with a repetition of the same burden expressed already in 9:1-3. Importunity is urgent, persistent pleading. Paul certainly manifests urgency and persistency in his pleading on Israel's behalf.

1. The end toward which Paul's burden is directed is expressed in the latter half of the verse: "that they (Israel) might be saved." This "salvation," in this particular context, probably has a deeper meaning than what we usually feel when we use the word. On the one hand, the personal element is involved: Paul wants to see as many of his countrymen "saved" as possible. But he is burdened for the whole people, so there is a nationalistic element involved too. Paul longs to see his nation delivered from the terrible situation now

198

experienced. By resisting the Messiah and the righteousness He offered by faith, the Jews find themselves rejected from that place of special love once known. That rejection spells an inevitable ruin, for the judgment of God will surely fall. Paul's repeated, importunate prayer is for Israel's deliverance from this threatening calamity and restoration to the favor of God.

2. *The nature of Paul's burden* is expressed in a two-fold way in the first part of the verse. First he speaks of "heart's desire." Literally, in Greek, this phrase is "the delight of my heart." The salvation of Israel would bring pleasure to Paul's heart. Indeed, it was the only thing that would, and thus Paul experienced intense longing for that unsatisfied desire.

Second, Paul speaks of his "prayer to God." The word for prayer is one that refers to a specific "petition." As Thayer's lexicon points out, the word, "gives prominence to the expression of personal need." It sees the prayer as a presentation of a specific, personal request to God. Paul's burden then was an intense, heartfelt, personal longing. The picture presented is certainly one that involved frequent and regular agonizing prayer to God on behalf of Israel's salvation.

Ignorance among the Jews (verses 2, 3a). Now Paul moves to his description of Israel's failure to take advantage of the righteousness God has offered by faith in Christ. That failure involves three elements, and the first of these is spiritual ignorance.

1. *The zeal of the Jews* is admitted in 2a. To this Paul himself can "bear record" (which means "bear witness," "testify," "give evidence"). Paul can give testimony of this zeal so effectively because he had been a prime example of the misguided zeal of unbelieving Jews. He understands well the feelings and forces that are at work in the hearts of Jews who reject Jesus as Messiah, because he has been there. He had given vent to those feelings far more forcefully than have most any other Jews.

The nature of the unbelieving Jews' "zeal of God" is to be seen best in their promotion of legalistic Judaism with its Mosaic ritual and the added rigamarole of rabbinic traditions. Literally, "a zeal of God" can mean "zeal for God." Indeed, the Jews were intensely religious. "Zeal" is ardor, fervor, hot—even competitive—pursuit. With just such zeal Paul himself had sought to rid his beloved Judaism of the "Christians" who would pollute pure religion. How well he understood that same zeal displayed by Jews against him and in favor of the hallowed traditions!

2. *The misdirection of that zeal* is pointed out in 2b. The words "not according to knowledge" expose the problem clearly. The Jews' zeal for the things of God is a misguided zeal, reflecting an erroneous understanding of Him and His requirements of men. The word "knowledge" here is not the usual simple word, but a more emphatic compound that refers to the fuller knowledge one has when he

experiences something for himself. The Jews know many things, but their knowledge falls short of the fulness and accuracy required for confident and correct direction of their zeal for God. Consequently their ignorance—for inadequate knowledge is really ignorance—causes them to fall short of attaining that for which they so zealously aim.

3. *Their ignorance of the righteousness of God* is indicated in 3a. This is at the heart of the Jews' failure. The expression is one that has several facets; it is at least four-pronged. First, it means they do not know how to get right with God. "God's righteousness" is the same, in Greek, as "the righteousness of God" (1:17). One thing this phrase means is right-standing with God, being right with God, standing before God righteous, innocent, justified. We have seen this meaning often in the preceding chapters of Romans. The Jews are ignorant of the method by which one achieves such right-standing before God.

Second, the expression "ignorant of God's righteousness" means that the Jews are therefore not right with God. Their ignorance of the method means they have, in fact, failed to achieve righteousness. They are not innocent before God. The ignorance is not only *intellectual;* their *experience* inevitably manifests their misconception.

Third, the expression implies their rejection of God's provision. In other words, more than negative failure is involved; positive resistance is included. "The righteousness of God" not only means "being right with God"; it also means "the righteousness God has porvided." That the Jews are ignorant of the righteousness God has offered implies that they have not hearkened to His offer. They have rejected His way.

Fourth, and perhaps most significant, one cannot help feeling that Paul himself sees "the righteousness of God" here in a very *personalized* sense. After all, *Christ* is our "righteousness" (cf., 1 Corinthians 1:30). This is the idea Paul seems to have below in verse 4. Thus, the Jews' ignorance of the righteousness of God is especially and specifically an ignorance of Christ. They do not know Christ, and in that ignorance is to be found the reason for all their misguided zeal and for the doom from which Paul longs to see them delivered.

Imitation by the Jews (verses 3b, 4). If ignorance of Christ's righteousness is the first element in the Jews' failure, an imitation righteousness is the second element. When one has not the real thing, he is apt to substitute an imitation. This the Jews have done. Failing to achieve true righteousness with God by Jesus Christ, they have invented an imitation righteousness that can only fail: self-righteousness.

1. *Their wicked substitution* is indicated in 3b: "going about to establish their own righteousness." Let it be said now that self-righteousness is pernicious and pretentious. When God has offered sinful man the gracious privilege of standing before Him

200

innocent by faith in Jesus Christ, it is rebellious and wicked to offer Him, instead, one's own works. All *our* righteousnesses are like filthy rags, said Isaiah (64:6), and this for two reasons: Filthy because we cannot really be righteous in our deeds, and so our efforts at self-righteousness are always sullied and spoiled. Like filthy rags because such rags are repulsive: God finds our self-righteous efforts repulsive because they manifest our resistance to His own plan.

2. *Their self-willed resistance* is spelled out in 3c: "(they) have not submitted themselves unto the righteousness of God." This points out clearly the aspect already mentioned above: The Jews' failure is more than a mere ignorant missing of the way; they have stubbornly refused to submit to the plan He has offered in Christ. The self-righteous always resist righteousness by Christ for they do not wish to admit their sins. And one cannot put saving faith in Jesus until he has owned his own sins. The Greek for "have not submitted" is more like a simple past action: they did not submit. Paul is thinking specifically of the Jews' rejection of Christ: The scene at Calvary is certainly before his mind.

3. *The plan they rejected* is briefly outlined in verse 4. Paul will expand on this at length in verses 6-11, the second half of this lesson. But for now he wants to make clear exactly what he has meant in verses 2 and 3 when he has spoken of their ignorance of and refusal to submit to the righteousness of God. And he makes clear that the essence of this ignorance and resistance is ignorance of and rejection of *Christ.* Though brief, the verse contains three aspects of the true plan for righteousness as found in Christ.

Second, this plan is truly in accord with the law. "The end of the law" does not mean the *finish* of the law, but the *purpose*, the *final goal* of the law. In other words, the real purpose of the law is achieved when one comes to the experiential knowledge of Jesus Christ. This truth we have emphasized earlier, as in the lessons dealing with 3:31 where Paul stresses that his doctrine does not make void but *establishes* the law. The Jews thought that the law provided a standard of conduct which one could observe and please God thereby. But this was wrong. God gave the law to manifest man's sinful sickness and drive him to Christ, the Great Physician (cf., Romans 3:19, 20). So Christ is the "end" toward which the law is at work in the world, and when men receive Him as the righteousness of God the law's work is done.

Third, faith is man's part in the plan, as seen in "to every one that believeth." The "every" means Jew or Gentile. The faith is the opposite of works, of efforts at self-righteousness. Faith in Christ as our righteousness involves the admission that we are sinners, the renunciation of our own self-righteousness, and the casting of ourselves on Jesus as the only hope to achieve right-standing with God. He alone has truly kept all God's requirements and possesses genuine *self*—righteousness. He too has fully paid the penalty for our own violations of God's requirements. In both these ways His righteous perfection can be imputed to us, and only so can we have righteousness before God.

Indebtedness for the Jews (verse 5). We see now the third element involved in the Jews' failure to achieve righteousness: The system they follow leaves them with an indebtedness they are helpless to pay. They who would justify themselves by the law find themselves bound to an impossible obligation.

Paul often tried to impress his readers with this truth. Galatians 3:10-12 teaches the same lesson, as you will recall if you have studied the commentary on Galatians. The phrase used here in Romans, "the righteousness which is of the law," does not admit that some actually achieve righteousness that way. It means "the righteousness which is sought by observing the law."

Paul quotes Moses to describe the kind of righteousness that would be if it were achieved. The passage is the same one quoted in Galatians 3:12 and is from Leviticus 18:5. Put in other words here is what Paul means: "The one who wants righteousness by law-keeping will find that law-keeping is the very thing this kind of righteousness depends on. He can 'live' only by doing every single thing the law requires." This standard is, however, beyond man's ability, and so this method is universally doomed to failure. The Jews have staked their lives on law-keeping and self-righteousness. In so doing, they have lost their lives.

2. SALVATION: THE WAY OF FAITH (Romans 10:6-11)

Paul turns now to a positive presentation of the gospel plan of righteousness which the Jews have rejected, substituting therefor their own imitation righteousness. This gospel method promises that God will graciously award righteousness to all who put faith in Jesus Christ. The Jews' rejection of this simple plan is the basic cause for their rejection from the favor of God.

An Observation about Achievement (verses 6, 7). First Paul makes the point that God's plan does not depend on human achievement. Man's own efforts at accomplishing salvation must be discarded. Justification is not the work of man. "The righteousness which is of faith" stands in contrast to "the righteousness which is of the law" in verse 5. Since Paul had quoted Moses there to describe that kind of righteousness, he now quotes Moses again to show what true righteousness has to say.

Verses 6, 7 (after "wise") are quoted freely from Deuteronomy 30:12, 13 where Moses had stressed the fact that the people should not regard their obligations to God as impossible; they should not say that to fulfil God's expectations they would have to climb up to Heaven or swim the ocean and back; they should not blaspheme God by claiming that He expected more of them than they could reasonably accomplish.

Here in Romans Paul borrows that same language, adjusts and expands it to refer to Christ's redemptive work. He says, in effect, that now the ancient words of Moses are genuinely true in Christ. God does *not* expect an impossible achievement of us; in fact he expects *no achievement at all!* Christ has done it for us. Only in Christ can Moses' words be fully realized. The righteousness which comes by faith calls on no one to climb to Heaven or descend to Hell: Christ has done both for us. Nor did anyone have to bring Christ from Heaven to earth or bring Him back from death: These were accomplished by Christ's own work, in the free and gracious provision of God. Man's efforts are totally out of place in *this* kind of righteousness.

An Observation about Availability (verse 8). Paul continues his quotation from Deuteronomy 30, now adding verse 14. Again he reapplies the words of Moses to the new situation in Christ. The point he makes is twofold.

1. The nearness of the "word" is first emphasized: "The word is nigh thee, even in thy mouth, and in thy heart." The "word" stands for "what God has *said* about getting right with Him." And what He has said makes righteousness as near to a person as his own mouth and heart. With the mouth one speaks; in the heart one has an attitude or conviction. Paul is saying that righteousness is as easy as saying some words, as easy as forming a conviction in the heart. He will tell us, in a moment just what one must say, what attitude one must hold, to attain to "the righteousness of God."

2. The nature of the "word" is then emphasized. If "word" means, as just noted, "what God has *said* about getting right with Him," the what God has said is this: "faith." God has announced *faith* as the answer to the question how to attain righteousness, and that is the method Paul preaches.

The point of all this about nearness and faith is that God's plan for righteousness is an easy one, freely available to any who will simply put faith in Christ. This easy availability is seen both in the fact that righteousness is as near as one's mouth and heart and in the fact that righteousness is by faith. Paul will expand on this method in the next two verses.

An Observation about Application (verses 9, 10). In the previous verse Paul said that salvation—righteousness with God—is as near as one's mouth and heart according to what God has said. He proceeds now to expand and explain the part played by these two bodily organs. This is the method by which salvation is applied to the individual.

1. The mouth's part is to confess, as indicated in verses 9a, 10b. This is the reason Paul indicated, in verse 8, that righteousness is as near as one's mouth. All one must do to attain righteousness is frame some words, express an idea. Of course the mere words would not be effective; they must come from the heart. The content of that expression might be worded in any number of ways, but the essence of that idea would always be: Jesus is my Savior. Note that confession is "unto salvation."

2. *The heart's part is to believe*, as indicated in verses 9b, 10a. This explains the reference to the heart in verse 8. Righteousness is as near as one's heart, for in the heart the conviction is formed that Jesus is one's Savior, and that conviction is faith. Note that faith is "unto righteousness."

The *faith* involved will cover more than the one item of Christ's resurrection, of course. But Paul selects this item because one cannot believe in the resurrection of the *Lord* Jesus by the power of *God* without believing all the rest of the gospel account of the Person and Word of Jesus. In a special way, then, the resurrection of Christ is the means of our justification (cf., Romans 4:25), and this doctrine alone will separate those who have genuine faith in Christ from those who do not.

The *confession* involved is really a particular aspect of faith and cannot be separated therefrom. The point is that God requires us who are saved by faith, rather than our own works, to *own* that *He* has saved us and is our Lord. Lack of such confession would mean we were still trying to save ourselves by our own efforts or merit. Thus confession and faith are not two distinct steps, but both aspects of the same basic fact. Nor need we overemphasize the literal bodily organs referred to. One cannot have genuine faith without confession, nor sincere confession without faith. Neither is the order significant, for the two verses reverse the order: both occur at the same time.

An Observation about Access (verse 11). The *ease* of the method of righteousness by faith is not its only good point. The plan is also for everyone. It is not just in reach for some; it is in reach of all.

A quotation from the Old Testament is made in verse 11. There is some doubt exactly which passage Paul is quoting, since he gives the sense freely rather than by a word-for-word reproduction. There are several statements in the Old Testament which express this basic idea: Isaiah 28:16; Isaiah 49:23; and Psalm 34:22 are good examples.

Once again, as before in Romans 1:16 and 5:5 (see those lessons), the word "ashamed" means to be disappointed, to fail to achieve that which is promised or expected. The one who believes in Christ will never experience the disappointment of God's plan failing. He will never be "put to shame."

The emphasis of this quotation, however, is on the "whosoever." This makes universal availability clear. Anyone, Jew or Gentile, may put faith in God through Christ and receive the gift of righteousness. Compare other places where the New Testament stresses the "whosoever": Acts 2:21 and Revelation 2:21 are good examples.

26 Righteousness by Faith: Gospel Proclamation

Study Text: Romans 10:12-21

Introduction
1. The Gospel and a Universal Purpose (Romans 10:12-15)
   a. A Universal People (verse 12)
   b. A Universal Plan (verse 13)
   c. A Universal Proclamation (verses 14, 15)
2. The Gospel and an Unbelieving People (Romans 10:16-21)
   a. Israel's Unbelief of the Gospel (verse 16)
   b. Israel's Unexcused Guilt (verses 17-21)

INTRODUCTION

We are in the midst of the section of Romans (chapters 9-11) in which he explains the current Jewish situation. Now that Messiah has come and offered salvation to all men by faith, the Jews find themselves outside the special favor they once knew. Paul explains many facets of this situation, emphasizing the righteousness of God in rejecting the Jews.

The heart of the matter lies in the Jews' efforts to save themselves by their own works instead of accepting by faith the justification made freely available in Christ. This truth Paul introduced in 9:30-33. In chapter ten Paul expands on this theme. The first eleven verses, as studied in the previous lesson, stressed the failure of the Jews and the simplicity of the plan God has announced: One need not bind himself to a law he cannot perfectly keep after all; one need only acknowledge, from a heart of faith, Jesus as his Savior.

The last half of chapter ten continues with this same basic

theme, concentrating now on the provision and proclamation of this gospel plan rather than on the simplicity of the plan itself.

EXPOSITION

A quick reference to the general study-outline in the back will show that this lesson covering 10:12-21 is entitled "Righteousness by Faith: Gospel Proclamation." This is the second of two lessons on the chapter, both of which relate Israel's rejection to the matter of God's provision of righteousness by faith.

1. THE GOSPEL AND A UNIVERSAL PURPOSE
(Romans 10:12-15)

Our previous lesson's coverage ended with verse 11 which emphasized the access all men have by faith to righteousness. The word, "whosoever," used in verse 11 sets the stage for Paul to emphasize the single plan of salvation that is for one and all alike, Jew and Gentile included.

A Universal People (verse 12). This verse stresses the truth that the people of God are not restricted by race. The gospel proclamation is for all without distinction. Several closely related truths are involved in this, and all of them have already been developed in this epistle. One truth is that Jews and Gentiles have equal access into the family of God. Racial distinctions are not considered. Righteousness by faith is as available to Gentile as to Jew. Verses like 3:22 and 3:29 have made this point clear.

Note one reason this is a universal people: "There is no difference between the Jew and the Greek." The idea used here has appeared earlier. In 3:22, 23 Paul said: "There is no difference: for all have sinned." See also 3:9: "We have before proved both Jews and Gentiles, that they are all under sin." This truth—that all alike are sinners—is the very backbone of Paul's whole doctrine that there is no difference in the plan of salvation. If all are sinners, then none can be saved by his own works; and all must come by faith in Christ who is God's provision for the unrighteous to become righteous. Then when Paul says there is no difference between Jew and Greek, both aspects are involved. As Denney expresses it, "There is no distinction between them in point of sin," so likewise "There is no distinction between them in that the same Lord is waiting to save all on the same conditions."

Note also that the oneness of the Lord is behind this universality in the outreach of the gospel. "The same Lord over all" presents this idea. The point is this: There is but one God for all men, and therefore there can be but one people of God and one plan for them to participate in that one family.

Further, the impartiality of God is involved too. When Paul says he is "rich unto all that call upon him," there is a clear implication that God deals with all alike, rewarding riches without partiality to any who meet the condition indicated. In 2:11 Paul has already emphasized that "There is no respect of persons with God." It would not be impartial of God to permit either Jews or Gentiles a special access to His favor not enjoyed by the other.

Finally, note the one method, or plan, that is provided for all: "all that *call* upon him." This same plan is for the Jew and the Gentile. Paul stresses this plan in the next verse.

A Universal Plan (verse 13). This verse is a quotation from Joel 2:32, cited here to prove and to emphasize that there is but one plan for all. Two sides of this truth need to be pointed up.

1. The oneness of the method is clear because of several things in both verses 12 and 13: the "no difference" (12), the "same Lord" (12), the "all that call" (12). The word "whosoever" makes this oneness plain. The very point of the word is that all men alike—Jew or Gentile—have equal access by this one method.

2. The simplicity of the method is to be seen in the use of the word "call." That is the word Paul is stressing in opposition to the Jews' notion that one must earn righteousness by law-observance. Remember that Paul is treating throughout chapters 9-11 the reasons for the Jews' rejection. The tragedy is that they have missed such a simple plan. God has graciously provided righteousness by Christ for any who will but call out to Him to save them. But Israel has stubbornly gone on in her refusal to acknowledge sinful need and in her commitment to the meticulous observance of the law as a hope for salvation.

We must understand that "call" here is not a different plan as compared to "believe" in verse 11. The two are the same after all. One will not call out to God, in Christ, unless he has confidence that Christ saves. Likewise, one who "puts faith" in Christ as Savior invariably expresses that faith as a call for Him to save. All put together then the method is quite simple: One owns his sin and need, is convinced that Christ saves, calls on God by Christ, and acknowledges Christ as his Savior. That is faith, and that is God's gospel plan for all.

"Israel" is not the only one who has tragically missed this marvelously simple way. Men almost unanimously prefer self-righteousness to any other kind. Such is the nature of human pride, and thus many reject Christ and the gracious righteousness He offers all who will but call on Him. Righteousness is as available to any as asking and receiving. Notice, by the way, that this quotation from Joel 2:32 is the very same one as was quoted by Peter at Pentecost.

One more observation about verses 12, 13. The "whosoever" doctrine is one that applies not only to the Jew-Gentile tension, but also in more current doctrinal arguments about the extent of God's provision, whether salvation is really available to all or only for the so-called "elect."

Some Calvinistic theologians teach that God provided redemption only for the chosen few, that Christ died only for these "elect" ones, that all others will go to Hell without having even had a genuine opportunity for salvation. One wonders whether they are aware how such notions sound so unlike the Bible!

This "no difference" argument of Paul's is a good one to use against Calvinism. Every time Paul argues that *anyone* and *all* may be saved, he argues it on the basis that *anyone* and *all* have sinned. In 3:22, 23 he says that righteousness by faith is for *all* because there is "no difference" in that *all* have sinned. Now again he says that "whosoever" may come because there is "no difference" in Jew and Greek, meaning there is no difference in men's need. The conclusion is clear: God's provision is as broad as man's sin. Jesus died for all. Any may come.

A Universal Proclamation (verse 14, 15). We will profit by looking at these verses from three points of view.

1. The Jews' point of view should be considered first, since the whole context of chapters 9-11 is concerned with the Jews' circumstances. The point here is this: The unbelieving Jews objected to the preaching of a man like Paul because he went out to Jew and Gentile alike, not observing the segregation barriers the Jews had carefully built to isolate them from Gentile "pollution." Paul's point is that since the gospel offers salvation to *any*—Jew or Gentile—who will call on the Lord, then it must be proclaimed to all without distinction or barrier. How can they call, Paul is asking rhetorically, unless we preach the word to them?

2. The missionary point of view should also be considered, and the implications are obvious from what has just been said. The gospel is for *all*, but all must hear if they are to call: foreign, home; city, country; black, white; rich, poor; inner city, suburbs. No cultural, economic, social, racial, ethnic, or geographic barriers should stand in the way of gospel outreach.

While Christ is the one who "sends" the "preacher," there is another sense in which it is the *church* that sends. In this sense the passage before us serves as an excellent indication of Christian responsibility to spread abroad the gospel, even unto the ends of the earth. The Christian community should take to heart the fact that men will not be saved apart from the gospel. And they will not hear unless proclaimers are sent forth. There is no *hearing* without *bearing*. The church at Antioch "sent forth" Paul and Barnabas (Acts 13:3); this is the example our modern churches ought to follow.

3. The salvation point of view is perhaps most interesting to us. We may consider these verses as indicating the basic, necessary steps involved in the salvation of any individual at any time or place.

The necessary steps to salvation are outlined in verses 14, 15. Each of these is an essential link in the chain of gospel-salvation as it moves from beginning to end. Each step is presented by a *verb:* Salvation is a moving, living, *active* thing. There are, in fact, *five* of these verbal steps, and we must take careful note of each.

The first step is to *send*. This verb in Greek is built on the same root as the noun "apostle," which Paul uses of himself in Romans 1:1 (see the first lesson). This means to send on a mission, to send as an emissary or official representative. Before anything else can happen toward a man's salvation, someone must be commissioned to go, sent from the Lord.

The second step is to *preach*. This verb in Greek is not the one that literally means to announce glad tidings, preach the gospel. That word would have been all right here, but it might have suggested formal sermonizing. The word used here is the one that means to *proclaim* something. It was often used in reference to the public herald, the "town crier" who went about informing people of the latest happenings or official notices. The emphasis is on spreading abroad the news. The man sent must proclaim what his sender entrusted to him.

We pause here to take note that there is absolutely nothing about these first two verbs that limits their performance to *ordained* persons! Every Christian ought to recognize himself as commissioned by Christ, sent as an official representative with the gospel to lost men. Likewise the "preaching" is not limited to pulpit oratory. Nothing more than telling someone else the gospel is required, and that is something all God's children ought to be doing.

The third step in the process is to *hear*. This verb switches us from the action of him who *gives* the gospel to that of him who *receives* it. And first he must hear. How simple a fact, but how sadly neglected! Men must hear; they must listen. We must tell them in such a way as to get their attention. We must give them what they must hear: the gospel, plain and simple.

The fourth step is also that of the hearer, to *believe*. The action of this verb in Greek is not continuous, but refers to *initial* faith, the placing of faith in Christ. This is the point at which one becomes convinced that Jesus is the Savior and accepts this truth, "latches on" to it, appropriates it for himself. And this cannot come apart from hearing.

The final step in the salvation of a person is to *call*. As already noted, this step is not really separable from the fourth. The two go so closely together that they must, in fact, be regarded as two ways of looking at the same action. Calling is faith directed personally to God for one's own personal need. It is not only believing that Jesus is Savior, it is inviting Him into the heart. It is admitting that God alone can save and asking Him to save. Here is the point we strive to bring men to; when reached, the work is done. This is the point to which the publican in Christ's parable came: "God, be merciful to me, a sinner!"

We have noted above the kind of action in the fourth step. To note this about each of these is helpful. Actually, only one of the five verbs is in continuing action in Greek, and that is the *preaching*. God "sends," and that is it. Men hear, believe, and call—all simple acts. But the one who preaches finds his duty not so once-for-all. He must go on preaching. Sometimes he must say it over and over before the intended fruit is produced. Perhaps Galatians 6:9 would apply here.

2. THE GOSPEL AND AN UNBELIEVING PEOPLE
(Romans 10:16-21)

Having expanded on the simple plan of salvation, universally preached for all—Jew and Gentile, Paul now returns to his main theme: the Jewish rejection of the gospel. That rejection is all the more tragic and disappointing in the light of the gospel's simplicity and in the light of the fact that the gospel has been so clearly proclaimed where the Jew himself could hear and be saved. But the Jews' unbelief has prevented the simple gospel plan from working in their behalf. God's universal purpose of salvation has not been accomplished among the unbelieving Israelites.

Israel's Unbelief of the Gospel (verse 16). The previous verses have proved that faith is for any, that the gospel is proclaimed for *all*. But the fact is, says Paul, not all have believed the gospel. For some then the gospel has not worked. Is this because the *gospel* is defective? No, it is because some have not met the simple condition.

1. The "not all" refers primarily in this context to the Jews of whom Paul is particularly thinking. Obviously, though, the same thing is true of any who do not believe.

2. "Obeying" the gospel means, in effect, the same thing as believing the gospel. Literally, obeying means "hearkening to," doing what the gospel asks: putting faith in Christ, calling on the Lord.

3. The quotation from "Esaias" (Isaiah 53:1) is given to prove that not all have believed. The unbelief of Israel is, in fact, not new in Paul's day, for Isaiah had experienced the same rejection of his preaching as has Paul. Indeed, unbelief is rather typical of Israel's whole history! The question form Isaiah used implies a negative answer to the "who"—like none, or not many.

Israel's Unexcused Guilt (verses 17-21). The remaining verses of the chapter undertake to show that Israel has no excuse for her unbelief. The section is in Paul's frequent argumentative style, asking questions that represent possible objections to his position and then forcefully answering those questions and reinforcing his views. There are, as we shall see, two basic factors with which Paul deals, two grounds that fail to provide excuse for Israel's unbelief.

1. Did Israel hear? Verses 17, 18 deal with this question, which appears in 18a. Our King James Version sounds like the question expects a positive answer, but in Greek the question is worded so as to expect a negative answer. The reason is that the question represents a possible objection to Paul's position, a possible excuse for Israel's unbelief. In other words, the objection asks this: Well, if Israel has not believed (16), and if "faith cometh by hearing" (17), then maybe Israel did not hear? Is this the case? Did Israel not hear? asks Paul.

Verse 17 must be seen in this light as the doctrine out of which this objection grows. Verse 16 has declared the fact that Israel has disbelieved the gospel. Verse 17 then reminds us that faith is produced by the hearing of the proclaimed gospel. The verse is basically a shortened summary repetition of the five steps of salvation outlined above in verses 14, 15. Here we have the middle three: the word (preach), hearing, and faith. After all, the first of the five (sending) is inseparable from the preaching; and the fifth (calling) is inseparable from the faith. So the three give us really as good a presentation of salvation as the five.

The objector to Paul's view then could ask whether Israel's unbelief is evidence she had not heard, since faith is produced by hearing. Paul's answer is clear and firm: *I* say they *have* heard! Israel's failure to put faith in God cannot be excused by any claim that she has not heard the gospel.

Paul proves his insistence that Israel has heard, in 18b, by quoting the Old Testament again. This time he quotes Psalm 19:4. Of course this psalm is referring to revelation in *nature*. "Their sound" and "their words" refer to the testimony of the heavens, the orderly passing of day and night, the sun, and all the rest of creation's marvelous display of the Creator's power. Israel had—like all the world—heard the gospel of nature. But Paul is probably not thinking primarily of nature; more likely he is borrowing these words about natural revelation and giving them a new application. What he means is that Israel has just as truly heard the gospel as has all mankind heard natural revelation.

We can add that Israel is not the only one who cannot excuse unbelief on the grounds of not having heard. Neither Israel nor any others can blame lack of faith on having been omitted from the gospel proclamation. As Paul puts it in Titus 2:11, "The grace of God that bringeth salvation hath appeared to all men."

2. Did Israel understand? Verses 19-21 deal with this question, which appears in 19a. "Know" is used in the sense of "understand," and it has a twofold meaning. Did they understand what they were doing? Did they understand what would happen if they did not hearken? Again, the question is worded so as to expect a negative answer and represents another possible objection that might be raised, another possible excuse for Israel's unbelief. In other words, the question goes like this: Well, if Israel heard, then maybe they did not understand?

Can that be so? asks Paul. Can we say that Israel did not understand? Again, his answer is quite forceful: They *did* understand; they were clearly warned. And again he makes this answer with quotes from the Old Testament rather than with affirmations of his own. In fact, there are three quotations; the first two prove one point, the third another.

The first two quotations prove that *Israel did understand the consequences of her unbelief* (and thus she understood that she was not really obeying and pleasing God). These two quotations demonstrate this because they relate times when God predicted He would replace Israel in His favor by the Gentiles.

The first citation (19b) is from Deuteronomy 32:21, showing that a "no people" and a "foolish nation" would take Israel's place, thus to provoke Israel's jealousy and arouse her anger. The lesson here is subtle, but clear: If a *"foolish* no-people" (Gentiles) are to take Israel's place, then Israel herself is contrasted to the foolish ones. Thus Israel is the *understanding* (opposite to foolish) people but will be replaced by those called foolish.

The second citation (20) is from Isaish 65:1 and is even more pointed: Israel would be replaced by a (Gentile) people who sought not God nor asked for Him. The implication is that the Gentiles did not know how to seek Him, and that *Israel did understand how.* Yet, understanding Israel was to be supplanted by ignorant Gentiles. Thus both quotations prove Israel's understanding, especially her understanding of the threatened consequences of her unbelief, her replacement in God's favor by the despised Gentiles.

The third quotation proves that *Israel did understand the fact of her own unbelief.* This comes from Isaiah 65:2. God is presented as saying that He had offered himself "all day" to a people who spurned Him. They are *not* a people who did not *know* Him, but a people who were disobedient and "gainsaying" (back talking).

All these Old Testament quotations in verses 19-21 had been true of Israel before. Paul is reapplying them to Israel's new rejection of Christ as the righteousness of God. Israel is but living up to her past history when she refuses to put faith in Christ. That she is now replaced in God's family by Gentiles who formerly had no understanding in the things of God proves how easily God can be found. Israel's rejection is certainly not because of lack of understanding; she knew far more than those who have received Christ by faith. It is not understanding which God requires anyway; it is faith.

The main point of verses 14-21, as of the entire chapter, is that Israel's rejection *by* God is caused by her rejection *of* God. Faith in Christ is God's plan for righteousness, not self-righteous observance of the law. And this faith comes simply by hearing the gracious gospel proclamation. This simple plan has been made available to all, Israel included. But Israel has rejected God's way. We are not surprised then that Israel—as a whole—now finds herself outside God's family; while multitudes not formerly included—Gentiles—repose therein at peace and righteous before God. Nor do we have any reason to impugn God's justice in having thus displaced unbelieving Israel.

27 Grace and Blindness : The Present Israelite Remnant

Study Text: Romans 11:1-10

INTRODUCTION

As we begin chapter 11 of Romans, a brief review of the past several lessons should prove helpful. You will remember that chapters 9—11 make up part 4 of Romans. In these three chapters Paul explains what has happened to the Jewish nation. Formerly, the Jews enjoyed a place of special privilege and favor in God's eyes. But now that Jesus has come and made plain the way of salvation by faith, the Jews stand judged. They have rejected God's plan for righteousness by Jesus Christ and attempted to substitute their self-righteous works performed in the diligent—if sometimes hypocritical—observance of the Mosaic Law.

Throughout these chapters Paul is conscious that some of his Jewish opponents will object to his views. They will say that God could not reject the Jews from His special favor without going back on His word. So Paul undertakes to show that God has rightly and justly rejected the self-righteous Jews.

215

Paul shows this by a series of arguments, and we have been tracing these arguments in the past several lessons (22-26). First, Paul showed that God never promised to show favor on the basis of mere fleshly descent (9:6-13). Second, Paul stressed the sovereign right of God to show favor to whomever He pleases (9:14-24). Third, Paul pointed out that the Lord had been saying all along, in Old Testament prophecies, that He would reject Israel and replace her in His favor with the Gentiles (9:25-29). Fourth, Paul proved that the real problem lay in the Jews' own rejection of the righteousness God had offered them by faith in Jesus Christ, as plainly proclaimed in the gospel (9:30—10:21). All these arguments show convincingly that God has not done wrong in His treatment of Israel (9:14).

But Paul is not through: There are yet more arguments that add to the picture. These arguments continue in chapter 11. There are three of these arguments, and so we will devote three lessons to this chapter. All three arguments reflect God's *purpose.*

EXPOSITION

The basic argument of this lesson (11:1-10) is this: God has not gone back on His promises to Jews because Jews are presently in God's favor—that is, any Jews who are saved by grace through faith. There is a remnant. Thus you will see, in the general study-outline in the back, that all of chapter 11 is listed as section C under part 4, and that this lesson is division 1 under C, entitled "Grace and Blindness: the Present Israelite Remnant."

1. THE REMNANT: A BELIEVING MINORITY
(Romans 11:1-6)

Paul is going to show us two apparently contradictory pictures in verses 1-10. One is a picture of Jews rejected, and that is the situation of the major part of the nation. But there are also Jews who are right with God and enjoying His favor and blessing, though they are in the minority. This picture Paul develops first.

A Present Exception (verses 1, 2a). Paul's first purpose is to assure us that the rejection of Israel is not a total rejection. There are clear exceptions to the majority situation, so that it can be said that God is still fulfilling His promises to "Israel." God has not cast His people aside—that is the point Paul expresses with confidence.

1. A question with an obvious answer is given in 1a. The Greeks had ways of asking questions in a way that the expected answer was shown in the question. The question in verse 1a definitely expects a negative answer. We could rephrase the words thus: "God has not rejected His people, has He? Absolutely not!" Paul will prove this in the verses that follow.

216

2. A personal testimony is used as the first proof in 1b. Paul speaks of his own experience, and that experience serves as an answer to the question already introduced.

Notice that Paul gives his full credentials as a Jew. He is "an Israelite." Israel (Jacob) was the chosen seed of Isaac, the father of the twelve tribes, the one whose name was taken to stand for the whole people. Paul is flesh and blood of Israel. Further, he is "of the seed of Abraham." Abraham was the revered Patriarch, the father of the Hebrew people, the one of whom all Jews boasted "Abraham is our father" (John 8:39). God had promised Abraham a blessed "seed" in the original covenant (Genesis 15:5). Paul is physically a son of Abraham, part of the promised seed. Finally, Paul is "of the tribe of Benjamin." The Jews were very careful to preserve their tribal genealogical tables. Paul can present his pedigree as testimony to the purity of his blood line as a Jew.

Do not miss the significance of Paul's testimony. What he is saying is simply this: "I am a Jew, and I am in God's favor. That proves God has not cast away *all* the chosen nation."

3. A confident conclusion is affirmed in 2a. This is the essence of the truth Paul is devoting this chapter to: God has not cast aside His people after all, because there are at least some Jews who are experiencing all the blessings God had promised the chosen seed. Paul is but one of many.

The only thing different about this affirmation, as compared to the original question (1a), is the addition of the words "which he foreknew." These words probably refer, simply, to the fact that God knew Israel before. We could read the words thus: "God has not cast aside His people, whom He knew before." Israel's special relationship to God during the Old Testament period is referred to in this expression.

A Past Example (verses 2b-4). Paul now turns to the idea that the "remnant" principle is not new. If only a minority of Israelites are now experiencing the blessed favor of God, this is not the first time. The past offers plenty of testimony that God often "knew" only a minority of the nation.

1. Elijah's mistaken complaint is introduced in 2b, 3 as the particular circumstance that revealed the existence of a remnant on one specific occasion. "Wot ye not," by the way, simply means, "Do you not know?" Paul's Jewish readers would be well aware of this story, as are we.

The original account of Elijah's discouraged complaint is given in 1 Kings 19. Elijah had just experienced the great triumph at Carmel over the prophets of Baal. God had answered with fire. Queen Jezebel, a Baal worshiper, vowed to get the prophet, and so Elijah ran for his life into the hills. He was distressed. He figured there were none left in Israel who loved the Lord. All had turned aside from the worship of Jehovah to the worship of Baal, he

217

thought, and there were none worthy of his efforts.

So in 1 Kings 19, verses 10 and 14, Elijah lodged the complaint recorded here in Romans 11:3: "Lord, the children of Israel have forsaken your covenant, thrown down your altars, and slain all the rest of your prophets. I am the only one left, and they are about to get me." Sometimes we are tempted to feel as discouraged as Elijah was. But we are no more apt to be right than he was.

2. *The Lord's answer to Elijah* is indicated in verse 4. In the original account we learn that the Lord instructed Elijah to go anoint another man, Jehu, to be king over Israel (only the northern kingdom at the time). That act was a promise of hope that things were going to change. God was about to judge the house of King Ahab, who had led Israel into strong Baal worship.

Then the Lord gave Elijah the reassurance referred to here in verse 4: "I have left me seven thousand in Israel, all the knees which have not bowed unto Baal, and every mouth which hath not kissed him" (1 Kings 19:18). Elijah was foolish to think he was the only loyal worshiper of the Lord. Still, the majority of Israel had clearly turned from Jehovah. There were but 7,000 men who had resisted the torrent of Baal worship that swept Israel.

The existence of that small group of 7,000 is the point Paul is making here in Romans 11. He cites that occasion to show that the Lord often had but a small remnant of Israelites left who were really in His favor. True, the whole nation reaped some of the external benefits of being God's chosen people; but only the minority were righteous. Indeed, this writer would go so far as to say there were few if any times in the history of Israel when most of the people were God's children in any spiritual sense.

The significance of Paul's example from Elijah's day is quite clear. What was true then is true now: Though the majority of Israel is out of God's favor, a remnant minority of believers still enjoys the blessings of the Lord's Covenant with Israel. God has no more cast aside His people in Paul's day than in Elijah's. In fact, there were probably many more than 7,000 who truly knew the Lord, by Jesus Christ, in Paul's day.

The Principle of Election (verses 5, 6). The thing Paul has been clearly implying in the first four verses is now openly declared, in summary this: Any believing Jews are saved by grace and form a faithful remnant of God's chosen people. Thus God has not cast aside His people.

1. *The existence of this present remnant* is first affirmed, particularly in the first part of verse 5. The "even so" carries over from the comparison with Elijah's day. The "present time" referred to by Paul would carry on throughout all the present church age when the gospel is just as freely preached to Gentiles as to Jews. This "remnant" of Jewish believers will, no doubt, always exist within the church. They, along with saved Gentiles, experience fully all the

permanent promises of God's original covenant with Abraham. And so God has not cast aside His people, after all. A "remnant," by the way, is a piece left over. The word suggests a small amount by comparison with the whole, a minority.

2. *The method by which this remnant exists* is discussed in 5b and 6. We are given two sides in this discussion, a positive and a negative, how the remnant does and does not exist.

On the positive side, we see that the remnant of believing Jews exists by "the election of grace." This phrase means the same thing as saying "a gracious election," but Paul's way of saying it puts greater emphasis on both words, *election* and *grace.*

When Paul says that there is a remnant of Jews in God's favor now by *election*, he means to stress God's free choice of them as objects of His favor. Election, on God's part, is the opposite of obligation. The Jews proudly thought God was obligated to keep them in His special favor. Paul is dousing that idea, as he has already done in 9:14-24, where he avows that God shows mercy to whomever He pleases. Remember, now, that this free choice by God to show mercy on some does not rule out the possibility that He will freely choose to establish a condition by which man can enter His favor. In fact, God has established such a condition, faith. This truth Paul has explained in detail earlier in the epistle, and so he does not go into the matter again here. But the use of a condition does not take away God's freedom or make the exercising of His mercy a matter of obligation. God has saved those He has freely chosen to save—that is Paul's emphasis here.

The other word Paul emphasizes is *grace.* This election, this choice to save, is a gracious one. We have already learned that grace is undeserved favor. This word also makes clear that the choice of those who will receive mercy is not by man's goodness or God's obligation. Man has not deserved or earned this favor, this right-standing. God has graciously and freely chosen to save all who put faith in Jesus Christ. By this method there is presently a remnant of saved Jews.

The negative side follows logically from the positive and is emphasized in verse 6. The method by which the remnant exists is not works. Works is the opposite of grace, and God's election of man must be by one or the other. Nor can this election be by works, for then God would owe His favor to those who earned it. This verse restates, in essence, the principle already affirmed in 4:4 (see lesson 9). Here Paul is especially aiming at those Jews who would have based their claim to God's favor on their own efforts to keep the law. That way has not provided an Israelite remnant who enjoy the blessings of God.

To summarize verses 1-6: Paul indicates that the gracious election of God, on behalf of any Jews who put saving faith in Jesus, has ensured that there is a remnant of Israel in His favor, that He has not cast aside His people after all.

2. THE REJECTED: A BLINDED MAJORITY
(Romans 11:7-10)

If there is but a minority of the Jewish people in God's favor on this side of the Cross, then obviously the majority of Israel does not enjoy right-standing before God. That is the sad truth of the matter, and to that other side of the coin Paul now turns.

Israel's Confusion in Seeking (verse 7a). The words "What then?" serve to introduce the conclusion that Paul's previous arguments have pointed to. That conclusion is a statement of the tragedy of the situation of the majority of Israel. In this verse, "Israel" means the fleshly Israel, the Jewish nation as a people physically descended from Jacob and Abraham. Thus when Paul speaks of Israel's failure, he means the failure of the majority. To put it another way, "Israel" means "being an Israelite merely in the flesh."

1. *Paul acknowledges that Israel seeks the favor of God.* The words "that which he seeketh for" show this. Paul has indicated this already in 10:2: "They have a zeal of God, but not according to knowledge."

2. *Israel's failure to obtain God's favor* is the tragic fact Paul is emphasizing here. The keenness of that failure is all the more sharply felt when one considers how tirelessly zealous the Jews were for the law. They sought God where He could not be found. They used a method He had not taught them. He gave them the law to show them their sins (3:20), and they foolishly tried to use it as a plan for obtaining righteousness.

Paul's emphasis here, however, is not so much on their faulty method of seeking God, as on the failure of flesh. As noted, "Israel" carries with it the idea of fleshly identity. Being of Israel has failed to bring one to God. Israel, prince with God, gropes helplessly after Him so long as he wears the name only, so long as he puts confidence in his fleshly identity. Compare 9:30-32.

3. *The only method of success,* which unbelieving Jews have rejected, is shown in the words, "but the election hath obtained it." The "election" referred to is "the election of grace" already indicated in verses 5, 6, and discussed above. The majority of the Jews rejected this election of grace when they rejected Christ. The "it" is "that which Israel seeketh for" and has not obtained: namely, the favor of God, right-standing with God, righteousness.

Israel's Condemnation to Slumber (verses 7b-10). Having failed to find God, Israel after the flesh has been condemned to a tragic state.

1. *The fact of Israel's present blindness* is stated in 7b in the plain words, "The rest were blinded." The *rest* includes all but the *remnant* saved by the gracious election. This blindness is the present condition ("unto this day," 8b) of the majority of physical Israel.

The way Paul states this makes it clear he sees this fate as a deliberate judgment of God on Israel for her wicked rejection of His Son. The blindness is spiritual, of course, but is a metaphor based on physical blindness. Just as the physically blind cannot see, so the spiritually blind are unable to grasp spiritual truth. They, too, cannot see where they are heading.

We should note that this blinding is presented not as a condition always true in Israel, but which became true at a specific time. Israel was not blinded until she first rejected God. We can also note that this blinding does not necessarily have to refer to some inner change in the Jews' own hearts. Whenever God removes His special favors and presence from a nation, blindness is automatic. Man is naturally blind anyway; when God leaves him alone, his blindness cannot be remedied. We must always be aware of the sobering truth involved here: Man's rejection of God's special influences invariably leads, sooner or later, to the removal of those special influences. And hopeless spiritual blindness is the inevitable result.

2. Prophecies of this blindness are cited in verses 8-10. As Paul so often does in Romans, he uses the Old Testament to back up his affirmations about Israel's condition. Her present spiritual blindness is not surprising. God had often predicted this condition by the old prophets. This is an approach Paul has already used in this same section, in 9:25-29 and 10:16-21. The Old Testament abounded with warnings of the condition to which God would condemn Israel if she did not follow Him.

Paul cites two Old Testament references here. The first, verse 8, is from Isaiah and more or less combines the wording of Isaiah 29:10 and 6:10. If you read the context of these references in Isaiah, you will see that Isaiah was first of all referring to the condition of Israel in his own day. Isaiah was being called to preach God's Word to a people who would not hear. Even in his time, God had sent spiritual blindness on an Israel who resisted His ways and went after idols.

So Paul sees Isaiah's reference as stating a principle that happens over and over, and thus a prophecy of what would happen for the worst time of all when Israel would reject God's Son as Her Messiah and Savior.

The "spirit of slumber" is, of course, the same as the spiritual blindness already referred to. Sleepiness and blindness are both metaphors frequently used in the Bible to represent spiritual ignorance and unconcern (compare 1 Thessalonians 5:6, 7, and 2 Corinthians 4:5). The "eyes that they should not see" and the "ears that they should not hear" are similar metaphors representing the same condition. Blind, slumbering, deaf—such is Israel's spiritual condition. We can say that this description pictures more than ignorance and unconcern, that hardness to be reached is also pictured. That is obviously so, only remember that man is universally hard to reach when the gracious, softening influences of God's dealings are missing or withdrawn.

The other reference Paul cites is a free rendition of Psalm 69:22, 23. The wording is not exactly the same but the meaning is, and Paul may be quoting the Greek translation of the Old Testament (Septuagint) instead of the original Hebrew. The reference is especially appropriate, because Psalm 69 is messianic. Verse 21 contains, in particular, words of Jesus referring to His death at the prompting of His own people (verse 8). Therefore, it is because of that rejection of the Savior that the judgment of verses 22, 23 (Romans 11:9, 10) is pronounced.

One's "table" is his delight, his sustenance—his most peaceful time, and the supplying of his greatest physical need. That this should become a trap, a snare, or a stumblingblock is especially ironic and tragic. Denney suggests that Israel delighted in the law, and that the law—misunderstood and abused—became her ruin. (Compare Romans 9:32, 33.) At any rate, as verse 10 shows, David is referring to the same spiritual stupor Isaiah referred to, and he adds the idea of spiritual bondage ("bow down their back"). The majority of Israel, who have trusted in their fleshly descent and self-righteous works of law observance, are condemned to spiritual blindness and bondage. Such helpless groping for God is the inevitable judgment that befalls any who reject the light He offers in His Son. Meanwhile, a remnant of Israel enjoys spiritual prosperity by the gracious election of God that is offered to any who will put faith in Him.

28 Gentile Branches : The Purpose of Israel's Rejection

Study Text: Romans 11:11-25

Introduction
1. Explanation to a Fallen People (Romans 11:11-16)
   a. The Purpose Involved (verses 11, 12)
   b. A Plea Indicated (verses 13, 14)
   c. A Promise Implied (verses 15, 16)
2. Exhortation to a Favored People (Romans 11:17-25)
   a. Cautions (verses 17-21)
   b. Conclusions (verses 22-25)

INTRODUCTION

Chapters 9—11 of Romans explain to us the Jewish situation after Christ's coming and rejection by His own nation. Paul shows that God has not acted unrighteously in rejecting Israel. In chapter 11, Paul continues with this line of thought, showing particularly how God's purpose relates to Israel's rejection.

In the first ten verses of the chapter, which we covered in the previous lesson, Paul shows that Israel has not been totally rejected. Even now, there is a remnant of Jews saved by grace through faith and enjoying the favor of God. Nor is this "remnant" situation new; the righteous Jews were quite often in the minority in Israel, as in Elijah's day. Thus God's purpose has not been abrogated at all. God has not cast aside His people.

This lesson, which covers verses 11-25, presents still another aspect of the picture, showing how Israel's situation fits into the

223

divine purpose and proving that God has not really cast aside His people. In these verses Paul shows that God has really *broadened* His "people." He has reached out to the Gentile world, and the rejection of Israel fits perfectly into the plan to make salvation available to all.

EXPOSITION

A quick check of the general study-outline in the back will serve to remind you how this lesson fits into the overall plan of chapter 11 and of Romans as a whole. This is lesson 28, the second of three lessons on chapter 11, and is entitled, "Gentile Branches: the Purpose of Israel's Rejection."

1. EXPLANATION TO A FALLEN PEOPLE
(Romans 11:11-16)

The verses immediately prior to verse 11 have spoken of the spiritual stupor which had possessed Israel as a whole and as a result of the rejection of Christ. That awful blindness of Israel after the flesh (11:7-10) was sharply contrasted with the blessedness of the small number of Jews who are saved by grace through faith in Jesus (11:1-6).

Paul now turns to a particular aspect of the situation of the blinded Jews, and that is to show us how this fits into the plan of God for the salvation of the world. In summary, Paul is going to show us that the fall of Israel has a purpose and effect that is good. The fall of Israel is not the ultimate purpose of her present stumbling.

The Purpose Involved (verses 11, 12). All along, Paul has been emphasizing that God is a Sovereign whose purposes are in control (9:15-24). The spiritual stupor of the fleshly Israel is no exception to this principle. God has not lost control of things, nor has He had to reverse His field because of unexpected interference with His dealings. Israel's blindness has come about because of Israel's own rejection of the one sent to save, but even that tragic situation works in perfect harmony with the plan and purpose of God.

1. A question introduces this subject in 11a. The question is worded so as to indicate that a negative answer is expected. The strong negative reply "God forbid" reinforces this. The ultimate purpose of Israel's stumbling was *not* Israel's utter fall. This appears to be the exact indication of the question. The word "stumble" and the word "fall" are Greek words in the same family. Probably the difference is that "stumble" is less serious and "fall" more drastic, though it is possible they mean the same thing and Paul uses them merely for variety. If this last is the explanation, then Paul is saying Israel has fallen but that fall was not the *true* purpose.

224

Either way, the final point is the same: God has a purpose for what has happened entirely beyond the fall of Israel. That purpose is indicated in the next part of the verse.

2. *An affirmation* is made in 11b, and this indicates the ultimate purpose of God that is being brought to fruition by what has happened to Israel. That purpose is the salvation of the Gentiles. The fall of Israel serves as an instrument by which salvation is freely offered to the Gentile world. This is true for two reasons, at least. First, in the plan of God—as prophesied even in Old Testament times—the rejection of Israel closed out the period during which God dealt specially through that nation and brought on the New Testament period during which the gospel is freely preached to all. Second, in a practical way, the gospel is preached to the Gentiles because they receive it freely after its rejection by the Jews. This was Paul's own personal experience on many occasions, as in Acts 13:46, for example: "Seeing ye . . . judge yourselves unworthy of everlasting life, lo, we turn to the Gentiles." Compare Acts 28:25-28, a passage that providentially closes the Book of Acts.

The last part of verse 11 mentions "provoking them to jealousy." The "them" refers to Jews. Paul hopes that the Gentiles' salvation will arouse the jealousy of the Jews for the things of God. Indeed he sees this as a part of the ultimate purpose of the whole situation. This idea will be returned to later.

3. *Another question* is asked in verse 12, and it indicates one thing clearly: Israel's fall has resulted in riches for the world. This is actually a restatement of 11b; the "riches" referred to are the spiritual riches of salvation. The "world" is the whole world, the Gentiles in particular. The "diminishing" of Israel is the same thing as her fall, a restatement in different terms.

The thing indirectly implied appears in the "how much more" part of the question. There is a "fulness" for Israel seen here that will be an even greater blessing for the world than the present diminishing. There are two possible interpretations of this; one that would be agreed to by both premillennialists and amillennialists, another that would be believed only by premillennialists.

The first interpretation is that Israel's "fulness" referred to here speaks of individual Jews who are saved now during the gospel dispensation, in spite of the resistance of the majority. If this is the primary meaning of Paul, then he is simply saying that the nation's blindness has offered the blessing of salvation to Gentiles, and that any Jew's spiritual fulness will be an even greater blessing and joy. There is no doubt that this is true, whether anything further is true or not, and both premillennialists and amillennialists can agree with this much. If this is taken as the primary implication of the question in verse 12, then this will also be the primary meaning of the "provoking to jealousy" in verses 11 and 14. To summarize this view, the majority of fleshly Israel has turned away from God and been rejected from favor. God's plan calls for the gospel now to be preached to all the world, and so Israel's fall means the Gentiles' opportunity. God also plans that the Gentiles' salvation should provoke the spiritual jealousy of many individual Jews who will hear the gospel and be saved, and their salvation will be a source of even greater joy in the world.

The second interpretation of verse 12 is one that only premillennialists believe. They see in this verse a confirmation of their expectancy that a time is coming when once again a sizable number of Jews will be converted and used as a special instrument in God's hands. Thus, according to this view, Paul expects (verse 11) that the salvation of the Gentiles, made possible by Israel's rejection, will some day arouse Israel's ancient jealousy for the things of God; and that anticipated "fulness" will be an even greater source of blessing for the whole world than the present rejection that brings the gospel to the Gentiles. Premillennialists see this implied future blessing in terms of a millennium, a thousand-year reign of Christ on earth.

We will not say much more about this disagreement in this lesson but will summarize again in the next lesson, where the matter is especially crucial.

A Plea Indicated (verses 13, 14). As already noted, Paul hopes that the conversion of the Gentiles will arouse the interest of many of his Jewish countrymen in the gospel. Paul's appointment as apostle to the Gentiles did not free him from a burden for his own people, as we have seen in 9:1-3 and 10:1. In verses 13 and 14 Paul inserts a plea that any Jewish readers will turn to God.

1. His office as apostle to the Gentiles is indicated in verse 13. Most of Paul's readers are Gentiles, so he "speaks to" them primarily. In saying this, Paul recognizes that he will always minister primarily to Gentiles, because that is the commission he had received from the beginning (Acts 9:15; Galatians 2:7).

It is difficult to tell exactly what Paul means by "I magnify mine office." "Magnify" means "glorify" or "bring glory upon." Perhaps he means that the faithful exercise of his ministry in preaching to the Gentiles glorifies his apostolic office. More likely, he means that the conversion of some Jews, as indicated in the next verse, will add glory to his office.

2. His hope for the conversion of some of his kinsmen in the flesh is expressed in verse 14. The words "provoked to emulation" translate exactly the same Greek as "provoke to jealousy" in verse 11. Paul, a Jew himself, never gives up hope for his countrymen. He continually longs to lead some of them to Christ. His hope is that the conversion of Gentiles under his ministry will arouse spiritual zeal in the hearts of Jewish observers and some of them will be saved. In so doing, as just indicated, an even greater glory will be attached to his office.

As noted in the earlier discussion, both amillennialists and premillennialists will agree to this much: that Paul sincerely longed to "provoke" many of his countrymen to Christ by his successful ministry among the Gentiles. Premillennialists also believe that Paul's desire to "provoke to jealousy" his kinsmen after the flesh is based on a hope for a future conversion of the people of Israel on a large scale.

A Promise Implied (verses 15, 16). These two verses appear to indicate that Paul's desire for the conversion of fellow-Jews is more than a hope, that Paul actually expects many to be saved and blessing to result. Basically, these verses imply the same truth as the question in verse 12, and in fact the same sort of question is used to imply the promise.

1. *Paul restates, first, the blessing that has resulted from Jewish rejection* (15a). The "casting away" is the same as the "fall" in verse 12, and that looks back to the spiritual stupor of the majority of the Jews described in verses 7-9. The "reconciling of the world" refers to the same thing as "the riches of the world" in verse 12, and those riches were explained in verse 11: "salvation is come unto the Gentiles." The Jewish rejection had led, in God's plan, to the open preaching of the gospel of reconciliation to the whole world.

2. *Paul asks, next, what effect the conversion of Jews may have* (15b). The question is more rhetorical than actual: He simply implies that Jewish conversions will bring even greater blessings and joy than Jewish rejection has brought. "Life from the dead" is a particularly appropriate expression, because the spiritual deadness of Christ-rejecting Jews is especially strong. You will immediately see that the promise implied here is subject to the same two possible interpretations—premillennial or amillennial—already discussed in reference to verse 12. See the explanation above on that verse.

3. *Paul indicates, third, a principle that applies to his implied promise* (16). He does this with two illustrations, both of which teach the same principle. The "firstfruit" and "lump" illustration look back to Numbers 15:19-21, when the first portion of the new bread-dough (after harvest) had to be given to the Lord for holy bread. The dedication of this small portion served to consecrate the whole; likewise, a holy "root" speaks of the holiness of the whole "tree" that would grow therefrom.

What Paul seems to be saying, then, is that Old Testament believing Jews were just part of a whole, like the firstfruits or the root. He expects, then, the salvation of many other Jews to make the whole complete. Again, however, the amillennialists and pre-millennialists would not agree completely about the implications of this principle. The amillennialists would see the "whole" completed by such Jews (and Gentiles) as are saved in our present age by personal faith in Christ. The premillennialists would say that the whole Jewish lump of dough will not be complete until a great turning to God (again, by faith in Christ, of course) in the future.

2. EXHORTATION TO A FAVORED PEOPLE
(ROMANS 11:17-25)

Paul has already explained that the Jewish fall has served to open the door of reconciliation to the Gentile world. That truth might be misunderstood by the Gentiles and give them a feeling of superiority or false security. So Paul hastens to address the favored Gentiles with some sobering exhortations.

Cautions (verses 17-21). The first thing Paul does is to caution his Gentile readers against any false conclusions they might reach. There are two main cautions.

1. A caution against a foolish sense of superiority is first expressed, in verses 17-19. The fact that Jewish rejection has meant salvation for Gentiles (verse 11) should not become a cause for conceit among Gentile believers, nor Gentile contempt of the Jews.

You will see that Paul's metaphor of branches grafted into a tree follows logically after the principle used in verse 16. He compared, there, the people of God to a tree. So now he continues with that figure and suggests that some of the natural branches (Jews) have been broken off and branches from a wild olive tree (Gentiles) have been grafted in to replace them. This is an excellent illustration of the change from Old to New Testament times and of the inclusion of Gentiles in the people of God in gospel times.

But this marvelous truth should not be misunderstood: Gentiles have no right to "boast" because of this. Paul makes two statements about this, both warning against the same danger. "The branches" against whom Gentile converts should not boast are the ones broken off in verse 17: that is, unbelieving Jews. Christian Gentiles should not feel contemptuous of or superior to the rejected Jews. The last part of verse 18 tells why: The Gentiles should remember that their faith rests on a foundation laid with Jewish believers in Old Testament times. The "root" is, of course, that Old Testament people of God, the same as in verse 16.

Verse 19 warns against the very same false conclusion that Gentile believers might reach. If they play up too much the notion that the Jewish branches were broken off just so they could be grafted in, they will be in danger of looking with wrongful condescension on the Jews.

2. A caution against a false sense of security is next expressed, in verses 20, 21. This warning is closely related to the one against boasting, and both of these dangers can only be avoided by seeing the whole truth. So Paul proceeds to make sure we see that whole truth. In doing so, he presents two very clear ideas.

First, Paul makes sure we understand just why the unbelieving "natural branches" were broken off the tree. Verse 19 had not stated this whole truth. The whole truth is that they were broken off because of their own unbelief—a truth Paul has already explained in

9:31—10:21. In other words, then, we must understand two aspects of the reason for Jewish rejection. On one hand, Jewish rejection ushered in Gentile opportunity. On the other hand, Jewish rejection resulted from Jewish unbelief. We must conlcude, then, that the Jews did not *have* to withhold faith from Christ and fall. Had they not done so, God would have provided for Gentile opportunity in a different way. But God knew the Jews would reject Messiah and so included that in His plan and used that to provide Gentile opportunity. God's plan, then, is not responsible for the Jew's unbelief, but He used that unbelief to work out His good purpose.

Second, Paul uses the truth of Jewish rejection as a warning to Gentile believers. If they, the natural branches, lost their place by unbelief, then we must recognize that we stand only by faith. Consequently, we must be careful to maintain faith."High-mindedness" (pride, false confidence) would be risky; the only security lies in the continued faith that results from fearing God. If He cut off unbelieving Jews, He will cut off unbelieving Gentiles, too. So let us not return to unbelief but hold fast our faith.

Conclusions (verses 22-25). The words "Behold therefore," introduce the conclusions we (especially we favored Gentile believers) are to see in the things Paul has been saying. These conclusions reinforce the warnings already given above.

1. A conclusion about God's severity is drawn in these verses. Verse 22 mentions this severity as having fallen on the natural branches broken off because of unbelief. Verse 22 also mentions that this severity might be manifested toward believing Gentiles should they not abide in Him. We see, then, that God does not show mercy where there is not faith. We learned in chapter 9, verse 18, that God shows mercy to whomever He will and hardens whomever He will. But He pleases to show mercy to those who keep faith with Him, and He judges severely those who do not. Israel has experienced this bitter truth, and so might we if we do not humbly hold fast faith.

2. A conclusion about God's goodness is drawn in these verses also. Verse 22 first mentions this goodness as the present experience of the Gentiles who have been grafted in contrary to nature (verse 24). The clear indication is that this goodness is experienced only by faith.

Verses 23, 24 continue with this theme of goodness by implying, once again, that any Jews who will not maintain their unbelief but will put faith in Jesus, can be grafted back into the "tree" and once again know God's goodness. This hope of Paul's is the same as has characterized this entire lesson (verses 12-16, especially) and has already been explained above. The same two millennial interpretations still apply. Amillennialists believe Paul is referring here, in verses 23, 24, only to any individual Jews who will put personal faith in Jesus in the present gospel age. Premillennialists see also the hope of a future Jewish restoration to favor," grafted again into their own olive tree.

    3. A conclusion about God's purpose in this age is drawn in verse 25. This conclusion serves as an appropriate summary for the entire lesson: Jewish rejection serves as Gentile opportunity. That is what Paul has been telling us in this lesson: Israel's situation fits perfectly with the plan of God to offer salvation by faith to all the world.

    Note that "blindness in part" has come to Israel. The "in part" indicates first that the blindness is not total. As Paul has pointed out in 11:1-6, there is a remnant now enjoying God's favor. The "in part" may also suggest that this blindness is not permanent. At least it need not be permanent, as Paul has kept holding out hope throughout this lesson: Any Jews whose jealousy for spiritual things is aroused may now be saved by faith.

    The word "until" may also indicate the temporariness of Israel's blindness. Premillennialists take this as an expression of a time now offered to Gentiles until their fulness be enjoyed and then Israel will once again experience God's favor. Amillennialists agree about Israelites' present opportunity to be saved by faith, but think the "until" is more a *purpose* word than a *time* word. More about this in the next lesson. Meanwhile God's present purpose to offer salvation freely to all the world is clear, and Israel's blindness must be seen and understood in that light.

29 God's Beloved: The Promise of Israel's Redemption

Study Text: Romans 11:26-36

Introduction
1. A Promise of Old Still Intact (Romans 11:26-32)
   a. The Matter of God's Memory (verses 26-29)
   b. The Matter of God's Mercy (verses 30-32)
2. Praise to One Still Inscrutable (Romans 11:33-36)
   a. Proclamation (verse 33)
   b. Proof (verses 34, 35)
   c. Praise (verse 36)

INTRODUCTION

With this lesson, we conclude our three-lesson treatment of Romans 11, and at the same time our coverage of chapters 9—11, in which Paul has dealt at length with the current Jewish situation. As you realize, Paul has explained just how God could be righteous (9:14) and reject the Jewish nation at the same time. At the close of this lesson we will summarize these three chapters (part 4 of Romans) by listing the various arguments Paul has used to defend and explain God's actions.

In chapter 11 Paul deals with the place of the Jewish rejection in terms of God's long-range purpose. The chapter was introduced with the question, "Hath God cast away his people?" The clear answer is No. One reason that answer is negative is the present existence of a remnant of Jews saved by grace through faith, Paul himself an example (verses 1-10, lesson 27). Another reason the answer is negative is this fact: The fall of Israel was not God's purpose, but His purpose was to make salvation freely available to the Gentiles (verses 11-25, lesson 28). To put it another way, God has not cast aside but has enlarged His people.

Throughout verses 12-25 Paul kept indicating a hope for the conversion of Israelites, as we noted in the previous lesson. Now, in verses 26-32, that hope is uppermost in Paul's mind, and reaches its climax with the affirmation: "All Israel shall be saved." God has not cast aside them who are really His people; all He has promised to save will be saved.

You already know, as was pointed out in the previous lesson, that this hope for Israel's conversion can be interpreted in two different ways. Amillennialists see this as hope and expectation of the conversion of many Jews, by the gospel, in our present age and as part of the regular New Testament church. No doubt Paul hoped for that. Premillennialists see this as more; they see here a hope for a future revival in Israel for a large-scale turning to God in a future time. This difference will have to occupy us some in the first part of the lesson.

EXPOSITION

One more check of the general study-outline in the back of this volume will confirm how this lesson fits into the scheme of part 4 of Romans. All of chapter 11 (section C) relates Israel's rejection to the divine purpose. This third lesson on chapter 11 covers 11:26-36 and is entitled "God's Beloved: the Promise of Israel's Redemption."

1. A PROMISE OF OLD STILL INTACT
(Romans 11:26-32)

What Paul does here is insist that God's old promise to save Israel has not been nullified by Israel's present rejection. God never goes back on a promise: Israel (whatever that word was intended to mean) will still be saved. The promise yet holds good. It is intact; it has not been broken by God's rejection of unbelieving Jews.

The Matter of God's Memory (verses 26-29). Paul bases his first assurance that God never fails to keep a promise on the memory of God. Men fail to fulfil their word when they forget, but God never forgets.

1. He remembers His promise, and that promise is cited in verse 26. "There shall come out of Sion the Deliverer, and shall turn away ungodliness from Jacob" comes from Isaiah 59:20, though you may note that the wording is a little different. Sion (Zion) means originally the hill on which the original portion of Jerusalem was built, and later the entire city. The Deliverer ("Redeemer" in Isaiah) is Jesus, of course, because He rescues from sin.

The original promise is that this Deliverer will turn away ungodliness from Jacob. The Isaiah wording says He will come to such as turn away from sin in Jacob. The truth behind both wordings is the same though, that Messiah's coming will definitely mark a successful turning away from sin among the Jews. "Jacob" is, of course, Israel's original name.

2. *He remembers His covenant,* as we are reminded in verse 27. This verse also is intended to present Old Testament words. Though the words are not exactly like any certain reference, they accurately present in summary a truth found more than once in the Old Testament. Note Isaiah 59:20, 21; Isaiah 27:9; and especially Jeremiah 31:31-37.

The "covenant" is the agreement God made with Israel, and as Paul puts it here that covenant included the promise to take away Israel's sins. God remembers this covenant promise, too.

3. *He remembers the fathers,* as indicated in verse 28. The "they" in this verse obviously refers to unbelieving Jews, now rejected. Paul looks at them from two points of view. On the one hand, they are viewed from the gospel point of view. Having rejected the gospel, they are at present enemies, both of God and of His people. The phrase "for your sakes" looks at the Gentile opportunity which has resulted from Jewish rejection (compare verse 11).

On the other hand, rejected Jews are viewed from the point of view of the "election." This "election" is the "choice" God made of Israel on His people, in Old Testament times, in a special way. From this point of view, even unbelieving Jews are to be seen as "beloved," objects of God's love. The reason lies in the Jewish fathers—Old Testament saints—who were specially close to God. For their sake, the Jewish people are still beloved of God. God remembers these fathers, and their children can benefit from that memory.

4. *He remembers His gifts and calling,* and this is stated in verse 29. This verse clearly indicates the unchanging nature of God. What He says He does; what He promises He delivers; the agreements He makes are kept; what He starts He finishes.

The word translated "repentance" is not the usual gospel word. This one indicates change of feeling and emotion. There is no such changeableness with God. His "gifts and calling" are based on stable commitments that grow out of His very purposes and decrees, not on changeable feelings. "Gifts" mean gifts of grace, and 9:4, 5 contains as good a list as any of the gracious privileges God bestowed on Israel (compare 3:2 and 2:4). The "calling" was the same, basically, as the "election": God called Israel to a place of special and unique privilege as His people. God remembers these gifts and calling. He has not changed them.

These, then, are the things God remembers: His promise to send a Deliverer to turn away sin from Jacob; His covenant to remove Israel's sins; His choice of Israel as His special people and promises to the fathers; and His unchanging gifts and calling. Based on these things, Paul affirms in verse 26a: "And so all Israel shall be saved." We must deal, now, with this promise, and with the different interpretations placed on it by amillennialists and premillennialists.

Let us take the *amillennial* view first. "All Israel" is interpreted here to mean all who are children of God by faith, whether Jewish or Gentile in national origin. In other words, a *spiritual* Israel is intended, an "Israel of God" (to borrow a phrase from Galatians 6:16).

Amillennialists do not believe that there is still a future restoration of the Jews—as a whole—to God's favor. They do not believe that there will be a thousand-year reign of a returned Christ on this earth. They believe, instead, that the kingdom of God is now, and in the hearts of God's children, a spiritual kingdom.

Thus amillennialists emphasize a truth we have met both in Galatians and Romans, that all who put faith in Christ are Abraham's children and spiritual seed. Review Galatians 3:7-9, 16, 29 and Romans 4:11, 12. They say, therefore, that the Christ-rejecting Jewish nation was once for all set aside from God's favor *as a people*, and that His "people" are now made up of any—Jew or Gentile—who are saved by faith in Christ. This people is the new Israel, the spiritual Israel.

So amillennialists believe that this spiritual Israel is the true Israel. They say that when God blesses this Israel, He is fulfilling all His promises to Israel. When He "turns away ungodliness" from any believer—Jew or Gentile—He is turning away ungodliness from Israel in this sense. The same thing applies to all the promises referred to in these verses.

Amillennialists believe, then, that Gentile Christians have largely replaced the Jews in "Israel." Gentile believers have been grafted in to the tree to replace the Jewish branches broken off because of unbelief (11:17). But the "tree" is still the true Israel and still the whole people of God to whom He made such wonderful promises as these in 11:26-28. So the amillennialist agrees that God has not cast aside His people. God knew all along that His people would be composed of Gentiles as well as Jews. God has not reneged on any promise, then: All Israel—the true Israel—shall be saved.

Now let us look at the *premillennial* view. Premillennialists look forward to a bodily reign of Christ on earth for a thousand years. They believe that this "millennium" (Latin word for 1,000 years) will be preceded by a large-scale revival among the Jews, that great numbers of them will be saved and that the nation will once again be used in a unique way during the end times. Of course this wholesale conversion of Israelites after the flesh will come only by their genuine spiritual renewal as a result of saving faith in Christ as Messiah and Savior. This renewal in Israel is still future, as premillennialists see it.

So when premillennialists read "All Israel shall be saved," and the Deliverer will "turn away ungodliness from Jacob," they take these promises to indicate this expectation of revival in the nation of the Jews. They see the present spiritual stupor of Israel (11:7-10) as only temporary (11:25). They believe God will yet fulfil the marvelous promises of 11:26-29 among a people who are really Jews in the flesh as well as children of God in the heart.

To conclude, then, both amillennialists and premillennialists believe that Paul keeps hoping Gentile conversions will challenge many individual Jews to put faith in Christ and be saved now. And this hope has pervaded chapter 11, especially since verse 12. The premillennialists go one step farther and see an expectation of a future restoration of "the chosen people" to God's favor.

The Matter of God's Mercy (verses 30-32). If Paul offered the memory of God as the first reason he believes God's old promises to "Israel" will still be kept, then he regards the mercy of God as another reason.

1. *The present Gentile experience of mercy* is referred to in verse 30. Paul looks back to the time when despised Gentiles were not believers and consequently did not experience God's mercy. (Compare Ephesians 2:11, 12.) Yet now, he says, the former outcasts have obtained mercy following, in God's timing, the Jewish unbelief and rejection of Messiah. Note that both the Gentiles' former rejection and the Jews' present rejection result from unbelief, not simply from changing whims of God.

Mercy is God's gracious (undeserved) help in response to man's helpless plight. Mercy only comes when the one helped cannot help himself. That Gentiles, who formerly disbelieved God and were not objects of His mercy, have now obtained mercy is a testimony that a situation is never utterly hopeless when God is involved. Thus Israel's present unbelief and rejection do not rule out access to the mercy of God for any Jew who will believe (and also for a large host of Jews in the future, if premillennialists are right).

2. *The potential Jewish experience of mercy* is indicated in verses 31, 32. "These" refers to the Jews, and verse 31 reminds us that their rejection, based on unbelief, ushered in the age of Gentile opportunity. But that need not be the end of the story, says Paul. Just as former Gentile rejection was not final or permanent, neither must present Jewish rejection. They, too, can turn to Christ and receive mercy. Paul expects the Gentile experience of mercy to lead to Jew's experiencing the mercy of God. Compare 11:14.

Verse 32 is a marvelous expression of Paul's confidence in the great, universal mercy of God. The "all" (both times) refers to every group of men, Jews and Gentiles. Paul is saying that all men naturally reside in unbelief, but that unbelief does not thwart God's purpose. His purpose is to show mercy to all, to any from any group, Jew or Gentile, who will believe. So His dealings with men have always been in such a way as to offer them opportunity of mercy. That may not always *seem* to be so from *our* viewpoint, but God's ways are too wonderful for us. Thus the old era of Gentile unbelief, when God worked specially with the Jews, had as its ultimate purpose the offering of mercy to the Gentiles. So, too, the present era of Jewish unbelief has as its purpose the offering of mercy to the Jews. This does not mean God caused the unbelief of any. Man is always personally responsible for his unbelief. But God does make the wickedness of men praise Him, and He has controlled the fortunes of men and nations—even their periods of unbelief—in such a way as to offer the greatest possible showcase for His mercy. That confidence adds to Paul's hope for the conversion of many Jews.

2. PRAISE TO ONE STILL INSCRUTABLE
(Romans 11:33-36)

Just above, we noted that we cannot always understand God's ways. They are too wonderful for us. We are assured He controls history so as to make mercy available to all in the most opportune way, but we cannot see this in our limited understanding of the changing historical scenes. We have to accept God at His word.

This limited understanding of ours is now uppermost on Paul's mind as he closes off part 4 of Romans. He has done the best man can do, even under the Spirit's inspiration, in explaining God's actions, and he has succeeded in clarifying matters—including the Jewish situation—immensely. But he is conscious, as are we, that much of God's ways lies beyond our current grasp. God is still inscrutable. He is too wonderful for us, and man can but submit in glad praise. Though we do not understand everything about Him, we are assured of His mercy, of His provision of salvation for all, of His control of all things for His eternal purposes. And so we utter praise to the one we still do not understand, but in whom we have utmost confidence. This is the way Paul's own heart responds.

Proclamation (verse 33). This exclamation proclaims God's greatness as being beyond our comprehension. The word "depth" often suggests a deepness man cannot plumb (cf. 1 Corinthians 2:10: "the deep things of God"). The exact relationship of the words "riches" and "wisdom" and "knowledge" is disputed in the commentaries. The King James version sees wisdom and knowledge as the two areas in which God's riches are manifested. But the Greek wording is such that the three words could all be parallel: the depth of God's riches, and of His wisdom, and of His knowledge. Many commentators take this as the correct relationship, and this seems the better way.

For the "riches," Denney points us back to 10:12, where God is said to be rich to all that call on Him by the gospel, and explains:

236

"What Paul adores is the unsearchable wealth of love that enables God to meet and far more than meet the appalling necessities of the world; love less deep would soon be bankrupt at the task."

The "wisdom" and "knowledge" of God refer to His "intellectual resources" (Denney's phrase). Thus God is omniscient (all knowledge) and has perfect wisdom in the application of knowledge to His actions. This inscrutable wisdom and knowledge (cf. 1 Corinthians 1:25) assure us that God sees the end from the beginning and wisely governs the universe by that perfect knowledge. Thus—though we cannot always see how all the pieces fit together—we know that nothing is out of His control, nor are His purposes formed—like ours—by faulty ideals, or His methods of achieving His purposes adopted out of incomplete knowledge.

God's "judgments" refer to all His decision-making in reference to man and the universe. (Compare Psalm 36:6.) "Unsearchable" means exactly what it says: God's decisive actions—whether of mercy or punishment—are not open to man's examination. The last phrase of the verse, "his ways past finding out," repeats, poetically, the previous one and so means the same thing in essence.

Proof (verses 34, 35). As often in Romans, Paul cites the Old Testament to sustain his point, this time to prove the inscrutability of God's ways. Verse 34 is a quotation of Isaiah 40:13. (The Old Testament used "Spirit" rather than "mind," but the truth is the same.) No man has come to the knowledge of God's mind. Note 1 Corinthians 1:21, 25. Even what we know by God's own revelation (1 Corinthians 2:9, 10) must be discerned by the Spirit-illuminated mind and not by natural, human understanding (1 Corinthians 2:14).

The second rhetorical question in the verse indicates no man has been called on to advise God. God does not need man's advice. He is independent of man, because His ways are so far above man's.

Verse 35 gives the meaning of Job 41:11. The point is that God's doings are not the results of man's actions. God's doings come first. As Denney expresses it: "God's ways *would* be finite and comprehensible if they were determined by what men had done, so as merely to requite that." In other words, God does not *react*, He acts. His course of action, His eternal purposes and plans are set in His own inscrutable wisdom and knowledge and are not dependent on man's puny doings.

Praise (verse 36). Paul concludes this section with a song of praise. The praise is based on the assertion that "of him, and through him, and to him, are all things." The "of him" refers to God as source of all being. The "through him" sees God as the agent by whom all things are created and upheld. The "to him" means that all things are ultimately for His glory and purpose. God is in absolute control of all things for His eternal purpose. To such a God goes our ascription—with Paul—of "glory for ever."

We summarize, now, chapters 9-11, part 4 of Romans. Paul's

overall purpose is to defend God's rejection of Israel. He does this with a series of arguments we have noted, as follows. (1) God never promised to deal with men on a fleshly basis (9:6-13). (2) God is Sovereign and shows mercy or punishment to whom He pleases (9:14-24). (3) God predicted, in Old Testament times, the present rejection of Israel (9:25-29). (4) Israel's own rejection, by unbelief, of righteousness by faith in Christ, is the reason for her rejection (9:30—10:21). (5) A remnant of Israelites still experiences the favor of God, by faith in Christ (11:1-10). (6) The Jewish rejection opened the door of Gentile opportunity (11:11-25). (7) The Jewish rejection does not exclude Jews from God's mercy, and so His promises to Israel will be fulfilled (11:26-32). Again, we praise God who fits all circumstances into His eternal purpose in ways far beyond our ability to comprehend.

30 Christian Service : The Self

INTRODUCTION

With this lesson we begin the fifth and final major part of Romans. In this whole section (12:1—15:13), Paul deals with the practical application of Christian doctrine to the saints' daily life. The first eleven chapters have taught us how we obtain righteous standing before God by faith in Christ. These last chapters teach us how that righteous standing ought to be demonstrated in righteous living.

Evidently, Paul was often accused of teaching that we are saved by grace in spite of our sins, and so it matters not how we live. This accusation seems to be behind Romans 3:8; 6:1; and Galatians 2:17. But Paul taught no such thing. He *did* teach that sinful men are saved by grace through faith and not by works (Ephesians 2:8, 9, for example). But he also taught that "grace" leads to holy living (Titus 2:11, 12, for example).

In other words, the individual's conversion involves more than a legal righteousness in position, a judicial act. Conversion also involves a work of the Holy Spirit on the individual, a regeneration, a new

239

birth; and this is the foundation for a *practical* righteousness that follows inseparably our *positional* righteousness. So in every epistle Paul followed doctrine by ethics. Romans is no exception.

EXPOSITION

This is a good time to consult the general study-guide in the back of this volume, especially since we are beginning a new part of the epistle. As you will see there, part 5 concerns the saints' practice of righteousness. Chapter 12, in a special way, will deal with "Christian service" (in three lessons). This first lesson covers verses 1-8 and is entitled "Christian Service: the Self." We must be in right relationship to God ourselves, and must have the right concept of ourselves, before we can be effective in Christian service to others.

1. EXHORTATION TO SURRENDER TO GOD
(Romans 12:1, 2)

These two verses are well-known in Christian circles as a text calling for total yieldedness to the will of God. Indeed, this is one of the few places in the Scriptures where we are told specifically what we must do to walk in God's will. The first requirement for living righteously in this world, and for living in effective Christian service, is being rightly related to God. So these two verses deal with the foundation of that right relationship.

A Reasonable Ministry (verse 1). The first requirement laid on us, if we are to be surrendered to God and walk in His will, is stated in verse 1. The verse contains several important ideas which must be examined one by one.

1. The foundation for this exhortation is first shown. The word "therefore" looks back to all Paul has already taught. The doctrine covered is the reason for the practice about to be indicated. "By the mercies of God" makes this foundation more specific. Paul is thinking of the merciful acts of God he has already explained in the preceding eleven chapters. Consider, for example, God's mercy in providing redemption by Christ, free for all (3:22-24; 5:8-10; etc.). Consider, too, His mercy in providing opportunity for the Gentiles to be saved (11:30). Therefore, says Paul, by such mercies as these I exhort you.

2. The nature of this exhortation is indicated next: "Present your bodies a living sacrifice." This clause, like the rest of the verse, uses the imagery of Old Testament animal sacrifices as a backdrop against which to speak of our total surrender to God. The word "present," in Greek, is one of many words that were used to speak of offering sacrifices. "Offer your bodies to God," says Paul. The word "sacrifice" proves this is what Paul means.

Still, Paul does not mean for us to offer our bodies in *exactly* the same way animal sacrifices were made, so he includes one more word to ensure our catching his idea: "living." Animals were killed and offered, but we are to offer our lives. Even that, however, does not remove the death idea completely from this sacrifice, for one must certainly die to all selfish considerations if he offers his body to live for God.

3. *God's response to our offering* is clearly seen by the words "holy, acceptable unto God." "Holy" is used in the frequent Biblical sense that anything God uses is holy because He is holy and because that thing is set apart from anything else by His use of it. Thus, the transfiguration mountain is called "the holy mount," for example, in 2 Peter 1:18; and the men used to write the Scriptures are called "holy men" in 2 Peter 1:21. "Acceptable to God" means the offering of ourselves pleases God, and so He accepts such an offering.

Count on it: Whatever you offer God, sincerely, He will accept and use, and thus make "holy." He most wants you.

4. *The "reasonableness" of this offering* is the final idea shown in verse 1. First, let us notice the word "service." This is not the usual New Testament word translated here, but one that refers to the priestly ministry. Paul keeps the Old Testament sacrificial system before our eyes with this word, comparing us to the priests whose duties included especially the ritual of sacrificial offerings. We can offer up sacrifices, too, he says; only ours will be our own bodies, alive, rather than dead animals.

The meaning of the word "reasonable" is probably not usually understood. We generally take it to mean realistic, not unreasonable, not too harsh or demanding. And certainly this sacrifice of ourselves is "reasonable" in that sense, when we consider all God has done for us. But "reasonable," here, probably describes the *area* in which we perform this sacrificial, worshipful "ministry" of offering ourselves to God. In other words, we do so in the sphere of reason, rather than in the real, literal sense. The old priests performed a literal, physical, tangible ministry. But ours is a rational, spiritual ministry, in the mind and soul instead of with literal tabernacles and altars and animals. Thus, "reasonable" in front of "service" (ministry) distinguishes it from Old Testament service just like "living" in front of sacrifice distinguished it from Old Testament sacrifice.

A Renewed Mind (verse 2). This verse gives us two other things we must do, beyond offering ourselves to God as living sacrifices, if we are to successfully follow His will. These two are, in fact, two sides of the same coin, a negative and positive.

1. *Avoiding conformity to the world* is the negative side. The Greek word literally means to be fashioned together with. The "world" is really the spirit of the *age*. The world system is a whole

way of life, under the supervision of Satan (the "god" of this world), and carefully organized to express the philosophy, the "mind," of the wicked one. Thus, we are always under pressure to be pressed into the mold of the age. We must resist.

Nor can we avoid this conformity simply by making out a list of a few specific "worldly" things we will not participate in. No, the world's philosophy cuts too deep for that and touches on values, standards, ideals, ambitions, fashions—in short, everything about life that expresses the very meaning of life. We have got to be determined, regardless how difficult and unpleasant, to refuse to let the world's "mind" set our life-style.

2. *Expressing transformation* is the positive side. The Greek word literally means a "metamorphosis." And Paul is not talking to sinners or looking back to one's conversion experience. That was a metamorphosis, all right. But *this* transformation is a continual, daily, Christian experience. (The Greek tense of both the negative and positive commands indicates continuing action.)

What, then, is this continuing transformation? The next phrase makes it clearer: "by the renewing of your mind." "Mind" is the way we think, our attitudes, our philosophy. You see, the world continues to bombard us, in a thousand ways, with its philosophy. We must be "brainwashed" every day, and so continually transformed, if we are to resist the world's way and walk, instead, by God's will. And the Word of God is the only source where we can find God's "mind" by which to renew our own. The choice, then, is clear: the world or the Word, the mind of this age or the mind of God. Which influence shall we let set our "minds"? If we are to walk in God's will, our minds must be renewed by God's way of thinking, and thus we will continue to experience transformation of life.

3. *The result of all this* is indicated in the last clause of verse 2: "that ye may prove what is that good, and acceptable, and perfect, will of God." "Prove" means "put to the test," and this implies both knowing God's will and practicing it with success and satisfaction at the results. Thus tested, God's will proves to be good and acceptable and perfect. God's will is the very best thing we can experience in life. Paul's thought here evidently drifts back to his discussion of God's purpose in 8:28.

2. EXERCISING SPIRITUAL GIFTS
(Romans 12:3-8)

Paul moves from the matter of our surrender to God to the matter of our particular places in that perfect will we have sought. What Paul wants us to know is that there is a place for each of us in God's work. Recognizing this is another part of getting *ourselves* in the right place before we worry too much about service to *others*.

There are, as Paul presents the subject in these verses, two aspects of seeing ourselves aright.

Seeing Ourselves Soberly (verse 3). The emphasis of this verse is on humility. We must not think more highly of ourselves than we ought. There is no place for pride in the service of God.

1. *The manner of Paul's instruction* is indicated in the phrase, "through the grace given unto me." Paul often called his place in the gospel ministry a "grace" (cf. Philippians 1:7). His office is a "grace" because he did not deserve it, and God gave it to him anyway. So when Paul says this, he avoids speaking contemptuously as though *he* had any right in himself to speak authoritatively. But still he shows that his words *are* authoritative because *God* is behind his teaching. God graciously gave Paul the responsibility of the apostolic office, and so Paul must give the teaching needed.

2. *The warning of Paul* is against pride. Each reader, each Christian is urged not to think of himself beyond what is proper. Christians, of all people, must not have blown-up opinions of themselves but must see themselves humbly. Compare Philippians 2:3: "In lowliness of mind let each esteem other better than themselves." This right attitude toward ourselves is essentially related to the surrender to God already urged on us in verses 1, 2. Denney quotes Gifford as saying that "Humility is the immediate effect of self-surrender to God."

3. *Paul's urging* is that we should think *soberly*, instead of with pride, when we view ourselves. This word means soundly, sanely, with self-control. In other words, we ought to strive to see ourselves objectively and not as we would *like* to see ourselves. We ought to try to see exactly what we are, to determine exactly what God expects of us individually, with humility. The next phrase makes this even clearer.

4. *The method of sober thinking* about ourselves is indicated by the words, "according as God has dealt to every man the measure of faith." We can only see ourselves accurately when we understand what God has given us. He does not deal with every man by the same measure, as will become plain in the following verses. Each of us ought to determine what God has given us and see ourselves sanely and sensibly in that light. This is further reason for humility, by the way, because we have nothing that was not *given*, graciously, to us (cf. 1 Corinthians 4:7).

The exact place of the word "faith" in this phrase is a bit difficult to fix. Probably Paul means that we each receive the particular measure God has meted out to us by faith. By faith each accepts the place God has given him to fill, and each must see himself as strictly having received this by faith, not by his own deserving or works. Consequently, each will see himself accurately, understanding his own unworthiness to deserve whatever God has dealt him, and thus not thinking proudly of himself.

Seeing Ourselves in Service (verses 4-8). But if we are not to think too highly of ourselves, neither are we to think too lowly of the place God has given us in His service. The last part of verse 3 introduced this thought by reminding us that God has dealt by different measures to different individuals, and each individual should discern his own place. Paul now proceeds to explain more in detail what he meant about the different measures God has measured out to us in faith. The doctrine involved here is the doctrine of "spiritual gifts." This means that every Christian is given, by the Spirit, a place to fill, a service to render, a function to fulfil, a part to play in the body of Christ.

1. The oneness of the body of Christ is first stressed in verses 4, 5. This is important, because a misunderstanding of spiritual gifts can lead to a spirit of competition and friction among brethren in Christ. We have to understand, though, that all the various gifts are for the *one* purpose of edifying the *one* body of Christ, the church.

Verse 4, by using the word "as," suggests a comparison with the human body. One body has a variety of "members" (parts)—hands, eyes, feet, etc.—with differing "offices" (functions). Yet the body is one, and all the parts work together, each with its own function, in harmony and for the common good of all in the one body.

Verse 5 indicates that this same principle applies to us as individual Christians in the church body. Like hands, eyes, and ears, we each have our own differing functions. But, as with the human body, we are all just parts of one spiritual body. And so we all work together in harmony for the common good of all.

If you would like to have a longer treatment of this very same truth, with the very same comparison made, study 1 Corinthians 12:12-27.

2. The variety of the spiritual gifts is suggested in verses 6-8. This doctrine is one that needs renewed emphasis in today's churches for two reasons. One is that current charismatic emphasis on spiritual gifts is distorted and needs correcting. More important, every individual Christian needs to have a sense of *usefulness* in the Lord's work and in the church. Many Christians seem to be at loose ends, wondering what their places are. A proper understanding of the scriptural teaching of spiritual gifts will help each Christian know he has a place to fill. Thus, while he will not be proud, as verse 3 warns against, he can still have a sense of his own God-given significance.

Notice, first, that these "gifts" differ according to the "grace" given to us (6a). This carries back to verse 3, the "measure" which God has dealt to every man. Further, as Paul said in 3a, he was merely operating by his own "gift of grace" when he wrote such instructions as these. We shall examine, in turn, each of the seven spiritual gifts Paul lists in these verses. In doing so, it will be helpful to compare the other three lists of spiritual gifts contained in the New Testament, in 1 Corinthians 12:8-10, in 1 Corinthians 12:28, and in Ephesians 4:11.

Prophecy is the first gift listed here, and is included in each of the other lists, though not first. Arguments have raged whether the prophet was a *fore*teller or *forth*-teller. Neither is accurate, though both are true. *For*-teller would be more accurate. The prophet, in the original Biblical sense (both Old and New Testaments), received his message directly from God and then spoke, for God, to man. In this technical sense, the gift of prophecy ceased when the apostolic period ended and the New Testament was complete. Men no longer obtain direct revelations from God. But the preacher, who speaks for God from the written revelation, is the "prophet" of our day. The modern capacity, like the old one, is a "gift."

Ministering is the gift listed next, and it does not show up in either of the other three lists. Ministering, in Greek, literally means serving. In fact, the Greek word is the very one from which our word "deacon" comes, and many think Paul is speaking here of the formal office of deacon (as qualified in 1 Timothy 3:8-13). The deacon's function is certainly one of the gifts; so would be *any* place of service.

Teaching comes next and appears in 1 Corinthians 12:28 and Ephesians 4:11. In this last place, the particular "teacher" referred to is the pastor. But all teachers, whether the pastor or Sunday school teachers, or others, receive their place as a gift by the Spirit for the edifying of the body.

Exhorting follows and was probably better recognized in the early days than now. This ability is certainly a gift. The emphasis is on the encouraging and comforting kind of exhorting, rather than instructional content. This gift is not mentioned in the other lists.

Giving is the next gift, and we ought not be too surprised. The ability to give comes not so much from a plentitude of possessions as from a generous spirit. This comes only from God. This gift also does not occur in the other lists. The "simplicity" Paul refers to means without hidden motives, openly.

Ruling is listed next and is probably the same as "governments" in 1 Corinthians 12:28. All church offices in which leadership authority is vested are included. Compare 1 Thessalonians 5:12. "Diligence" is zeal, earnestness, urgency.

Showing mercy is the last gift in this list and is not to be taken lightly. The spirit of compassion is a gift from God's Spirit. Many Christians ought to possess this ability to be moved by men's needs—whether physical, economic, or spiritual—and respond in mercy. And cheerfulness ought to characterize such a service.

Many more "spiritual gifts" could be listed. The four lists are all different and thus open-ended. *Any* place of usefulness in the life of the body of Christ is such a "spiritual gift," and the Spirit of God has one—or more—for *every* Christian. Sometimes these are natural talents surrendered to God and sanctified by His Spirit for the Lord's

245

service. Others are special abilities or functions developed after the individual's conversion. Either way, the emphasis ought to be on the fact that everyone has a place to fill: nursery workers, singers, pray-ers, and many others, just as surely as the ones here or in the other lists.

Every Christian, then, ought to get ready for service to others by seeing *himself* aright: not with pride but with a sober understanding of the place God has for him. And every Christian ought to be concerned to develop his gift—or gifts—and exercise them faithfully.

31 Christian Service : The Saints

Study Text: Romans 12:9-13

Introduction
1. A Selfless Affection (Romans 12:9, 10)
   a. An Honest Love (verse 9)
   b. An Honoring Love (verse 10)
2. A Spiritual Ardor (Romans 12:11, 12)
   a. Spiritual Fervor (verse 11)
   b. Spiritual Faithfulness (verse 12)
3. A Sharing Attitude (Romans 12:13)
   a. The Exhortation (verse 13a)
   b. An Example (verse 13b)

INTRODUCTION

This is the second of three lessons on Romans 12 which deals with Christian service. Service is, after all, the expression of our Christianity in daily life, especially as that expression is related to others, either within or without the Christian fellowship.

The particular emphasis of this lesson is on our service to others within the fellowship. When we are saved, we are baptized by the Holy Spirit into the body of Christ. The local church is the most practical way in which that "body" unity is manifested, because the local church is like a miniature copy of the great universal body of Christ. One of the most meaningful blessings of being saved is belonging to a fellowship of fellow believers. We are not left to go it alone, because we have the help and encouragement of each other.

This fellowship is not all receiving; there is giving, too. We have obligations to one another, responsibilities to help each other in the church grow in grace and prosper spiritually. This is what Christian service involves.

EXPOSITION

You may want to glance at the study-guide in the back of this volume to remind yourself how this particular lesson fits into the general plan. As you can see, this is the second lesson on Christian service, from Romans 12. The lesson covers verses 9-13 and is entitled "Christian Service: the Saints."

1. A SELFLESS AFFECTION
(Romans 12:9, 10)

The subject of these two verses is "brotherly love." This is one of the finest expressions that the New Testament uses to express the nature of our relationship to each other in the church. We are as concerned about each other as are members of a closely-knit family. In fact, the Christian fellowship *is* a family, and these ties often outweigh flesh-and-blood family ties. Our Christian service to our fellow-saints is built on this concept.

Compare these two verses with 1 Corinthians 13, especially with the similarity in plan. Both there and here, Paul discusses love immediately after a discussion of spiritual gifts (here, verses 4-8; there, 1 Corinthians 12). The lesson we are to see in this is that our love for one another in the church is the highest consideration of all in our service to one another. This consideration must condition all others. The spiritual gifts must be exercised in a spirit of love, a genuine concern for each other's welfare and progress. Without love, as Paul puts it in 1 Corinthians 13, all our service is as nothing.

An Honest Love (verse 9). The first thing Paul wants us to know is that Christian love is not a silly, sickly sentiment that hides the truth or refuses to face the facts. Nor does Christian love float adrift to be cast about by every changing whim of fancy. Christian love is open and honest, anchored to the truth.

1. The principle: love without hypocrisy. The first exhortation in verse 9 is "Let love be without dissimulation." Dissimulation is the same word, in Greek, as is usually translated *hypocrisy*. The "hypocrite," in the ancient Greek world, was an actor, a stage-player. An actor plays a part he really does not fulfil. He pretends to be someone he is not. Hypocrisy, then, is pretense, acting. Hypocrisy is manifesting something outwardly that one does not really feel inwardly.

The first characteristic of Christian brotherly love, then, is genuineness, sincerity. Let your love for one another in the church be genuine, real, heartfelt—that is what Paul is saying. And when such sincere love lies behind our deeds, then the service rendered is worthy Christian service.

2. The application: love that faces reality. Sometimes we hear it said that love is blind. Not Christian love. Christian love faces facts, sees the good and the evil in those loved, and responds properly to both. Any other attitude is not genuine love.

In this sense, the last half of verse 9 explains the unhypocritical love of the first half. When we see evil in those we love, we recognize it for what it really is and, without pretending it is something good, reject it. When we see good in those we love, again we recognize it for what it really is and, without coloring it falsely, commend it. Only in this way can we practice sincere love for our fellow Christians. As Denney expresses this truth, "Love is not a principle of mutual indulgence . . . like Christ Who is the only perfect example of love, it has always something inexorable about it. *He* never condoned evil. "

So Paul indicates that we should, in genuine Christian love, "abhor that which is evil." Abhor means shrink from. The word suggests revulsion and rejection. Rebuke is certainly included. Love is not blind, not an anemic covering of evil. When we really love a brother in Christ, we will understand that any evil must be exposed in order to be recognized and expelled and overcome. That brother's own spiritual welfare is at stake. We do not love him if we fail to help him purify his life. To accept his evil as though there were nothing wrong would be to partake of his sin and encourage his failure. That is not love. That is a sickly, sentimental indulgence and helps him not at all. But by the same token, neither will love rejoice in his sin (1 Corinthians 13:6) or cut off the offender without a loving effort to restore him (Galatians 6:1). Unpretentious love sees the evil in a brother, mourns over that evil, rejects that evil, and spares no energy toward rescuing the fallen brother.

Likewise, Paul says we must, in Christian love, "cleave to that which is good." If Christian love cannot hide its face from evil in those loved, neither can the eyes be closed to the good. Love is not jealous, you see, and so we rejoice to see good in those we love. Most pernicious and destructive of all is withholding praise from that which is praiseworthy or—worse still—hypocritically pretending that it is something other than praiseworthy after all. Cleave to means hold on to, embrace. This suggests acceptance and appreciation, approval and commendation being implied. And this is as much a necessary ingredient of love without hypocrisy as the rejection of evil.

An Honoring Love (verse 10). If Christian love is open and honest, it also honors those loved. Here is real Christian *family* love expressed.

1. The attitude involved is made plain in the first half of this verse. There are two key words here that give us the essence of this clause. The first is "kindly affectioned." This is the only place this (Greek) word occurs in the entire New Testament. It comes from two words that, put together, refer to the mutual love of parents and children, or of husbands and wives. In other words, this is the tender love of a closely-knit family. Thayer's lexicon suggests that "loving

249

affection" or "tender love" might be good translations.

The other word Paul uses is "brotherly love," which means exactly what it says. The "brotherhood" referred to here, however, does not encompass all men but the Christian brotherhood only. While we are certainly to love all men, we have a special bond to our fellow believers. Love is manifested "especially unto them who are of the household of faith" (Galatians 6:10). Christians are brothers in a unique way. Putting this word with the first one, then, Paul is saying this: "In the matter of your love for one another as brethren in the Lord, have the tender affection of a closely-knit family."

2. *The application to be demonstrated* is indicated in the second clause in verse 10: "in honour preferring one another." Literally, the Greek word translated "preferring one another" means counting them before you. In other words, we put our brethren first. This shows that real Christian affection is selfless. We are more interested in promoting our brethren than ourselves, in pushing them forward, in seeking their spiritual welfare and prayers. This is often said in the Bible: Compare 1 Corinthians 10:24; 13:5; and Philippians 2:4.

Honor is the key word here: We honor our brethren. And because we hold them in such esteem we promote them. We consider their needs before we consider any selfish ends. And when we do, we render Christian service in its best sense, because such selfless choices of a brother's benefit in preference to selfish desires will move us out of the stands of feeling and emotion into the arena of action. We will wash the brother's feet and then go out and render him true service.

2. A SPIRITUAL ARDOR
(Romans 12:11, 12)

These two verses speak directly of our spiritual zeal for God. Consequently, we might at first glance think these verses have little to do with our service to each other in the Christian fellowship. But on second thought, we recognize that part of the purpose of our congregational life together is to maintain spiritual fervency. Thus part of our service to our brethren consists in keeping a healthy spiritual temperature ourselves, as examples for others, and in helping cultivate such a climate in the whole church.

Spiritual Fervor (verse 11). There are three phrases in this verse, and each must be examined for its own point. The three seem to be loosely tied together as expressing a zeal for spiritual things, an eager and warm service for the Lord.

1. *Eager in zeal.* The first phrase is "not slothful in business," which is often misunderstood to apply to a need for industry in our secular professions. But that is not the meaning. First, you must understand that the Greek word translated "business" is exactly the same one as was translated "diligence" just above in verse 8 (see the

previous lesson). The word is translated in a variety of ways in the New Testament: carefulness, care, earnest care, diligence, forwardness, haste. The idea involved is that of zeal, eagerness, enthusiasm, dedication—with a sense of urgency thrown in.

The word translated "not slothful" means not holding back, not dragging one's feet, not reluctant. Instead, one is eager, willing, ready. Put these words together, then, and Paul's phrase comes out like this: "not reluctant to exercise zeal," enthusiastic and ready. Paul is condemning those who are slow to serve. He wants us to be zealous and ready for service, for spiritual things, for the development of our various callings and gifts.

2. *Burning in spirit.* This phrase does not suggest a totally different idea but merely expands on the first and expresses a similar substance in different words. "Fervent" literally means burning. We might argue whether Paul refers to the Christian's spirit or the Holy Spirit, but such an argument would ultimately be pointless since both must be involved. Paul wants the saint's soul to be on fire but not with wildfire; the Holy Spirit is the true fire that should make one's blood boil for the things of God. The spiritual temperature of the individual believer and of the community of believers ought to be maintained at a high level all the time.

3. *Serving the Lord.* The word for service is the usual one referring to bondservice. This means full and unquestioned submission and obedience, recognizing Him as Lord with absolute authority over us. Probably this third phrase is intended to add more specific content to the ideas suggested in the two previous phrases. By themselves, those two phrases might remain somewhat vague. We must have an eager zeal, but zeal for what? And for what should our spirits burn with that Spirit of fire? The answer is the service of the Lord. All together, then, verse 10 refers to our devotion to the Lord Jesus that results in fervent service to Him.

Spiritual Faithfulness (verse 12). If verse 11 speaks of our zeal for service that grows from warm devotion to God, verse 12 speaks of our consistency and perserverance in this devotion. Again, there are three phrases that are loosely tied together to give this picture.

1. *Rejoicing in hope.* The "hope" we have is our confident expectation of participation in heavenly glory. This hope has been referred to previously in Romans. In 5:1-11, especially, this hope was defined as "hope of the glory of God" (5:2) and an assurance that "we shall be saved from wrath" (5:9). In 8:17-25, this hope was defined as an expectation that we will be "glorified" with Christ (8:17, 18) and that our bodies will be redeemed (8:23).

Here, then, Paul urges us once again to have a constant gladness in our hearts (the Greek verb "rejoicing" is continuing action) over this hope. Compare 5:2. He knows that this continuing exultation will help sustain us in our spiritual ardor and keep us faithful. We do not say enough, these days, about the joy that ought to be a consistent characteristic of the Christian life. Paul had a lot to say about it (cf. Galatians 5:22; Philippians 4:4; 1 Thessalonians 5:16; etc.).

2. *Persevering in affliction.* The second phrase in verse 12 indicates that we may expect circumstances, at times, that are unhappy and troublesome. Such "tribulation" may result from the opposition of the wicked, or from natural calamity, or from the flesh's ills, or a hundred other causes. But whenever afflictions come, we can "bear up under" them. This is the literal meaning of the word translated "patient" (persevering).

We must not allow such affliction to dampen our spiritual ardor. We remember Romans 5:3: Not only do we rejoice in the hope we possess, but we rejoice in tribulation too, because we know that tribulation works to produce patience, and ultimately our hope is stronger as a final result. When we see affliction in this light, we are encouraged to be faithful in the maintaining—and even the strengthening—of our zeal for God. Compare 2 Corinthians 4:17: "Our light affliction . . . worketh . . . a far more exceeding and eternal weight of glory."

3. *Persistence in prayer.* Here is an especially important part of the spiritual faithfulness we need to preserve our zeal for spiritual service. "Continuing instant in" means "to give constant attention to." Compare 1 Thessalonians 5:17, "Pray without ceasing," which has the same meaning. In both places Paul does not mean a round-the-clock vigil of conscious prayer but a consistent, regular, habitual prayer life. He knows we must be faithful in prayer if our spiritual temperature is to remain hot, if we are to burn always with spiritual fervor for the service of God.

Do not forget, now, that all this comes in the middle of a section that deals with our Christian service to our fellow believers. We must be consistent and persevering in the spiritual disciplines so that our own spiritual devotion will remain strong and enthusiastic. Glad hope and perseverance in trouble and consistent prayer will help us maintain eager zeal and a burning spirit in submissive service to the Lord Jesus. In this way we serve each other, both because our fervor and faithfulness will serve as examples for our brethren to emulate and because we are helping the whole body to maintain that same level of spiritual ardor.

3. A SHARING ATTITUDE
(Romans 12:13)

A few verses back (9, 10) Paul spoke of the principle and application of genuine, Christian brotherly love. He turns now to a particular way in which that brotherly love will manifest itself. He gives us first the particular type of demonstration he has in mind, and then cites one very specific illustration how that demonstration will be put into effect.

The Exhortation (verse 13a). This injunction is brief: "Distributing to the necessity of saints." But it is packed full of meaning. This particular demonstration of brotherly love in Christian service to fellow believers could take on an infinite variety of forms.

1. The persons involved can be noted first: "saints." As observed above, in verse 10, fellow believers are involved in a special way, not all people in general. Christians are obligated to all men, of course, but in a unique way to each other. Note that Christians are called "saints" (compare 1:7). "Saints" mean "holy ones," "set apart ones." We qualify not because we have achieved some special place that makes us revered, but because the Lord has set us apart to wear His name and bear His Spirit. Thus we are consecrated to Him and called to holy lives and Heaven's service. This is our sainthood.

2. The situation involved is to be noted next and is indicated by the word "necessity." Actually, in Greek, this word is plural, not singular: "the needs" of the saints. Whenever the saints have needs, we must respond.

The particular kinds of needs are not limited. Saints have varying needs at different times. Sometimes these needs are economic. Sometimes there is need for material provisions. These kinds we are more used to. But there are other needs: emotional needs—for attention, for love, for sympathy, for understanding, for acceptance; and there are spiritual needs—for teaching, for encouragement, for discipline even. The list could be almost endless.

Christians must not be unmoved by the needs of fellow believers. We must be responsive and compassionate. If we are not, then John makes it clear that the love of God does not dwell within us (see John 3:17).

3. The fellowship involved in such a time is interestingly portrayed in the word "distributing." Literally, this word means "being partners with" or "being in fellowship with" or "sharing with" or "having in common with." At least two things must be involved for this kind of response to a brother's needs. First, is identification. We must see ourselves as one with our brethren. Then comes sharing. We act to meet the need by sharing what we have because we hold that what we have is theirs, too (cf. Acts 2:44b). This is Christian service to others in its most blessed form. Such selfless, sacrificial giving in response to the needs of fellow believers is everywhere commended in the Word (as in 2 Corinthians 8 and 9) and is one of the most significant expressions and experiences of Christian fellowship.

An Example (verse 13b). In the little phrase "given to hospitality," Paul cites one very specific illustration when the opportunity to share with saints in need would arise. "Hospitality," literally, is "love for strangers." In Paul's day, there were many traveling preachers who moved about from one area to another in the service of the gospel. He was one such "missionary" himself. And there were not good hotels and motels like we have now. So there was need for Christians to be hospitable, to share their homes and food with such. (Many New Testament references relate to this kind of situation, like 2 John 10, 11; 3 John 5-8; Hebrews 13:2; Philemon 22; etc.)

We should not think the need for such hospitality is over, even though our present American affluence often makes the motel more convenient than the home. We can still respond, in various ways, to the needs of those who serve the Lord, even to the sharing of our homes and goods when that is the need. Again, there is no higher expression of Christian service to our fellow believers than sharing what we have when they are in need.

32 Christian Service : The Sinners

Study Text: Romans 12:14-21

Introduction
1. Attitudes Toward Others (Romans 12:14-16)
   a. Submission (verse 14)
   b. Sympathy (verse 15)
   c. Same Mindedness (verse 16)
2. Actions Toward Opposers (Romans 12:17-21)
   a. Accepting Reproach (verse 17)
   b. Advancing Reconciliation (verse 18)
   c. Avoiding Revenge (verses 19-21)

INTRODUCTION

The lessons on Chapter 12 of Romans are emphazing Christian service. We have seen, in the past two lessons, that Christian service involves a right relationship to God and a proper concept of oneself. Then Christian service involves one in a special relationship to the other members of the Christian community, a relationship characterized by brotherly love.

But Christian service also involves one in duties toward the unsaved in the world around him, as well as to the saints in the fellowship of the church. We may prefer to spend all our time with the saints: They are much more lovable, and certainly there is a special tie between us. But God intends for us to be out in the world, too. In fact, He has put us here as lights in the world, to shine and thus to be a testimony for His grace and glory (Philippians 2:15). Our service to sinners, then, is especially important, even though they do not really understand us and sometimes mistreat us.

255

EXPOSITION

A glance at the general study-outline in the back of this volume will show that this third lesson on chapter 12 covers 12:14-21 and is entitled "Christian Service: the Sinners." Actually, not every single thing said in these verses is limited to our relationship to sinners. Some of the instructions speak of Christian relationships in a way very similar to that of the previous lesson. But the sinner's needs are primarily in view, and so that will be our emphasis here.

1. ATTITUDES TOWARD OTHERS
(Romans 12:14-16)

In these verses Paul deals with our "minds" (the word occurs twice in verse 16). In the writings of Paul, "mind" means mind-set, attitude, the way we think. Attitudes come before actions. We have to have the right attitudes toward others (of all kinds, sinners and saints) if we are to manifest real Christianity in service to men.

Submission (verse 14). The first requirement of Christians is that we be submissive to others, even to sinners who oppose us and mistreat us. Submission is an important prerequisite to service. No one will ever serve others if he has not submitted to them, regardless how they treat him. In particular Paul refers to our response to those who persecute us, knowing this is the best possible test of our submission to others. Paul will return to this matter for greater detail below. If we can react rightly to our persecutors, we can react rightly to most anyone.

1. That some will persecute us is assured. The way Paul puts this does not suggest that persecution is the exception but the expected thing. That may have been more true in his day than in ours (cf. 1 Thessalonians 3:4). Always, though, real Christians must expect to be misunderstood by the unsaved, to strike friction because of the differences in beliefs and behavior. And that tension inevitably leads to opposition that is more or less open.

2. We should bless our persecutors. Paul stresses this positive by twice repeating the words. There is some difference of opinion as to the meaning of the word "bless" as it is used here. Literally, the Greek word means to "speak well." So does this mean to say good things to and about our persecutors? Or does it mean to pronounce a blessing on them, thus in essence asking God to bless them? The word is clearly used in both ways, at various times, in the Scriptures.

Considering the contrast with "curse," perhaps the best way to understand "bless" here is in the sense of invoking a blessing or pronouncing a blessing on the persecutors. This is the sense many modern versions see in the word, and some translate, "ask God to bless those persecuting you." Either way, the idea is to seek good things for those who would do us evil, thus manifesting our submission to them, our desire to serve them. This is the attitude Christ himself commended in such passages as Matthew 5:44, where the wording is very similar.

3. *We must not curse our persecutors.* If curse is the opposite of bless—and it probably is—then this negative means we must avoid the natural temptation to wish evil on those who abuse us. To curse them, then, is not as much to condemn or blaspheme them as to invoke a curse or pronounce a curse on them. Just as the "blessing" is in effect a prayer for God to bless (an invocation), the "curse" is in effect a prayer for God (or is it some other supernatural power?) to curse (an imprecation). But if we are submissive to all men, and thus can *accept* their abusive treatment of us in our desire to serve them, we will not wish them ill.

Sympathy (verse 15). It is a real question whether this verse speaks of our attitudes toward saints or toward sinners. Probably the best answer is that both are included, that Paul is thinking broadly of all men without any particular consideration of unique duties toward the saints. If so, then certainly the unsaved are included, and perhaps even the primary reference.

1. *Sympathetic identification with those who rejoice* is first enjoined. This may be harder than the next, because, as Denney says, "Those who rejoice neither need, expect, nor feel grateful for sympathy in the same degree as those who weep." Furthermore, it is easy to feel jealous when "good fortune" has been others' lot. It is much easier to rejoice over one's own blessings than those of others. Perhaps this is what Paul meant in 1 Corinthians 13:4: "Charity [love] envieth not" (when others rejoice, but joins with them in their happiness). Surely that must be included in the meaning of Romans 12:10 (see previous lesson): "in honour preferring one another."

What Paul means is that we must show our concern for and desire to serve others in such an attitude as this, that the good of others and their gladness thereby is occasion for our rejoicing too. And they must be made to know that we enter into their joy, thus demonstrating our genuine concern for their welfare. As already noted, this attitude should apply to all men, saints or sinners, and even to those who (as in the previous verse) persecute us. That we sought their "blessing" should certainly mean we would rejoice in their good fortune.

2. *Sympathetic identification with those who weep* is likewise enjoined upon us. As already observed, this may be easier, both because others welcome sympathy more in grief than joy, and because we are ourselves more easily moved by others' suffering than by their joys. Except, again, we must not forget that these who weep may, at times, include our enemies. Then we may be tempted to gloat, but that is not Christian. If we should not curse them, neither

should we be glad when they must suffer. Is that what Paul means in 1 Corinthians 13:4 when he says "Love is not proud or boastful" (when others—even if they appear to deserve it—must suffer ill fortune)? Even our persecutors must know we want to spare them grief, that we weep when they weep, and that we enter into their sorrows as well as their joys.

Empathy is a word often used to describe such sympathetic identification with others. Literally, the word means "to feel with." Christians ought to have such ability, to share in others' joy or to share in their grief, to feel their gladness or pain in our hearts. That is an essential ingredient in Christian service.

Same mindedness (verse 16). As already pointed out above, this section stresses the Christian's mind or attitude. Verse 16, in particular, speaks of our mind-set, using "mind" twice.

1. A harmonious spirit is indicated by the first instruction in this verse, "Be of the same mind one toward another." While most of the passage we study in this lesson deals with our service to sinners, this expression certainly speaks of harmony within the church. But even that inner harmony, that "loving unanimity" (Denney), is necessary for our service to sinners. They must see a church with unity of mind and purpose if they are going to respect the church and listen to the Christian.

This expression "be of the same mind" (literally: "think the same") is a frequent one of Paul's. Note Philippians 2:2 and 4:2, and 2 Corinthians 13:11, for examples. In all these, Paul emphasizes the fact that the Christians in a congregation ought to be of "one accord" (Acts 2:1). This means they have the same philosophy and purposes. It also means they regard each other with mutual love and respect; no one thinking himself an exception to the rules that apply to all, or better than the others; each eager to serve the others as his brethren in Christ. As Gifford puts it, "Let each so enter into the feelings and desires of the other as to be of one mind with him."

Some modern versions see in this expression an idea of equality as well as harmony. In other words, regarding all alike. That is certainly required for real harmony.

2. A humble spirit is required for this harmony to exist in the church. Paul uses, in the remainder of verse 16, two instructions to emphasize this humility. The first is, "Mind not high things, but condescend to men of low estate." This instruction cautions us against pride that would hold us back from lowly tasks and simple men. With this verse compare 12:3.

Minding high things is seeking self-exaltation, considering oneself better than others and thus too good for such menial tasks or places as one considers beneath his dignity. Some Christians seem willing to accept only such offices as they regard truly important, but that is not the spirit of Christianity. Selfish ambition will always kill the possibilities of harmony in the church and is the very opposite of the submissive spirit required for real Christian service.

Condescending to men of low estate means that no persons, however humble or lowly or poor or simple, are considered "beneath" us. We serve *all* men because we are "same minded" toward all. There is some doubt whether the Greek word used here means *men* of low estate or *tasks* of low estate. Either way, the ultimate truth is the same. The spirit of Christian service regards no person, no task, no office, no function as too humbling or undignified.

The question can easily be raised whether this instruction, and the next one, are speaking exclusively of our attitude toward the saints or toward all. Because of the first instruction in this verse (see the comments above), we could limit this to inner-church relationships. Somehow, though, this writer cannot avoid the feeling that Paul is thinking of our condescension and humble service to *all* men, and not merely to fellow believers.

The second instruction Paul uses to teach us humility is, "Be not wise in your own conceits." If the previous instruction warned against pride that would hold us back from lowly *deeds*, this one warns against a pride that exalts one's own *knowledge* and judgment, our opinions. Same mindedness in the church tends to unanimity of opinion. But such harmony is inevitably broken by one who considers himself wiser than all the rest. Likewise, a person conceited will be unable to win the respect of sinners and serve them. No doubt it is difficult for any of us to examine our own views and judgments as objectively as those of others, or to consider those of others as worthy as our own. But such is the genuine Christian same mindedness that is required for serving others as a Christian should.

2. ACTIONS TOWARD OPPOSERS
(Romans 12:17-21)

If attitudes are first right, right actions will follow. Paul is especially concerned about our actions, as Christians, toward those who mistreat us as our enemies and enemies of God. To this concern, which Paul first expressed above in verse 14, he now returns for closer consideration.

Accepting Reproach (verse 17). This verse contains two distinct, but closely related instructions.

1. *We are not to pay back those who evil treat us.* "Recompense" means pay back, reciprocate. "No man" includes all, saints or sinners; but the unsaved are especially in view, as being more likely to treat us with reproach. The word "for" means "in exchange for": The Christian does not desire to swap off evil treatment with those who reproach him for Christ's sake.

This is, of course, a frequent Biblical teaching. One is reminded of Christ himself, "Who, when he was reviled, reviled not again" (1 Peter 2:23). And He taught us the same, as in Matthew 5:44. Paul often gives such instruction: See 1 Thessalonians 5:15, for example. Someone has said that to return evil for good is devil-like; to return evil for evil and good for good is man-like; but to return good for evil is Christ-like. The Christians who would serve others must manifest this spirit.

2. *In this we are to win men's respect.* This is the meaning of the second instruction in verse 17, "Provide things honest in the sight of all men." The word translated "honest" is really much broader and refers to anything that men recognize as good, worthy, or honorable. Paul means that if we will accept men's reproach with submission, all men will agree that this is good and honorable.

The word "provide" means careful forethought on our part. In our actions that respond to men's evil treatment, we must not merely react but give careful consideration to our response with the goal that all will regard our deeds as good. The "all men" is as emphatic here as the "no man" in the preceding instruction: saints and sinners alike. If we are to serve all men, we must win their respect as being genuinely good and honorable. And our response to reproach is an especially crucial testing for our conduct.

Advancing Reconciliation (verse 18). This verse is often misread, with the emphasis on the word "possible." But the emphasis ought to rest on the word "you." Paul knew we could not always be at peace with the world around us, for unsaved men often react unreasonably to our Christian lives. For this reason he uses the "if it be possible." But we can keep *our* side of the relationship with others right, regardless how others act, and even when others abuse us. So what Paul means is that as far as *our* part is concerned, be at peace with all. If the peace is broken, let it be *their* responsibility, not *ours*.

One is reminded of Christ's beatitude, "Blessed are the peacemakers" (Matthew 5:9). Our aim, even when men mistreat us, ought to be reconciliation, to make peace between ourselves and them. Our actions, when attacked by those with bitter enmity against us for Christ's sake, ought to be such as would promote healing and advance the cause of peaceful relations with all. We should not react in such a way as to widen the breach or increase the enmity.

Another way of looking at this verse, and the last half of the preceding one, is this: Our actions should never be such as would provide men with any excuse for reproaching us. Compare 1 Peter 4:14-16. We should carefully consider all our deeds ("provide things," verse 17) so that all men must respect them as honorable and upright. We should make sure *we* are never responsible for arousing enmity (verse 18). Consequently, our behavior is blameless and none can justify their evil treatment of us. It is far easier to respond to reproach without striking back when our own consciences are clear. Then we know that the "evil" they do to us is really enmity against our Lord, and we can respond with compassion and kindness. And so we advance the cause of reconciliation and enhance our opportunities for service.

Avoiding Revenge (verses 19-21). In a very special way Paul wants us to avoid a vengeful spirit in our dealings with men who wrongfully treat us. Already he has said this twice (verses 14, 17), and now he says so again.

1. *Meekness and patience* are to be our responses when abused for Christ's sake. Verse 19 makes this clear. First we are told what *not to do:* "Avenge not yourselves." It is not our place, as Christians, to seek vengeance. The word translated "avenge," by the way, is one based on the concept of justice. Punishment is just, but such justice is not to be sought for ourselves, certainly not to be inflicted by us. We do not demand justice.

Next we are told what *to do:* "Give place unto wrath." This clause can be interpreted in either of two ways. It may mean to submit meekly to the wrath manifested by those who evil treat us. Or it may mean to yield to God's wrath, to wait patiently for *His* punishment instead of taking wrath into our own hands. Either way, the result is the same: We must submit meekly to evil treatment and wait patiently for God's vindication. Wrath is not ours.

Finally, Paul quotes a Scripture verse (Deuteronomy 32:35) to remind us that God will ultimately right such wrongs as those to which we must now submit. He is the only one who can be trusted to bring truly just vengeance on the wicked. Vengeance is *His,* not men's. He *will* justly repay His enemies who oppose His people. His *Word* is faithful.

2. *Good deeds of service* ought to be rendered, now, by us to those who afflict us. If we give an enemy food and drink we will (metaphorically) heap coals of fire on his head (quoted from Proverbs 25:21, 22). This tells us two things. First it reminds us that we are serving the sinner, even him who reproaches us. Thus we are committed to his welfare and good, and so we offer him food for his hunger and drink for his thirst (or respond to any other need he has).

Second, this tells us that our good deeds will affect him in a definite way. The "coals of fire" refer to the "burning pain of shame and remorse which the man feels whose hostility is repaid by love . . . the only kind of vengeance the Christian is at liberty to contemplate" (Denney). Sometimes, the persecutor so "burnt" will respond with even greater anger; sometimes, with remorse and repentance. We always hope for the latter, but either way the responsibility is his and we have done right.

3. *The meaning of this* is summarized in verse 20. If we practice Paul's teaching, as given above, the real victory will be ours. There

are these two alternatives, you see. We could respond to abuse like our human nature would incline us, with retaliation. But in so doing we ourselves would become evildoers, and thus we would be overcome by evil. Evil would triumph. Or we can respond, as Paul has urged us, with meekness and patience, "punishing" the persecutor only by our deeds of loving service to him. In so doing, the good has prevailed: first in ourselves, and then—hopefully—even in the winning of the enemy to our faith. Thus the good triumphs over the evil. And our Christian service to sinners is effective.

33 Christian Submission : Law

Study Text: Romans 13:1-7

Introduction
1. The Principles Involved (Romans 13:1, 2)
   a. The Responsibility Concerned (verse 1a)
   b. The Reason Considered (verse 1b)
   c. Resistance Condemned (verse 2)
2. The Power Invested (Romans 13:3-5)
   a. The Right of the Sword (verses 3, 4)
   b. The Reasons for Submission (verse 5)
3. The Practice Indicated (Romans 13:6, 7)
   a. Helping Them as Ministers (verse 6)
   b. Honoring Them as Men (verse 7)

INTRODUCTION

Part 5 of Romans (12:1—15:13) deals with Christian practice, with righteousness as it is manifested in daily conduct. In the past three lessons, on chapter 12, we have viewed the implications of complete consecration in our duties toward God (12:1, 2); toward ourselves (12:3); toward our functions in the church (12:4-8); our love for others, especially the saints (12:9-13); and our service to others, especially the unsaved (12:14-21).

There are other duties we have as Christians. One of these is the subject of this lesson and may be introduced with one of our Lord's own instructions: "Render to Caesar the things that are Caesar's" (Mark 12:17). On the occasion of those words Jesus was questioned as to whether it was right to pay taxes as required by the civil government. He made clear that the Christian has obligations to civil authorities. The law must be obeyed. The Christian must submit.

263

Thus Paul echoes the words of Christ himself. One of the ways the righteousness of the believer is practically manifested is in subjection to law and order as enforced by civil rulers. In this lesson Paul dwells on the reasons for this duty and the ways our submission should be shown.

EXPOSITION

A glance at the general study-outline of Romans in the back of this volume will show that there are two lessons on chapter 13. Both deal with the Christian's submission. This lesson covers 13:1-7 and is entitled "Christian Submission: Law."

1. THE PRINCIPLES INVOLVED
(Romans 13:1, 2)

Subjection is the word Paul uses here. Literally it means "to place oneself under." We are obligated to be in such subjection to the "higher powers." In the first two verses Paul speaks both of the *nature* of our submission (the responsibility) and of the *reason* therefor.

The Responsibility Concerned (verse 1a). The responsibility is simply expressed: "Let every soul be subject unto the higher powers." At least two key questions must be discussed here.

1. The powers we must submit to are indicated by the broad phrase "the higher powers." Theoretically, that phrase is broad enough to include all authorities to which Christians rightfully submit, whether at home, on the job, in the church, or in civil government, or elsewhere. We are always under some properly constituted authority, and the Christian ought always to manifest a properly submissive attitude toward any such authority. Paul even told slaves to manifest such subjection toward their masters as a testimony of God's saving grace in their hearts (Titus 2:9, 10, for example).

The context here in Romans 13, however, is such that Paul is probably talking primarily about our subjection to civil authority. The rest of the passage speaks almost exclusively of the governors of the land, and so "higher powers" should be taken in that sense here.

2. The attitude we must manifest is seen in the words "be subject." As noted above, the Greek word literally means to place oneself under. That expression pictures subjection well. The verb is in continuing action in the Greek tense, so a habitual practice is meant. Note, too, Paul's use of "every soul." The "every" means none are excluded. All must submit. The "soul" may mean that Paul knows such subjection cannot be merely external or superficial but must come from the very heart of our being. We must demonstrate, in conduct, a habitual and heartfelt subjection to those who have authority over us. Note, too, that we do not just submit to the *rules*, but to the *rulers*.

The Reason Considered (verse 1b). The principle Paul expresses in the second part of verse 1 is simple and clear: The civil authorities that exist (others, too, of course) do so by the ordinance of God himself. The reason we must obey them, then, is seen in the fact that God's own authority is behind them.

1. *The general fact* is shown by the last part of the sentence: "the powers that be are ordained of God." The word for "powers" means authority more than ability. Authorities exist. And they have been ordered by God. "Ordained" means arranged, placed in order. Civil authorities exist as God has arranged them. In a real sense, then, the authority of civil rulers is the authority of God himself.

2. *The universality of this fact* is shown by the other clause: "there is no power but of God." Literally, these words say, "Authority exists not, except by God." We understand, then, that the very principle by which any civil ruler operates anywhere is a principle established by God. No power on earth could exist except as ordered by the God of Heaven and earth. Was this not what Jesus meant, in John 19:11, when He spoke of Pilate's "power" that was given him from above?

The question can easily arise whether Paul means that the universal principle derives from God, or that every single person who bears authority is providentially placed there by God. In other words, are there ever any individuals wielding power (a Hitler or a Stalin, for example) who are there contrary to God's will? Well, even if we could satisfy ourselves that Paul's general rule has exceptions, we still must see that Christians are not to take it on themselves to determine that the civil ruler is wicked and must be resisted. Most civil rulers do not acknowledge God; nonetheless, they occupy their places as God ordains civil rulers to exist. And Christians manifest their Christianity by submission to them, wicked or good.

Resistance Condemned (verse 2). The Christian will not resist civil government, because the Scriptures condemn such resistance. Paul gives us two specific reasons in this verse.

1. *Resisting civil authority is resisting God.* This truth is a logical application of the principle laid down in the previous verse: All existing civil authorities have been arranged by God. Consequently, when we resist civil authority, we are resisting "the ordinance of God."

The word "resist" means to set or place oneself against. The "ordinance" is the same basic word as the "ordained" in verse 1: arranged, placed in order. Since God has arranged the powers that be, then God's own authority is behind them. And so we are rebelling against God himself when we rebel against properly constituted authority. This writer has heard one preacher carry this principle so far as to say we ought not "boo" the umpire at a ball game. Well, maybe we boo only in fun, but for sure the players should not resist the umpire's calls. And should not we accept the fact that the speed limits represent God's ordained authority?

We hear a great deal about "civil disobedience" these days, a practice when some deliberately break laws they have decided are bad. Now there are certainly bad laws at times, and they need changing. But there is a lawful way to work for change. And until the change is made, the Christian ought to manifest his subjection to God by practicing subjection to civil government.

2. *Resisting civil authority leads to judgment.* Resistance earns its own punishment, and that is another reason resisting civil rule must be avoided. The word "damnation" here may be a little strong for the context. Actually, the Greek word used can refer to any kind of judgment or chastisement, whether temporal or eternal, civil or spiritual. "Condemnation" would be an accurate translation, as would "judgment." Paul is probably referring to the "judgment" that will be inflicted by the civil rulers themselves as punishment for law breaking. He *could* be referring to a chastisement from God (as in 1 Corinthians 11:32, where the very same Greek word is involved). But the context here makes it more likely that he is talking about the normal penalty one will expect to receive when he has broken the law.

This does not mean, however, that one is at liberty to say he will break the law and take his punishment like a man if he be caught. No, there is still the truth made clear in verses 1 and 2 above, that the law represents God's own law. Any form of disobedience is still disobedience to God.

2. THE POWER INVESTED
(Romans 13:3-5)

Paul has told us about the authority behind civil rulers. Now he proceeds to tell us about the specific power invested in those civil rulers, thus giving another reason for our submission to the laws of the land.

The Right of the Sword (verses 3, 4). In these two verses Paul indicates that the right of punishment is definitely invested in civil authorities by God himself. Thus Paul is explaining further the point already introduced in verse 2b when he spoke of the judgment that law violators can expect to receive.

1. *Those who must fear civil rulers* are spoken of in verse 3a. These are those who do evil, and naturally they have to fear because the civil rulers do have the right to punish offenders. This is what Paul means when he says "rulers are not a terror to good works." That is, those who do good things will find themselves "in step" with

266

civil authorities. They will not have to be afraid of civil rulers. They will not find it difficult to be in submission to the powers that be.

"But to the evil," Paul says, there will certainly be terror. People who want to do wrong things will be justified to fear the authorities and can expect punishment for their wrongdoing. It has often been pointed out that those who want to do right do not mind rules and regulations anyway. But those who really want to do wrong resent law and order, both because their desires are curbed and because of the punishment they fear.

2. *The solution to fear of civil rulers* is suggested in verse 3b. Paul uses a rhetorical question to introduce this: Do you want to be able to avoid having to be afraid of the authorities? Then do what is right. This affirmation makes clear the fact that men's laws usually are close enough to God's so that one who really wants to do right in God's eyes will not find himself violating the civil laws. Indeed, that is almost always true. Of course man's laws never are as complete as God's. We can "get by" with far more toward earth's laws than toward Heaven's. But if we keep God's, we will not have any trouble with man's, even godless man's.

Occasionally a situation arises in some country when civil law would call for one to violate God's law. In such a situation as that, one would naturally have to yield to the Higher authority of Heaven. When loyalties conflict, man's greatest loyalty is to God. The truth is, though, that such situations do not often arise, even in such countries as those now governed by communistic infidels. We who live in the United States can be grateful that we never face such conflicts.

Note that Paul promises, to the one who does right, *praise* from the civil ruler rather than the threats that cause fear. The solution, then, and the Christian attitude, is to do right and obey all laws. Then one need not fear the magistrates but can even expect recognition and appreciation from them.

3. *The civil ruler's office as minister of God* is twice affirmed in verse 4. The word "minister" means *servant.* Every civil ruler is a servant of God in the sense that he occupies a place God has ordained as necessary for the government of men. The ruler's office as servant of God carries us back to verse 1b: "the powers that be are ordained of God."

This does not mean that the particular ruler involved must be a Christian to be such a "minister" of God. Even a godless man, or one who refuses to acknowledge God, is such a servant of God. He fills a place and performs a function that God has established and that God uses in superintending the affairs of man. So he serves God whether he knows God or not. The words of Cyrus in Ezra 1:2 provide a good illustration of this.

Paul gives two ways—or two aspects of the one way—a civil ruler serves God. First, in 4a, "to thee for good." That is, the civil ruler helps maintain good on earth and especially encourages men (even if only by his threats) to perform the good. He thus promotes the cause of moral order among men. Second, as in 4b, the civil ruler serves God "to execute wrath upon him that doeth evil." These two are positive and negative of the same truth. The civil ruler serves God by making and enforcing laws against wrong. When the civil ruler sentences law breakers to be punished, he is taking vengeance as a representative of God himself.

4. *The civil ruler's right to punish* is thus fully proved and clearly indicated in the clause, "He beareth not the sword in vain." "The sword," here, is the most extreme form of civil punishment, used here to represent all civil punishments. That the ruler admimisters these punishments not in vain means they are not for nothing; they are full of serious and divinely-given import; and they are effective when rightly executed.

That "the sword" is mentioned here, even in this New Testament setting, proves that the State has the right to administer capital punishment. The sword was a common method of execution in those days, as our electric chair or gas chamber is today. Paul might well have said, he administers not the gas chamber in vain. Only today's misguided authorities have almost completely allowed capital punishment to fall into disuse, to our nation's hurt.

Note that the civil ruler's use of punishments for the violation of civil laws is a form of *vengeance* exercised on God's behalf. Compare verse 19 of the previous chapter. Not *all* of God's avenging wrath awaits the last judgment. God has invested in earthly authorities the power to punish wrong and so to promote moral order. When men persist in wrongdoing and go to Hell, they do so not only against the influence of the gospel but also against the influence of human government.

The Reasons for Submission (verse 5). Paul gives us, by way of completing his discussion of the power invested in civil rulers, two reasons for being in subjection to them. These have already been stated or implied logically in the verses above.

1. *For wrath's sake* we are subject to the powers that govern us. This carries us back to verses 2b and 4b. If we violate the law, we expect the ruler's wrath and the punishment he prescribes. So one reason we submit ourselves to his laws is our desire to avoid that punishment, that wrath he administers as a servant of God himself.

2. *For conscience sake*, too, we are subject to our rulers. This reason is more important than the first one, because it reaches into the realm of our hearts and character. We can avoid law breaking because of fear of punishment without ever really *wanting* to do right. In such a case, only *external* conformity is attained, though that is better than no conformity at all. But when we really allow a consciousness of the divine authority behind earthly authorities to sink into our hearts, then we will respect the rulers as the ministers

of God they are. And our consciences will tell us that obedience is right. And then obedience will come from the heart because it is right, and not just because of the fear of punishment.

3. THE PRACTICE INDICATED
(Romans 13:6, 7)

These two verses contain Paul's positive conclusions about our duties toward the civil rulers. These conclusions, as shown by the phrase "for this cause" (verse 6), are based on the principles explained in the preceding five verses. We can summarize our obligations in two categories.

Helping Them as Ministers (verse 6). This verse presents a very positive attitude we should take toward civil rulers, an attitude that causes us to want to help and support them in their work, to strengthen their hands.

1. *We remember they are ministers of God.* Paul reminds us of this point again by repeating the words already given twice in verse 4: "They are God's ministers." We must have this right conception of their work if we are to have a helpful attitude. We must see them as performing God's own work on earth. It is interesting to note, in passing, that the Greek word for "minister" is different here from the one used twice in verse 4. Here the word is the one commonly used for priestly service. This does not make civil rulers priests, of course, but it stresses their official capacity as representatives of God in the performance of their duties.

2. *They are employed full time in this ministry.* The last part of verse 6, "attending continually upon this very thing," means that the civil rulers must give all their attention to the work they do in governing. Paul's point is quite clear: Because of this, they must live by their "ministry." Like the ancient priests (with whom Paul has compared them by the word just used for "ministers"), they must be able to devote full-time to their employment in government, and so the people must support them.

3. *Therefore, our taxes must support them.* Paul says clearly, "Pay ye tribute." When we realize they are full-time servants of God and must be free to devote constant attention to their ministries, then we can understand why our taxes are necessary for their support. We are helpers in their ministry, partners in their service, when we pay the tribute money required to sustain their work in governing us. Jesus himself laid the foundation for this, as in Mark 12:17. We should pay taxes honestly and happily.

Honoring Them as Men (verse 7). Paul concludes by grouping together several words that serve to represent all the various

269

obligations we might have toward civil authorities. All together they mean we ascribe genuine honor and respect to the individual civil servants who govern us as men, though not simply because they are men but because they represent God as men.

"Tribute" is repeated from the previous verse. Together with "custom" these two words represent *monetary* obligations. Such monetary requirements as may come in various forms—taxes, duties, assessments, etc.—are all included. We do not rejoice in wasteful government programs, of course, but we recognize the necessity of the use of our money to govern us effectively for our good. And so we pay honestly and without resentment if we are Christians and in proper submission to law.

"Fear" and "honor" speak of obligations of *attitude* and *behavior* rather than money. We owe the civil ministers of God respect and obedience as well as support in taxes. The places they fill entitle them to our honor. We manifest Christian submission to the law by manifesting a respectful attitude toward those who make and enforce the law. Disrespect for the officers of the law has no place in Christian circles.

We conclude by asking, again, whether there are *any* exceptions to the requirement that we honor and obey the civil authorities who are properly constituted to govern us. Only one. If submission to a civil ruler in a given instance would bring one into direct disobedience of God, then he must "obey God rather than men" (Acts 5:29), though even then being respectful of the rulers involved. Though governments have, at times, represented the evil purposes of wicked men instead of the good purposes for which God ordained them, we must leave such problems to the providence of God and meanwhile perform our duty as Christians to "Fear God. [and] Honour the king" (1 Peter 2:17).

34 Christian Submission : Love

INTRODUCTION

The previous lesson has shown us that Christians must be in submission to the law of the land. They *owe* it (13:7, "dues") to the civil authorities to be subject to them, both in paying taxes and in giving them proper respect.

Today's lesson deals with another debt the Christian has, the obligation to love one's neighbor. You will remember that Jesus summarized the law in two basic obligations, to love God with the whole of one's being and to love one's neighbor as oneself (Matthew 22:35-40). Nor was Jesus the first to speak of these two great duties of man. His "first" commandment is a quotation from Deuteronomy 6:5; his "second" is from Leviticus 19:18.

Our duty to honor and obey civil rulers comes under the first of the two great commandments, since the ruler is God's representative, God's ordained servant to govern. This was the subject of the first half of chapter 13. Now Paul turns to the second of the two great commandments and reminds us of our primary obligation to men, to love them as ourselves. Our submission to this obligation to love others will mark us as practicing Christians.

271

EXPOSITION

Note the general study-outline of Romans given in the back of this volume. This lesson is the second on chapter 13, about Christian submission, and is entitled "Christian Submission: Love." The lesson covers 13:8-14.

1. A DEBT: THE WORKING OF CHRISTIAN LOVE
(Romans 13:8-10)

In these three verses Paul lays down a principle we must observe. That principle is selfless love for others. You will recall that 12:10 spoke of *brotherly* love. But here in chapter 13 Paul speaks of the love we owe *all* men.

Love's Debt Realized (verse 8). Paul approaches this subject by instructing us to realize that the one primary obligation we have toward all men is this duty to love them.

1. Our only unfulfilled obligation: This is the way our debt is presented in 8a. Many people have pondered Paul's exact meaning in saying "Owe no man anything, but to love one another." Does Paul mean we should never make a debt of any kind? Some think so. But if that were the case, then we could not even finance a car or home. We could never borrow for any reason or even promise anything for some future time. Admittedly, there are always certain kinds of problems connected with obligations. When we are "beholden" to others, they have a claim against us. They can make certain demands over us that restrict our liberty. The only complete freedom is freedom from any debts to anyone.

Still, when we make our mortgage payments on time we stay paid up. Paul probably means, then, that we should not take on any obligations that are beyond our means. We must not allow any debts to stand unpaid. The tense of the verb "owe," in Greek could well mean, do not continue in any man's debt. In this sense, Paul may mean, "Pay your debts on time." It is definitely a shameful thing, and a hindrance to Christian testimony to allow debts to stand without meeting our promised obiligations.

But there is one obligation under which we live and which can never be "paid off." That is our Christian duty to love our fellow men. This debt will continue to rest upon us so long as we live, and we must always recognize and honor it. You might say that we are always paying but never pay in full.

2. The fulfilment of the law: This is the way love for others is presented in 8b. Here in verse 8, unlike most Scripture passages, the "one another" probably is not used in the narrow sense of Christian fellowship. All our fellow men are included, not merely the Christian brotherhood. Paul's use of "neighbour" (verses 9, 10) makes this

272

opinion likely. Furthermore, even here in verse 8, when Paul says "he that loveth another," the Greek word for "another" means someone different.

To love others, then, is to fulfil the law's requirements in respect to our duties toward others. This does *not* mean, as we soon shall see, that love for others fulfils the law in respect to our duties toward *God*. Nor does it mean that love for others can be substituted in place of the law's regulations about inter-personal relationships. We cannot love others *instead* of honoring the law's demands. That would be a travesty of justice, a perversion of the law.

No, love is the fulfilling of the law for two reasons. First, because when we truly love others we will keep the law. When we love men, we will not want to harm them. We will find our hearts in tune with the law's rules. Second, and more important, love is the fulfilling of the law because love goes deeper than law. Law is always limited in that it can only write out just so many rules. And these rules can never cover every possible situation or secure anything more than external conformity. But genuine love for others will be from within and will apply even when the written rules run out.

Love's Duty Revealed (verse 9). Paul gets specific here, listing the basic commandments that speak of our duties toward others and affirming that these are summarized in our obligation to love our neighbors.

1. The "second table" of the law is itemized by Paul. He quotes the last five of the Old Testament ten: (1) Thou shalt not commit adultery; (2) Thou shalt not kill; (3) Thou shalt not steal; (4) Thou shalt not bear false witness; and (5) Thou shalt not covet. That Paul does not quote here the *first* table of the law is significant. The first five commandments outline our duties toward God, and to our parents as over us in the Lord (God's representatives in the home, just as civil rulers are God's representatives in the land). "Thou shalt love thy neighbour as thyself" does *not* summarize the first five commandments. God and parents are not our neighbors, not our equals.

The same significance is to be seen in Jesus' dealing with the "rich young ruler" in Matthew 19:16-22 (cf. Luke 18:18-23). Jesus quoted only the commandments that speak of our duties toward *people* (though He did include the fifth, or parents) and used "Thou shalt love thy neighbour as thyself" as a summary of these (Matthew 19:19). The "one thing" lacked by the young man was his duty toward *God*. Though he zealously tried to do right by others, he loved his possessions more than he loved God. He missed the first table of the law while he tried to observe the second. He would keep the second great commandment but not the first.

The one who loves others as himself will certainly observe these five commandments. Lust leads to adultery, not love. Love is the very opposite of the hatred that leads to murder. Love is not selfish and so does not take from others what is a joy to them. Love will not wish to hurt others and so will not lie against them. Love will not jealously covet that which others possess. Love seeks the welfare and happiness of others instead of selfish pursuits and so resists any hurt of those loved.

2. *Love as the comprehension of all laws* relating to the neighbor's good is Paul's teaching. As already indicated, Paul is but quoting Jesus and Leviticus 19:18 when he gives the "saying," "Thou shalt love thy neighbour as thyself." "Comprehended" means "headed up," "summed up." Love for others sums up the second five commandments and any other relating to our neighbor's welfare. As explained above, love goes beyond all rules and covers situations that could never be expressed in rules.

Love's Desire Reflected (verse 10). Paul summarizes his reason for teaching that love for one's neighbor will fulfil the law. That "love worketh no ill to his neighbour" means that love always operates in such a way as to seek the neighbor's good, not his hurt. Love desires others' happiness, not misery; others' advancement, not hindrance; others' welfare, not poverty. Consequently, we desire to help others, to see them prosper when we love them. We will not hold back that which they need, whether material or spiritual need is involved.

And so love for one's neighbor as oneself fulfils the law; as Denney puts it, "has done all that law requires." We might raise the question raised by the "lawyer" in Luke 10:29: "Who is my neighbour?" The answer Jesus gave in the parable of the good Samaritan is still sufficient for us. The Jews and Samaritans were bitter enemies. Even an enemy is a neighbor. Every man, especially a man in need, is my neighbor.

By the way, Paul gives us this very same teaching in Galatians 5:14, preceding the summary by these words, "By love serve one another." The law could only secure negative action, refraining from injury to another. Love secures positive action as well, in Christian submission and service to others, seeking their welfare instead of our own (1 Corinthians 10:24; Philippians 2:4). To love one's neighbor *as oneself* means selfless love. Selfish considerations will not hinder service to others when the other's welfare is as truly desired as one's own. James makes the same kind of summary of specific commandments in this duty to love one's neighbor as oneself and calls this "the royal law" (James 2:8-11).

2. A DEMONSTRATION: A WIDE-AWAKE CHRISTIAN LIFE
(Romans 13:11-14)

One could almost think that Paul turns to an entirely new subject here. The content of verses 11-14 does not seem, at first reading, to have much to do with loving others. A deeper study of these verses shows, however, that Paul is still on the same track, even if he moves a bit farther along. He wants us to demonstrate, to practice in our daily lives, the duty of mutual love. The first two words in verse 11, "and that," look back to the teaching just given, to love one's neighbor as oneself. Paul is going to introduce the subject of the soon coming of our Lord as a special impetus for Christian love and indeed for a clean and wholesome, watchful and alert Christian life.

The Vigilant Watch (verses 11, 12). As often in his writings, Paul speaks of our spiritual alertness. Compare 1 Thessalonians 5:4-8 for example.

1. *Awareness of the time* is referred to in verse 11. Note that "time" occurs twice, although two different Greek words are used. The first "time" means season, opportunity. The second "time" means hour, a fixed time. That we "know the time" means we are aware, knowledgeable, about the times that are in God's hands. We understand what era we live in, that these are the last days. We know how our times fit into the program of God. Indeed, we recognize the shortness of time (1 Corinthians 7:29, same Greek word), and thus the urgency behind wide-awake Christian living in these days.

That it is "high time" for us to awake from sleep means we cannot afford any delay. The moment for alertness and watching is already here. We understand the suddenness with which Jesus may come (Revelation 22:12). No time, then, for lazy dozing in the sun. We must be awake and watchful.

2. *The nearness of Christ's coming* is also indicated in verse 11 and is the reason for a wide-awake Christianity. The return of Christ is called "our salvation" in the same sense as is spoken of in Romans 5:9: "We shall be saved from wrath through him." Final salvation is meant, when the body, too, is redeemed (Romans 8:23); when we are perfectly conformed to the image of God's Son (Romans 8:29); and when we are glorified together with Christ (Romans 8:17).

That salvation is nearer than when we put faith in Him. This is a timeless truth, of course, because every passing day brings us nearer to Christ's coming and our final salvation. But the meaning is not altogether this vague or uncertain. The point is, we are to understand Christ's coming as *imminent*. What Paul meant is that His return had been near all along, ever since He went away. Now, with the passing of many days, that presence is even nearer. He may come today, and that is the reason we must be wide-awake and demonstrating every day our regard for our debt to love one another. If He comes today, or tomorrow, or the day after, we must stand before Him. And we will want to be found discharging our Christian duty of love for all men. As Denney puts it, "We must all appear (and who can tell how soon?) before the judgment seat of Christ, that every one may receive the things done in the body."

3. *The need for changed lives* is indicated in verse 12 and is based on the nearness of Christ's coming. The expression, "The night is far spent, the day is at hand," means exactly what has just been said about the nearness of Christ's return. The time we live in is called "night" because Christ is not here. The spiritual darkness of our age, and its ignorance of God, means that our times are more like night than day. When Jesus comes, and only then, it will be day. Compare 2 Peter 1:19, where we are told to take heed, now, to the Scripture as a light shining in a dark place, awaiting the dawning of the true day.

In particular, though, note that the night is "far spent." The spiritual darkness of the world has about run its course. Jesus will soon come. We are in the *last* days. Therefore, we must allow this truth to influence our daily behavior with deeds appropriate for the light that will soon dawn when Jesus comes. The "works of darkness" are those that are fit to be done only in the dark, where others cannot see. As Jesus said it, "Men loved darkness rather than light" because their deeds are "evil" (John 3:19; cf. 2 Corinthians 4:2; and Ephesians 5:12). Every genuine Christian wants to cast off, to put aside such works if he carries with him a consciousness of the Lord's soon coming (cf. 1 John 3:3). We do not want to do things that the light of the soon dawning day will expose to our shame.

Instead, the Christian who stays awake and aware will want to "put on" such deeds as he will not mind being exposed to the light. These deeds include, in our context, such deeds as grow out of our recognition of the Christian's debt to love others. But notice that Paul used "armour of light" rather than mere "works of light." The reason is that the Christian's wide-awake daily life is a *battle*, not a sleeping time. Good deeds, including submissive service to others, are part of our weapons against the darkness, part of our armor for the battle against evil and for the light. That Christ is soon to appear is especially strong motivation for staying in the fight for light. We must be vigilant, sober, awake, alert, intelligent, informed in our Christian lives, and on guard with the weapons and defenses of genuinely Christian conduct.

The Virtuous Walk (verses 13, 14). Paul now speaks in more detail of the code of conduct that will sustain us as we wait for Christ's return.

1. *The positive: decorous deeds for the day.* The first instruction in verse 13 speaks of what we seek to do, as Christians, in the *light* of Christ's soon coming. The word "honestly" is broader in Greek than it sounds in English. It means seemly behavior, proper living, comely, orderly, attractive, becoming, decorous conduct. (The same word is translated "decently" in 1 Corinthians 14:40.) The word emphasizes the way our lives will appear to others and to the Lord. The Christian wants a life that is attractive, orderly, beautiful to others who view it.

276

"As in the day" means the opposite of the "works of darkness" in verse 12. Deeds done in the day are those we do not mind being seen. Again, we are concerned how our lives appear to those who view us and with the influence we have on them. This, too, is testimony of our love for our neighbors.

2. *The negative: avoiding evil.* The last part of verse 13 contains three pairs of words suggesting the evils we avoid. These are suggestive of "the works of darkness" (verse 12) and are particularly chosen for their appropriateness as manifesting the deeds of men *not* aware of the times, *not* careful about the soon coming of Christ.

The first pair, "rioting and drunkenness," refers to excessive indulgence on the stomach's side of the flesh. The rioting is reveling, carousal. Originally this was the practice of drunken celebrants who paraded through the Greek city with torches and music in honor of the god of wine, Bacchus. Thus rioting can refer to any feast and drinking-party characterized by unrestrained celebration and revelry. The "drunkenness" refers to any intoxication, whether at a party or alone, what Trench calls a "drinking-bout": a binge, a drunken spree. These two are together again in Galatians 5:21.

The second pair, "chambering and wantonness," refers to excessive indulgence on the sexual side of the flesh. "Chambering" is the Greek word *coitus,* and thus refers to illicit sexual relations. "Wantonness" literally means without restraint and refers to any lack of sexual self-control: lust or any of the fruits of lust. Especially does the word carry with it an idea of shameless abandon.

The third pair of words, "strife and envying," refers to sins of attitude and emotion, especially in relationship to others (thus bringing us back to our duty to love others). Strife is contention or wrangling. Envying is jealousy or hatred. Real love for others will not tolerate such emotions or the actions that grow from them. These two are together again in Galatians 5:20 and 1 Corinthians 3:3.

3. *The solution: putting on Christ.* Above, we were told to "put . . . on" the weapons (armor) of light. Now we are told to "put . . . on" Christ. Gifford says this means a "clothing of the soul in the moral disposition and habits of Christ" (quoted by Denney); and that pretty well gets the idea. There is a certain mystical aspect to this, for when we lose ourselves in Christ, His attitudes and desires become ours. We can cultivate the mind of Christ (Philippians 2:5) by immersing ourselves in His word and teaching. This is, according to Peter, growing in the knowledge of Christ (2 Peter 3:18).

Paul means, then, that we should take on the habits and character of Christ himself, that we should clothe ourselves with the attitudes and behavior He manifested (cf. 1 John 2:6).

4. *Success: denying the flesh.* If we follow Paul's instruction we can expect success. We will deny the unredeemed flesh the satisfaction it illicitly seeks (by such sins as those listed in verse 13). Paul's verb is continuing action in Greek: Do not be making

provision for the flesh's lusts. We can only avoid this as we put on Christ and imitate Him. We must be determined to deny to flesh the lusts it seeks to fulfil.

In conclusion, then, let us remember our overall theme. The Christian submits to a special obligation to love others. The impending return of Christ makes us determined to demonstrate this love in our daily lives, to be watchful and wide-awake, conscious of the time.

35 Christian Self – Denial : Respecting Each Other

Study Text: Romans 14:1-12

Introduction
1. Disagreement Without Contempt or Condemnation(Romans 14:1-4)
    a. The Free Must Avoid Contempt (verses 1-3a)
    b. The Fearful Must Avoid Condemnation (verses 3b, 4)
2. Disagreement With Common Concerns (Romans 14:5-9)
    a. A Matter of Persuasion (verse 5)
    b. A Matter of Purpose (verse 6)
    c. A Matter of Possession (verses 7-9)
3. Disagreement with Consciousness of Christ (Romans 14:10-12)
    a. A Consideration in Attitudes (verse 10)
    b. A Conclusion for All (verses 11, 12)

INTRODUCTION

Throughout chapters 12—15, we are concerned with the implications of justification by faith for Christian living. Redemption not only provides man a righteous standing before God but also provides man with the real possibility for righteous living.

Perhaps *service* is the single best word to describe the practical side of Christian living, especially as that life relates to others, both in and out of the church. Thus Christian service was stressed in three lessons on chapter 12, including service to God, to the saints, and to sinners. The two lessons on chapter 13, using Christian submission for a theme, have also dealt with serving. This was especially true of 13:8-14 (see the previous lesson), where we were given the truth that we must, by love, serve all our neighbors.

Now, in 14:1—15:13, Paul takes us one step farther in this matter of Christian service to others. He deals with times when self-denial will be necessary in seeking the spiritual welfare and benefit of our brethren in the faith. Though we have "liberty" in Christ, that liberty must be regulated and limited, not so much by law as by love for others. If you have ever studied 1 Corinthians, chapters 8—10, you will soon see that this section of Romans deals with exactly the same ideas as there. Whenever there are questions or disagreements among Christians about standards of conduct, these two great passages of Paul's provide sure direction for us.

EXPOSITION

The general study guide in the back of this volume will confirm that there are three lessons, from 14:1—15:13, on Christian self-denial. This first lesson from this section is entitled "Christian Self-Denial: Respecting Each Other," and covers 14:1-12.

1. DISAGREEMENT WITHOUT CONTEMPT OR CONDEMNATION
(Romans 14:1-4)

Clearly, there was disagreement among believers at Rome (probably elsewhere, too) about certain practices. Verses 2 and 5a introduce two particular questions there was disagreement about, certain matters of food and certain observances of "days." Both these will be discussed further below when these verses are commented on.

By way of introduction here, we simply note that some of the brethren felt more restricted and fearful, more scrupulous about these questions. These are the ones called "weak" in this whole section (more about that word below, too). Others felt more relaxed and free about these questions and had a greater sense of liberty. These are called "strong" in this section. Evidently, the disagreement between the weak and the strong threatened the harmony of the church. So Paul addresses some serious words to both sides.

The Free Must Avoid Contempt (verses 1-3a). As just noted, Paul has instructions for both sides in this agreement. He speaks first to those called the "strong" (15:1). These are they who feel freer in their Christian lives, who have a greater sense of liberty in regard to certain disputed matters.

1. The nature of the disagreement should be discussed first, as it is indicated in verse 2: "One believeth that he may eat all things [the strong, the free]: another, who is weak, eateth herbs." There has been much speculation among interpreters about this difference, but the truth is we do not know anything more than we read right here. Thus the best thing to do is take the words exactly as they are. One side felt free to eat all foods, various meats included. The other side evidently insisted on leaving meat from the diet, thus being vegetarians.

If this were the problem, it was not quite the same as that the Corinthians faced, as dealt with in 1 Corinthians 8—10. There the disagreement was over eating any food that had been offered to idols. Some felt free to do so; others were fearful of such liberty and scrupulously avoided the practice. Here, however, the difference is between vegetarians and meat eaters.

Then neither was the problem at Rome a purely Jewish versus non-Jewish practice. Jews never insisted on vegetarianism altogether. Certain meats, like pork especially, were prohibited. But these "weak" ones at Rome ate *only* vegetables. We can guess, however, that there was an element of Judaism involved in the background thinking of these vegetarians, because history has often seen that an extreme, Old Testament based legalism can lead to complete vegetarianism. Witness the Seventh Day Adventists or Armstrong's Worldwide Church of God for examples. But though some Jewish influence may have been involved, there was more to it than that.

What else? We cannot be positive, but perhaps there was some sort of early ascetic tendency at work in this argument. All religions, Christianity included, have always known some who zealously and scrupulously practice a misguided separatism and self-denial, teaching that real religion includes the denial of all luxuries and the living of as simple and pious a life as possible.

Enough speculation about what may have been the reason for the difference at Rome. Though we cannot be sure of the background, we can understand that some overly scrupulous ones taught complete vegetarianism. Others felt free to indulge in a more usual, meat-based diet.

2. *The responsibilities of the free* side are given in verses 1 and 3a, and there are two: one positive, *to receive* the weaker ones; one negative, *not to despise* them. Let us look at these separately.

First (verse 1), the stronger ones must receive their weaker brethren. The tendency would be to reject and ignore such misguided, scrupulous brethren. But they must be *accepted.* That acceptance involves, for one thing, a recognition that they are brethren, and thus part of the fellowship. One does not reject a part of his body. The acceptance involves, further, an attitude of love and consideration for the apparently misguided brethren in spite of their peculiar views. The acceptance involves, finally, a recognition of one's obligations to them.

Note that this acceptance is "not to doubtful disputations." This means that the acceptance of the weaker brother must be wholehearted and unselfish. The stronger brother might be tempted to take the brother he disagrees with into fellowship just to argue with him. But that is not the proper spirit. The word translated "disputations" literally means judgments, discernments, or opinion passing. The "doubtful" refers to the uncertain debate over foods, the questions the two sides disagree about. In other words, then, the so-called stronger brother is not to receive the other in a conceited spirit and with the purpose of passing judgment on the weaker brother's doubts. Denney: "The strong . . . welcome him . . . unreservedly, not with the purpose of judging and ruling his mind by their own."

Second (verse 3a), the stronger ones are warned not to be contemptuous of ("despise") their weaker brethren. Paul knows they will be tempted to look down their noses at the peculiar scruples of the other side. But such a spirit must be avoided. The weaker brethren are to be received fully, with genuine love, concern, and respect. The stronger ones must be considerate and careful about them. All Christians must be thus with other brethren, regardless of differences of opinion.

The Fearful Must Avoid Condemnation (verses 3b, 4). If the free-minded brethren have a responsibility to receive their more scrupulous brethren with love and respect, so must it work the other way around. Paul has words for the "weak" brethren, too. These men on the other side of the dispute face dangers in their attitudes, also, only the dangers are different.

1. The danger of judgmentalism is clear in verse 3b. "Him that eateth not" is the vegetarian referred to above. The trouble with those who observe rigorous, detailed rules in their religion is that they have a tendency to be censorious and intolerant of other brethren who do not observe the same rules. And that attutude, on their part, is as much a threat to brotherly fellowship as contempt on the other side. Both sides can easily be wrong in such a disagreement. What each side must have is genuine respect for the Christianity and views of the other, and a spirit of acceptance and brotherly love.

2. The foolishness of judgmentalism is exposed in these verses. "God hath received him" (3b) indicates to the scrupulous brother that God has accepted the free-minded brother. How, then, can we do less? Verse 4 develops this thought further, with a question and an answer. The question (4a) makes it plain that one's brother in Christ is another's (God's) servant. Then God must be the one before whom he stands for judgment, not us. His standing or falling relate to his Master, God, not to us. Indeed, as Paul assures us in 4b, God is able to make him stand. The point here is that only God has such power. We must trust Him and His love for His children. We cannot make them stand, not even by our most careful instruction of them in our smallest scruples. So if God cannot make them stand, when He is their Master and the very one interested in their success, then we cannot.

You see, then, that Paul was well aware of the dangers on both sides. He does not take sides or try to settle the dispute. Instead, he speaks up for mutual respect and acceptance. The free-minded brethren must not reject or lord it over the others. Likewise, the fearfully scrupulous must not condemn the others. As Denney expresses this, Paul was aware that "He who eats will be inclined to contempt—to sneer at the scruples of the weak as mere prejudice or obscurantism." That must be avoided. Likewise, "Paul . . . was alive to the possibility of a tyranny of the weak . . . . It is easy to lapse from scrupulousness about one's own conduct into Pharisaism about that of others." That must be avoided, too.

One further observation about Paul's use of "strong" (15:1) and "weak." In this writer's personal opinion, Paul is more or less using these words *in quotes,* as the identification they would be familiar with. If this is right, then he is not necessarily agreeing that the one side is really "weak" and the other side "strong." But these were the words the "strong" side used of their side and the other side. They thought themselves strong in their sense of liberty and the other side weak in their legalistic scrupulousness. There is a certain truth in those terms, of course, else Paul would not have even partially accepted them. We *do* possess liberty from legalistic rules and regulations in Christ. We *are* saved by faith and not by meticulous and fearful observance of such matters as diets and days (below). To that degree, the free-minded ones were stronger in faith. Still, liberty can lead to libertinism when carried to an exaggerated place. These brethren will only be truly "strong" if they learn to limit and regulate their liberties (self-denial) for the sake of others and of themselves. It is no accident, then, that Paul has much more to say, in the whole section (14:1—15:13), to the so-called strong side.

What sort of disagreements do Paul's observations apply to? The answer is *not* to matters of basic morality, where right and wrong are clearly indicated in the Bible. On these there is no need for tolerance about differing views. But to matters about which the Biblical principles are not altogether clear, matters about which true Christians can disagree with each other, Paul's principles apply. Each side must manifest Christian attitudes toward the other. There is room neither for contempt on one side nor censorious judgmentalism on the other.

2. DISAGREEMENT WITH COMMON CONCERNS
(Romans 14:5-9)

In verses 1-4 Paul spoke separately to each side. Now he speaks about the common concerns of both sides. These mutual interests must be kept in mind by both the strong and the weak in the midst of their disagreement over practice.

A Matter of Persuasion (verse 5). The first common concern Paul mentions is a fully-persuaded mind. Each side must have this.

1. Another matter of disagreement is introduced in 5a. This is the observance of certain days. One side "judges" (esteems) every day alike; the other regards some days as special. Again, we are not told enough to enable us to fully understand this disagreement. For one thing, we do not know whether the two disagreements of verses 2 and 5 are related to one another or completely separate issues. For another thing, we do not know which side was which ("strong" or "weak"). Finally, we do not even know the nature of the disagreement. Was the Sabbath or the Lord's day involved? Or were some other types of "holy" day observance involved? Or was it a matter of connecting certain days (verse 5) with the eating or abstaining from certain foods (verse 2)? All we know is that this was a matter of religious practice not made absolutely clear in the Bible. Thus some Christians took one position, some another. Probably the "strong" were those who ate all foods and regarded all days alike.

One observation made by Denney is important enough to repeat here. The weak brethren "were certainly not legalists in principle, making the observance of the Jewish law or any part of it an essential condition of the Christian salvation; otherwise Paul, as the Epistle to the Galatians shows, would have addressed them in a different tone." Paul would not have stayed neutral but would have rebuked them sharply had they been teaching that their justification depended on their diet and days.

2. The main concern is found in the last sentence of verse 5: "Let every man [those on each side of such questions] be fully persuaded in his own mind." This simply means that *none* of us ought to be doing things about which we have doubts, regardless which side we are on. Compare verse 23 below. All Christians must live with clear consciences and be confident about their own practices.

A Matter of Purpose (verse 6). The key words in this verse are "unto the Lord." All Christians should have the common concern of doing whatever they do for the Lord and for His glory. Both sides must remember this and keep this consideration uppermost, with each side trusting the other to be guided by this same principle. That is part of what "acceptance" and respect for each other mean.

1. Devotion to the Lord is the main concern of all Christians. Thus on both questions at Rome, the observance of special days and the eating of meats, it was the *Lord's* interest that should be served, not *men's*. Both sides should respect the other's sincerity in this devotion. The ones who ate all foods and/or observed no special days did so with devotion to the Lord. Likewise, they who refused meats and/or observed special days did so with devotion to the Lord.

2. Thanksgiving to the Lord. Furthermore, as Paul adds to the matter of eating vegetables or meats, both sides do so with thanksgiving to the Lord. "Thanksgiving to God consecrates *every* meal, whether it be the ascetic one of him who abstains from wine and flesh, or the more generous one of him who uses both . . . . The thanksgiving shows that in either case the Christian is acting for God's glory (1 Corinthians 10:31), and therefore that the Lord's interest is safe" (Denney).

A Matter of Possession (verses 7-9). These three verses take the matter one step farther. Not only must all Christians act in the Lord's interest and for His glory but specifically with a consciousness that they *belong* to the Lord.

1. *We cannot isolate ourselves* from this consideration, says Paul in verse 7. At first glance we might take this verse to rule out selfishness in relation to other people; but the next verse shows that Paul is thinking about our relation to the Lord Jesus. We do not live for ourselves or even die for overselves if we belong to the Lord. Compare 1 Corinthians 6:19, 20: "Ye are not your own, For ye are bought with a price." Paul uses living and dying here to show that this basic principle applies to far more than small matters like eating meats and observing certain days. All of life is involved.

2. *We belong to the Lord in life or death* says Paul in verse 8. Thus the fact that we belong to Him must rule every consideration. They who eat freely and regard no special days must recognize His ownership of them in their decisions. And they who eat only vegetables and observe certain days must also recognize the Lord's ownership in making their decisions. And each side must still believe in the other's sincere regard for this principle, in spite of the disagreement. After all, if both belong to the *Lord*, in *life* or in *death*, then each can trust the other to the Lord's direction for life and judgment in death.

3. *Christ died to purchase us* says Paul in verse 9. Though he mentions Christ's resurrection as an essential part of His redemptive work, the emphasis is on His death, as the ransom price with which we have been bought (1 Corinthians 6:19 again). We are therefore His, whether living or dead. The "lordship" stressed here involves not only possession but control and judgment. We are all subject to Him and must give answer to Him, an idea which Paul now moves to expand on.

3. DISAGREEMENT WITH CONSCIOUSNESS OF CHRIST
(Romans 14:10-12)

The idea in the previous verses, that Jesus Christ is Lord of all believers, leads naturally to the truth that Jesus is the Judge before whom all must stand. Paul has already used this truth, in verse 4, as a basis for warning the "weak" side against condemning their "strong" brethren. Now Paul returns to this fact that *Jesus* is the Judge, *not man*, and uses it to speak now to *both* sides of the disagreement. Both sides must stay conscious of the Lordship and Judgeship of Christ in their dispute.

A Consideration in Attitudes (verse 10). The fact that Jesus is our final judge is a consideration that should affect us in our attitudes toward each other. Paul makes this point in verse 10.

1. Questions for both sides appear in 10a. The first question, "Why dost thou judge thy brother?" is addressed to the overly cautious "weak" side who harshly censored their more free-minded brethren. Compare verse 4. The second question, "Why dost thou set at nought thy brother" is addressed to the "strong" side who were flippant and contemptuous of their brethren's scruples, and (without any concern for their welfare) ignored them. "Set at nought" is the same Greek word as "despise" in verse 3.

The questions are, of course, rhetorical. In each case Paul means the question as a rebuke, to indicate that each side is wronging the other in doing what the question asks. Probably brother is the key word. Both sides were ignoring the bond of Christian brotherhood and the responsibilities that this bond puts on us for each other's welfare.

2. A sobering fact for both sides appears in 10b: "We shall all stand before the judgment seat of Christ." This fact makes the attitudes of both sides foolish. In the light of our necessary appearance before the judgment seat, the weaker brethren ought not to pharisaically condemn their freer brethren. And in the light of that appearance of all before Christ, the free-minded brethren ought not conceitedly ignore their more cautious brethren's spiritual welfare. Both sides, all Christians, will stand on equal ground before Christ as Lord and Judge.

We ought to note, here, that Christians are to be judged in reference to their attitudes and actions even when their salvation is not in question (compare 1 Corinthians 3:12-15 and 2 Corinthians 5:9, 10). Some (premillennialists) think that the Christians' judgment will be at a time different from the sinners'. Others (amillennialists) think both are judged at the same time. The time is not as important as the fact that we must be judged. How careful, then, we should be in all our attitudes and actions here. One of the prime questions in the judgment will concern our attitudes and service to others, especially our brethren.

A Conclusion for All (verses 11, 12). Paul reinforces the fact indicated in 10a in two ways.

1. A Scripture affirms the fact, as seen in verse 11. Isaiah 45:23 is the place Paul quotes, showing that the judgment must finally be universal (whether at the same or different times matters not here). The "bowing" and "confessing" do not necessarily represent true heart-felt submission, but the enforced submission of all before the Lord as Judge.

2. Paul reaffirms the fact in verse 12. This statement basically repeats 10b. However, the emphasis is more individual than above. There, both sides were in view. Here, each indivual is in view. Every

one will answer for himself. We will not answer for others, nor will others answer for us. Thus the "weaker" brother will not have to answer for the more carefree brother, or vice versa. Nor will either be judged by the other's standards—a comforting thought! But each will be judged by God's standards—a not-so-comforting thought!

How, now, shall we apply this lesson to contemporary problems? We should not attempt a thorough application yet, because we will not have finished with Paul's coverage of the problem until two more lessons. Meanwhile, we can say this. When genuine Christians disagree on a matter of practice not clear in the Scriptures, they must maintain respect for each other and commitment to each other's welfare in spite of their disagreement. And both must remember their obligation to the Lord of them both.

36 Christian Self-Denial: Regarding Each Other

Study Text: Romans 14:13-23

Introduction
1. Principles to Obey (Romans 14:13-16)
   a. The Principle of Consideration (verse 13)
   b. The Principle of Conscience (verse 14)
   c. The Principle of Charity (verse 15)
   d. The Principle of Consequences (verse 16)
2. Priorities to Own (Romans 14:17-19)
   a. Peace with Our Brethren (verses 17-19a)
   b. The Progress of Our Brethren (verse 19b)
3. Practice to Observe (Romans 14:20-23)
   a. A Concern for Others (verses 20, 21)
   b. The Conscience of Ourselves (verses 22, 23)

INTRODUCTION

In the previous lesson we began examining Paul's treatment of a dispute that arose at Rome about certain practices for Christians. In the disagreement Paul has not taken sides to try to settle the issue, and thus he may be admitting that each side has its points. But Paul's objective is to make sure that both sides remain Christian in their attitudes and actions toward their brethren.

Paul is saying, basically, that our relationship to each other, and our obligations to each other, outweigh the individual's freedom to act just as he pleases. In other words, we cannot consider merely our own selfish desires or even our "rights." We must consider our brother's views and welfare, too. Thus our liberties have to be regulated by love.

Since this is true, the side with the greater liberties (the "strong") must finally bear the greater responsibility for self-denying concern for their brethren. Their greater maturity in the faith makes it so. Thus, whereas verses 1-12 (the previous lesson) spoke almost equally to both sides, verses 13-23 speak almost exclusively to the strong side, admonishing them to regard their brethren's spiritual welfare as more inportant than their own liberties in practice.

EXPOSITION

Check the general study-guide in the back of this volume to remind yourself how this lesson fits into the scheme of things. This is the second lesson on C under part 5 (Christian Self-Denial) and is entitled "Christian Self-Denial: Regarding Each Other," covering 14:13-23.

1. PRINCIPLES TO OBEY
(Romans 14:13-16)

You will remember, from the previous lesson, that there were some matters of practice about which there was disagreement among the Romans. On one side, some very cautious brethren refused to eat any meat and observed certain special days. We do not know much more than this about their views, but perhaps they were inclined toward a Christian asceticism. Their views may have been somewhat like a false emphasis that existed at Colosse (cf. Colossians 2:16, 17, 20-23), though the Roman teaching was obviously not connected with a more serious false doctrine like that which existed at Colosse. Anyway, these brethren were very scrupulous about certain religious practices and harshly condemned others who did not agree with them. These brethren evidently did not base their justification on these scruples, else Paul would have strongly condemned the doctrine, as he did at Galatia. But they evidently felt fearful about the full favor of God if they did not observe these "requirements." These brethren are the "weak" ones in this chapter. "Weak" is a word the other side used in describing them, but the word is at least partly right in that these brethren's fears and cautions would naturally result from immaturity in the faith. In verses 1-12 (the previous lesson), Paul reminded these weaker brethren of their bond with the other side and warned them not to be caustic and censorious toward their brethren.

The other side called themselves "strong," and they were so in at least one sense. They understood more clearly the doctrine of justification by faith and their freedom from legalistic rules and regulations. But in their free mindedness they tended to write off their weaker brethren, to ignore them in their own conceit. Paul told

289

them, in verses 1-12, not to reject or ignore their brethren, nor even to look down on them. In the last half of the chapter, which we cover in this lesson, Paul speaks almost entirely to this "strong" side, telling them how to be *truly* strong. In verses 13-16, he lays down some basic principles these brethren must go by in their relationship to the weak brethren.

The Principle of Consideration (verse 13). This verse lays down the one chief principle that undergirds the whole lesson: consideration, regard for a brother's spiritual welfare. Here is the story in a nutshell: The spiritual welfare of a brother is more important than one's own personal liberty. Thus liberty must be regulated by love and limited when there is danger of hindering a brother's spiritual progress. A mature Christian refrains from doing some things he feels free to do if the doing will threaten a less mature Christian.

1. A "judgment" that is permissible is suggested by verse 13a. This looks back to the previous section, where Paul warned against "judging" each other in this disputable matter. Such a judgmental attitude is not permissible, says Paul, but there is one "judgment" we can all make: namely, that we will not hinder our brethren.

2. The wrong of "offending" a brother is the basic principle involved. What is said here in 13b is exactly like 1 Corinthians 8:9-13 (and, indeed, of all 1 Corinthians 8—10). "Watch out," says Paul, "lest your liberty become a stumblingblock in the path of the weak brethren" (cf. 1 Corinthians 8:9). Again: "If eating meat offends my brother, I will not eat meat!" (cf. 1 Corinthians 8:13). The Greek word translated "offend" is the very same as "stumble." Thus Paul is not referring to something that one's brethren will merely dislike but something that threatens the brother's spiritual progress, that may make him stumble into sin.

So if one feels free to do something, but that something may cause a brother to stumble into sin, or otherwise hinder his spiritual progress, thus endangering his soul, then that freedom must be curtailed for the sake of the "weaker" brother who does not have the same sense of freedom about the particular matter involved.

The Principle of Conscience (verse 14). In the discussion above, you may have wondered how *my* doing something I think is all right can risk causing a brother who *does not* think it is all right to stumble into sin. 1 Corinthians 8:10 answers that question: If I do what I know my brother feels is wrong, he may be "emboldened" to do it, too. But then *he* will be sinning against his conscience and thus against God. This is the same idea Paul presents here in verse 14.

1. Paul's own free conscience is indicated in 14a. His "persuasion" is a confidence begotten "by the Lord Jesus": that is, as a result of Christ's own teaching. Paul is thinking about such gospel passages as Matthew 15:11: "Not that which goeth into the mouth defileth a man; but that which cometh out of the mouth, this defileth a man" (cf. Matthew 15:17-20, which interprets this).

That "there is nothing unclean of itself" means, for one thing, that sin does not lie in the physical or external. Sin issues from the *heart*, from motives and attitudes. Thus one may—to use a crude illustration—drive a knife into a man either to kill or to do helpful surgery. The one is a sin, the other not. The physical act is not the factor but the motive of the heart.

What Paul means, then, is that knowing Christ *does* set one free from the kind of legalistic rules that reflect external observances. Thus there are now no "unclean" foods, and there are now no ceremonies and rituals like those on which Old Testament religion was based. One is not "unclean" because of accidentally touching a dead animal, nor does he have to "sanctify" certain festive days and be ceremonially clean for their observance.

The conscience, then, is the thing. But even here a problem remains. Some Christians have a more cautious and fearful conscience. They still regard certain externals as "unclean." They sincerely fear that certain practices will "defile" them with God. Immature they may be, and "weak in faith" they are, but they are brethren for whom Christ died; and we must consider *their* consciences as well as our own. Note 1 Corinthians 10:29: "Conscience, I say, not thine own, but of the other." Sometimes a freer Christian must live by the conscience of a less mature one lest he ignore that brother's spiritual welfare. As Paul asks so pointedly in 1 Corinthians 8:11: "Through thy knowledge shall the weak brother perish, for whom Christ died?" And then he adds: "When ye sin so against the brethren, and wound their weak conscience, ye sin against Christ" (verse 12).

How can it be wrong for a brother—weak or not—to sin in doing something that is not a sin? It is if he considers it a sin. In his own heart he is disobeying what he truly thinks God has said, so he is consciously disobeying God and thus committing sin in his heart— and that is where sin is anyway. Further, when he is provoked to violate his own conscience, by the example of a bolder brother. he may go on to other sins much more easily. Thus his spiritual welfare is in danger.

The Principle of Charity (verse 15). If one's own exercise of freedom, even *Christian* freedom, hurts others, then one is not manifesting love, charity toward others. Thus the principles of Romans 12:10; 13:8 are not kept. Two words are used here by Paul to suggest some of the harmful effects our unregulated liberty might have on weaker brethren.

1. We must not grieve a brother. The "grief" involved here is the pain and distress the weaker brother will feel when he "sees the strong pursue a line of conduct which his conscience cannot approve. Even to cause such pain as this is a violation of the law of Christ" (Denney).

2. We must not destroy a brother. This contemplates the

possiblity, as discussed above, that the weaker brother will be provoked to violate his own conscience by the bolder brother's uncautious actions. Then, having violated his own conscience, he may follow on in the path of sin thus begun and may even finally come to spiritual ruin. We who believe the Bible's warnings about the real possibility of apostasy must be all the more careful about this implication of our doctrine: Our own deeds must not be cause of a brother's fall.

The Principle of Consequences (verse 16). "Let not then your good be evil spoken of" is addressed to the strong side in the disagreement. Their "good" is the practice they feel free to do as being all right in itself (in this instance, eating meat or not observing certain holy days). But if their freedom, when exercised, have harmful effects on their weaker brethren, then that "good" of theirs becomes something that can be justly charged as "evil."

Thus we see another way something innocent in itself may be *sin*. If the "innocent" deed is done without regard to the welfare of a brother who will be hindered, it is sin for this reason though not in itself. Again, the heart and motive count. Note 1 Corinthians 8:12 again.

We see, then, that we are responsible for the consequences of our deeds as well as for the deeds themselves. It is not sufficient to know that a thing is all right in itself; we must consider the effects our deeds may have on others. Genuine Christian love will cause us to restrict our liberties when those liberties risk harm to others or be interpreted as evil and thus tarnish our testimonies.

2. PRIORITIES TO OWN
(Romans 14:17-19)

The principles outlined above lead to certain priorities that we must own or acknowledge in our decisions about practice. First things must be put first. In essence, our own liberties are not as important as our brother's welfare.

Peace with Our Brethren (verses 17-19a). What Paul says here, in summary, is this: Peace with our brethren in Christ is more important than our personal liberties. If we must restrict ourselves for the sake of peace, we will gladly do so.

1. The priority of spiritual values as the reason for our commitment to peace is seen in verses 17, 18. "The kingdom of God," in verse 17, stands for the spiritual relationship we have to one another as subjects of God, as members of His family and citizens of Heaven. In this "kingdom," we are not concerned with material things like meat and drink but with spiritual values. This difference helps get our priorities straight; compare Matthew 6:33.

Key spiritual values sought by subjects of the heavenly Kingdom are such things as righteousness (right living as growing out

292

of right standing with God), peace (peaceful relationships with others as a result of being at peace with God), and joy (the exultant gladness of the justified and the manifestation of this hope in their daily lives). Note that all these are "in the Holy Ghost," which reminds us that these are *spiritual* fruits produced by the Holy Spirit.

Verse 18 tells us that the "service" of Christ in such things as these three spiritual graces will please both God and men. This statement speaks both to the strong and the weak. The strong must not think more of their freedom and meat than of these spiritual values. Neither must the weak think their observance of external rules will please God like these spiritual fruits will. Still, Paul is speaking mainly to the strong. They can please both God *and men* (i.e., their weaker brethren), if they will let love for righteousness, peace, and joy rule and regulate their Christian liberty.

2. The pursuit of peace is urged on us as a *command* in verse 19a. To "follow after" is to pursue faithfully, to seek with full commitment. If the strong will do this, they will not grieve their weaker brethren with their freedom and meat.

The Progress of Our Brethren (verse 19b). Paul adds, almost as an afterthought, the words, "and things wherewith one may edify another." But the brief words give us the consideration that must get highest priority: the spiritual progress of our brethren. That is far more important than our own liberties.

This is what Paul means in 1 Corinthians 10:24, where the same truths are being discussed: "Let no man seek his own, but every man another's wealth." "Wealth" means welfare, spiritual well-being. 1 Corinthians 14 likewise emphasizes mutual edification as a matter of paramount importance; note verse 26b: "Let all things be done unto edifying." If the exercise of one's own "rights" hinders a brother's growth in the Lord, the right is better foregone. More, if the limitation of one's liberty can serve the purpose of others' edification, then that limitation ought to be gladly accepted. This is keeping proper spiritual priorities in view.

3. PRACTICE TO OBSERVE
(Romans 14:20-23)

With the principles and priorities made clear, not much doubt remains about the actual practice we should observe. Such curbing of one's liberties (self-denial) as will benefit others and enhance spiritual values is to be readily adopted.

A Concern for Others (verses 20, 21). The first and foremost element of our practice will be to manifest genuine concern for others and their welfare. Paul groups several cautions together to make this point, cautions addressed to the strong.

1. Consider God's work, and for that reason restrain yourselves.

This is the point of 20a. "For meat" means "because of meat." "Do not destroy a work of God over meat"—this is the meaning. The strong knew they could eat meat without guilt, but a headstrong insistence on that right, regardless of its effects, was not Christian. They should have more regard for God's work than for their own liberties. And their brethren are God's work!

2. *Consider the effects of your actions*, and for that reason restrain yourselves (20b). Things pure in themselves, done carelessly to the hurt (offense) of others, are evil in consequences and therefore to be avoided. The "all things" here is an expression not completely unlimited but universal only in regard to the context. Paul means "all sorts of things" *like* eating meat.

3. *Consider possible hurt of brethren*, and for that reason restrain yourselves (21). The word "good" gets emphasis here. Remember that the whole argument was about what was "good," and the strong were inclined to insist on their right to do "good" as they saw it. This was the point of verse 16, above. Paul's point, now, is this: The *true* good is to avoid hurting a brother.

Three words are used to express possibly harmful effects on a brother that ought to be avoided, even at the cost of giving up one's liberties. "Stumble" means, literally, to strike one's foot. "Offended" means to be caused to stumble. "Made weak" means to be spiritually weakened. A mature Christian gladly restricts his liberty to avoid such consequences.

Note that one matter of practice is mentioned here which had not been discussed above, in verses 2 and 5, where the main matters of disagreement were suggested. That is "drinking wine." The vegetarians also refrained from wine, evidently; and the free-minded brethren evidently permitted it. Since this question comes so late in the discussion, we can assume it was not as important a part of the debate as the other two issues. So we will not enter at length here into an old argument about wine. For now, do not forget that the Greek word translated "wine" refers to *all* juice of grapes, fresh or fermented. The ascetic denial of meat in the diet probably forbade *any* product of the vine, as a luxury, in the same manner as the Old Testament Nazarite vow. The Roman's argument, then, would not have been over alcohol but over grape juice (*or* wine) as a luxury, like meat, to be denied.

The Conscience of Ourselves (verses 22, 23). Our practice, as Christians, must not only be such as to manifest Christian concern for others but also such as to keep our own consciences clear, as thus to avoid self-condemnation and divine condemnation. Both sides are addressed on this matter of clear conscience, but still the strong are expected to bear the burdens of the weak.

1. *The clear conscience of the strong* is seen as a blessed state that must be preserved for its great value (verse 22). Paul approaches this with a rhetorical question, "Hast thou faith?" That is what the

strong said of themselves and rightly so. They understood clearly that justification is by faith and not by careful observance of rules for externals and ceremonies. Well, then, says Paul, if you have faith, "have it to thyself before God." This means that they must not flaunt their faith before their weaker brethren. Nor must they attempt to force off their concept of faith as the standard whereby others' actions must be judged.

Verse 22b, "Happy is he that condemneth not himself in that thing which he alloweth," reminds the strong of the blessedness of a clear conscience. The observation has a double edge. First, they are to remember and rejoice in the happiness they have in Christ, in the clear consciences they possess, in the freedom they know as a result of justification by faith. But second, and most important, they are gently prodded here to avoid "offending" their weaker brethren and thus by another route to defile their consciences. They will not keep their consciences clear if they carelessly ignore their brethren's welfare and exercise their own liberties to the hurt of their brethren.

2. *The clear conscience of the weak* is maintained by acting in accord with faith (verse 23). The weak ones "doubt," that is, they waver back and forth thinking sometimes the questionable thing (like eating meat) is wrong and, at other times, thinking perhaps it is permissible. But the doubts mean they must not indulge; else, as we have seen in verse 14, they will violate their consciences and thus bring themselves under both *self* condemnation and *God's.* ("Damned" means "condemned.")

That which is "not of faith" means that which cannot be done with a clear conscience when one is conscious of his faith in Christ, that which one cannot do in terms of his own faith. That which one does against this faith is sin—as we have noted earlier because sin is of the heart and motives. The strong brethren must remember this matter of the weak brother's conscience and must not provoke or pressure him to violate his conscience. The strong bear special responsibility in helping both sides keep clear consciences, because that state is a blessed one indeed.

In conclusion, let us note some observations about applying this lesson to modern problems. We are not faced with exactly the same debate about meat (or even of food offered to idols, as in 1 Corinthians). But we do face questions about which genuine Christians disagree, not basic moral matters like stealing, adultery, and the like but debatable matters of style, dress, amusements, and so on. In such matters we must observe the principles, priorities, and practice laid down in this lesson. Especially must the more mature restrict their freedom for the sake of the weaker, more scrupulous believers. True Christianity stands not on one's own rights but on one's responsibilities to others. Whatever limitations we impose on ourselves for the sake of our testimony, of our influence with others, and of our desire to help others are marks of the mature Christian.

37 Christian Self-Denial : Receiving Each Other

Study Text: Romans 15:1-13

Introduction
1. Avoiding Self Pleasing (Romans 15:1-6)
   a. The Exhortation (verses 1, 2)
   b. An Example (verses 3, 4)
   c. The End (verses 5, 6)
2. Avoiding Self Praise (Romans 15:7-13)
   a. The Manner of Receiving One Another (verse 7)
   b. A Motivation for Receiving One Another (verses 8-13)

INTRODUCTION

You have no doubt been perplexed by arguments among Christians about certain matters of right and wrong. We all agree about the basic morality clearly spoken of in the Bible. But when we try to apply those principles to questions of style, amusements, or appearance, we inevitably uncover areas that genuine Christians disagree about.

So what do we do in these doubtful matters? What about hair styles, dress styles, and ball games? Most movies, these days, we do not have any doubt about; but what about the few that might otherwise be clean? Some Christians will feel a sense of liberty for some of these things or similar ones. Yes, but what do we do when we know some other sincere Christians are sure that the thing we feel liberty for is wrong? Do we ignore their views? Must we be ever straightjacketed by every foolish whim and fancy of anybody?

These questions are difficult, but Romans 14:1—15:7 (like 1 Corinthians 8:10) contain some answers for mature believers. As we have seen in the two previous lessons on this passage, the Lord expects all believers to have respect for the views of other believers. And the more mature (and therefore freer) brother must have Christian regard for his more cautious brother, limiting his own freedom whenever his brother's spiritual welfare might be threatened. This final lesson on the subject concludes our study in self-denial by reminding us that we must each receive the other in the fellowship of Christ.

EXPOSITION

As you can see clearly in the general study outline (given in the back of this volume), this is the third lesson on Christian Self Denial, from Romans 14:1—15:13. This lesson covers 15:1-13 and is entitled: "Christian Self-Denial: Receiving Each Other." Therefore 15:7 (compare 14:1) is the key verse: "Wherefore receive ye one another, as Christ also received us."

1. AVOIDING SELF PLEASING
(Romans 15:1-6)

If we must deny ourselves to receive our brethren, then we certainly cannot be controlled by a self-centered desire to please only ourselves. Such self centeredness will disrupt fellowship among brethren, dishonor Christ, and endanger the spiritual welfare of the weaker brethren.

The Exhortation (verses 1, 2). Paul starts with a direct exhortation. This exhortation begins with the matter of the conflict between the "strong" and the "weak" and then moves on to give us a principle by which both sides—and, in fact, all Christians always—should be governed.

1. *The specific exhortation to the strong* is given in verse 1. First, note that Paul generally identifies himself with the "strong" ones at Rome. This probably needs explaining. He could not identify himself with their contemptuous disregard of the "weaker" brethren, an attitude he warned against in 14:3, 15. But he could identify with their stand that justification is by faith and not by the meticulous observance of external rules. Their consciousness of liberty in Christ, their sense of freedom from the old Judaistic ceremonies was, in fact, the result of the kind of gospel of faith Paul himself preached. No doubt the "strong" ones rightly felt Paul's teaching had produced their maturity, and they held up Paul as their hero. This much Paul accepts when he includes himself as one of the "strong." But he disassociates himself from any attitude that would abuse that liberty and hurt fellow believers when he adds, "We then that are strong

ought to bear the infirmities of the weak." He always limited the exercise of his liberty for the sake of the needs of others, saints or sinners, as is clearly seen in 1 Corinthians, chapter 9. Compare Galatians 5:1-15, in which he firmly proclaims, "Stand fast therefore in the liberty wherewith Christ hath made us free," and then warns, "Only use not liberty for an occasion to the flesh, but by love serve one another."

Note also that the weaker brethren's scruples are regarded as "infirmities" to be "borne" by the more mature believers. We have seen two primary scruples in this section: One was against eating any meat (14:2) and the other was for the ritual observance of certain holy days (14:5). A third one, perhaps not as important, was the ascetic denial of the luxury of the fruit of the vine (14:21). Paul calls these "infirmities" because they were manifestations of spiritual weakness and immaturity. These practices, all right in themselves, showed that these brethren still failed to stand strong on the freedom from externals one has by faith in Christ. The word "bear" means to bear as a burden. This probably has a two-fold implication here. For one thing, the restrictions we must place on ourselves because of others' narrow consciences will be something of a burden to bear, though a willing one for their sake. More important, however, is the fact that the weaker brethren are infirm and thus need help to stand. In their immaturity they cannot stand alone, and "bearing" their imfirmities will include helping support them. Compare 1 Thessalonians 5:14, where "support the weak" includes this very matter.

How then do we "bear the infirmities of the weak" in our own time and with the somewhat different problems we face? Space will not permit us to deal with the great variety of similar questions here, so one such disagreement will have to suffice as an illustration. Let us consider men's hair. Some believers feel it is morally wrong for men to have long hair. Others say that such an external matter cannot possibly affect one's spiritual condition. Without debating the matter here, let us suppose that the first group compares to Paul's "weaker" brethren and the second group to the "strong." How can they be truly strong? By restricting the liberty they have for the sake of their brethren. Now they *could* say that they are not going to be so narrow, that they are not going to encourage their foolish, meticulous brethren by going along with them, that they are going to wear their long hair as a testimony to their maturity and freedom, that they are not going to submit to such silly notions. But that is not what Paul says. In the end, there are really three groups, not two. The "weak" insist their externals *must* be meticulously observed. Then the so-called "strong" flaunt their liberty to be different and hold the weak in contempt. But the third group, the really strong, know they could take that liberty but gladly forego the freedom for the sake of the weak.

You may ask whether the truly strong ought not try to teach the weak and bring them from their immaturity. Certainly they should. But that is a slow process, and one cannot teach those he cuts himself off from by violating their consciences. One of the problems of our day is that the truly strong—who sense their Christian freedom from externals (Matthew 15:11), but who teach self-discipline and the restriction of liberty for the sake of weaker, overly-scrupulous believers—are themselves held in contempt by the middle crowd who loves to throw off all restraints and "stand on their rights." Paul never insisted on his "rights" but on how he could by love serve his brethren. (You will enjoy applying these same principles, questions, and attitudes to various others of the debatable matters of our day.)

Note, finally, the self-denial taught in the last words of verse 1: "and not to please ourselves." Pleasing ourselves is the opposite of bearing the infirmities of the weak. Pleasing ourselves is the opposite of restricting our liberties for the sake of disagreeing (and sometimes disagreeable) brethren. Pleasing ourselves is generally the *reason* we refuse to identify with the meticulous conscience of the other brethren. We may cloak our lack of self-restraint under other pretenses: insisting that the thing is good; saying we do not want to encourage the brother in his mistaken notion; even saying we want to identify with another group so we can win them. But our profession of a "principle" involved is most often a disguise for wilful self-pleasing. There is only one absolute principle, love for our brethren; and there is only one absolute "good," his edification.

2. *The general principle for all* is given in verse 2. Both the strong and weak are to obey this principle. All Christians are to obey this principle. Instead of seeking to "please ourselves" (which includes standing up for our "rights," "doing your own thing," and "doing it my way"), we must seek to please our neighbors. And "neighbor" includes the broadest number of people: not the brethren only, but the sinners too. The consciences of others must be respected. If others generally, either saints or sinners, believe that Christians must do or not do certain things, then Christians better act accordingly. Compare 1 Corinthians 10:24-33. No "freedom" is as important as the spiritual welfare of others.

Can we *always* "please others"? Of course not, but that should be our goal in the way this context indicates, not violating others' sincere consciences. Of course there are always some "nuts" around who propose some silly rules that do not represent a sincere concern for Biblical and Christian principles. But sincere convictions, even when we disagree, must be respected.

Note the last part of verse 2. The "pleasing" of others that we must always be finally concerned about is in their edification. Building others' faith is more important than insisting on our own rights. See how Paul calls this a "good." Compare 14:16: The strong insisted their free practice was "good." The true "good," Paul says, is the spiritual strengthening of your brethren, not the parading of your own liberties. If self-denial aids one's ministry to others, then self-denial is far better than exercising one's liberties.

An Example (verses 3, 4). Paul does not leave his exhortation to stand alone but gives us the best example of self-denial we can have, Christ.

1. *The fact of Christ's self-denial* is affirmed first, in verse 3a. That "Christ pleased not himself" means the same thing as Philippians 2:7: He "made himself of no reputation" (literally in Greek, "He emptied himself"). Both in Philippians 2:4-8 and here in Romans the point is plain: Christ made His decisions about actions on the basis of others' needs and not His own desires. He too gave up His rights to minister to others.

2. *A Scripture picturing Christ's self-denial* is quoted in verse 3b. The quotation is from Psalm 69:9. He took on himself, in His human person, the reproaches of men who hate God. In doing so, they vented against Him all their pent-up hatred of God and so cruelly mistreated Him. As Denney puts it, this "shows that He was no self-pleaser. If He had been, He would never have given Himself up willingly, as He did, to such a fate."

3. *A parenthetic explanation of the use of the Old Testament* is given in verse 4. Paul tells why he used the Old Testament to back up his teachings. He had just done that, using Psalm 69:9 to support his claim that Jesus did not practice self-pleasing. Futhermore, Paul has used the Old Testament frequently throughout the Book of Romans.

In essence, then, verse 4 is a defense, a justification for Paul's free use of the Old Testament both here and elsewhere in the epistle. And that defense is simple: Whatever things were written before (the Old Testament Scriptures) were written for our learning (that is, to instruct us), with the purpose that we may have (that is, keep a hold on) hope, by means of the patience and comfort which these Scriptures produce in us. Paul always taught that the Old Testament was for our instruction in the Christian era. Note 1 Corinthians 9:11. Compare 1 Peter 1:10-12.

Note, too, Paul's concept of the part the Scriptures play. They give us a firm hold on *hope*, the word that was so important in Romans 5:1-11, and was summarized there in this expectation: "We shall be saved from wrath through him." The Scriptures nourish this firm hope by teaching us (and thus helping us have) perseverance—endurance—and comfort.

The End (verses 5, 6). The ultimate end, or result, of our bearing the infirmities of the weak and pleasing others rather than ourselves, is suggested here. That end is unity—harmony—in the church. The edification of our brethren was one objective that made self-denying restrictions of liberty worthwhile (verse 2). The peace of the fellowship is another such end that is more important than the personal freedoms of the individual.

1. *The immediate goal* is given in verse 5, that Christians may be "like-minded" toward each other. To be like-minded is, literally, to think in accord, to share the same basic attitudes and concepts. This is the same expression as was used in 12:16 (see lesson 31). Compare Philippians 1:27; 2:2. Paul was very concerned that believers be in accord in purpose and doctrine. The disputes over debatable practice have disrupted that harmony. But that one-mindedness can be restored if all will seek each other's good instead of self's pleasure.

Paul expresses this objective in the form of a prayer. God must grant this harmony; it cannot come by natural means. But even God cannot grant it if they persist in self-seeking! Note, too, that He is "the God of patience and consolation." These are the very same two words as were used in the previous verse, as graces wrought by the Scriptures to produce hope. That association shows two things: first, that the God of patience and comfort (consolation) *is* the God of the Scriptures; and second, that He will use the Scriptures to produce these and ultimately to produce the desired harmony. So the Romans must make use of the *Scriptures!*

Note also the expression "according to Christ Jesus." This is evidently intended to point back again to the example of Christ cited in verse 3. This desired unity can come only if the example and mind of Christ controls.

2. *The ultimate goal* is given in verse 6. The harmony desired will, in turn, glorify God. And the glory of God is the final end of man. The one mind (harmony of thought and purpose) will lead to one mouth (harmony of expression and testimony), and that one expression will be the glorification of God.

2. AVOIDING SELF PRAISE
(Romans 15:7-13)

If the edification of believers be a goal that makes self restriction worthwhile, and if the harmony of believers also does, then finally the glorification of God is likewise worthy of the restrictions one must place on his own liberty for the sake of the brethren.

The Manner of Receiving One Another (verse 7). As was noted earlier, the words "receive ye one another" express the sum and substance of this whole section from 14:1—15:13. Receiving others is denying self. Receiving others is restricting one's own liberties for them. Receiving others is respecting their convictions (even when one disagrees) and regarding their consciences. Receiving others is refraining from harsh condemnation of their liberties, on one side; on the other side, it is accepting their stringent consciences without contempt (14:3).

1. *We receive each other as Christ received us.* This truth is

two-pronged. First, it reminds us of His reception of us against our deserving and at such great personal cost. When we have been received so graciously and self-sacrificingly, how can we possibly hold back from receiving our brethren?

Second, this truth reminds us that Christ has already received *both sides*. Then neither of us can reject one whom *Christ* has received. So we are not only moved by His example but also given by Him the very content of our fellowship. The fellowship consists of just those who have been received by Christ. Compare 14:4.

2. We receive each other to the glory of God. In verse 7, surely the phrase "to the glory of God" modifies *both* verbs ("receive" and "received"). Christ received us to the glory of God. We receive each other to the glory of God. Indeed, God will be glorified—as has already been pointed out in the previous verse—when believers receive each other and sacrifice their own pleasures (and "rights") for others' welfare.

In other words, we must be concerned about the ultimate objective of glorifying, praising, and exalting God rather than ourselves. Those who insist on their own rights are seeking both their own pleasure (above, verses 1-6) and their own praise. Self-centeredness is their problem, and that is the opposite of self-denial. The best expression of self-denial is the glorification of God.

A Motivation for Receiving One Another (verses 8-13). The use of Christ as an example in receiving us, in the previous verse, moves Paul to expand on His gracious reception of us and the glory of God which results. In other words, verses 8-12 make up an explanation of 7b.

1.Christ's reception of all is emphasized in verses 8, 9. You will notice that these verses play up His ministry both to the Jews (the "circumcision" and "fathers" in verse 8) and to Gentiles (verses 9-12). In other words, Christ received all alike, without distinction. So should we all receive each other.

This point may reach a little deeper. Paul may be using Jews and Gentiles here because the tension at Rome was between Jewish and Gentile believers. You will recall that we wondered earlier (lesson 35) if the "strong" were mostly Gentile believers and the "weak" mostly Jewish believers still confused over the ceremonies of the law. If that were the case, then Paul is saying here, again, that Christ received both and so each must receive the other.

2. The two-fold results of Christ's reception of Jews and Gentiles are given also in verses 8, 9. In verse 8, Christ ministered to and received Jews on behalf of the truth (truthfulness) of God, that the ancient promises given to the Old Testament fathers might be confirmed (fulfilled). Such promises as were contained in the Abrahamic covenant are meant here but especially all promises of the true forgiveness of sin and salvation for "Israel" (compare 11:26-29). This was one result.

The other result, and the one Paul is primarily concerned about here, is that Christ also received Gentiles that He might be glorified for His mercy. Actually, even the salvation of Jews was of mercy (compare 11:32), but most of the Roman believers were probably Gentile, and so Paul emphasizes the merciful salvation of the Gentiles here. That is a special manifestation of God's mercy even in contrast to Jewish salvation, for they were in a sense already "insiders" when the Gentiles were still "outsiders" (compare Ephesians 2:11-13, 19). To put it another way, they were "the natural branches" and Gentiles were "wild" branches grafted in "contrary to nature" (Romans 11:24).

3. *The propriety of praise to God* is stressed (in verses 9-12) as the intended result of Christ's reception of all, especially of the Gentiles. He received us and we glorify God for His mercy. This humbling truth becomes a special motivating force to move us to receive each other and even thus contribute to the glorification of God.

Paul uses four Scriptures to back up his claim that we are to glorify God for His mercy on all, especially on us Gentiles. The first (9b) is Psalm 18:49, which speaks of the Jew who praises God out among the heathen nations, rejoicing in his own and in their salvation. The second quotation (verse 10) is Deuteronomy 32:43 and speaks of Jew and Gentile rejoicing together over God's mercy. The third (verse 11) is Psalm 117:1 and speaks directly of all heathen nations praising and glorifying God. The fourth (verse 12) reflects Isaiah 11:1, 10 and refers clearly to Gentile salvation by Christ, the root of Jesse (father of David: Note the connection between the *royal* family and the *reigning* of Christ over the Gentiles). All four of these citations do two things: First, they speak clearly of God's mercy to Gentiles and of the glorification of God that results. Second, they cleverly link together the salvation of the Gentiles with that of the Jews, reminding us (and Paul's original readers) that Christ received *both*, and thus that both must receive each other.

4. *This glorification of God leads to a benediction* on Paul's readers (verse 13), a benediction that concludes this section and the main body of the epistle. The benediction is a beautiful one and deserving of more space than we have here. We can only take note of the key elements and how they relate to each other.

First, the epistle has been about justification by faith. So Paul's blessing on his readers is for them *in a believing* state. These blessings are only for believers. Next, he wants them to be *filled with all joy and peace.* "All" means "utmost." These graces are the rejoicing and exultation of the one who has peace with God. Next, he knows that *the God of hope* is the one who must so fill them. The God of hope is the one who promises final salvation and thus gives hope. Next, Paul intends that this filling of joy and peace by the God of hope will result in *the abounding*—confident flourishing—*of their hope* (for

303

final salvation). Note that joy, peace, and hope are bound together here again as they were the key elements in 5:1-11. Finally, Paul knows that all this is possible only through (the manifestation of) the power of the Holy Spirit. Such Christian graces are, in fact, the fruit of the Spirit (compare Galatians 5:22, 23).

38 Paul's Situation and Future

Study Text: Romans 15:14-33

Introduction
1. The Reason for the Passion of Paul (Romans 15:14-16)
   a. His Confidence (verse 14)
   b. His Concern (verse 15a)
   c. His Commission (verses 15b, 16)
2. The Responsibility in the Preaching of Paul (Romans 15:17-21)
   a. The Boldness of His Ministry (verses 17-19a)
   b. The Breadth of His Ministry (verses 19b-21)
3. A Revelation of the Plans of Paul (Romans 15:22-29)
   a. At Rome in the Future (verses 22-24)
   b. Another Responsibility First (verses 25-29)
4. A Request for Prayers for Paul (Romans 15:30-33)
   a. For Fulfilment and Paul's Protection in Jerusalem (verses 30, 31)
   b. For the Fruition of Paul's Plans in Joy (verses 32, 33)

INTRODUCTION

With the previous lesson, we completed our study of the five great parts of the main body of Romans. We have seen man's universal *need* for righteousness (1:18—3:20); God's gracious *provision* for righteousness by faith through Jesus Christ (3:21—4:25); the new life of the believer in the *experience* of this right standing with God (5:1—8:39); the sobering lessons involved in the Jews' *rejection* of Christ and His righteousness (9:1—11:36); and finally the *manifestation* of this right standing in the daily practice of the believer (12:1—15:13).

The fifth section closed (15:13) with a benediction, a prayer of Paul's that his readers—including us!—will be full of joy and peace and abounding hope. Then, at 15:14, Paul departs from the great doctrinal and practical themes and begins to close his letter on a more personal note. This conclusion is much longer than in most of his letters. He has many things to say about why he has written them, his plans, and many greetings for and from his friends. In the midst of these, he keeps putting in brief personal observations and exhortations about the spiritual welfare of the Romans. This conclusion shows us a great deal about the keen personal interest Paul took in all the the folks he might minister to, including those at Rome.

EXPOSITION

As you will see in the general study-guide to Romans (printed in the back of this volume), we will devote two final lessons to the concluding portion of the epistle. This first lesson of the two covers 15:14-33. We call it "Paul's Situation and Future."

1. THE REASON FOR THE PASSION OF PAUL
(Romans 15:14-16)

In these three verses, Paul justifies the concern he felt for the Romans, the strong passion he had for their spiritual welfare. He is, in effect, explaining why he has written this bold letter.

His Confidence (verses 14). Paul begins his explanation by admitting that his Roman readers had certain things going for them even if he had not written. He gladly recognizes these spiritual qualities and abilities they possessed, and his extensive letter was not meant to cast doubt on this.

1. *They were full of goodness and knowledge.* The goodness referred to is the practical manifestation of inner character. Thus the word often refers to kindness, benevolence, generosity, and similar demonstrations of inner goodness. Their knowledge includes comprehension of the basic doctrines of Christianity. "All" knowledge means utmost knowledge, knowledge that is thorough and detailed.

2. *They were capable of teaching each other.* "Admonish," in Greek, is more like our "instruct." Paul recognizes that the believers at Rome—at least some of them—were well enough taught to be able to teach. The "utmost knowledge" just referred to would imply this, but they also had the ability.

The two admissions of Paul might seem to imply that his letter was not really necessary. But such "compliments"—fully sincere, of course—served two purposes: not only to give rightful recognition and encouragement to them but also subtly to prod them to seek to become even more skilled and capable of teaching each other.

His Concern (verse 15a). Though their spiritual qualities and abilities might have made it unnecessary for Paul to write, he has done so. The "nevertheless" amounts to such an admission. In fact, Paul admits he has been rather "bold" (daring) to write. Why has he written? For one thing, because he is concerned about them and their spiritual progress.

This concern is manifested in the phrase "putting you in mind," a phrase often used by the Biblical writers to refer to their desire to help their readers. Compare 2 Peter 1:12, "put you always in remembrance of these things, though ye know them" and 2 Peter 3:1, 2, "I stir up your pure minds by way of remembrance: That ye may be mindful . . . . " Such phrases acknowledge that the readers are already aware of the truths being taught but need to be reminded of and to consider again the implications of those truths.

His Commission (verses 15b, 16). Here is the main justification Paul gives for having written this letter to the Romans: It is part of the job, the ministry, Christ has given him. If Paul's concern for their welfare were the *reason* he wrote, then this commission is the *right* he has. These verses give us an interesting insight into the concept Paul had of his ministry.

1. His ministry is a gift of grace. This last phrase in verse 15 recalls Romans 12:4-8, where God is said to have "given according to the grace," to each Christian a place to serve, a ministry to fulfil, and a work to do for Him. Thus when Paul writes Rome, he is merely exercising his own spiritual gift for the church's welfare. Compare 1:5; 12:3; Philippians 1:7; Ephesians 3:2; Colossians 1:25; in all of these, Paul calls his apostolic office a "grace" given to him. All spiritual gifts are gifts of grace, since we no more deserve such places of service than we deserve salvation itself.

2. His ministry is representing and serving Jesus Christ. "Minister of Jesus Christ" encompasses the servant and apostle of Jesus Christ used in 1:1 (see the comments on that verse in lesson 1). Since Jesus is the one who has sent him and whom he serves, the Romans cannot very easily reject his ministry.

3. His ministry is "to the Gentiles." See Acts 9:15. Most of the Roman believers were Gentiles, so Paul was operating within the bounds of his commission when he became concerned enough to write them.

4. His ministry is with the gospel of God. This shows the nature of his work. He was a preacher of the gospel. He was to get the gospel out and understood. The "Gospel," for Paul, included the whole counsel of God, all that was needed for doctrine and deeds. And this very letter was a systematic presentation of the gospel, as is clear in 7:15-17.

5. His ministry is to make an offering to God. This presents Paul's ministry in terms of priestly service (compare 12:1). Verse 16 is filled with words suggestive of this concept. "Minister" refers to the priestly ministry. "Ministering" means temple service. "Offering up" indicates a sacrifice. "Acceptable" reminds us that God accepted some sacrifices and rejected others. Paul sees himself as something of a New Testament priest, who deals not with the tabernacle-temple ritual, but the service of the gospel; who offers not animal sacrifices but living persons to God, a sacrifice He will be pleased with, a sacrifice "consecrated" by the work of the Holy Spirit within those He offers. Paul's sacrifice offered to God consists of the souls he wins and establishes in the faith. Compare Colossians 1:28, where also he sees his objective as presenting mature believers to God. He is but performing his ministry when he writes to Rome to establish them.

2. THE RESPONSIBILITY IN THE PREACHING OF PAUL
(Romans 15:17-21)

In these verses Paul expands on the ministry just outlined in verses 15b, 16. Here he explains the broad responsibility he has accepted and therefore the boldness he has to preach the gospel wherever he can, including Rome.

The Boldness of His Ministry (verses 17-19a). In verse 18, the word "dare" is the same, in Greek, as the "boldly" in verse 15. And the verb "glory," in verse 17, though a different word, has a similar idea. Paul is showing that the "boldness" he spoke of in verse 15, a boldness he showed in writing Rome, does have justification. He has good reason for bold confidence in reaching out to minister to others on the Lord's behalf. The previous verses (15b, 16) showed those grounds in so far as his commission was concerned. These verses show those grounds for boldness in so far as his actual practice is concerned. In other words, 15b and 16 show what God told Paul to do; verses 17-21 show what Paul has done. Both show that he has full right to reach out to Rome with the gospel.

1. His work "pertains" to God. Paul would not assume a bold posture as one who boasts of his own identity or abilities or accomplishments in his own affairs. He is not doing his work, but God's work. He is bold, then, only in spiritual matters and not in natural or material things. And his boldness is centered in God, not in himself.

2. His confidence is in Christ. Two phrases suggest this, one in a general way, the other giving more detail. "Through Jesus Christ" shows, in general, where his boldness and confidence really lie. Paul's own identity and recognition were never very important to him. The credit for what he did, as well as the reason for doing it, lay with his Master, Jesus Christ. Paul would say, as it were, "Do not give me credit, I cannot help myself; I am only doing what He said I must do. And I can do so boldly because I represent Him, and He controls me."

"I will not dare to speak of any of those things which Christ hath not wrought by me" shows that Paul gave Jesus credit for whatever specific work was done, for whatever particular things were accomplished. The only things Paul boasts about are those things Christ has done.

What has Christ wrought? He has made "Gentiles obedient by word and deed." The "word" is the preaching Paul has done, the verbalization of the gospel (whether in person or in letter). The "deed" refers to the effort of Paul, the work he has done, the energy he has expended, even the suffering he has experienced—all to get the gospel out to the Gentiles. Remember, though, *he* does not take credit for this: Christ has done this through him to bring Gentiles to submit to the gospel. The letter to Rome is but one more thing Christ has compelled Paul to do for the sake of the church of the Gentiles.

3. His power is by the Spirit. Here Paul explains the secret of his success, the reason for his effectiveness. All this is still part of what Christ has wrought to bring Gentiles to Him. Specifically, there have been miracles performed in connection with the ministry of Paul. Again, Paul—though he has, in one sense, performed those miracles—does not take credit. The Holy Spirit did the work; His was the power demonstrated. Paul always said he depended not on his own abilities but on the Spirit's power. Compare 1 Corinthians 2:4, 5; 1 Thessalonians 1:5.

Still, a reference to these miracles, along with all the other works being listed here, serves to verify the apostolic authority Paul claimed (and was exercising when he wrote Rome). Compare 2 Corinthians 12:12, where he calls such miracles the "signs of an apostle."

The Breadth of His Ministry (verses 19b-21). If verses 17-19a have stressed the *effectiveness* of Paul's ministry as being for God, by Christ, and through the Spirit, then verses 19b-21 stress the *extent* of his ministry. Two factors, in particular, are mentioned, as manifesting Paul's policies in reaching out with the gospel.

1. The wide and thorough preaching of Paul is emphasized in 19b. "From Jerusalem, and round about unto Illyricum" stresses the breadth; "fully preached" stresses the thoroughness. Illyricum was a country adjoining Macedonia on the far northwest. Paul considered that territory his, reaching out from Jerusalem in a semicircle through Antioch (in Syria), through Asia Minor, and across the Aegean into Greece. All three missionary journeys had been in that territory. He had covered that area with the gospel.

2. Paul's preaching to new places and people is stressed in 20, 21. His objective was to preach where Christ was not already being preached, to open new territory for the gospel. This also means Paul deliberately wanted to avoid "building" on foundations laid by others. He wanted to build churches where churches were not already established. In so doing, he helped fulfil an ancient prophecy of Isaiah 52:15, quoted in verse 21.

Paul's reference to his thorough preaching across Asia Minor and Greece and to his policy of entering new areas will serve two purposes here in reference to the Romans (in addition to supporting his apostolic authority for writing them). For one thing, this extensive work will explain—as Paul specifically says in the next verse—why he has not yet had time to get to Rome. He had, no doubt, often promised many of them there he would come. For another thing, this expression of his policy for avoiding another man's foundation will serve to gently remind the Roman believers that they are essentially one of Paul's churches. He would not write this letter if this were another man's church.

3. A REVELATION OF THE PLANS OF PAUL
(Romans 15:22-29)

Paul proceeds now to share with the Roman Christians his personal plans for the days ahead, primarily because those plans involve Rome.

At Rome in the Future (verses 22-24). The important thing Paul reveals here is his intention to visit Rome in the foreseeable future.

1. *He has had an intense desire to visit Rome a long time.* Verse 23b refers to this. "Many years" had, in fact, been involved. Compare 1:13 where Paul even says he "often" purposed (made specific plans) to go to Rome, but was "let" (hindered) from doing so.

2. *He has been hindered in the past.* Again, compare 1:13. But here in verse 22 we learn how he was hindered. The work occupied him. The "which cause" refers back to verses 19b-21, where Paul's extensive ministry "from Jerusalem to Illyricum" is mentioned. The opportunities and needs in that area were so great he had not been set free by the Spirit to leave and minister elsewhere.

3. *The completion of the work elsewhere now frees him for Rome.* This is what verse 23a means. "No more place in these parts" means he has thoroughly covered that area of his first calling in the districts named above, not that all in these areas had been converted, nor even a majority of them. But Paul's work of evangelizing new areas and establishing churches there was done.

4. *A proposed trip to Spain will provide occasion to visit Rome.* This is the substance of verse 24. Obviously Paul felt strongly about going to Spain, so much so that he calls it "my journey into Spain" (Greek: "whenever I go into Spain"). We cannot be absolutely certain he ever got there, though there is a strong tradition in the early church that he was released from the two years' imprisonment referred to in the final chapter of Acts and did evangelize Spain afterward. Anyway, he plans such a trip and expects Rome to be an

important point in that journey.

Paul has at least three things in mind: to *see* the Romans, to *be helped* on toward Spain by them ("to be brought on my way thitherward by you," and to be (at least partly) satisfied in his long-standing desire for *fellowship* with the Romans ("somewhat filled with your company").

Another Responsibility First (verses 25-29). Paul is still not quite free to go to Rome and Spain.

1. *He must take a collection to Jerusalem*, and verses 25-27 speak of this duty. The fact is indicated in verse 25, the purpose in verse 26, and the purpose is defended in verse 27. "Ministering" to the saints means attending to their needs, serving them (it is the word from which "deacon" comes). The funds had been raised in Macedonia and Achaia. The collection was sponsored by Paul during the closing months of his third missionary journey. (Remember that Romans was written at this time, from Corinth in Achaia, near the end of that third journey.)

Other New Testament references to this same collection are in 1 Corinthians 16:14 and 2 Corinthians 8 and 9, where he urges the Corinthians to participate liberally in this effort. Compare also Acts 24:17.

In justifying this effort (verse 27), Paul calls this Christian duty (compare 1 John 3:17; James 3:14, 15). He also calls it a *debt* of the Gentile believers (in his churches) to the Jewish believers (at Jerusalem). Since Gentiles had benefited in a spiritual way from God's dealings with Israel (Romans 9—11 again; 11:11, for example), then should not Gentile believers share material ("carnal") blessings in return?

2. *Then he will come and be a blessing at Rome.* Verses 28, 29 say this. He must first "perform" his responsibility in the matter of the collection for the Jerusalem saints. Note he calls this "sealed to them this fruit." This expression is a little vague, but this writer thinks Paul means that the money will be presented to the Jerusalem church as a seal and fruit of the genuine Christianity of the Gentiles in his missionary churches.

Anyway, Paul expects to be a blessing when he does get to visit Rome. How? With the gospel. In fact, the word "blessing," like "gospel," literally means a "good word."

4. A REQUEST FOR PRAYERS FOR PAUL
(Romans 15:30-33)

Paul's plans (above) are not like those of an ordinary traveler who lays out his itinerary and buys his tickets. There are too many unforeseen eventualities that may interrupt. In the light of these uncertainties, there is a need for prayer.

For Fulfilment and Paul's Protection in Jerusalem (verses 30,

31). Paul first requests prayers about his impending ministry in Jerusalem.

1. *The Romans' help in prayer* is desired in verse 30, and this is a very interesting exhortation. When Paul urges them "by our Lord Jesus Christ," he is invoking Christ's name as the authority behind his charge to pray. But when he does so "for the love of the Spirit," he is pleading with them in the name of Christian love, a love for each other produced as a fruit of the Spirit (Galatians 5:22). Note also the expression "strive together with me in your prayers." "Strive," in Greek, is an athletic term, referring to the intense struggle of a wrestler or boxer against his foe. Prayer is such a struggle, and satanic powers oppose us. Paul wanted the Roman Christians to join with him in the struggle.

2. *The two-fold need at Jerusalem* is indicated in verse 31. First is the need for protection, for "deliverance" from unbelieving Jews there. Paul knew he would be in danger. The Holy Spirit was already revealing, through various prophets in the local churches, that Paul faced arrest and suffering in Jerusalem. In Acts 20:22, 23 (spoken shortly after writing Romans), he says: "I go . . . to Jerusalem, not knowing the things that shall befall me there: Save that the Holy Ghost witnesseth in every city, saying that bonds and afflictions abide me." Acts 21:4 and 21:10-14 illustrate that Paul's fears were justified. He would indeed be arrested and imprisoned in Jerusalem and would spend the next four years in jail.

Paul's other need in Jerusalem was the successful fulfilment of his intended ministry there. Verse 31b refers to this. The "service" for Jerusalem is the collection he is carrying. He desires that this offering will be accepted by the Jerusalem believers with genuine pleasure and as a recognition of the true Christianity of the Gentile believers Paul represents. Thus a bond of fellowship between the two groups of believers will be established and strengthened.

For the Fruition of Paul's Plans in Joy (verses 32, 33). Paul's second major request concerns his intended ministry at Rome. In essence, his request is that he may get to Rome and enjoy blessed fellowship with the believers there.

1. *The will of God must be done.* With "by the will of God," compare 1:10, where also Paul wants to go to Rome only if and when God wills. This writer ventures to observe that even though Paul finally went as a prisoner, instead of on a voluntary journey toward Spain as he hoped, he went "in the will of God" (consult Romans 8:28).

2. *Joy will be experienced* in such a journey. This joy will be Paul's, because he has longed to go so long and because the trip *will* be God's will. So this writer ventures to say, too, that Paul went "with joy" even as a prisoner.

3. *Mutual spiritual refreshing will result.* Paul not only expects to *carry* a blessing to the Romans but to *receive* one as well. Each

will be blessed by the other. Compare 1:11, 12 where he expects both the Romans and himself to be mutually strengthened by witnessing each other's faith.

Verse 33 is another "benediction" (compare 15:13). Paul is "concluding" again, though the final personal greetings remain. Here he wants the "God of *peace*" to be with them. In 15:13, it was the "God of *hope*." Both peace and hope come only from God.

39 Paul's Salutations and Farewell

Study Text: Romans 16:1-27

Introduction
1. The Business of Phebe (Romans 16:1, 2)
   a. Recommendation Indicated (verses 1, 2b)
   b. Reception Invited (verse 2a)
2. Blessings from Paul (Romans 16:3-16)
   a. A Special Couple (verses 3-5a)
   b. Several Christians (verses 5b-16)
3. Beseeching for Purity (Romans 16:17-20)
   a. Watching (verses 17, 18)
   b. Wise (verses 19, 20)
4. Brotherhood Pledged (Romans 16:21-24)
5. A Benediction of Praise (Romans 16:25-27)

INTRODUCTION

We come, now, to the final chapter of Romans and to our last lesson on this great book. After having traced the tremendous themes of this letter, the sixteenth chapter may seem a bit common, with all its very personal matters.

Still, even this chapter has a significant lesson for us and gives us important insight into Paul's character. We see that he was concerned about his personal relationships, and we learn that the pursuit of so majestic a theme as the righteousness of God does not decrease the importance of our attention to such relationships.

Being a Christian, after all, is being in a family. In this lengthy list of greetings Paul shows his consciousness of the fellowship he enjoyed with other believers. Our relationship to fellow-believers is a sacred and significant one, created by the Holy Spirit himself (1

314

Corinthians 12:13; Ephesians 4:3, 4). We should always have time to attend to this brotherly unity.

EXPOSITION

The general study-outline of Romans in the back of this volume will show that this closing lesson covers the entire sixteenth chapter and is entitled "Paul's Salutations and Farewell." The chapter is much like the concluding portion of all Paul's epistles, only longer.

1. THE BUSINESS OF PHEBE

(Romans 16:1, 2)

In these two verses Paul takes time to speak of a matter relating to one person, a Christian woman who was about to visit Rome, evidently on some business.

Recommendation Indicated (verses 1, 2b). Paul will ask the Romans to assist Phebe, but not without first telling them more about her. So he "commends" (Greek: present, introduce) her to them by making three statements about her.

1. Phebe is a sister in the faith. The "our" probably means Paul, as in 1 Thessalonians 3:1: He often uses the plural pronoun when thinking primarily of himself. Still, he often includes others with him in such plurals, and Phebe was "sister" not only to Paul but all believers.

2. Phebe is a servant of the church. Cenchrea was a seaport suburb of Corinth, where Paul was when he wrote this letter. The Christians in Cenchrea and Corinth would have been well acquainted with each other. No doubt Paul would have ministered to several "congregations" in the vicinity. Phebe obviously was in a group in Cenchrea. That she "served" may mean almost anything. Service is ministering and would suggest a humble and helpful work of some sort. She may well have waited on the poor and sick or fed the hungry. Since she may have been a businesswoman, she might have "ministered" with her money.

3. Phebe is a succorer of many, and of Paul. This last attribute (verse 2b) may well define more clearly Phebe's "ministry," at least in one aspect. The Greek word "succorer" means, literally, "one stationed in front" and refers originally to a guardian or protector. But then one who protects can do so in the milder sense of a patron, provider, or sponsor, and that is probably the sense the word has here. The guess is that she had filled this office in a monetary way, underwriting the needs of many Christians on various occasions and on at least one occasion for Paul. Or she may have "ministered" in a more personal way, as in nursing sick ones back to health. It is even possible she—if she were a businesswoman of position—used her influence to rescue Christians who (as Paul often was) would be falsely accused and in trouble with the authorities. One can imagine numerous ways she might have served the church and succored various believers. A pity we do not have more details.

Reception Invited (verse 2a). With the introductions made, Paul now urges the Roman believers to receive this godly woman.

1. *The manner of her reception* should be one that "becometh" (is appropriate for, *worthy* of) saints. Both the Roman Christians and Phebe are meant: They should act like saints, and they should receive her as a saint. In other words, the welcome will be such as can only be shown between believers, manifesting the unique fellowship of Christians.

2. *The matter of her business* is suggested, without definition. The word translated "business" is vague and can mean business, affair, matter, or thing. The usual view is that Phebe was some kind of businesswoman (cf. Lydia, Acts 16:14), and that she had business to transact in Rome. The particular secular matter she had to attend to need not be mentioned, but Paul wants the Roman believers to render whatever assistance she might need. The word "assist" is almost the same Greek word as "succourer" mentioned earlier. "In complying with this request, they will only be doing for Phebe what she has done for others" (Denney).

One concluding observation about Phebe: In all probability she was the one who would carry this letter to the Roman Christians. Perhaps she would be there for a time. This commendation would serve to certify her genuine Christian character and trustworthiness.

2. BLESSINGS FROM PAUL
(Romans 16:3-16)

In these verses Paul "greets" (or "salutes": both English words translate the same Greek word in these verses) a number of believers in Rome. We should understand that this "salutation" means more than a mere "hello." Thayer's lexicon notes that the word implies a well-wishing. Such greetings were warm expressions of fellowship and indications of a desire for the others' good. They would remind those who received the salutations of Paul's concern and prayers for them, of his interest in their welfare, and of his consciousness of the bond between them. The force of the word, then, is almost like "Give my blessings to . . . ."

This section is quite remarkable. No less than twenty-five persons in Rome, known to Paul, are called by name. Yet Paul had never been to Rome. The explanation lies in the fact that these all had been met by Paul elsewhere and now lived in Rome. In a few cases, as will be noted below, we can tell where Paul met them. With Rome as the big-city capital of the Roman Empire, we should not be surprised that many moved there. Phebe herself provides an example of what was common.

A Special Couple (verses 3:5a). The first greetings are for Aquila and Priscilla, a twosome that had often ministered in the gospel with Paul. This Jewish couple had first met Paul in Corinth on his second journey; he stayed at their home while there because they were—like him—tentmakers. See Acts 18:1-3. When Paul had left Corinth on that same journey, he took Aquila and Priscilla to Ephesus with him, where they played an important role in laying the foundations of the church there. See Acts 18:18-26.

These two have now moved back to Rome, where they had once lived before they first met Paul (Acts 18:2). Probably they had Paul's encouragement to return to Rome for the very purpose of building up the church there. Verse 5a would seem to show they are doing this. Paul brags on this couple (verse 4), probably both to express his gratitude and to inform the Roman believers about them, ensuring that they will be respected and appreciated in the church at Rome. They are in Rome in a more or less official capacity.

That these had "laid down their own necks" for Paul's life means that on some occasion—we know not when—they had risked death on Paul's behalf and for the service of Christ. Paul owes and expresses his gratitude. The Gentile churches likewise owe them a debt of gratitude, not only because they had evidently saved Paul's life—and he was the minister to the Gentiles—but also because they personally worked with Paul in his ministry of establishing Gentile churches.

Verse 5a reminds us that churches, in those days, most often met in people's homes. One such congregation gathered regularly in the home of Aquila and Priscilla. Probably there were other groups that met elsewhere, though all the believers regarded themselves as one in that time before modern denominations came necessarily to exist. The groups usually stayed small because they had not yet begun building church houses. Paul greets the group at this couple's house too.

Several Christians (verses 5b-16). Twenty-four more names are given in these twelve verses, though in two cases the persons' families are greeted rather than the persons themselves. About some of these, more is said. About others, nothing further is mentioned.

Epaenetus (masculine, verse 5) is loved by Paul. He was one of Paul's first converts (firstfruits unto Christ) in the Greek province of Achaia. *Mary* (verse 6) "toiled much" in behalf of Paul (and his co-workers, perhaps), though we know not where or how. Nor do we know whether these two were related in some way.

Andronicus and *Junia* (perhaps man and wife, verse 7) are called "kinsmen," probably meaning they were Jews. Compare "kinsmen" in Romans 9:3. They had been in jail with Paul ("fellowprisoners") on some occasion. They had a good reputation among the apostles as Christian workers, and had been saved longer than Paul.

Amplias (verse 8) and *Stachys* (verse 9) were especially loved by Paul in Christian brotherhood, but we do not know anything further about their relationship to him. *Urbane* (verse 9) was regarded as a helper (Greek: co-worker), and again the "our" may mean Paul and others. We have no background information on this. *Apelles* (verse 10) was one whose Christian character had been particularly tested and found solid ("approved in Christ"), but we know not how. All four of these are masculine names.

Aristobulus and *Narcissus* may not themselves have been Christians. Some in their "households" certainly were. In those days, all the servants were regarded as members of one's household, so we know not whether the ones meant here were blood kin to Aristobulus and Narcissus, their slaves, or some of both. Some think this Aristobulus is the famous grandson of Herod the Great who lived in Rome, and it would perhaps be more likely that some of his servants would be Christians than some of his immediate family. (But that is merely a *human* consideration!) The limitation added after Narcissus' name certainly means that not all his household were believers, a situation probably true with Aristobulus, too.

Herodion (masculine, verse 11) is another of Paul's Jewish kinsmen. Since he is mentioned here right after Aristobulus, he may have been one of Aristobulus' family servants, and thus may have been named after Herod (again, assuming this Aristobulus was of the family of the Herods).

Tryphena and *Tryphosa* (verse 12) may have been sisters, judging from their similar names and our knowledge of ancient customs. They are recognized by Paul as "toilers" in the Lord's service. *Persis* (also feminine, verse 12) is also noted and beloved as one who has toiled in many things (or many times) for the Lord's work.

Rufus (verse 13) is regarded as a "choice" Christian. His mother had (on some occasions of being in their home, probably) "mothered" Paul, and she is greeted, too. The two groups in verses 14 and 15 (all names masculine except Julia, and even that should perhaps be Julian), each including "the brethren with them" probably refer to small assemblies of saints that met in some homes, like the group that met with Aquila and Priscilla (verse 5). The expression in verse 16 is intended to catch all the rest not mentioned by name and includes not only Paul's own "blessings" but remembrances from his churches also.

3. BESEECHING FOR PURITY
(Romans 16:17-20)

318

Paul cannot quit without one last word. And an important word, too: one that warns the Roman believers of false teachers who will divide the flock and disrupt the fellowship. These must be watched for and avoided, that peace and purity may be maintained.

Watching (verses 17, 18). These verses give Paul's specific points concerning the particular danger he is concerned about.

1. *Watch for false teachers.* The word "mark" means to be on lookout for and thus to recognize and identify. Who are those to be thus watched for? They are those who teach "contrary to" the sound doctrine these Roman believers had already learned, many of them either from Paul or from some of his co-workers. And by such teaching, these false teachers will cause divisions (Greek: "To stand apart") and offenses (Greek: "stumbling-blocks"). They will thus divide and injure, causing splits and hindrances to the progress of the church and the believers. For this reason, the Christian must not be naive and foolishly accept everything that comes along. He must closely observe and intelligently inspect all teaching lest insidious false doctrine ruin the church.

2. *Avoid them.* It would be foolish to watch and identify false teachers and still allow them access to the flock of God. Identified, they should be removed. The word "avoid" means, literally, to turn away from. The protection and purity and peace of the fellowship is the goal of such decisive action. The imperative "avoid" is *continuing* action, too.

3. *Understand them.* This is the point of verse 18. These false teachers are not serving Christ, as they claim, but their own selfish ends. We must not be fooled by them. Paul uses "belly" to emphasize the base, selfish, fleshly nature of anything that perverts true Christianity. These teachers' "fair speeches" serve to aid them in deceiving the naive ("simple") believers. We do not need, in the church, a naive piety that believes everything and everyone is good. We need courageous, intelligent exposure of hurtful heresy.

Wise (verses 19, 20). Paul's mention of the "simple," trusting believer who is so easily deceived by false doctrine reminds him of the need for informed, judicious observation and action. This is the wisdom he now mentions.

1. *Wisdom must accompany submission.* Verse 19 expresses this. The word "obedience" means subjection or submissiveness. Evidently the Roman Christians had a reputation for humble, submissive spirits. "That is fine," says Paul. "And yet in your meek, accepting manner I do not want you to be foolish and naive, accepting just anything without testing it. I want you to be wise and careful, observing, testing, and rejecting the evil that exists and threatens."

So be submissive, both to the Lord and to fellow believers, even to sinners, in your acceptance of their reproach (Romans 12:17-21) and your service of their souls. But be cautious, observant, informed, and firm, too. False doctrine inevitably approaches and must be turned aside for the church's sake.

Does this mean we must become suspicious and harsh? No. Nor need we become so well informed and "experienced" in evil that we believe everything and everybody is evil. This is the reason Paul adds the last words in verse 19. He wants our "wisdom" to result in our good and in our thorough familiarity with and experience of that which is good. We will try to stay "simple"—inexperienced, pure, undefiled, and undeceived—about evil. We will be intelligent and informed enough to recognize and turn away from evil but innocent enough that evil is not our own expertise. We want to be experts in the good.

2. *Confidence in God must accompany our own wise efforts.* Verse 20 makes this point. Ultimately we need not rely on our own acumen or strength to withstand false teaching. All such teaching comes from Satan, and God will one day destroy his power and work forever. We trust, then, in God for final victory. We do not have to be sharp enough to ferret out all the little distinctions that confuse us, nor to separate all the good and bad that are abroad. Paul means for us, however, to keep the flock pure, to be alert for dangerous doctrine and turn aside from it. Then, in the end, God will destroy Satan and his influence.

"Bruise Satan under your feet" reflects Genesis 3:15: The church will finally participate in Christ's victory over the devil. The "blessing" at the end of verse 20 closes this brief exhortation: God's grace will sustain us in our battle with Satan and with the false teachers he sends.

4. BROTHERHOOD PLEDGED
(Romans 16:21-24)

Above, in verses 3-16, Paul expressed salutations *to* his Christian friends in Rome. Now, in verses 21-24, he sends similar salutations *from* his Christian friends who are closely associated with him (in Corinth) at the time he writes the letter. In studying the salutations above, we noted that these should be taken as more meaningful than mere "hellos," that Paul was actually wishing them well, spiritually. The same is true here. These associates of Paul mean more than a simple observance of the social amenities. They want their brethren in Rome to know they are concerned about them, praying for them, and conscious they are one with them. These Christian greetings, then, are special manifestations of brotherhood, almost like a pledge of interest.

Eight men, in all, send these greetings. *Timothy* is first, and we know enough about him to understand he was, indeed, Paul's "workfellow" (co-worker, partner in the work). Timothy first joined

Paul's team in Lystra on the second journey (Acts 16:1-3) and had been with him ever since. Paul could count on Timothy to go where he was needed and do what must be done.

Lucius, Jason, and *Sosipater* are fellow Jews ("kinsmen"), but we know nothing more about them. Nor do we know anything further about *Tertius,* except that he is identified here as the scribe who took down in writing Paul's dictated letter. This is a unique reference, being the only one like it in all Paul's letters.

Gaius (probably the same one as mentioned in 1 Corinthians 1:14) is Paul's "host" in Corinth, meaning Paul stayed there. That he was also "host" for the "whole church" means either that a congregation met in his home or that Gaius was hospitable (cf. Romans 12:13) to any Christians visiting in Corinth. *Erastus'* office in city government is (or had been) that of "city treasurer," an important function. *Quartus* is "a brother" in the faith, as are all these. Verse 24 provides yet another (almost) benediction to conclude yet another section (cf. 16:20b; 15:33; 15:13; and perhaps 16:16, all of which are almost stopping places).

5. A BENEDICTION OF PRAISE
(ROMANS 16:25-27)

At this stopping place Paul really is going to stop. So he chooses an appropriate "doxology," a song of praise to God, as a fitting conclusion for this great epistle. It is appropriate that our treatment of Romans close with this same doxology, for the content of Romans has certainly been such as to merit an outburst of praise to God.

These three verses say, in summary, "To God be glory." But Paul is a bit more detailed than that and a bit more personal (with reference both to himself and to his Roman readers).

1. God has power to establish the Romans, thus Paul can confidently leave them in His hands, having himself done what he could by this letter. That establishing will take place in perfect accord with the "gospel" Paul preached—and here "gospel" includes *all* his teaching about justification and Christian duty and development.

In that gospel, Paul had primarily "preached Jesus" (25b, 26). In preaching Jesus, the gospel revealed a "mystery" that had been previously unrealized but is now fully manifested. This "mystery" is that "all nations" (Gentiles) are admitted into God's family through the "obedience" called faith. Compare Ephesians 3:1-7, where exactly the same point is made. This truth, though unknown to Old Testament saints, is still in full accord with Old Testament prophecy, says Paul, and was accomplished by the commandment of the eternal, unchanging God. Compare Romans 1:1-5.

2.*God is wise*, a point Paul makes in verse 27, and which means that God's gospel provision for all men (above) is in perfect accord with His eternal and perfect wisdom. He knows how to accomplish His own good will in the wisest way.

3. *God is glorified by Jesus.* Jesus himself glorified God, and what He has accomplished results in God's glory. Paul is glorifying God's Son along with the Father, and that is proper because all God's redemptive work is done through Jesus. Jesus is the power and wisdom of God. Here Paul intends that we remember the honored position he has given Jesus throughout the epistle.

So we have studied this great epistle through, following the great themes of redemption. We have examined man's desperate need and then seen how God has moved through Jesus to meet man's need and provide righteous standing for him and the possibility of righteous living as well. When we consider how this has been done in spite of man's sinfulness, we too can conclude with Paul:

TO GOD BE GLORY THROUGH JESUS CHRIST FOREVER.

ROMANS: GENERAL STUDY OUTLINE

Printed in the United States
58005LVS00003B/26